Three
week lo

rn on before the la

WORKING WOMEN AND
SOCIALIST POLITICS IN FRANCE

Working Women and Socialist Politics in France

1880–1914

A Regional Study

PATRICIA HILDEN

CLARENDON PRESS · OXFORD
1986

Oxford University Press, Walton Street, Oxford OX2 6DP
Oxford New York Toronto
Delhi Bombay Calcutta Madras Karachi
Petaling Jaya Singapore Hong Kong Tokyo
Nairobi Dar es Salaam Cape Town
Melbourne Auckland
and associated companies in
Beirut Berlin Ibadan Nicosia

Oxford is a trade mark of Oxford University Press

Published in the United States
by Oxford University Press, New York

British Library Cataloguing in Publication Data
Hilden Patricia.
Working women and socialist politics in France,
1880–1914: a regional study.
1. Women and socialism—France—History
2. Women in politics—France—History.   3. France—
Politics and government—1870–1940
I. Title
335'.00944   HX263
ISBN 0–19–821935–0

Library of Congress Cataloging in Publication Data
Hilden, Patricia.
Working women and socialist politics in France,
1880–1914.
Bibliography: p.
Includes index.
1. Women textile workers—France—Lille Region—
Case studies.   2. Women in trade–unions—France—
History.   3. Socialism—France—History. I. Title.
HD6073.T42F84   1986   331.4'877'0094428   85–15487
ISBN 0–19–821935–0

Set by Cambrian Typesetters, Frimley, Surrey
Printed in Great Britain
at the University Press, Oxford
by David Stanford
Printer to the University

TO TONY AND
TO THE MEMORY OF ELIZABETH PENN AND
PATRICK BRAY

ACKNOWLEDGEMENTS

MANY people have contributed their advice, encouragement, and assistance to this book. Heading the list is Tony Judt, without whom there would be no book. For many years he has been unstinting with help and critical advice.

In addition, I have been extraordinarily fortunate in having many friends willing to listen and to advise. In Britain, I have found both the example and the friendship of Olwen Hufton more essential than I think she realizes. She has been a tireless reader as well as a stimulating adversary throughout the writing of this book.

Other British friends include Jane Caplan, Maurice Larkin, Tim Mason, Richard Mitten, Gareth Stedman Jones, Jonathan Steinberg, Gillian Sutherland, David Travis, and many of my students in Cambridge. To participants in the social history seminar in King's College I also owe thanks. An anonymous publisher's reader read the typescript with unusual care.

On the other side of the Atlantic, I have many more friends who have helped along the way. Firstly, I must thank Ted Margadant who first suggested that I research the women textile workers of the Lille area. I am also indebted to Fran Anderson, David Brody, Tom Dublin, Eric Foner, Joe Fracchia, Ray Jonas, Sheila Lichtman, Eugene Lunn, Marjorie Murphy, Jonathan Prude, and Ruth Rosen. My brother, William Penn, and Caroline Beasley-Baker provided a much needed and extremely tolerant audience while I wrote.

My friends and students at Emory University's Graduate Institute of the Liberal Arts, especially Elizabeth Cocke, have contributed their enthusiasm and interest throughout.

I have also been fortunate in having a good deal of assistance from many institutions. M. Pierre Petitmengin generously allowed me to work for many months undisturbed in the library of the *École normale supérieure*. Without that library and the generous help of its staff, I should never have discovered some of the richest sources. I also worked extensively in the *Musée social*, where both Mlle Colette Chambelland and her staff were unfailingly helpful. All the people at the International Institute for Social History in Amsterdam were similarly generous with their time and resources.

The staff in the *Archives départementales du Nord* in Lille worked very hard to supply all my requests, as did the women who work in the *bibliothèques municipales* of Lille, Roubaix, and especially Tourcoing.

Finally, the staff of the newspaper library at the University of California, Berkeley, discovered numerous sources I had not known existed.

Much of the research for the book was made possible by the Master and Fellows of Trinity Hall, Cambridge, who elected me to a research fellowship. The Warden and Fellows of Nuffield College, Oxford, have generously given me the academic year 1983–4 amongst them to write the book. Christine Kennedy and her staff also gave me every help I required in the Nuffield library during the year.

I must also take this opportunity to thank all the institutions from which I received financial support. These include the London School of Economics, King's College, Cambridge, the American Association of University Women, the British Academy, the British Social Science Research Council, the *Centre nationale de recherches scientifiques*, and the American Council of Learned Societies.

Finally, I should like to acknowledge those historians whose work has been essential to me. These include Pierre Pierrard, Marcel Gillet, and Félix-Paul Codaccioni, all of whom write about the Nord department and its people. Without Madeleine Guilbert, Charles Sowerwine, Daniel Armogathe, Maïté Albistur, Huguette Bouchardeau, Alain Dalôtel and many others, the history of politically active French working women would not be as rich as it has become. Marie-Hélène Zylberberg-Hocquard's work has also provided much useful information about women in the syndicalist movement. Of course, no one can write about the Guesdists without referring constantly to Claude Willard's work. And finally, there are those historians whose work, though not specifically related to my own interests, has been a model. For me, these include George Lichtheim, Marc Bloch, Geoffrey Elton, Donald Coleman, and Robert Brentano.

CONTENTS

ABBREVIATIONS

ADN	*Archives départementales du Nord*
AN	*Archives nationales*
APP	*Archives de la préfecture de police*
BMD	*Bibliothèque Marguerite Durand*
BS	*La Bataille syndicaliste*
CdF	*Le Cri du forçat*
CDl'O	*Le Cri de l'ouvrier*
CdT	*Le Cri du travailleur*
CGT	*Confédération générale du travail*
É	*L'Égalité*
Égalité de R-T	*L'Égalité de Roubaix-Tourcoing*
Enquête sur l'industrie, 1904	France, Assemblée nationale, chambre des députés, session de 1904, *Procès-verbaux de la commission chargée de procéder à une enquête sur l'état de l'industrie textile et la condition des ouvriers tisseurs,* vol. ii (Paris, 1906)
FS	*La Femme Socialiste*
GdFS	Groupe des femmes socialistes
GFS	Groupe féministe socialiste
H	*L'Humanité*
ICSW	International Congress of Socialist Women
IISH	International Institute of Social History, Amsterdam
LF	*Le Forçat*
LT	*Le Travailleur*
MS	*Le Mouvement socialiste*
OT	*L'Ouvrier textile*
PJ	*Le Petit Jaune*
POF	Parti ouvrier français
PsdF	Parti socialiste de France
RdF	*La Revanche du forçat* (July–Sept. 1883)
	La Réveil du forçat (1885–6)
RdN	La Reveil du Nord (1889–1914)
	Le Revue du Nord (1950–)
RS	*La Revue socialiste*
SFIO	Parti socialiste, section française de l'Internationale ouvrière
VdP	*La Voix du peuple*

INTRODUCTION

THE link between the organized French left and women's collective struggle for equality is a very old one. Since the French Revolution, every movement aimed at broadening political and economic rights has encompassed—to a greater or lesser extent—a parallel movement of women, organized to demand their admission to the *pays légal*. Since the late nineteenth century the relationship between the two movements has become more direct, between socialist parties rooted in a Marxist analysis of class relations in industrial society, and groups of women who have perceived themselves as both socialists and feminists. Moreover, this connection between the class struggle and the women's movement continues within the modern French left. Both mass-based left-wing political parties in contemporary France, the *Parti socialiste* and the *Parti communiste*, claim women (especially, but not exclusively, working women) as a special constituency for their projects of revolutionary change.

Nevertheless, despite this lengthy historical tie between women and socialists, relations have been, and continue to be, difficult. Not only do women—even proletarian women—present a theoretical dilemma for Marxists, but they also present special organizational problems which arise out of the particularity of their private and public experiences within a male-dominated world. It is not surprising, then, to discover that women were always on the margins of organized left-wing politics in France. Their numbers among party members were—and remain—few; fewer still their numbers among activists and leaders.

Of course when writing about organized socialist politics in France it is important to keep in mind the fact that relatively few workers of either sex have joined socialist parties. Thus one must not exaggerate the importance of the fact that few women were found on membership lists. But even keeping in mind most French workers' reluctance to enroll in mass organizations, women's much greater absence from socialist parties is striking. Women's collective greater indifference to socialist parties, as well as those parties' inability to overcome that indifference, provide the underlying problematic of this book.

At a more specific level, this book represents an enquiry into the historical origins of one set of relations between working women and socialists, those which developed between the Marxian socialists of the *Parti ouvrier français* (which unified with other socialist groups in 1905 to form the *Parti socialiste, section française de l'Internationale ouvrière*, or *SFIO*) and a substantial female proletariat, the women textile workers of the industrial conurbation formed by the three cities of Lille, Roubaix, and Tourcoing in the period 1880 to 1914.

In the *belle époque*, Jules Guesde's *Parti ouvrier* (*POF*) built a solid base of support among the textile workers of French Flanders. Voters in Lille sent the party's co-founder, Paul Lafargue, to the *Chambre* in 1891. Roubaix's voters followed suit by electing a socialist municipal council in 1892, and a socialist deputy—Jules Guesde—in 1893. Lille's municipal council fell next to the Guesdists, in 1895. Socialist conquest of Tourcoing lagged behind. It was not until just before the First World War that Tourcoing's voters began to elect socialist councillors in substantial numbers. And it was only in 1914 that they finally chose a long-standing Guesdist militant, Albert Inghels, as their deputy.

Throughout this period of intense socialist organization the presence of an active, vocal female industrial work-force in the area helped shape the Guesdists' politics. These politics were grounded in a wide-ranging commitment to women's equality, expressed in the resolution passed at the 1879 workers' congress in Marseilles. That resolution (passed by the great majority of delegates) outlined a far-reaching programme designed to bring women into the mainstream of left-wing political life. Not only did it promise to include women specifically in all workers' movement activities, but it also placed the goals of women's public and private emancipation high on the movement's agenda.

Most of these goals found their way into the official programme of the *Parti ouvrier*, promulgated at the party's founding in 1880. That programme's strong commitment to women's rights subsequently formed the basis for what were, for the time, highly egalitarian political practices in the workers' communities of Lille, Roubaix, and Tourcoing. Throughout the 1880s and early 1890s, local working women were specifically included in all party activities, including meetings, election campaigns, and socialist-sponsored unions (albeit in the last case with conditions).

Not surprisingly, the Guesdists' efforts evoked a positive response from local women. Not only did they join *en masse* in all the various informal, unstructured socialist activities of the time, but they also founded several socialist women's groups which joined the many small, *quartier*-based social study groups. The women's groups met monthly either in members' homes or in socialist *estaminets* in both Lille and Roubaix. They joined in local municipal reform campaigns, including especially those which benefited textile workers' children. Moreover, until the second half of the 1890s, the women's groups sent delegates to represent them at all *POF* congresses.

Parallel with these local efforts to mobilize working women ran an attempt to develop an ideology of women's emancipation which neither contradicted nor compromised the Marxist ideology of proletarian revolution, upon which *POF* politics rested. In the first fifteen years after the party's founding, this attempt produced an amalgam of radical feminist ideas (borrowed mainly from Hubertine Auclert but also from ideas prevalent in earlier radical movements in France) and concepts derived from the Marxist analysis of production relations in industrial capitalist societies. Not surprisingly, the efforts to mould the two projects into one often resulted in a hopeless theoretical muddle. Nevertheless, the Guesdists discovered that a discourse compounded of feminism and Marxism had great appeal among women workers in the Lille *arrondissement*.

The *POF*'s success among local working women was bolstered by the presence of several prominent women among the pleiad of socialist militants who appeared on party platforms during these early years. These women included the radical feminist, Léonie Rouzade, as well as two popular ex-*communardes*, Paule Minck and Louise Michel. In 1893 these women were joined by Aline Valette, who in that year became the only woman to serve on the *POF*'s administrative council (where she remained until her death in 1899).

In addition to these national socialist figures, a few local women began to emerge as leaders of the local working women's movement. Unfortunately little is known about these women save their names and the positions they held in the socialist women's groups. They included Maria Delory Devernay, Anna Ghesquière, Mme Carrette, and Mme Collignon. The first three women were related to local *POF* leaders, and doubtless helped to shape the party's strikingly progressive policies toward local working women.

Despite these early successes, however, they did not portend any long-term success. By the mid-nineties, in fact, both the local women's groups and their leaders had begun to fade from sight as male Guesdists increasingly turned their attentions toward shaping a formal, centralized political party designed to win elections. In this process, the issue of mobilizing non-voting working women side by side with working men disappeared from the Guesdist agenda in the Lille area. By 1900, no remnants of women's earlier organizational militancy remained.

From then on, in spite of continuing evidence of textile *ouvrières'* continuing collective resistance to steadily worsening industrial conditions, a gap grew between them and the party which still claimed to represent their interests. Concomitantly, theoretical pronouncements regarding the position and role of working women in socialist movements changed their tone. A greater emphasis upon women's traditional roles as mothers and wives superseded a commitment to their equal place in the waged work-force. This shifting focus helped to justify the marginalization of working women from organized politics. Gradually, in both theory and practice, working women began to form a silent auxiliary to male political activities. Although still present in mass demonstrations and political campaigns, they were increasingly absent from formal meetings and congresses. All the earlier Guesdist efforts to overcome the special problems by organizing women party members ceased.

This did not mean, however, that women's absence from formal socialist politics in any way signalled their growing quiescence. In fact quite the contrary. Most officials of the Third Republic, including local police informers, paid increasing attention to local women after the turn of the century. Official documents recorded a growing worry about *ouvrières'* collective militancy. Ironically, then, just at the moment when the socialist party hierarchy was turning its attentions away from mobilizing working women, most non-socialist observers began to cite what they perceived as the dangerous development of *ouvrières'* organized resistance.

But this change in the official perception of women's collective behaviour provoked no change in the socialists' policy of neglect. In fact, until just before the First World War, socialist party leaders continually refused to consider organizing—or allowing women to organize—separate socialist women's groups, despite the success of that tactic in the Nord department in previous years. When in 1912 the *SFIO* did at last agree to allow women's groups they confined them to the periphery of the party by limiting the groups' membership to women who already belonged to the *SFIO*.

Between 1880 and 1914, then, relations between women textile workers and the organized socialist movement followed a curious trajectory in the Lille area. An initial upward curve described the earliest period of grass-roots organizing. This peaked in 1896, when several socialist women's groups were active in local politics. Rather suddenly, however, the curve turned downward. A rapid disappearance of every vestige of organized socialist women's activities followed. When in 1913 the *SFIO* decided to allow the organization of socialist women's auxiliaries, organizers in the Lille area were forced to begin all over again to try to gather women in the new groups. The search for an explanation for this story of deteriorating relations between the socialists and women textile workers forms the basis for the following chapters.

The subject is not only of interest to historians of socialism. For historians of working women, the retrieval of the history of a hitherto neglected group of *ouvrières* offers empirical evidence upon which broader generalizations about the patterns of women's work and politics might be based. Moreover, the day-to-day story of relations between a mass of working women and a party which purported to represent them helps to explain the vexations encountered by other groups of women who have attempted (and continue to attempt) to mobilize within an organized socialist movement.

Both the time and the place have been chosen with some care. Because the *POF/SFIO* organized a strong base in the textile working communities of French Flanders in the *belle époque*, and given the fact that the factory work-force was nearly half female, it is possible to examine in detail the ways in which the two groups met, coalesced for a time, and ultimately grew far apart over the later years. Moreover, the fact that the major national textile union was both led by the Guesdists and headquartered in Roubaix makes it possible to see close up how union policies

shaped women's mass economic behaviour in these years, and how
ouvrières, in their turn, affected the strategies adopted by a major
socialist union in their dealings with female workers.

On the other hand, it must be said that the region was not
chosen because it was in any way representative of industrial
France as a whole—or even of industrial cities in the provinces. In
fact, quite the contrary. These three great textile cities which lie in
a triangle along the Belgian border form the heart of urban French
Flanders. Throughout the nineteenth century, the constant movement of people between Belgium and France gave a special flavour
to the cultural, social, and eventually the political lives of the
common people of the Lille area. Until the Second Empire, in
fact, most workers in Lille, Roubaix, and Tourcoing continued to
speak the local patois (which sounds to the francophone ear rather
like rapid French spoken with a Flemish accent). Even in the final
years of the nineteenth century, patois continued to be spoken in
many workers' *quartiers* in the region, though it was dying out.

Moreover, daily life in the workers' communities of our three
cities shared many characteristics with the experiences of working-
class Flemings on both sides of the border. By long tradition ·
Flemings of both nationalities were highly communitarian in their
private, as well as their public, activities. As Claude Willard
discovered, it was this characteristic that assured the success of the
socialist message when it arrived on the scene in the 1880s.
Politically skilled local leaders quickly capitalized on the shared
nature of Flemish cultural life, most aspects of which they
assimilated. Ultimately all local mass activities took on a distinct
socialist identity, and often a clear political content, in the years
following the founding of the party. Socialist politicians discovered
that they had little need to preach the importance of class
solidarity to the textile workers of Lille and Roubaix; most
understood it intuitively. Even in Tourcoing, where class divisions
were less apparent than in the neighbouring cities, local textile
workers gradually shifted their lingering loyalty from the wider
community to that defined by their class.

This community-centred Flemish society harboured another
anomaly in the context of nineteenth-century France. Women of
the popular classes were nowhere excluded from public life. Nor
did they inhabit what could clearly be identified as a separate
women's sphere. Instead, women both worked alongside men in

the mills and socialized with them in the ubiquitous *estaminets* which dotted the Flemish landscape. It is not surprising, then, to find that sex divisions had only minimal effect on the mass political activities of the Nord in our period.

This does not mean, of course, that women and men of the local working class lived identical lives. Women's private lives were, as we shall see, far more restricted. Moreover, they were the particular victims of mill owners' efforts to control the work-force during the volatile years of the *belle époque*. Because of their different experiences, women did share some aspects of life mainly with one another. To some extent they developed some of their own habits and customs—not least among these the most popular festival of the Lille workers' year, *Broquelet*, which was the ancient fête of the lace-makers. But, more than was the case elsewhere in France, women were integrated into the family-centred community life of the popular classes of French Flanders.

Furthermore, the textile industries of the three cities were unlike those elsewhere. The Lille area's mills processed a wide variety of raw materials, including cotton, wool, flax, hemp, and jute. With the exception of a very few remaining skilled hand workers—the wool-sorters—most textile workers did not normally experience the occupational stability which came from working with only raw material. Instead, most workers moved from mill to mill as well as from job to job within the mills. Moreover, few jobs in the mills were clearly assigned by sex—a fact which led to widespread bourgeois horror at the 'immorality' of such daily fraternization on the shop-floors. Given the fact that this mixing of the work-force occasioned so much adverse publicity, many mill owners expended considerable effort in trying to keep men and women workers from socializing in the mills, especially during the infrequent rest breaks.

The constant daily contact between the sexes in the mills did not cease when women married, or even after they began to have children. Instead, most *ouvrières* remained in waged work throughout their lives—escaping only when death, debilitating illness, accident, or unemployment drove them out.

The fact that they worked side by side, however, did not mean that women and men enjoyed perfect equality at work. In the mills, women consistently earned lower wages than men, even when they worked at identical tasks. Furthermore, work routines were different for women. Far more often than the men, they were required to add attendance at mass to their work activities. Both mass and obligatory confessions often occurred within special chapels built on to the mill by religiously zealous mill owners. In addition, many *patrons* employed nuns who paid special attention to the behaviour of *ouvrières*. As a result women workers' activities were controlled more than were those of the men.

Relations between women and men at home were also nowhere near equal. Instead, family relations mirrored those in French families everywhere. Women were resonsible for virtually all domestic tasks, including care of the children. Politically active women carried their children to mass meetings and demonstrations. The necessity of keeping their many children quiet and amused through strike or political meetings helped to curb women's freedom to concentrate on what was being said, as well as to take an active part in discussions.

In many respects, then, the women textile workers of Lille, Roubaix, and Tourcoing shared the experiences of their working sisters everywhere. At the same time, however, their lives were never as clearly separate from men's as many historians of working women have assumed them to be. Rather, the picture is more nuanced; relations between women and men at the grass-roots level were generally just as complex as were relations between the mass of working women and the socialist party.

My aim is to address these various issues coherently. The first half of the book sets out in detail the geographical, social, economic, and cultural context which provided the background for organized political activity in the area. The second half describes the interaction between the attitudes and the behaviour of the textile workers on the one hand and the *POF/SFIO* on the other. Chapter 4 deals with union politics in the area. Chapters 5 and 6 examine the development of socialist politics among the textile workers' communities first during the early period from 1880 to 1897, and subsequently in the later years, to 1914. The conclusion draws these chapters together, and speculates briefly on the extent to which the history of relations between Lille area women textile workers and the *POF/SFIO* and exemplary of such relations elsewhere in France in our period. It concludes with some speculation as to the lessons for organized socialists, as well as for some feminists, which might be drawn from this history.

1

LILLE, ROUBAIX, AND TOURCOING
IN THE *BELLE ÉPOQUE*

i

IN the early years of the Third Republic, the three great textile cities of French Flanders sprawled along the Belgian border. Row upon row of red-brick factory chimneys spewed black smoke into the low northern skies. A pall hung over miles of identical grey rooftops, and scudded across the open fields which bordered the cities on all sides.

Although the effects of rapid industrialization had tended to merge the three cities together, the process was not yet complete in the final years of the nineteenth century. Instead, Lille, Roubaix, and especially Tourcoing retained unique characteristics, rooted in their differing pasts.[1]

As the remaining medieval walls suggested, Lille was the oldest of the three cities. Called 'l'Insula', it appeared in ancient chronicles and was marked on the earliest Latin maps.[2] But its major growth awaited the nineteenth century, when Lille was rapidly transformed from a commercial centre based amidst a thriving artisanal sector into a huge industrial city, the wealth of which came mainly from the products of massive red-brick factories which sprawled everywhere in the city by the opening years of the Third Republic. The development of Lille's major industries, moreover, was accompanied by a great surge in the city's population. A high birth-rate, the steady immigration of workers from nearby Belgium, and the annexation of most of Lille's neighbouring towns in the Second Empire changed Lille from a city of 55,000 in 1816 to a major urban centre with 203,491 inhabitants in the mid-1880s.

---

[1] Ardouin-Dumazet, in *Voyage en France, région du Nord* (Paris, 1903), p. 8, describes Tourcoing's ancient past. For the absence of a past in Roubaix see Gaston Motte, *Roubaix à travers les âges* (Roubaix, 1946), preface.

[2] Léon Bocquet, *Villes meurtries de France. Villes du Nord: Lille, Douai, Cambrai, Valenciennes, Bergues, Dunkerque* (Brussels and Paris, 1918), p. 5.

In spite of this rapid growth, however, Lille's old neighbourhoods, buried in the heart of the ancient city centre, remained mostly intact. Workers' *quartiers*, including the pestiferous Saint-Sauveur[3], stood separate from bourgeois districts which housed both mill owners and the denizens of Lille's thriving commerce. This characteristic geography of class, moreover, was even more striking in many of Lille's outlying areas, annexed in the 1860s. Saint-Maurice, for example, housed Lille's *petite bourgeoisie*, including the *employés* of Lille's industries and commercial houses. Fives, on the other hand, was solidly *ouvrier*. Wazemmes was likewise a workers' district, but its inhabitants were Belgian textile workers. In our period, Wazemmes was popularly known as 'petite Belgique', where, it was said, no French was ever heard.

Fin de siècle Lille, was a city built of neighbourhoods, each defined by class, and some by ethnicity. The integrity of these neighbourhoods, moreover, was not broken by the rapid industrial building of the late nineteenth century. Most mills sat on the outskirts of the city centre and the interstices between Lille's annexed suburbs. Thus the city centre retained its medieval character, with, in the words of one visitor, 'tortuous streets, . . . houses of brick and chalk . . . ornamented with curious sculptures'. Linking this ancient centre with its outlying districts was a 'vast *cité americaine*, of endless, characterless roads set at right angles to each other'.[4]

The inhabitants of Lille, unlike those in the neighbouring cities, found a variety of employment within the city's borders. In the *belle époque*, thousands of *Lillois* worked in railway yards, sugar mills, machine works, oil refineries (which processed flax, rape, and poppy seeds), chemical factories, garment manufacturers, smelting works, chicory mills, and the various building trades. In addition, the production of certain traditional luxury goods, including lace, survived into the early twentieth century.

Moreover, Lille was still a great commercial city. Banking and trade employed many more thousands of Lille's inhabitants. And the fact that Lille was a garrison city as well meant employment for

---

[3] See Pierre Pierrard, *La Vie ouvrière à Lille sous le Second Empire* (Paris, 1965), pp. 45 ff.
[4] Ardouin-Dumazet, *Voyage*, p. 70.

still more workers in the various service trades associated with military centres—including, of course, prostitution.[5]

Despite this complex economic and demographic infrastructure, however, the Lille familiar to most late nineteenth-century textile workers was a simple one. Most workers lived together in tightly knit neighbourhoods, located either in the old city or outside the walls in workers' *quartiers*, or in nearby workers' towns, such as Croix, which sat between Lille and Roubaix.[6]

Each of these workers' areas, however distant one from the other, shared one thing in common: all were overcrowded, poor, and miserable. Every traveller who ventured near these workers' 'ghettos' reacted with horror. One described them as 'leprous and sordid *quartiers*, swarming with workers, who suffer, who sweat, and who end as nothing in the shadowed, narrow, hovels'.[7] Nevertheless, these districts supported a vital community life in the *belle époque*, the traditions of which provided fertile ground for socialist politics when organizers appeared on the scene in the late 1870s.

Roubaix in the early Third Republic was a rather different place from its more venerable neighbour to the south-west. In the words of a local poet, it was 'a city without a past, without art, without beauty, without history'.[8] But a closer look suggested that though the city of Roubaix lacked a past, the village out of which it sprang in the nineteenth century did not. Roubaix village, in fact, dated back to the seventeenth century, when its inhabitants had first begun to weave luxury cloth in their scattered cottages. This artisanal trade continue for over two hundred years, carried on in the traditional manner by families of weavers, working at home to produce cloth for Lille's merchants.

This home-based, artisan production of fine cloth continued well into the nineteenth century. The first major influx of Belgians in mid-century in fact strengthened the trade, as they brought with them similar work practices from their villages across the border.[9]

---

[5] Ibid., and Pierrard, *Vie ouvrière*.

[6] Croix, which fell rapidly to the socialists in the 1890s, lies between Lille and Roubaix. It was entirely a community of textile workers—proud of their mill which, they claimed, had the tallest chimney in the world. See Ardouin-Dumazet, *Voyage*, p. 70.

[7] Bocquet, *Villes meurtries*, p. 8.

[8] Quoted anonymously in Motte, *Roubaix à travers*, preface.

[9] Ibid., p. 46.

But this home-based production of textiles disappeared rapidly in the second half of the century, overwhelmed by the factory production of cloth. Mills to house the new textile machines sprang up higgledy-piggledy, with little regard for the pattern of the existing village. Each new mill, moreover, was rapidly surrounded by a haphazard mix of workers' slums, the small brick terraces of *employés*, and the great ornate mansions of the *patronat*.

This speedy and unplanned expansion created a city where stark contrasts between rich and poor sat side by side. As a result, no one of either group could avoid a daily confrontation with the evidence of the growing gap between affluent manufacturers and their poverty-stricken workers. The bigger and richer the mansions, the more plentiful the workers' slums. One late nineteenth-century visitor warned of the consequences: 'In no other city in France is the demarcation between employer and employed clearer than in Roubaix.'[10]

The overcrowded city quickly lost any remnants of its earlier, rural character. Elm trees and pear orchards, fields and tiny farmhouses were swallowed up overnight by brick and cobble-stones. The few green spaces that remained at the end of the century were walled off, providing gardens for the mill owners' mansions. What had once been clear streams became, in one writer's words, 'infamous sink-holes'. These, in their turn, quickly turned the large rivers flowing through Roubaix into 'open black drains'.[11] The Espierre, which ran between Roubaix and Tourcoing,[12] horrified one traveller who wrote: 'It is now only a current of swill coming from the factories. This current carries ten times more solid matter than the sewers of London, elsewhere celebrated for their impurity.'[13]

Of course, these depredations did not stop at the borders of the old village of Roubaix, but instead spread outside, absorbing many small neighbouring villages and transforming them into squalid terraced housing for Roubaix's growing textile work-force. Wat-trelos, for example, on the eastern edge of Roubaix, housed 22,731 workers and their families in 1903. All that remained of

[10] Ardouin-Dumazet, *Voyage*, p. 20.
[11] Ibid., p. 5.
[12] *ADN*, 'Plan no. 470 (Lille—Roubaix—Tourcoing)'.
[13] Ardouin-Dumazet, *Voyage*, p. 29.

Wattrelos village was a 'squat church, surrounded by row upon row of identical, red-tiled workers' terraces'.[14]

Roubaix, then, had become a city of extremes—of wealth and poverty, of rural past and urban present. For many contemporaries, this unique character provided the explanation for the development of similarly extreme politics in the *belle époque*. On the one side stood the apparently monolithic, conservative, Catholic textile *patronat*. On the other were masses of militant workers, rapid converts to the revolutionary socialism of the *Parti ouvrier*.[15]

Directly north of Roubaix, on a hill near the Belgian border, stood the third of our cities, Tourcoing. Still surrounded by fertile fields at the end of the century, Tourcoing retained much of its ancient town character. A small, ornate Flemish square stood at the town's centre. Curving streets, bordered by the squat, narrow buildings characteristic of Flanders radiated outward from the *Grande Place*. Some features of that square, including an elaborate bell tower, dated back to the eleventh century.[16]

Shortly after the textile trade arrived in Roubaix, it spread to Tourcoing. Many *Tourquenois* were hired to spin wool yarn for *roubaisien* weavers. Tourcoing's yarn, prepared and spun in homes throughout the town, was traded in the square, where trading halls and commercial offices quickly appeared. As more people filled the town centre during the day, market traders spotted a potential market for their goods and began to erect market stalls around the edges of the *Grande Place*. A full-scale open market thus grew up in the heart of the city, and some aspects of it remain to this day.

This little Flemish town, then, built around a thriving centre, formed the nucleus for Tourcoing's textile industry when the first mills began to arrive in the mid-nineteenth century. As they had in Lille, factory-builders left the town centre intact, building their great red-brick mills on the open land which encircled the city.

Partly because of the social cohesion symbolized by Tourcoing's ancient town centre, the inhabitants did not shift overnight to the

[14] Ibid.

[15] See, e.g., A. Siegfried, *Tableau politique de la France de l'Ouest sous la Troisième République* (Paris, 1913), and Tony Judt, 'On the use and abuse of geography in historical explanation' (paper delivered at the French History Seminar, Corpus Christi College, Cambridge, Nov. 1977).

[16] Ardouin-Dumazet, *Voyage*, pp. 8, 35.

factory production of textiles. Unlike Roubaix, Tourcoing in the *belle époque* continued to support both a thriving class of wool-traders and many skilled manual textile workers, employed in anachronistic, but still viable artisan workshops, weaving intricate textured cloth, mainly used for upholstery fabric.

In addition, Tourcoing's greater proximity to the Belgian border gave its inhabitants access to a second source of ready income. This was smuggling. Items heavily taxed in France were brought across the border in darkness, when smugglers were helped by the heavy fogs of the Flanders night. One visitor remarked that 'every hamlet, suburb, or Belgian village near the gates of Tourcoing is crowded with workers seduced by the low prices . . . of sugar, coffee, matches, tobacco, and so on, all sold much cheaper than in France.'[17] This smuggling trade was often carried on with the tacit approval of the local textile manufacturers (though not with that of the local republican officials), who saw in smuggling a safety-valve for frustrations engendered by the sporadic employment pattern of factory textile production in the period.

These various characteristics help to explain the greater harmony which existed between classes in Tourcoing throughout the early years of the *belle époque*. Tourcoing's workers proved much more reluctant recruits for the socialist movement which swept rapidly through the workers' *quartiers* of Roubaix and Lille in the 1880s and 1890s. Nevertheless, the pressures of a growing industry, together with a massive immigrant population, gradually weakened the social stability of the city. By 1914, only superficial remnants of the old Tourcoing remained, and thus on the eve of the Great War Tourcoing's socialists at last began to enjoy some success in the municipal and national elections.

ii

Industrialization did not only alter the district characters of Lille, Roubaix, and Tourcoing in the late nineteenth century but it also began to tie the cities together into what eventually became a single urban mass. The most important elements in the growing connection among the three cities were new roads,—such as the broad, paved *boulevard Gambetta*, built to link Tourcoing and

17 Ibid., p. 39.

Roubaix in 1872—railway trains, and, most importantly for workers, trams.

Horse-drawn trams were first constructed in the 1870s to link workers' districts in all three cities. By the time steam power replaced horses in the eighties and nineties, a vast web of iron rails ran throughout the area. Moreover, because tram rides were relatively cheap, they were the workers' form of public transport *par excellence.* Every morning, in the early pre-dawn hours, thousands of textile workers mounted the trams for the ride to work. For many observers, this daily scene evoked romantic images: gas lights flickering in the morning mists and engines' steam, tram bells ringing, echoed in the distance by the whistles of the great factories . . . Such images softened the harsher reality that coloured the lives of most textile workers in the era. For most tram-riders the trams were, more than anything, eminently practical. By 1900, over half the daily passengers were workers.[18]

Because they provided a cheap and popular form of transport among the cities, these trams had important consequences for political developments in the Lille area in the *belle époque.* Firstly, the relatively low second-class fare (from 15 to 45 centimes, depending on distance) made quick trips between factories easy. At the first sign of a major strike both strike leaders and local organizers could move freely about the textile districts of the cities, spreading news, soliciting support, gathering strike funds, and so on. Secondly, mass meetings, upon which socialist leaders came to depend for the oral dissemination of propaganda, became possible for the first time. Thirdly, the network of trams facilitated the all-important rapid distribution of newspapers, strike bulletins, and broadsides, which poured from the socialist press in Lille. Not only did the trams carry printed material from one workers' area to another, but they also carried a few literate passengers, who either read their papers aloud during the journey from city to city, or left papers behind on seats, to be picked up by other passengers. Fourthly, and concomitantly with the previous point, tram journeys provided regular, informal contact between workers, who were usually prevented from casual conversation during

[18] J.-E. Van den Driessche, *Histoire de Tourcoing* (Tourcoing, 1928), p. 192; Motte, *Roubaix à travers*, p. 63; Pierrard, *Lille et les Lillois* (Paris, 1967), pp. 231–4.

working hours, both by stringent factory rules and by the oppressive noise of the textile machinery. For these people, the tramcars provided a place to socialize as well as a forum for political discussions safe from the prying eyes of the *patronat*.

Not only did the trams provide a venue for workers' politics in the *belle époque*, they also provided the means by which leaders and militants travelled from district to district during strikes or demonstrations. It is arguable, in fact, that without these trams the rapid spread of the mass general strikes of 1880, 1890, 1903–4, and 1909 might well have been slowed considerably. But with them, news of workers' activities anywhere within the three cities' perimeter spread like wildfire. This movement of leaders from city to city, moreover, helped to break down some of the barriers which prevented the development of class solidarity which crossed city boundaries. When the trams eventually spread to Belgium, this development of a wider class-consciousness began to cross even national boundaries.

Amidst all the good, however, lurked one negative factor. Although the tram fares were relatively low—and certainly much cheaper than those on trains—they were still beyond the reach of the poorest textile workers of Lille, Roubaix, and Tourcoing, most of whom were women. For the great majority of *ouvrières*, even a 30 centime return ticket ate up a large part of a day's wages (which averaged, throughout our period, just under 2.50 fr. a day). For most of them, regular use of the trams was out of the question. The immediate effect of this was that most working women could not afford to travel very far from home in search of new employment with higher wages or better conditions than they found in mills nearer their homes. Thus they were effectively tied to jobs within walking distance. Not surprisingly, this restriction contributed to their greater unwillingness to risk their jobs by rebelling against conditions—a luxury many of the higher-paid men could more readily indulge, because they could travel further afield in search of alternative work.

A second problem which arose from the cost of tram fares was women's inability to attend more than a few of the all-important mass political meetings of the eighties and nineties, through which both the socialist party and its textile unions spread their message. Because such meetings were also the place where most unions and party sections were organized, many women found themselves left out of official groups. In the early years of the eighties and nineties, women organized their own groups within their *quartiers*, and held meetings near members' homes. But when the various socialist groups of the area began increasingly to group together into a more centralized, area-wide structure, the women's groups found it impossible to follow suit. They remained instead an unconnected cluster of small, *quartier*-based groups, whose potential collective strength was diluted by their lack of co-ordination.

Railway train fares were equally beyond the means of women textile workers, just as they were too costly for most men workers. But their development in the area proved a boon to socialist politics. Not only did they bring national political newspapers to the area but they also brought socialist leaders from all over France—indeed, from all over Europe—who packed the public meeting halls of Lille and Roubaix with potential socialist recruits. In the early years, several famous women socialists and left-wing political figures appeared on local platforms, encouraging women as well as men to join the *Parti ouvrier*. The visits of such figures gave local workers a sense that they were joining a much larger movement—one which encompassed industrial workers all over Europe.

For most local workers, however, the system of new, paved roads was more immediately important than the other new forms of transport. Not only did the new roads ease the daily trip from home to mill, but they also provided a venue for the activities of fête days—not least for the endless parades to which Flemish workers were addicted. Moreover, because these roads allowed the parades to go beyond the borders of the cities, they drew local workers closer together. By the end of our period, most fêtes included workers from all three cities in their activities. This fact, in turn, reflected the extent to which the working class of the area had grown into a single entity.

iii

Despite these connecting links, however, most workers' lives unfolded within their own *quartiers*. And in the *belle époque*, there was nothing 'pretty' about any of them. Indeed, workers' slums in our period were at least as squalid as those which had caused

Adolphe Blanqui to declare Lille a 'city of pariahs' in 1849.[19] And, of course, there were many more of them in *fin de siècle* Lille, Roubaix, and Tourcoing, crowded to overflowing with workers and families. One observer remarked with horror: 'At every step one confronts scenes of frightful misery.'[20]

Part of the reason for the extreme wretchedness which lurked in every workers' *quartier* in the early Third Republic was the massive population growth in the three cities. Whereas the national population growth had settled near to a zero growth by mid-century, that of the Lille *arrondissement* remained extremely high. Lille nearly quadrupled its population between 1816 and 1885, from 55,000 to 204,000. In roughly the same period, Roubaix grew from a town of just over 12,000 to a major industrial centre of 100,000. Tourcoing lagged behind—growing from 14,500 to 56,000.[21] In the French context—though not in the context of other European industrial nations—this was a staggering rate of growth. There were two sources for it: Belgian immigration and a continuing high birth-rate.

Go on any Monday morning, between 7 and 8 o'clock, to the place where Roubaix meets Lannoy, at the square called 'la justice'. There you'll see children from 12 to 16 coming into Roubaix, walking from Hainaut-Belgique, carrying their pots of butter and their week's supply of bread.

So wrote one visitor in the early autumn of 1896.[22] This weekly wave of 'pots du beurre' (as they were popularly known) swelled the already bursting workers' *quartiers* of Lille, Roubaix, and Tourcoing throughout the *belle époque*.

Although the movement of Belgians across the French border was not new, it increased in the early years of the Third Republic as textile workers were attracted to the higher wages paid in the French mills. At first, most Belgians came only on a weekly basis, and took little part in the community life of the French workers,

[19] Adolphe Blanqui, *Des classes ouvrières en France pendant l'année 1848* (Paris, 1849), p. 33.

[20] Mathilde Bourdon, *Marthe Blondel, ou l'ouvrière de fabrique* (Paris, 1862).

[21] Population figures taken from: France, *Annuaire statistique 1886* (Paris, 1886); Pierrard, *Lille*, p. 234; F. R. Codaccioni, *et al.*, *Histoire d'une métropole: Lille, Roubaix, Tourcoing* (Toulouse, 1977), p. 317. See also André Armengaud, *La Population française au XIXᵉ siècle* (Paris, 1971).

[22] IISH 'Dossier Jules Guesde' 637/5.

preferring to stay in rooming-houses located in predominantly Belgian districts. Gradually, however, perhaps inevitably, some began to settle permanently in the three cities, some in Belgian districts but others throughout the area. When an 1889 law encouraged foreign settlers to take French citizenship (the government having an eye to increasing the numbers of potential military conscripts), many Belgians did so.

The precise numbers of Belgian workers in Lille, Roubaix, and Tourcoing in the *belle époque* are impossible to discover. Contemporary sources offered wildly varying estimates, their confusion increased by the mixture of Flemish-speaking and French-speaking Belgians (though the latter were relatively few). However, sources make it clear that the numbers were substantial. In 1904, the Lille sections of the national socialist textile workers' union declared that at least 40 per cent of the total textile work-force in that city was Belgian. That same year, the *conseil des prud'hommes* of Tourcoing estimated that some two-thirds of that city's textile work-force was Belgian, though only one-third were permanent residents in France. The best estimate for Roubaix in 1904 suggested that between 35 per cent and 40 per cent of all textile workers in that city were Belgian, 'most' of them living permanently in France.[23]

The presence of so many Belgians had two important consequences. Firstly, they brought with them their experience with socialist food co-operatives which helped transform the small French co-ops of the area into vast food stores by the end of the nineteenth century. Secondly, in a less positive vein, the Belgians initially weakened textile workers' solidarity by offering convenient scapegoats for native-born workers' wrath at the growing rate of unemployment in the 1880s. The Belgians' experience, of course, mirrored that of immigrant labourers everywhere during depression years. But there was a second aspect to their situation which arose from the presence in the local industrial work-force of so many women. Elsewhere in France, lower-paid women workers usually bore the brunt of male workers' fear of competition. In our area, the Belgians absorbed such hostility, allowing the relations between men and women workers to remain as amicable as Villermé found them to be in the 1830s. Accusations of 'job

[23] Figures used are from *Enquête sur l'industrie, 1904*, pp. 425, 420, 212.

stealing' were aimed almost exclusively at Belgians rather than at women.[24]

Moreover, the rhetoric in which such accusations were couched bore a striking resemblance to that more commonly employed against women's work. Native-born workers complained that the Belgians were 'naturally more docile'—willing to accept the worst jobs at the lowest wages without protest. One Tourcoing magistrate told a parliamentary committee in 1904 that the Belgians endured any hardship imposed by the *patronat* 'without a murmur'. Maxence van der Meersch, the Roubaix-born novelist, corroborated this view. The Belgians, he wrote, 'worked with the courageous patience of the labouring beast'.[25] (Such stereotypes continue to provide the basis for French mockery of their Belgian neighbours.)

Belgian passivity in the face of low wages and difficult conditions was, needless to say, a result not of national character but rather of dire economic necessity.[26] Furthermore, most observers from outside the area saw little distinction between the behaviour of French-born textile workers and those who came from across the Belgian border. In fact, long before the massive influx of Belgians, Villermé had remarked 'the sweetness, patience, and resignation' which, he wrote, 'lay at the heart of the Flemish character'.[27]

In addition to the massive Belgian immigration, all three cities felt the effects of a birth-rate that was higher than any in France. In 1870, the rate in Lille, Roubaix, and Tourcoing was nearly 41.54 per thousand—compared with only 25.9 per thousand in France as a whole. This high rate was nearer those in other industrial countries, including Germany, with its birth rate of 38.5

---

[24] A classic expression of some men workers' hostility to women workers is found in 'Le Travail féminin en concurrence avec le travail masculin', *Libres Entretiens* (10 jan. 1909), p. 132. In the article, the writer argued, 'It is no longer necessary to protect the women from the exploitation of manufacturers of middle-men; it is now necessary to protect the man against the woman.'

[25] See *Enquête sur l'industrie, 1904*, 'déposition, juge de paix de Tourcoing', p. 448, and Maxence van der Meersch, *Quand les sirènes se taisent* (Paris, 1933), p. 29.

[26] Eugen Weber, in *Peasants into Frenchmen, the Modernisation of Rural France, 1870–1914* (London, 1977) has argued that this sense of national identity had overwhelmed most French people by the end of the century.

[27] Louis-René Villermé, *État physique et moral des ouvriers des manufactures de coton, laine . . .* (Paris, 1840), vol. i, p. 103.

per thousand, and England and Wales with their rate of 35.2 per thousand in the same year.[28]

In the years around the turn of the century, the birth-rate began to drop to a figure more nearly resembling that of the rest of the country. By 1891, the rate was 29 per thousand, and by 1908 it had dropped to 25.2 per thousand. In spite of the decline, however, the Lille *arrondissement* continued to rank high among the rapidly growing areas of France.[29] In the last census taken before the Great War, in 1911, there were 217,807 *Lillois*, 122,700 *Roubaisiens*, and 82,600 *Tourquenois*. Most of these were workers. According to the historian Félix-Paul Codaccioni, the 'popular classes' constituted over 67 per cent of the local population, and 80 per cent of these popular classes were *ouvriers* (properly so-called).[30]

iv

Of these vast numbers of workers, a substantial proportion filled the work-rooms of the textile mills, especially in Roubaix and Tourcoing, where alternative employment was scarcer than in the more mixed economy of Lille. For women, especially, textiles provided their most likely source of steady income.

How many workers actually found work in the mills of Lille, Roubaix, and Tourcoing during our period is difficult to estimate. Employment figures were highly volatile, as the situation in the industry varied almost from day to day.[31] The fact that virtually all

[28] For France, see Pierrard, *Lille*, p. 234. For Britain and Germany, see B.R. Mitchell, *European Historical Statistics 1750–1970* (New York, 1978).

[29] The reasons for this anomaly remain unclear. Possible hypotheses are found in Marcel Gillet, 'Présentation générale', in Gillet, ed., *L'Homme, la vie et la mort dans le Nord au 19ᵉ siècle* (Lille, 1972), p. 9; Angus McLaren, 'Doctor in the House: medicine and private morality in France, 1800–1850', *Feminist Studies*, ii (Autumn 1975), pp. 39–54. It seems likely that each of these historians is partly correct. In other words, it was probably a combination of residual Catholic beliefs plus a lack of effective birth control, plus a traditional Flemish love of children.

[30] France, *Recensement de la population, 1911* (Paris, 1912), and Félix-Paul Codaccioni, *De l'inégalité sociale dans une grande ville industrielle: le drame de Lille de 1850 à 1914* (Lille, 1976), pp. 110, 142.

[31] *ADN* M 572, 6, 7, 'Situation industrielle 1885' includes a *chambre de commerce* report to the effect that no figures were available as the situation in textiles varied from day to day. See also *AN*, C 3019, 36, 'Enquête des situations ouvrières, 1872–85' in which a Roubaix mill owner claimed to employ 'between 2,500 and 9,000 workers'. See also *ADN* M 591, 1, 1–10, 'Travail dans l'industrie, 1891'.

official statistics in the early decades of the Third Republic were at best of questionable reliability further compounds the historian's problem.[32] Then, too, most local observers including both employers and union leaders were frequently more concerned with supporting a political point than with providing accurate numbers. Thus, the numbers which follow are, at best, informed approximations.[33]

With these caveats in mind, however, it is possible to estimate the numbers of women and men textile workers in the period 1880 to 1914. In 1882, the prefect of the Nord department reported that there were 7,385 adult (i.e. over 18) women working in textiles in Lille, 4,958 in Roubaix, and 4,160 in Tourcoing.[34] There were a further 30,000 adult men working in the mills of the three cities, making a total of 46,503 workers. (These figures were lower than in previous years because 1882 was a year of widespread unemployment in the industry, and the prefect did not count unemployed workers.) In addition, several thousand children of both sexes—many only 10 years old—further swelled the work-force. But their employment was even more sporadic than that of

---

[32] More than one historian has discovered the inaccuracy of official French statistics in this period. The early Third Republic lacked any coherent policy on gathering such data. Enquiries sent to prefects were often casually passed on to mayors. Some of these, in turn, asked the *patronat* for data, or the local *chambre de commerce* or *conseil des prud'hommes*. No controls existed; no sources were given. Only manuscript data, sometimes found in local archives, hints at the total absence of method in the collection of what became the official, published statistics for the period. Two other discussions of these statistics are found in Michelle Perrot, *Enquêtes sur la condition ouvrière en France au dix-neuvième siècle* (Paris, n.d.), pp. 13–20, and Tony Judt, *Socialism in Provence, 1871–1914* (Cambridge, 1979), pp. 337–42.

[33] This does not mean, of course, that social historians should avoid using quantitative materials altogether, but only that these sources must be checked carefully against qualitative data. Moreover, numbers do not, in themselves, explain change or supply explanations for attitudes or behaviour. Yet a popular preoccupation with what Ernest Gombrich has called *Idola Quantitatus* often veils the inadequacies of numbers. It is this preoccupation that evoked Tony Judt's criticism in 'A Clown in Regal Purple: social history and the historians', *History Workshop Journal*, vii (spring 1979), pp. 66–94. Numbers, in Judt's view, have too often served as 'pompous words' which often conceal a 'vile conceit'. ('A vile conceit in pompous words express'd / Is like a clown in regal purple dress'd', Alexander Pope, *Essay on Criticism*.

[34] *ADN* M 611–18, 'Travail des femmes adultes dans les manufactures. Enquête, 1882–3'. Numbers of male workers are derived by using the 1896 ratio of eight males to every female working in textiles.

the adults, and their numbers, consequently, even more difficult to estimate. And, of course, the textile *patronat*, mindful of the ever-increasing pressure to minimize the employment of young children in the mills, were reluctant to admit the actual extent of their presence, thus complicating the problem further.

By 1896, the government estimated that the total number of textile workers in Lille, Roubaix, and Tourcoing had increased to 81,710, of whom 30,000 were adult women. Factories situated in the suburbs of Lille added an additional 30,596 men and 20,518 women, bringing the total textile work-force of the area to 132,824.[35]

Despite the gravity of the economic crisis which brought increased suffering to the textile workers of the Lille area after 1899, the total textile workforce—mostly employed only seasonally—continued to grow. By 1904 there were 128,459 textile workers in the three cities proper (that is, excluding those working in the suburban mills), of whom 38,119 were women.[36] These figures increased, though the numbers available for 1914 are even less reliable than earlier ones. One 1914 observer counted 50,000 women textile workers in Lille and its suburbs.[37] If the ratio of women workers in Lille to those in Roubaix and Tourcoing remained roughly the same in 1914 as it had been in earlier years, then there were 31,000 more women working in Roubaix, plus 19,000 in Tourcoing, for a total of 70,000 women textile workers on the eve of the Great War. If the proportion of women to men held steady, then the total textile work-force in all three cities in that year numbered 241,500 adults, well over half the population in the area.

This 1914 estimate seems high, however, despite a recovery in the industry, the effects of which began to be felt in 1911. Nor was the vast increase in women workers explained by the replacement of men workers with women, as was the pattern in other French

---

[35] France *Résultats statistiques du recensement des industries et professions, 29 mars 1896* (Paris, 1896). Because most figures in this source resulted from the efforts of factory work inspectors, working within the *Office du travail* (founded in 1891) they are probably more reliable than those collected willy-nilly by a variety of people—though the *Office* did not prescribe standard procedures.

[36] These figures are taken from *Enquête sur l'industrie, 1904*, vol. ii, pp. 223, 427, 338, 339.

[37] See *BS* (20 Ap. 1914).

industry in the period. In fact, between 1896 and 1904—two years for which there are relatively accurate figures—the proportion of women to men actually dropped, from 36 per cent of the total work-force to only 29 per cent. (This drop was due to protective labour legislation which shortened women's hours, making it difficult for employers to retain them in mills which could work men for twelve hours and even longer. Not every—or even most— of the mill owners complied with the new laws, as we shall see, but those who did often chose to let their women workers go.)

Thousands of children also worked in the mills, though the pattern for girls and boys was different. In the 1880s most children entered the factory between the ages of 10 and 13. The girls, however, typically remained working in the mills until one of three things forced them out. In descending order of importance these were ill health, a debilitating factory accident, or the presence of too many children at home. Once in the mills, most girls remained there throughout their lives. On the other hand, although boys entered the factories at the same age, they were more likely to leave for some period during their adolescence.[38] The army, of course, took a large number of youths from the mills for two years. But in addition, young men frequently chose to leave textiles to seek alternative employment—which was more available to them than to the girls. Not least among their choices was smuggling which, while not exclusively a male preserve (many young women served prison sentences for it in our period[39]), certainly attracted many more young men and women. Furthermore, youths could pick up various odd jobs about the cities—hauling, packing and unpacking, cleaning rail and tram tracks, and loading and unloading barges on the canals which criss-crossed the region in the late nineteenth century. They could also try working in other kinds of factories. Chicory-processing and metalwork employed substantial numbers of local men.

[38] These data are found in Tony Judt, *Marxism and Labour in France* (Oxford, forthcoming, 1986).

[39] See B. Broutchoux, 'Celina Renoir: le régime des prisons—Une fille torturée', *L'Action syndicale* (6 Man. 1904), which documents the arrest and imprisonment of a young Lille woman convicted of bringing twenty boxes of matches across the border. After ten days in solitary confinement, in a cellar without heat, her feet froze. Both had to be amputated. The prison warden was subsequently fired by the prefect, M. Vincent. The girl got 50 fr. compensation from the prefecture.

The fact that girls remained in the textile mills had important implications in the formation of their political behaviour. Work habits inculcated in childhood stuck. In addition, girls who had no experience of life beyond the mill or *quartier* were less likely to imagine anything very different from what they knew. Thus their long unbroken years in the mills narrowed their mental horizons. As a result, many were less ready to embrace the socialist dream, especially in some of its more radical guises.

v

The great masses of textile workers created an enormous housing problem in Lille, Roubaix, and Tourcoing in the early Third Republic. By the 1880s, the extent of squalid housing became obvious to even the most sanguine local authorities, though it did little to arouse the sympathies of the local textile *patronat*. The fact that nothing was done to alleviate the misery in which most workers lived may have been due to the rapidity of social change in the century, which Pierre Sorlin has argued left the bourgeoisie 'stunned, unable to react'.[40] But whatever the cause, massive local indifference allowed the appalling squalor to increase in the thirty-four years after 1880. As a result, conditions in the workers' *quartiers* grew worse.

The most notorious of local workers' *quartiers* was Saint-Sauveur, which horrified every visitor to Lille throughout the nineteenth century. In 1840, Villermé painted a grim portrait of the 3,687 workers ('weavers, spinners, and lace-makers') he discovered huddled beneath the city's streets in the infamous cellar dwellings of the district. These people, the prefect told him, were effectively 'entombed' below ground. A local poet added that these 'caves' contained 'twisted souls and bodies' inhabiting 'basements, more muffled than the Avernes . . .'.[41]

These cellars of Saint-Sauveur deserved their evil notoriety. Dug below the pavements of the district, they were entered by a street-level trapdoor. A narrow ladder led down into the single room in which an entire family lived and worked. By day, the

<hr>

[40] Pierre Sorlin, *La Société française, 1840–1914* (Paris, 1969), vol. i, p. 125.
[41] Villermé, *État physique*, vol. i, pp. 79–80; Verhaeren, quoted in Claude Willard, *Les Guesdistes: le mouvement socialiste en France (1893–1905)* (Paris, 1965), p. 229.

trapdoors were left open, providing limited access to light and air. At night they were closed in an effort to preserve any heat that the cellar had accumulated during the day.[42]

Lille's massive growth in the second half of the nineteenth century ensured that these cellars continued to house many workers throughout our period. But they were nowhere near numerous enough to provide housing for the soaring numbers of workers who crowded the area. Gradually, therefore, every one of the old, multi-roomed houses of the district was subdivided into as many rooms as possible, each one holding a whole family. Even the tiniest attic was rented by workers desperate for shelter.

Those workers who could not find a home in the various *quartiers* of 'vieux Lille' gathered instead in Lille's working-class suburbs. In 1881, the south-west canton of Lille, which included four workers' districts—Moulins-Lille, Wazemmes, Fives, and Esquermes—housed more people than the other four Lille cantons combined. More than 50,000 workers lived in Wazemmes, 19,819 in Moulins-Lille, 10,952 in Esquermes, and 21,247 in Fives.[43] Conditions in these swarming districts were only slightly less appalling than those in Saint-Sauveur. One traveller described Wazemmes: 'Streets are sad', she wrote, 'muddy lakes flow between the paving stones. Everywhere there are *estaminets*, filled with drunks of both sexes.'[44]

Most families in these four *quartiers* on the edge of Lille occupied part of a narrow, terraced house. Few families enjoyed more than two rooms, and the poorest had only one. Most of these terraces were built along narrow, partially paved alley-ways, into which sunlight shone for only a few hours a day, if at all. Sewage and rain water ran in the streets; mud was an ever-present fact of life.[45]

Entrepreneurs in Roubaix found a different solution to that city's housing problem. There, beginning in mid-century, they built what became Roubaix's infamous 'courées', or courtyards. Terraces were built around a square, which backed up to another

---

[42] Léon and Maurice Bonneff, *La Vie tragique des travailleurs* (Paris, 1914), pp. 24–8.

[43] Pierrard, *Lille*, p. 126.

[44] Marcelle Capy, 'Industrie textile. Pour oublier', *BS* (19 Ap. 1914).

[45] See Georges Sueur, *Lille, Roubaix, Tourcoing: Métropole en miettes* (Paris, 1971), p. 9.

square, which, in turn, backed up to yet another square. The *courées* sat at right angles all along a main road. A narrow opening allowed passage from the road into each *courée* and served as well as drainage for the water and sewage which collected in a channel running down the centre of the interior yard. So efficient were these red-brick beehives in housing thousands of workers at low cost and for high profits that speculators in Tourcoing and Lille rapidly caught on and began to fill their cities' empty spaces with similar constructions.[46]

Conditions in the *courées* were horrific. One journalist, Marcelle Capy, wrote a detailed account of Roubaix's *courées*. She described 'tiny, narrow streets, with a narrow waste canal running down the centre. On each side stand a row of low houses. There are no cellars, no air, no sun, and constant damp. For these, the inhabitants pay high rents to house their huge families in single rooms, where all functions take place. There may be as many as 10 people living crowded together in one room.' Capy visited two *courée* interiors. In the first, she found a woman, her daughter, and her three grandchildren, aged 7, 2, and a few months, living in a single first-floor room. The room was furnished with one bed, one cradle, one table, and one stool. During Capy's visit, the baby crawled around the floor 'half naked' in the bitter cold, while the 7-year-old was sick in one corner. Freshly washed clothing and bed linens were draped along the walls to dry. A single window was closed against the cold. A small smoky stove heated the room. In a similar home nearby, Capy found a family of six sharing a single room.

Both these dwellings formed part of a *courée* built along Roubaix's notorious 'via dolorosa', the *rue des Longues-Haies*. The forty *courées* of this single short road housed more than 10,000 people, 250 in each.[47]

A typical *courée* lodging (which was usually subdivided into single-room dwellings or occasionally rented as a whole to the more fortunate) contained 'two up, two down'. Windows existed on the front wall, looking into the central yard, as most houses backed up to those of another *courée*. Dwellings typically

---

[46] Bonneffs, *Vie tragique*, pp. 24–8 and Sueur, *Lille, Roubaix, Tourcoing*, pp. 16–17.
[47] Capy, 'Industrie textile. Mal logés, mal nourris', *BS* (16 Ap. 1914).

measured about 18 feet across. Inside, the two ground-floor rooms measured respectively 8½ feet by 11 feet and 9½ feet by 13½ feet. The two upstairs rooms shared these dimensions, but the ceilings were much lower—just over 5½ feet high. Although the low ceilings suited these rooms for little more than sleeping-lofts, photographs from the period, as well as contemporaries' accounts, suggest that many families shared the plight of Capy's subjects, and inhabited a single upstairs room.[48]

Outside, in the courtyard itself, stood two or three privies. These communal toilets were cleaned, if at all, by the women of the *courée*. (Most observers were surprised by the cleanliness of the *courées*, which the Flemish women achieved in spite of the filth and mud.) In more affluent *courées*, the yard was cobbled. In most, however, it was little more than a puddle of mud, sloping toward a central drainage ditch. In dry weather, the women hung their laundry on ropes and wires which criss-crossed the yard. Somewhere in each *courée* a single tap provided water for all the inhabitants.

A great surge in *courée* construction came in the two decades before and after the turn of the century. Whereas, for example, Roubaix had only 156 *courées* in 1891 (housing 16,109 people), by 1896 it had 205, by 1904, 1,050, and by 1912, a total of 1,524 *courées*, housing 156,972 people.[49]

Though there are no figures for the precise number of *courées* in neighbouring Tourcoing in the *belle époque*, it is clear from contemporaries' comments that they existed there in their hundreds. As Ardouin-Dumazet travelled along the tram line from Belgium through Tourcoing and on to Roubaix just after the turn of the century, he remarked on the number of *courées* he saw on both sides of the line. He described them as '*cités sombres*, filling every square foot of space—all identical, all running with foul sewage and filled with barefoot, tow-haired children, playing in the mud of the unpaved paths and courtyards'.[50]

---

[48] Photographs are found in Jacques Borgé et Nicolas Viasnoff, eds., *Archives du Nord* (Paris, 1979), pp. 70, 89.

[49] Many *courées* are still inhabited in Roubaix and Tourcoing. See Jacques Toulemonde, *Naissance d'une métropole: Roubaix et Tourcoing au XIXe siècle* (Tourcoing, n.d.), p. 79, and Codaccioni, *et al.*, eds., *Histoire d'une métropole*, p. 360.

[50] Ardouin-Dumazet, *Voyage*, p. 18.

Lille, with less open space available for building, was slower to copy Roubaix's lead, but by 1911 local speculators had constructed 882 *courées*, the majority of them in the five working-class districts which bordered the city on the south-west.[51]

Conditions in the *courées*, as well as in other types of workers' housing, varied, of course, depending on such amenities as paving, the size of each dwelling, and so on. Nevertheless, tight over-crowding was the salient feature of working-class life everywhere in Lille, Roubaix, and Tourcoing. One housing survey taken in 1911 found, for example, 32,442 *Lillois* living in homes with less than one-quarter of a room per person. A further 69,925 lived in lodgings where each person had 'more than one-half, but less than one' room. In Roubaix, investigators found 4,288 people living in less than a quarter of a room, and a further 29,555 in just over one-half a room each. These figures are even more shocking when one learns that the definition of a room was 'any space large enough to allow one person to lie down'.[52]

Not surprisingly, these slums were ideal incubators for a variety of diseases. Furthermore, the structure of the *courées*, in which all dwellings faced each other across a yard, prohibited privacy. Families spilled out into the muddy courtyards in good weather and bad. All the inhabitants shared equally the noise, the odours, the filth produced by hundreds of people living in close proximity without adequate sanitation. It was no wonder that observers were shocked. In one novel Maxence van der Meersch described a Roubaix *courée*. 'Throngs of miserable people', he wrote, lay 'buried in ramshackle, evil-smelling tenements, in tortuous courts and alleys at the heart of the great city. There were dubious beds, nightdresses that were dirty and full of holes, grimy feet, and suspicious flesh that one approached holding one's breath.'[53] And the inhabitants themselves were no less conscious of the horrors. One worker wrote eloquently to a local socialist newspaper in the spring of 1882, 'I live in a filthy hovel, into which death oozes: not a violent death, but rather a slow one.'[54] The adjective most

---

[51] Pierrard, *Lille*, p. 226.

[52] France, *Statistique générale de la France. Statistique des familles et des habitations en 1911 (Paris, 1912).*

[53] Maxence van der Meersch, *Bodies and Souls*, trans. Eithne Wilkins (New York, 1948), p. 409.

[54] *LF* (14 July 1882).

frequently employed in *fin de siècle* descriptions of these *courées* was 'nauséabonde'.

These stark facts do not, however, tell the whole story of workers' domestic lives in the region at the end of the nineteenth century. Relief from crowding and misery, though temporary, was found in the ubiquitous *estaminets* which occupied a corner of every *courée* or road. In these warm and brightly lit café-bars, families found comradeship, cheap food, credit, help in times of need, and, most importantly of all, a constant supply of the beer and gin which were popularly believed to wash the deadly textile dust from workers' lungs. Furthermore, those *estaminets* which were run by sympathetic *cabaretiers* or *cabaretières* offered a rare haven from the prying eyes of the *patronat* or their minions—the priests, nuns, and police, who felt no compunction about entering workers' homes at will on a variety of pretexts. Protective of this valuable privacy, workers rarely welcomed outsiders in their *estaminets*. When Villermé peered into some local café-bars earlier in the nineteenth century, he met daunting hostility (a hostility that continues to the present day). Intent on his researches into workers' private lives, he persisted. A successful, if furtive, glimpse into the interior of one *estaminet* revealed a shocking sight. Women, he discovered, were drinking side by side with men. (Elsewhere in France women were prohibited by long custom from entering bars unless they were there as prostitutes.[55]) Not only women, but children as well, were welcome in the *estaminets* of French Flanders. In fact, these *estaminets* were, in addition to the *courées* themselves, the major centre of workers' social lives in our period. But the bourgeois view of these vice dens continued to echo Villermé's concluding remarks: 'I must affirm: I have never seen, all at the same time, so much beastliness, so much misery, so much vice, and nowhere in an atmosphere more hideous, more revolting.'[56]

Contrary to the opinions of outsiders, however, the atmosphere in most *estaminets* was neither beastly nor revolting. In addition to

---

[55] Respectable women were excluded from café-bars throughout Provence, for example. This exclusion effectively barred them from participating in most of the day-to-day political life of the area. As Flemish tradition made no such division by gender, working women of Lille, Roubaix, and Tourcoing were more involved in a shared public life than elsewhere.

[56] Villermé, *État physique*, vol. i, p. 85.

shared drink, food, local gossip, and news (frequently read aloud by the literate few), workers enjoyed both singing and the recitations of local street poets, who recorded, in the local patois, events of everyday life. According to one visitor, these poets spoke not of the vanished 'fields and woods' of pre-industrial Flanders, but rather 'of life in the *quartier*'. Moreover, he added, 'At Lille, one cannot find even a single cross-roads without its appointed poet. All year long, these street minstrels forge their couplets, telling about the events unfolding in their narrow world. They sing them in the *estaminets*. Then, when carnival time comes in mid-Lent, societies are formed, of which the local bard becomes the leader.' The most popular songs told 'little stories of the streets', chastised wayward husbands or wives, or simply recorded the details of workers' humble lives.[57]

vi

Most of the efforts which made life in the workers' *quartiers* tolerable came from the women. They finished a day of work in the mills only to confront an evening of domestic work. In the short hours before they fell into bed, the working women of Lille, Roubaix, and Tourcoing struggled to maintain some order and cleanliness in the constant mud and detritus of their slums. And, however loudly local socialists proclaimed their opposition to women's 'double toil', the *belle époque* saw no lessening of this work.[58] Daily domestic drudgery filled most women's hours away from the mills. And, as was the case with factory discipline, girls learned their domestic chores in early childhood. Thus, most adult women accepted them as a fact of life.

When 1892 factory legislation aimed to alleviate some of working women's misery by prescribing a 'day of rest' from mill work, the results were far from helpful. The day away from the mill only meant more time for housework. One sympathetic woman work inspector described a typical Sunday in Lille:

In effect, Sunday's work stoppage permits the man and boy to enjoy a prolonged sleep on Sunday morning, and gives them leisure time to get

[57] Ardouin-Dumazet, *Voyage*, p. 104.

[58] A more positive though no less critical view of *courée* life is found in van der Meersch, *Quand les sirènes* . . .

exercise, to go for walks, and to entertain themselves for the rest of the day. It is not the same for the mother or for the girls. It is necessary for them to put in order all the housework which was neglected during the rest of the week because there was not time for it: there is washing to do, general house-cleaning, repair of husbands' and childrens' clothes. When all this is finished, the 'day of rest' has passed.[59]

These domestic routines of selfless, never-ending labour, learned early in childhood, together with the habits of the mill shaped most women textile workers' experiences throughout their lives.

[59] Caroline Milhaud, *L'Ouvrière en France* (Paris, 1907), p. 125.

2

LA VIE INTIME

i

'IF a boy or girl goes to work in a spinning mill at an early age, he or she will die young, usually before 45.' Thus one Lille professor assessed the life expectancy of local textile workers at the beginning of the twentieth century. Divided by gender, the prediction for women was grimmer still: most working women died in their mid-thirties.[1]

Mindful of popular stereotypes of bourgeois women in France in the *belle époque*, observers remarked with particular horror the physical toll exacted by women's work in the mills. One visitor wrote:

In the cities of the Nord, at the gates of spinning and weaving mills, one sees puny, thin, deformed bodies, pale skin, sunken eyes, hollow cheeks, bloodless lips. These women are old before they are young. Misery and consumption stalk them, tracking them towards the death that awaits them on a street corner, carried on a fatal wind, or even in their miserable slums, without air, without heat, without cheer.[2]

Two union militants, the brothers Maurice and Léon Bonneff, visited the three cities in 1913. They were similarly shocked by what they found in the workers' *quartiers* of Lille. During one visit, their guide asked them, *sotto voce*, to guess the age of the dying woman whose home they were entering. 'Between 45 and 50?' they ventured. 'She is twenty-six,' their guide replied.[3] However shocking the circumstances of this ex-textile *ouvrière*, they were far from unique, as the Bonneffs quickly discovered.

[1] A. Aftalion is quoted in Léon and Maurice Bonneff, *La Vie tragique des travailleurs* (Paris, 1914), p. 29. See also Marcelle Capy, 'Drames du travail', *BS* 17 Apr. 1914); M. Leclerc de Pulligny, 'Les Conditions de l'hygiène dans les filatures de lin', in France, *Bulletin de l'inspection du travail 1902* (Paris, 1903), p. 233; and Désiré Descamps, *Les Crimes de la misère* (Lille, 1892), which shows the higher local death-rate among the poor.

[2] P. Brisson, *Histoire du travail et des travailleurs* (Paris, 1906), p. 443.

[3] Bonneffs, *Vie tragique*, p. 23.

The director of the local tuberculosis hospital, Dr Verhaeghe, told them that most textile workers, of either sex, were in such precarious health that their fatal illness almost always struck between the ages of 25 and 35.[4]

Thus all textile workers in Lille, Roubaix, and Tourcoing faced an early death if they continued to work in the mills. But women's shorter life expectancy put them at greater risk than their male co-workers. Three main factors help to explain women's earlier deaths. Firstly, they were less likely to have a break from mill work once they entered the mills as children. Once most girls had signed on at the mills, they were textile workers for life. Thus their exposure to the health-destroying conditions of the textile factories was unbroken, except by periods of unemployment, which exacted its own toll on women workers.

The second and third factors which contributed to women's shorter life expectancy were marriage and child-bearing, each of which further weakened women's precarious health.

ii

Most women textile workers married, and by marrying added further labour to their already exhausting working day. Unlike working women in certain other industries in France, or in other industrialized countries, few northern workers found in marriage an escape from mill work. The statement that married textile workers continued to work in the mills after marriage at first seems unproblematic, especially given the absence of any contemporaries' evidence to the contrary.[5] However, much of the historiography concerned with the political attitudes and behaviour of European working women at the turn of the nineteenth century has rested arguments about women's putative political quiescence upon the assumption that most working women left the factories after marriage or childbirth. This assumption is, in turn, often adduced to support an argument in favour of women's exclusive preoccupation with domestic—rather than public—concerns. Consequently, it has been the view of several historians that upon marriage working-class women assumed a marginal position in

---

[4] Ibid., p. 30.
[5] See Appendix.

labour or political movements and were likely to involve themselves in public activities only when their familial interests were threatened.[6]

It is the prevalence of such arguments that makes it important to emphasize that the textile mill workers of Lille, Roubaix, and Tourcoing did not usually find that marriage provided them with a way out of the factories. On the other hand, highlighting this fact is not meant to support the argument that a break in working patterns—such as that brought about elsewhere by marriage and childbirth, or, for that matter, by extended periods of unemployment—necessarily produced either political indifference or ignorance of public issues. Only the most vulgar of Marxists would suggest that the daily work experience, carried out continuously over a lifetime, alone provided the necessary conditions for the formation of political consciousness. More questionable still is the assumption that domestic work necessarily produced a reactionary political consciousness while factory labour provoked its opposite. Nevertheless, this study is concerned with the political lives of women who did not cease waged labour, and whose consciousness was shaped as much by life in the mills as it was by life in the slums of the three cities.

Moreover, the view that marriage allowed working-class women to escape factory or other waged labour was not widely held in

---

[6] Among historians who have argued this case are Eric Hobsbawm, 'Man and Woman in socialist iconography', *History Workshop Journal*, vi (autumn 1978), p. 131. (Hobsbawm has conflated the cases of England and France. In England in the late nineteenth century, working-class married women *were* less likely to remain in industrial employment, as was demonstrated by Kathleen Gales and P.H. Marks in 'Twentieth-century trends in the work of women in England and Wales', *Journal of the Royal Statistical Society*, series A, vol. cxxxvii (1974) pp. 60–70.) Others include Louise Tilly and Joan Scott, *Women, Work and Family* (New York, 1978), esp. pp. 188, 208, Patricia Branca, *Women in Europe since 1750* (London, 1978), and, surprisingly, Michelle Perrot, who does not argue that marriage was an escape from factory labour in France but who does lean toward the view that married women who worked at home, whether for wages or not, were less political and less concerned with public affairs. See 'Les Ménagères et la classe ouvrière', unpublished paper delivered at a colloquium at Vincennes, 'Les Femmes et la classe ouvrière' (16 Dec. 1978). Unfortunately both the view that marriage freed women from waged labour and the view that home workers were politically quiescent have become received wisdom. It should be added that these ideas have a long history. Paul Brisson wrote in 1906 of pre-industrial women, 'Parce qu'elles restaient chez elles, les historiens et sociologues n'ont pas pris garde qu'elles étaient des ouvrières,' *Histoire du travail*, p. 432.

France at the turn of the century. The facts would not support such
a view. The syndicalist feminist Claire Gérard, for example, found
that in 1912, out of every 100 households in France including every
socio-economic category, at least 50 included a wife who was a
waged labourer. Furthermore, in cities with textile industries, 65
households out of every 100 were partly, or entirely, supported by
the wages of wives or mothers.[7]

On the other hand, married women's double responsibilities, in
addition to shortening their lives, did circumscribe their behaviour.
At the noon whistle, for example, married women were first out of
the factory, hurrying to gather up their waiting children to feed
them lunch. The men, and those single women who did not have
responsibilities for younger siblings, made their way at a more
leisurely pace to the local *estaminets*, where they had time for
lunch and a glass or two of beer or gin. Again, at the end of the
factory day, married women rushed straight home, past the
estaminets where their husbands and sons were pausing for a drink.
Once home, they faced a second round of work: cleaning the
house, washing the children, preparing supper, doing laundry,
mending clothes, and so on. Only the most efficient—or careless—
women finished their tasks in time to join their husbands for a
drink before the family supper.

A married woman's lot, then, was harder than her husband's. In
the words of the socialist leader Aline Valette, 'Just as the word
"proletarian" applied to men is synonymous with work, with
suffering, how much more is it, in its application to women, a
synonym for double work, double suffering.'[8]

Pregnancy was the third factor which contributed to working
women's shorter life span. During their fertile years pregnancy
was, for most women, a constant fact of life. And pregnancy
brought little rest from the wearying round of mill and home.
Instead their poverty meant that most women ceased mill work for
only a brief period before and after childbirth; they needed wages
more than they needed rest.

A 1904 parliamentary commission, examining France's textile

[7] Claire Gérard, *Syndicalisme féminin et bourses du travail* (Paris, 1912), p. 4.
[8] Aline Valette, *LT* (16 May 1894). Women's double toil is vividly described by
a textile union leader outside the Nord department. See Louise Chaboseau-Napias,
'Les Femmes et le socialisme', *H* (19 Feb. 1907).

industry, was startled to discover the brevity of women's maternity break. Witnesses told that group that most women in Lille, Roubaix, and Tourcoing worked in the mills right up until their babies were born—not infrequently on the factory floor. Further, all those who testified before the deputies, including both workers and mill owners, agreed that new mothers returned to the factories as rapidly as possible, generally between two and three weeks after giving birth. So widespread was this practice among working women, in fact, that the Third Republic finally passed a law requiring paid maternity leave of one month in 1909 (the Engerand law)—though that law, like most other factory legislation, was widely ignored by both workers and owners in the Nord department.[9]

Childbirth, moreover, was nearly continuous among most textile workers. The working people of Lille, Roubaix, and Tourcoing upheld the stereotype of prolific *flamandes*, producing large families throughout the years before the war. Average family size among local workers was high. In the 1880s, estimates of the average numbers of children in textile families ranged from four to six per family—and these figures included only living children. In France as a whole, by comparison, the average was only 2.2 children per family.[10]

Although the birth-rate dropped slightly after 1880, the number of children in textile workers' homes remained high. Of a sample of 970 such families in Lille in 1914, 872 (89.9 per cent) included children, with an average of four per family. Many of the families,

---

[9] *Enquête sur l'industrie, 1904*, 'déposition, Fédération nationale des ouvriers en textile, Lille', p. 301; 'deposition, Syndicats des ouvriers de l'industrie textile, Roubaix', p. 174; 'déposition, Chambre de commerce, Roubaix', p. 155. Two other contemporaries concerned with the effects of this practice were Dr Henri Thiroux and A. Vallin. See 'Assistance et hygiène sociale', *MS*, vol. i (Jan.–June 1902), p. 313, and *La Femme salariée et la maternité* (Paris, 1911), p. 25, respectively. The *loi Engerand* is discussed in Yvonne Knibielher and Cathérine Fouquet, *Histoire des mères du Moyen Âge à nos jours* (Paris, 1977), p. 245.

[10] In 1896, the average number of children per French family was only 2.2. See *AN* C 3019, *pièce* 36, 'Enquête des situations ouvrières, 1872–1885', and Jean-Marie Mayeur, *Les Débuts de la Troisième République* (Paris, 1973), p. 56. Local population trends are analysed in detail in Marie-Pascale Buriez-Duez' 'Le Mouvement de la population dans le département du Nord au XIXᵉ siècle', in Gillet, ed., *L'Homme, la vie, et la mort dans le Nord au 19ᵉ siècle* (Lille, 1972), p. 24. The percentage of workers in the local population is found in Codaccioni, *et al.*, *Histoire d'une métropole*, p. 378.

of course, had more than four children; some had between eleven and twenty.[11]

Of course women gave birth many more times than these numbers suggest. Infant mortality in the workers' *quartiers* of Lille, Roubaix, and Tourcoing was appallingly high. In Lille in 1898, 381 out of every thousand children of textile workers died before the age of 2. In 1899, that number grew to 401 out of every thousand.[12] In 1899, Roubaix and Lille headed the list of large French cities with high infant mortality.[13]

Even more poignant than the bare figures were the words of northern textile workers themselves. In 1890, one Lille worker told Aline Valette: 'My wife has had 12 children. She worked 8 years on the night shift in carding factories. The 7 children born during that period are dead. Since then, she has worked selling newspapers; the 5 children she has brought into the world in that time are living.'[14] A decade later Jean Jaurès heard a similar story from four Armentières textile workers. When he asked them if they had lost any children, they replied in turn, starting with the oldest, 'I've lost 4; 4 remain to me'; 'I've lost 2 of 3'; 'I lost mine at 20 months'; and, 'I've lost 1 of 2'. The oldest child to die was 2 years old.[15]

Tragic as these figures were, the fact was that infant mortality was lower in Armentières than in Roubaix, Tourcoing, and Lille. In 1904, in those cities the infant mortality rate was 190–200 per thousand births, compared to 144 per thousand in France as a whole.[16]

One need not look far to find the villains in this bleak picture of infant death. As we have seen, women typically worked in the mills up until the last moment before giving birth. Childbirth usually occurred at home, in the tenements or *courées*, where even the most rudimentary hygiene was absent. Virtually no textile

---

[11] Bonneffs, *La Vie tragique*, p. 37.

[12] Figures on infant mortality are found in Aline Lesaege-Dugied, 'La Mortalité infantile dans le département du Nord de 1815 à 1914', in Gillet, ed., *L'Homme*, p. 104.

[13] Georges Franchomme, 'L'Evolution démographique et économique de Roubaix dans le dernier tiers du XIXe siècle', *RdN* (Apr.–June 1969), p. 207.

[14] Aline Valette, 'La Femme dans l'usine', *LT* (3 Feb. 1894).

[15] *Enquête sur l'industrie, 1904*, 'déposition, L'Association des ouvriers de l'industrie textile d'Armentières et d'Houplines', p. 72.

[16] Ibid. Figures for France are taken from B.R. Mitchell, *European Historical Statistics 1750–1970* (New York, 1978), p. 42.

workers were attended by doctors, and few had the luxury of a trained midwife. Instead, most women were helped by neighbours or by local 'sage-femmes'. A few of these 'wise women', such as Dame Victoire of Saint-Sauveur[17], became well-known folk heroines because of their kind and knowledgeable attentions to women during childbirth. But most had little expertise, and their ministrations were often extremely dangerous, particularly if they had attended more than one birth in a day. Sterility was unknown and *sages-femmes* often spread the fatal illness of new mothers, puerperal fever. Although the spread of this disease, which had peaked in 1857 (when, in one workers' district in Lille, half of all new mothers contracted the illness[18]), had begun to decline during the *belle époque*, childbirth remained, for working women, a dangerous affair.

Because most women returned to the mills shortly after giving birth, infants were usually reared by others. Sometimes an older sister was available for the job. In other cases, a neighbour too ill with tuberculosis or brown lung to work or an elderly relative charged a few centimes a day to look after workers' children. The poorest women had recourse to their grandmothers' solution, drugging the babies in the hope that they would sleep until the lunch break when they could hurry home to tend them. For a very few, crèche care was available—particularly after the election of socialist municipal councils in Lille and Roubaix in the 1890s. But most women were forced to leave their infants with women known as 'professional guardians'—whose general lack of care earned them the frightening sobriquet, 'faiseuses d'anges' (makers of angels). Needless to say, the carelessness of these professional guardians was a substantial cause of the high mortality among babies born to local textile workers.[19]

---

[17] Alexandre Desrousseaux wrote a song about Dame Victoire which is quoted in Pierre Pierrard, *La Vie quotidienne dans le Nord au XIXe siècle* (Paris, 1976), p. 24.

[18] Figures about maternal deaths come from Knibielher and Fouquet. *Mères*, p. 234.

[19] Such guardians are described in Aline Lesaege-Dugied, 'La Mortalité', p. 105. Villermé's critical observation of this practice earlier in the nineteenth century is found in *État physique*, p. 107. Local municipal crèches became increasingly available in all three cities over time. Marcelle Capy described such facilities in 'Industrie textile. Mal logés, mal nourris', *BS* (16 Apr. 1914). (It should, perhaps, be noted that 'faiseuses d'anges' was also commonly used in nineteenth-century France to describe abortionists.)

Few workers, of course, were able to breast-feed their infants.
Few babies even received regular feeding with good quality milk.
When textile workers were able to buy milk, it was usually a rather
weak skimmed milk, known as 'lait battu'. This milk was neither
sterile nor pasteurized, and many local cows were tubercular.
Some reformers, conscious of the effects of depriving infants of
good quality milk, demanded that textile factory owners provide
nurseries within the mills where nursing mothers could feed their
children during the day. But most mill owners preferred to blame
the high infant deaths on parents' supposed indifference; thus
pleas for reform fell on deaf ears.[20]

Children's survival, then, remained mostly a matter of chance
throughout our period. Even the founding of a local *Comité de
protection de l'enfance*, by a few guilt-stricken members of the
Lille bourgeoisie in 1893, had few positive implications for the
health of workers' infants. Instead of working to improve workers'
housing, or to provide medical care for mothers and babies, that
committee, like its successor, the *Goutte du lait* (founded in 1903),
concentrated its attention on criticizing local child-rearing practices,
and on distributing layettes and limited quantities of pasteurized
milk to 'deserving' families. In Lille, the deserving poor were
those who had married in church, who were practising Catholics,
and who avoided any political activities. Single mothers, or
mothers who were not married to their partners, were ineligible
for help from these charities.[21]

iii

In their harsh and constant condemnation of illegitimacy, the local

[20] Wet-nursing was little practised in our period. See Knibielher and Fouquet,
Mères, p. 221 ff. Also see A. Vallin, *La Femme salariée*, p. 25; George Sussman,
Selling Mothers' Milk (Champaign, Ill., 1982), and Pierre Pierrard, *Lille et les
Lillois* (Paris, 1967), p. 243. Bonnie Smith, in *Ladies of the Leisure Class*
(Princeton, 1981), implies that more crèche care was available before 1880,
although her lack of figures for places available to working mothers leaves the
matter unclear (see p. 140).

[21] See Gaston Motte's sympathetic account of these employer-run charities in
Roubaix à travers les âges (Roubaix, 1946), p. 80. Employer response to the misery
of the textile workers is examined in more detail in chapter 3. In the judgement of
two recent historians, 'les classes riches du Nord de la France, bardées d'un
catholicisme rigoriste, sont impitoyables à l'égard des mères sans mari.' It is a
judgement with which I concur. See Knibielher and Fouquet, *Mères*, pp. 234–5.

Catholic bourgeoisie demonstrated the gap between their attitudes and those of the local working class. The latter rarely censured unmarried mothers, or differentiated between 'legitimate' or 'illegitimate' children. Instead, all children were welcomed into the Flemish textile workers' community.

Given this fact, together with the high cost of a church marriage, relatively few young people in Lille, Roubaix, and Tourcoing concerned themselves with formal marriage rites in our period. The rate of illegitimacy therefore remained exceptionally high in the nineteenth century. The figures of Claude-Hélène Dewaepenaere show that in 1880 the Nord department had an illegitimacy rate of 10 per hundred, compared with 7.4 per hundred in France as a whole (and to only 4.7 per hundred in neighbouring late Victorian England). In our period, local illegitimacy increased, reaching a peak of 12.1 per hundred in 1895, and then dropping slowly back to its original level in 1910.

Illegitimacy in the Lille *arrondissement* was higher than in other cities in the Nord department. Dewaepenaere has shown that in 1885 the Lille area had a rate of 13.6 per hundred compared to 9.9 per hundred in Valenciennes and 11.8 in Cambrai. Ten years later, the figures were 14.4 per hundred, 11.8 per hundred, and 10.9 per hundred, respectively. Finally, in 1905, Lille area figures dropped to 13.3 per hundred.[22]

Workers' failure to ostracize illegitimate children or their mothers distressed most local bourgeois Catholics. They acted on their distress by putting pressure on workers to marry. Their methods included withholding charitable help from unmarried mothers (including help from the city *bureau de bienfaisance*, over which they had control until the socialist takeovers in the nineties) and even, in some cases, withholding employment.

Statistics show that such efforts bore no fruit, however. Moreover, neither abortion nor infanticide found many takers among the working people of the Lille area. In fact, Dewaepenaere has calculated that only a tiny minority of infanticides in our period occurred in any of the Nord's great urban centres. According to her research, in 1875 only 205 out of 1000 infanticides were perpetrated by urban dwellers. All the rest

[22] Figures are found in Claude-Hélène Dewaepenaere, 'L'Enfance illégitime dans le départment du Nord au XIXe siècle', in Gillet, ed., *L'Homme*, pp. 141–67.

occurred in rural areas.[23] Furthermore, Dewaepenaere agrees with Pierre Pierrard that abortion was little practised in the workers' districts of the Lille *arrondissement*.[24] Not only was the cost prohibitive, but long religious teaching, coupled with traditional Flemish pride in large families, had their effects.

In addition to the community's willing acceptance of illegitimate children, three additional factors contributed to the high birth-rate in the three cities at the end of the century. Firstly, there was widespread informal prostitution—so common that it was known among textile workers as the 'fifth quarter of a woman's day'. One sentimental but far from untypical description of this 'fifth quarter' appeared in Lille's socialist newspaper in 1890 in a poem called 'Pauvre Mère':

> Night falls, it is December.
> There is no wood, there is no bread.
> From the depths of the tiny room
> Comes a child's cry: 'I'm hungry!'
>
> The mother stands stunned, eyes wild,
> Suffering for both of them;
> Then one senses she has made a frightful decision.
> What has she decided?
> First she takes from a drawer
> A poor scrap of lace
> And the remains of an old mirror.
> Then, shaking like a skeleton
> Shaken by the winds of stormy skies,
>
> She dresses up in some old chiffons.
> Stupefied she looks at herself:
> Onto her thin body she has thrown
> Everything that this sad household had
> Saved from the pawnshop.
> What a frightening apprenticeship.
> A blush covers her face
> As into her narrow bodice she imprisons her round breast.
> The child says to her: 'Little mother,
> Are we going out for a while?'

---

[23] Ibid., p. 158.
[24] Ibid., and Pierre Pierrard, *La Vie ouvrière à Lille sous le Second Empire* (Paris, 1965), p. 124.

She thinks, 'Oh what one must do for these poor angels of God!'
They hug: he is very pale.
Though very hungry, he goes to bed.
She quickly pins on her shawl,
Casts her eyes once toward heaven, then leaves.[25]

Widespread misery in the textile areas of three cities, plus the indifference of the textile *patronat* ensured that such scenes were repeated frequently in the workers' *quartiers* in the *belle époque*.

Even among workers who might have wished to limit their families, however, a second problem arose. Ignorance of contraception was the rule.[26] Thus the fact that some urban areas of France at the end of the nineteenth century had a much higher birth-rate than was prevalent in more rural areas was partly due to this ignorance. It seems likely that urbanization meant for many women the loss of ties with older women who knew ways to control births. Nothing replaced such village ties. Moreover, in the Lille area, the organs of popular propaganda were in the hands of either the predominantly Catholic bourgeoisie or the socialists. The former had both religious and economic reasons for maintaining a high birth-rate among the working class. The latter, too, took no steps to help women control reproduction. Even after the rival workers' movement, the syndicalists, launched a neo-Malthusian birth control campaign after the turn of the century,

---

[25] Clovis Hugues, 'Pauvre mère', *CdT* (13 Sept. 1890). It should be added, however that formal (i.e. registered) prostitution was less widespread in the Nord department than elsewhere in urban France. In 1872, the Nord had between 8 and 14 prostitutes per 10,000 women aged 15–49 (as compared to more than 45 in the Seine, the Bouches du Rhône, and the Var). And 'maisons de tolerance' began to disappear by the 1880s—from 23 in 1876 to only 6 in 1888. See Alain Corbin, *Les Filles de noce: misère sexuelle et prostitution (19ᵉ siècle)* (Paris, 1982), pp. 67, 171. Even though Lille was a garrison city, then, prostitution remained highly informal, and therefore less regulated.

[26] See Pierrard's remarks about this ignorance in *Vie ouvrière*, pp. 127ff. Also see Angus McLaren, 'Doctor in the House', *Feminist Studies*, ii. (autumn 1975), pp. 39–54, and Linda Gordon, *Woman's Body, Woman's Right* (Harmondsworth, Middx., 1977), esp. pp. 149, 154, 215. Problems encountered by would-be historians of birth control in France are discussed in Michel Rouche, 'La Recherche historique sur la femme, l'amour et le mariage', in *RdN*, iii (Apr.–June 1971), pp. 313–18, and in Jean-Paul Enthoven 'Tu ne feras point périr ton fruit: un entretien avec Jean-Louis Flandrin', *Le Nouvel Observateur* (22–28 Oct. 1979), pp. 76–9.

the Nord department's socialists remained silent about the issue.[27]

Overall, then, several factors taken together help to explain the crowds of children in the streets and courtyards of the workers' *quartiers* in Lille, Roubaix, and Tourcoing in the *belle époque*.

Motherhood, like most other features of workers' lives, was not altogether onerous. Mothers were, in fact, honoured in Flemish tradition. One of the most popular heroines of local Flemish folklore was a lace-maker and mother of P'tit Quinquin. She was immortalized first in patois by a local poet, Alexandre Desrousseaux, then in a sculpture erected in Roubaix by the socialist municipality in 1902. Desrousseaux's poem became a lullaby, which told of P'tit Quinquin's mother's efforts to get him to sleep so that she could finish her lace-making. First, she promised him toys and treats if he would sleep. When that failed, she tried two more bribes: new clothes and a visit to the marionettes. These also failed, and finally she threatened him with a visit from St Nicholas, the ogre featured by all naughty Flemish children. At this, he slept. The song concluded tenderly:

> Dors, min p'tit Quinquin
> Min p'tit puchin, min gros rojin,
> Tu m'fras du chagrin
> Si tu n'dors pas qu'a d'main.[28]
>
> (Sleep my little Quinquin,
> My little chicken, my chubby rooster
> You will give me sorrow
> If you don't sleep until tomorrow.)

The song highlighted the mixture of joy and difficulty which the birth of children promised women textile workers in our period.

---

[27] It is interesting to note the dearth of socialist (as opposed to syndicalist) attention to the issue of birth control. Even the national socialist-feminist journal, *La Femme socialiste* (in 1901–2, 1912–14), made no reference to the issue. The *CGT*'s neo-Malthusian propaganda was, by contrast, widely disseminated throughout the non-socialist union movement. See, e.g., D. Sieurin, 'Familles ouvrières', *VdP* (21–28 Sept. 1902), which argues the characteristic *CGT* line: that increasing the numbers of working-class children only increased the amount of working-class flesh available for exploitation. *L'Action syndicale*, which began in 1904 in Lens featured a regular birth control column which both urged its practice and even hinted (with as much specificity as the law allowed) at various methods. The column was signed, 'Adultérine'.

[28] Alexandre Desrousseaux, 'L'Canchon Dormoire' (Paris, 1938).

Unlike most men, women had primary responsibility for their children, whose needs interrupted every break from the equally heavy demands of the mills. Motherhood constrained women's time far more than fatherhood limited the time of their male counterparts, and it sapped their meagre strength.[29]

iv

Except in so far as they resulted from childbirth, health conditions for male and female textile workers were similarly terrible. It is impossible to separate those illnesses contracted as a result of life in the slums from those linked to work in the textile mills. Conditions in one place simply exacerbated conditions in the other. However, because this section addresses the private, rather than the working, lives of women textile workers, I have somewhat artificially separated diseases among textile workers from those factors which produced and exaggerated them in the factories.

The major killer of all textile workers, as one might guess, was lung disease, especially tuberculosis. Tuberculosis cut a large swath through the *courées* of Lille, Roubaix, and Tourcoing as it did throughout France in this era.[30] Moreover, although the fatalism with which most workers greeted the onset of the disease was the despair of local health officials, it was little more than a realistic assessment of their chances of survival once the disease had struck. Few had any chance of a cure.

The Bonneff brothers were among the first outsiders to investigate the extent of tuberculosis in the textile areas of Lille, Roubaix, and Tourcoing early in this century. They were shocked by the ravages of the disease. They visited several victims, as well as the local hospital where people received treatment. They found one woman in a Roubaix *courée*, on her knees scrubbing her doorstep:

She was thin and pretty. She got up, smiling, wiping her hands on the sacking tied around her waist as an apron, and called her children, who

---

[29] Details of the toll exacted by constant child-bearing are given in Dr Henri Thiroux, 'Assistance et hygiène. . .', p. 313, and Pierrard, *Vie quotidienne*, pp. 24–5.

[30] In 1901, France led western Europe in deaths from tuberculosis, with 150,000, as compared with 58,000 deaths in England, Scotland, and Ireland combined.

were crawling around in the *courée* mud, or on the floor of the small room, all nearly naked. Inside the one-room dwelling were 1 bed, and 1 small cradle. Eight people lived in that room. The woman, who was 30, had borne one additional child, who had died of tubercular meningitis. The father was at work at a weaving factory where the woman had used to work. Dr Verhaeghe has told us that this woman was in the early stages of the disease, and could be saved if she got adequate food, air, and so on. But if she remained in the *courée*, she would die.[31]

Dr Verhaeghe's study of 1,065 textile workers in Lille—all of whom were unusual in so far as they had visited his hospital voluntarily—showed that 68 per cent had chronic respiratory disease, including tuberculosis. From this sample, the doctor concluded that just over one-quarter of all textile workers suffered at the very least from 'chronic bronchitis'. Further, he added, a 'huge' number of workers between 25 and 35 were forced to leave the mills because they could not breathe well enough to do the work. Finally, when he interviewed 25 widowers in Lille, whose wives had been textile workers, he discovered that 19 of the men had lost their wives to tuberculosis.[32]

Of course, given local housing conditions, if one member of a family contracted tuberculosis, the rest were more than likely to get it as well. And the tragedy of the doctors at the local tuberculosis clinic was that all they could do was diagnose: no effective treatment was possible under the circumstances, though they made heroic attempts. When a family member was diagnosed as tubercular, a clinic worker disinfected the home, provided spittoons and paper handkerchiefs to the patient, boiled all the family's clothing and bed linens, and brought a ration of milk to the consumptive once a week. These measures doubtless did some good, particularly in helping to halt the spread of the disease through the family. But they did little more than postpone the inevitable death of the patient, for whom there was no rest cure, no 'magic mountain'.

Although textile workers were well aware of the slow march of death once they began to work in the textile mills, they preferred to remain ignorant of its proximity. Thus they avoided the TB hospital in Lille. Union representatives told the 1904 parliamentary

[31] Bonneffs, *Vie tragique*, p. 27.
[32] Dr Verhaeghe's work is reported in Marcelle Capy, 'Drames du travail', *BS* (17 Apr. 1914).

commission that most textile workers feared the TB clinic, knowing that a diagnosis of tuberculosis was a 'death sentence'.[33]

A second scourge of the working population of the textile cities was alcoholism, ironically tied in the popular imagination to the lung problems suffered by most textile workers. As noted earlier, workers believed that alcohol chased the dust from their lungs. This widely held idea encouraged those worst affected by textile dust, the flax-workers of Lille, to drink even while at work. Visiting one flax-carding mill, Marcelle Capy wrote, 'the gorge rises, the brain catches fire. The *ouvrières*, in order to resist, drink alcohol.' One of these women told Capy that many women drank as much as 10 sous worth of gin every morning.[34]

And of course there were the *estaminets*, locus of workers' social lives. 'There, in these *estaminets* where one is served bitter beer and sinister spirits, beats the heart of the *roubaisien* proletariat,' exclaimed one visitor in 1903.[35]

Alcoholism was more prevalent among men textile workers than among the women, though it was by no means rare among the latter. But its presence in French Flanders was not caused by the coming of the factory system, nor by urbanization. In the seventeenth century one *Intendant* had written of the Flemish inhabitants of northern France: 'They are prompt at mass and at sermons, neither of which prejudices their view of the *cabaret*, which is their dominant passion.'[36]

It was a passion undiminished in our period. Textile workers usually began drinking seriously after work on Saturdays and continued until late Monday night. The resulting foreshortened workweek, which ran from Tuesday morning to Saturday noon, was popularly known as 'la semaine flamande'.

Although alcohol provided a substantial portion of most textile workers' diet in this period, it was hardly sufficient to maintain the energy needed to work in the mills. In addition to alcohol, working

---

[33] *Enquête sur l'industrie, 1904*, 'déposition, Fédération de l'industrie textile de Lille et environs, p. 309, and Dr Jules Thiercelin, 'La Lutte contre la tuberculose', *MS*, vol. ii (July–Dec. 1901), p. 279.

[34] The problem of alcoholism in the Nord textile cities is discussed in Bonneffs, *Vie tragique*, p. 41, and Marcelle Capy, 'Pour oublier', *BS* (19 Apr. 1914), and 'Visite d'une filature d'étoupe', *BS* (31 Mar. 1914).

[35] Ardouin-Dumazet, *Voyage*, p. 22.

[36] Quoted in Villermé, *État physique*, p. 106.

people typically ate bread spread with lard, a few vegetables, potatoes, whey milk, and coffee heavily diluted with chicory. Meat of any kind was rare and, when available, usually went to male family members only. Women normally lacked any special nourishment, even when pregnant, or in those rare instances when they nursed their babies. Furthermore, like working women everywhere, the *ouvrières* of Lille, Roubaix, and Tourcoing frequently went hungry so that their many children could eat.[37]

V

In the midst of all these appalling problems, however, the textile workers of Lille, Roubaix, and Tourcoing created a rich community life, centred on the *courée* or street. Centuries of Flemish tradition shaped the necessarily public experiences of the workers' *quartiers*. Fortunately, local traditions were grounded in deep commitment to the collectivity, a sentiment which helped to smooth over the inevitable frictions produced by overcrowding and constant deprivation. Moreover, these local communitarian traditions proved fertile soil for the Marxian socialism of the *Parti ouvrier* when it arrived in the area in the 1880s.

But, long before the socialists arrived on the scene, the Flemish workers' traditional collectivism had proved resistant to externally imposed change. In the mid-nineteenth century, Armand Audiganne noted the Flemish workers' expressed hostility to the code of individualism accompanying industrial capitalism. He wrote, 'Unwelcoming to the spirit of individualism, the soil of Lille is very favourable to the spirit of association.'[38] Thus, as Audiganne noted, local workers quickly reacted to the coming of the factory system by forming mutual aid associations. As early as 1836, Villermé counted 106 such groups, with 7,329 members.[39] Such associations continued to flourish throughout the century—though many came and went rapidly, only to be replaced by new ones with slightly different goals and different costs and benefits. Nevertheless, they were an early form of community-based response to

[37] See Marcelle Capy, 'Industrie textile. Mal logés, mal nourris', *BS* (16 Apr. 1914), and Bonneffs, *Vie tragique*, p. 40.

[38] Armand Audiganne, *Les Populations ouvrières et les industries de la France dans le mouvement social du dix-neuvième siècle* (Paris, 1854), p. 22.

[39] Villermé, *État physique*, p. 104.

social and economic change, grounded in long-standing Flemish habits of co-operation.

The Flemings' addiction to community life was supported by rich, oral cultural traditions, transmitted from generation to generation in the *estaminets* and courtyards of the workers' *quartiers*. Before describing this oral culture, however, it is important to note that it continued unbroken in our period, not least because of widespread illiteracy among the common people of French Flanders. In fact, few textile workers were literate, even in the later years of our period. In 1880, the prefect reported that only one in three of those under 20 in Lille, Roubaix, and Tourcoing could read. And it is likely that even fewer girls could read than boys. One historian has noted that, in 1870, a full 95 per cent of all the women of the three cities over the age of 50 were unable to read or write.[40] This unhappy situation improved slightly toward the end of the century, particularly as factory legislation shortened children's working hours and raised the age at which they could enter the mills. But even in 1914 Marcelle Capy was horrified to discover that most of the women textile workers she visited could not read, not even the 'penny dreadfuls' (known in France as the '13-sous novels') so popular among working women elsewhere in France.[41]

The reasons for this low literacy level were not hard to discover. Every factor which limited the education of all working-class children was doubled in the case of girls. In Lille, in the 1880s, the few free municipal lay schools available to workers' children had places for only 50 girls.[42] Even when more places became available with the spread of free primary education in the late 1880s and 1890s, few children were able to take advantage of them. Because their wages were essential to family survival, most textile children of both sexes went into the mills as soon as possible—at age 12, or earlier if it was possible to fool the employers about the child's age. Moreover, when parents' wages allowed schooling for some

---

[40] See Léon Diagoras, *La Genèse d'une métropole* (Roubaix, 1969), p. 42, and Pierre Pierrard, *Vie ouvrière*, p. 353 for the earlier figures. For the 1880s, see *AN* C 3019, *pièce* 37, 'Enquête sur les situations ouvrières 1872–1885'. The study by François Furet and Jacques Ozouf, 'Literacy and Industrialisation: the case of the Département du Nord in France', *Journal of European Economic History*, vol. 5, no. 1 (spring 1976), pp. 5–44, supports the low literacy figures.

[41] Marcelle Capy, 'Industrie textile. Quelques réflexions', *BS* (20 Apr. 1914).

[42] Françoise Mayeur, *L'Enseignement secondaire des jeunes filles sous la Troisième République* (Paris, 1977), p. 156.

children, girls were less often the beneficiaries. Not only did tradition dictate the choice of male children over females, but custom also demanded that girls take a share in domestic work. The more siblings a girl had, therefore, the less likely she was to attend school regularly. As for secondary education, it was virtually unknown among poor children of either sex.[43]

As the socialists came to power in the municipalities of Roubaix (1892) and Lille (1895), more primary schooling was opened for workers' children, as well as night-schools for workers themselves. The socialists accompanied these practical measures with a lengthy campaign to encourage workers to send their children to school rather than to the mills.[44] But, while some body benefitted, few girls did. Even when they were allowed to attend school, their attendance was regularly interrupted by the domestic demands which their working mothers could not meet.

Of course, the cities offered another form of education in the form of church schools, not all of which were reserved for the children of the bourgeoisie. Some of these schools in fact actively competed with lay schools for workers' children, as we shall see in chapter 3.

The educational level of workers' children rose slowly in the early years of the twentieth century, thanks to a combination of lay schools, Catholic schools, and socialist efforts to educate workers at night-schools. Nevertheless, the literacy level of most textile workers remained low. The primary beneficiaries of a wider spread of schooling were young men, who built upon their primary schooling by attending night-classes and participating in socialist study groups. Women, still burdened by double work, rarely

---

[43] See ibid., p. 186. According to Mayeur, the period 1886–1905 saw a decrease in the percentage of secondary school scholarships for workers' children in France – from 18.1 per cent to only 3.1 per cent. Only a very tiny number of scholarship children were girls.

[44] *Le Cri de l'ouvrier* launched its campaign in favour of schooling at the end of 1884. See also *Le Travailleur* (3 Dec. 1892, and Jan. 1893). Henri Ghesquière, the son of textile workers, who got his own education via night-schools in the 1860s and 1870s and ultimately became both a socialist municipal councillor in Lille and editor of *Le Réveil du Nord*, wrote a lengthy report of the socialists' educational policies in 'L'Assistance intellectuelle à Lille', *MS*, vol. i (Jan.–June 1899), pp. 230–4. For Roubaix see Félix Chabrouillaud, 'La Municipalité de Roubaix', *MS*, vol. iii (Jan.–June 1900), pp. 545–55. Chabrouillaud was born in Roubaix, and ultimately became secretary-general of the *mairie*, but only after a career as a radical and radical-socialist in Limoges.

found the time to join their male colleagues at workers' schools in the evening.[45]

Fortunately, however, French Flanders was rich in oral culture. Early in the nineteenth century, Audiganne remarked that Flemish workers sang constantly—and when they were not singing, they were writing little poems or songs in patois.[46] Despite the laments of local folklorists about the loss of most of these Flemish traditions in the last quarter of the century, they were by no means moribund.[47] Quite the contrary, in fact. New songs and poems emerged steadily from the workers' *quartiers* of Lille, Roubaix, and Tourcoing—though they were more and more frequently written in French than in the dying local patois.[48]

Furthermore, workers' communities created a formal setting for these songs and poems in the many musical and dramatic societies which flourished throughout the *belle époque*. In Roubaix, for example, in 1900, there were twenty-eight instrumental groups and thirty-seven singing societies registered with local authorities.

[45] Only two letters to the local socialist press were clearly written by women in the eighties and nineties. See *LF* (15 Oct. 1882), which contains a letter signed, 'Une lectrice désirant la suppression de la propriété individuelle'. A second letter, signed 'Une servante' is found in *LF* (14 Jan. 1883). This letter ends, 'Oh! go, friends of the people, destroy the corrupt society. Neither I nor my friends will regret it because it is sad for a woman to abnegate her dignity in order to serve as the sport of another woman.' It should be noted that women textile workers in other regions were literate in this period. The Isère's mills had a high quotient of literate women who organized and led that department's textile union. See, *inter alia*, Louise Leyssieux, 'Protestations du syndicat des ouvriers et ouvrières en soiries de Vizille', *VdP* (12–19 May 1907), and Lucie Baud, 'Les Tisseuses de soie dans la region de Vizille', *MS*, vol. ii (Jan.–June 1908), pp. 418–25. The activities of these women are discussed in Raymond Jonas, 'From Radical Republic to the Social Republic: the example of the Isère, (Ph.D., University of California, Berkeley, 1984). Marcelle Capy's remarks are found in 'Quelques réflexions', *BS* (20 Apr. 1914), and in her report of working women's lives in a Paris light bulb factory, 'L'Usine de la lampe Osram', *BS* (2 Oct. 1913). So widespread were these '13 sous novels' among working women that left-wing feminists campaigned against them on the grounds that they diverted women from the class struggle. See Fanny Clair, 'Littérature malsaine', *BS* (2–7 Apr. 1913), and 'Le Militarisme', *VdP* (9 Dec. 1900). A recent study, produced under the auspices of the *Parti communiste français*, suggests that both the habit of reading romance literature and party leaders' concern about that habit remain. See Louisette Blanquart, *Chiffres et commentaires sur la 'Presse féminine'* (Paris, 1978).

[46] Audiganne, *Les Populations ouvrières*, p. 40.

[47] In the introduction to his collection of Flemish customs, Alexandre Desrousseaux lamented the rapid loss of tradition in the region. See Desrousseaux, *Moeurs populaires de la Flandre française*, 2 vols. (Lille, 1889), p. vi.

[48] Ardouin-Dumazet, *Voyage*, p. 102.

At least as many amateur theatrical groups thrived there as well. And the Roubaix groups had counterparts in both Lille and Tourcoing. These popular clubs staged weekly events and frequent competitions, at which prizes were awarded to the best writers and composers.[49]

As workers began to organize into socialist political groups and into unions, beginning in the 1880s, these songs and poems were integrated into the local political culture, as we shall see in chapter 4. Two examples, however, suffice to suggest some of the flavour of the mixture of politics and popular culture in the *belle époque*.

In the autumn of 1888, a cotton worker, G. Brennes, sent a poem to the prefect, demanding shorter hours in the textile mills of Lille. The local socialist newspaper, *Le Cri du travailleur*, published it under the title, 'Simple question'. It read, in part,

> La journée de travail
> Dans ce beau pays de Flandre
> Beaucoup plus longue qu'ailleurs
> Épuise les travailleurs:
> Vous semblez ne pas comprendre.[50]

A few years later, a group of Lille workers composed a song objecting to a new overseer hired from Lyon—called, variously, 'Fatso', 'the raging lion', and 'le porc-épic'. The rhythm of the song is typically Flemish, echoing the click-clack of wooden sabots on cobbled roads:

> M. Joseph, le porc-épic
> Retournez à votre boutique
> Il ne faut pas essayer
> De combattre l'ouvrier.
>
> Faites attention, buveur du sang
> De ne pas faire si tyran
> Car les femmes, à main levée
> Ont juré de vous dompter.
>
> Les choses en sont là.[51]

---

[49] Gaston Motte, *Roubaix à travers les âges* (Roubaix, 1946), pp. 84–5.

[50] G. Brennes, *CdT* (19–26 Oct. 1888). It is interesting to note that this poem, and most of the others published in the local press, was not written in the local patois, as it most probably would have been if written twenty years earlier. Like Eugen Weber's French peasants, the workers of Lille, Roubaix, and Tourcoing were becoming French men and women by the early Third Republic.

[51] 'Lille. Chez Boutry', *LT* (18 Oct. 1893).

On a more formal level, local popular culture spread through the *courées* and slums via local music-halls, or 'cinémas'. These were usually held outdoors on a rough wooden stage facing rows of benches, with standing-room at the rear. Every Sunday evening, workers found at least one such place open, where entire families could spend an evening watching amateur theatricals, hearing singing groups perform, and, later in our period, viewing films. Most such evenings ended in group singing. A careful family, in periods of employment, could enjoy such evenings fairly frequently; the cost was 60 centimes for the 'plutocrats' in the front rows and 40 centimes for those in the rear. Children, moreover, were free.[52]

Marcelle Capy spent one evening at a local music-hall in the spring of 1914. She wrote that 'everyone' from the local *quartier* was there, washed and brushed, dressed in their finest clothes. A 'feminine instinct seizes them as they listen to love-songs. The men are calmed. These sweet songs, these simple films—it is their revenge, their ideal, their poetry . . . they relax there for hours. . . . The melodies pierce their misery.'

When the songs displeased them, however, they were merciless, hooting the singers off the stage. 'Used to working like beasts', Capy concluded, 'they lack sympathy for those who let them down.'[53]

In the lives of Flemish workers, these music-halls played a role similar to that played by sentimental 'penny dreadfuls' in the lives of workers elsewhere. Here, however, this culture of sentiment was shared by men and women alike rather than by women only. Thus as the socialists co-opted these music-halls, turning them into venues for the spread of socialist propaganda, they found themselves addressing a mixed audience of women as well as men, a situation not often encountered elsewhere in provincial France where men and women traditionally led more separate social lives.

In addition to their evenings spent at music-halls, workers enjoyed a full calendar of community fêtes, long characteristic of social life in the Nord. These fêtes were both formal and informal. Impromptu celebrations sprang up in the *courées* or narrow streets of workers' *quartiers* virtually every time the sun shone. These

---

[52] Notices and reports of such evenings are found in, *inter alia*, *CdT* (4–7 July 1888, 3–15 Sept. 1888) and a piece by O.B. titled 'Roubaix', *LT* (8 Mar. 1893).

[53] Marcelle Capy, 'Pour oublier', *BS* (19 Apr. 1914).

little spontaneous fêtes were likely to include a marionette show (put on by an unemployed or disabled worker), accordion players, children's games, and much singing. On a Sunday afternoon, Marcelle Capy discovered one such informal fête in a *courée*. Little boys played games to 'show off their pitiful muscles' to the little girls. Men without families wandered into the local *estaminet* where 'girls with hair-ribbons' (which identified them as prostitutes) offered companionship.[54]

The more formal fêtes which dotted the Flemish calendar were events of mass celebration, eagerly anticipated throughout the long months in the mills. Every fête occasioned great excitement. One visitor wrote: 'Today, as from time immemorial, from every street and crossroad, bursts an effervescence, a marvellous tumult . . . the famous parades which are so beloved of the common people of the Nord.'[55] As these annual events soon became vehicles for socialist expression in Lille, Roubaix, and Tourcoing in the *belle époque*, they require a closer look. The three most famous fêtes in the Flemish year included two held in September—the festival of the lamplighters and the market fête, called the *Grande Braderie*—and one in May which was the best-loved fête of all, the ancient fête of the lace-makers, *Broquelet*.

The lamplighters' fête was primarily a celebration for the children. Held on the last Monday of September, it was, in Ardouin-Dumazet's opinion, 'the most gracious fête of that region'. Factories closed their doors at noon and workers gathered in the public gardens of the three cities to picnic, sing, play boule, and so on. But for children the fête began after dark. Once the sun was gone, bands of children, singing 'Des cafotins / Pour ouvrer du matin / Des allumoirs / Pour ouvrer du soir', paraded through the streets of the cities, all carrying candles which lit their faces with 'artificial fire', and gave the streets, at least for a moment, 'a fairy aspect'. The processions ended in *estaminets*, with a meal of traditional sausages ('pirreux' in patois, 'pierrots' in French), potatoes, and beans.[56]

[54] Ibid.

[55] Léon Bocquet, *Villes meurtries de France. Villes du Nord: Lille, Douai, Cambrai, Valenciennes, Bergues, Dunkerque* (Brussels and Paris, 1918), p. 19.

[56] Ardouin-Dumazet, in *Voyage*, p. 8, witnessed this 'gracious fête' early in this century. A longer description of it is found in Desrousseaux, *Mœurs populaires*, p. 67.

September's other festival, the *Grande Braderie*, was primarily for adults. According to Léon Bocquet, who visited the fête in 1918, its origins were very old. Held on the Monday following the first Sunday in September, it, too, was an occasion observed by the mill owners, who released their workers early on that day. All around the church of Sainte-Cathérine, in Lille, and extending down the roads behind Saint-Maurice, and well into the tortuous narrow streets of Saint-Sauveur, a great jumble sale was set up, featuring old clothes and used household items. Interspersed with rows and rows of market stalls and display tables were marionette shows, performing *saltimbanques*, and various local games. 'Unique in Flanders', according to Bocquet, it was a combination fair and fête, with a practical purpose. Each year, at the beginning of winter, people bought winter clothes and household necessities. Those who could not buy could sell or trade. Those who could do neither could at least enjoy the festivities.[57]

In May came the most joyous fête of the textile workers' year, *Broquelet*. Although it celebrated a vanishing craft, lace-making, the fête showed no signs of disappearing in the *belle époque*, although it began to lose its primary identification as a women's fête, as it increasingly included all textile workers. The poet Alexandre Desrousseaux has left a detailed description of the fête as he recalled it from his own childhood in Lille.

Early on the first morning a trumpet summoned all the working population to the *Grande Place*. Children crowded together beneath the tower of the church of Saint-Étienne to catch cakes thrown to them from the top of the tower by local working women, who had baked them the night before. Apprentices (originally only lace-making apprentices, but in our period including all the older children) gathered before the *Hôtel de Ville*, where they retrieved varicoloured candies which had been tossed from every window.

Toward mid-morning, a great banner floated from the church tower, which signalled local people to decorate their streets and *courées* with garlands of flowers, leafy boughs, and draperies of local textiles. Soon, Desrousseaux recalled, every inch of the squalid house fronts was covered over.

---

[57] Bocquet, *Villes meurtries*, pp. 20–1. See also Desrousseaux, *Mœurs populaires*, p. 66.

At noon, a parade formed. The earliest parades, which were women only, comprised groups of workers from each lace-making workshop. As these workshops disappeared, however, groups were formed instead by mill. These groups included, for the first time, workers of both sexes. Each group carried its own banner, and most women carried bouquets of spring flowers. The parade circled through every workers' *quartier*, singing, and ended up at the city centre for a dance which lasted until the mid-afternoon dinner.

After the public dinner, people filled the parks, coming from the villages and towns near by—and, thanks to the trams, from Roubaix and Tourcoing, and even from Belgium. Traditional games, puppet shows, and travelling entertainers occupied people until the evening, which ended in a formal ball.

The traditional *Broquelet* lasted for eight days, with all public events organized by the women lace-makers of Lille. Only on the final day of the original *Broquelet* had men and boys been invited to join in—in a last, great procession led by a man dressed as St Nicholas. When the parade reached the river, 'St Nicholas' was thrown into the water, ending the fête.[58] (It will be remembered that St Nicholas was the local bogey-man.)

The ancient origins of *Broquelet* proved a problem for local socialist leaders, who tried to assimilate the fête to the workers' May Day, first observed in the Lille area in 1890. To this end, socialists tried to limit the fête to only one day (a goal they shared with textile mill owners). But the workers rejected socialist efforts as well as similar efforts of the *patronat* during most of our period, and *Broquelet* frequently signalled the beginning of a lengthy strike in the textile mills—strikes which tradition demanded should last at least eight days. Nevertheless, during the course of the 1880s and 1890s, *Broquelet* gradually became identified as a socialist fête, though it retained most of its customary activities.

Before leaving this outline of the social lives of textile workers in the *belle époque* it is important to discuss in some detail one last form of community life, which also provided socialists with a potential form of propaganda. This was what might loosely be called community gossip, to which Flemish workers were particularly addicted. This informal story-telling based on both approval

---

[58] See Desrousseaux, *Mœurs populaires*, pp. 31–4.

and criticism of individuals' activities was the social cement which held together the lives of workers in each neighbourhood. Virtually no anti-social or benevolent behaviour escaped the watchful eyes of neighbours in *courées* or tenements. Even more effective than the little poems of everyday life, gossip knitted together all the inhabitants of an area—sanctioned their good deeds, punished their bad. Above all, gossip held families together by condemning any behaviour that shook family, or community life. Moreover, it was the means by which help was solicited for families in need, and support gathered for people in conflict with outsiders, particularly the *patronat* or police.

The narrow world of the *courées* and slums thus promoted gossip as an important means of community social control. A constant running commentary on individuals' activities merged private with public life. So intense was the local commitment to sharing in public every detail of daily experience that Ardouin-Dumazet found himself comparing life in the workers' *quartiers* of the Lille area with that of 'ancient Greece, Tyre, and primitive Carthage'.[59]

Local gossip had two important outlets in our period, one more clearly efficacious than the other, but both key forums for community views. These included local police records and local newspapers which were increasingly socialist papers in our period.

Local police reports in the *belle époque* invariably included the testimony of the accused's neighbours—an eventuality of which every wrongdoer, or potential wrongdoer, was aware. One's neighbours could offer both negative and positive evidence—the latter often sufficing to allow the prisoner to avoid punishment, or at least to weaken it. Negative testimony, however, had the opposite effect. Morever, the nature of that negative infor-mation—i.e. what workers thought constituted wrong behaviour—reveals a very strict, if unusual, code of morality in the *courées*.

---

[59] For figures on place of birth of *Roubaisiens* in 1886, see Georges Franchomme, 'L'Évolution . . . de Roubaix', p. 210. He shows that of 45,756 French citizens in Roubaix in that year, 29,524 were born in the commune where they lived, and 11,297 in another commune of the Nord. Only about 4,000 people came from outside the Nord. Of the 54,423 non-citizens, 24,240 were born in the commune they inhabited, and 3,702 in neighbouring communes. Also, of course, the vast majority of the remaining 26,081 non-citizens were born in Belgium. Ardouin-Dumazet's comment is found in *Voyage*, p. 21.

One of the most interesting series of such police records comes from the period just after the assassination of President Carnot in 1894. Five local people were arrested for sedition—usually for expressing approval of the murder. Of the five, one was acquitted, one was lightly fined, two were heavily fined and given prison terms, and one was let off without a trial.

There were two main types of evidence which shaped a defendant's ultimate treatment. One was testimony suggesting that the accused had left-wing sympathies. The second was a claim that the defendant had failed to support his or her family. Of the two accusations, the worst was the second; most of the accused could have been presumed to have some political views of the 'wrong' kind, else they would not have applauded the assassination.

The most severely punished among the defendants had both these defects in equal measure. Émile Guilmot, a local painter, was said by his neighbours to hold left-wing views, but also to neglect his four children, whose support was entirely in the hands of his common-law wife. The second failing was complicated by the fact that he had already abandoned a family in Belgium, before coming to France and setting up house a second time. His neighbours' testimony earned Guilmot a 500 fr. fine and a month in gaol.

A second defendant, Joseph Henri Verdant, a Tourcoing weaver, also received a 500 fr. fine, as well as fifteen days in gaol. He had no previous convictions, and only a vague reputation as a political activist. What condemned him was his reputation as a layabout who forced his wife (also a textile worker) to support their two children. His earnings, according to his neighbours, went into the pockets of local bar owners.

Just as those convicted were condemned by the negative opinions of their neighbours, so the one prisoner acquitted was rescued by her good reputation. Léonie Marie Bombeck, a *cabaretière*, was reported to have 'good morals', though she lived in what her witnesses called 'concubinage'. She was said not to drink, or to engage in any 'debauchery'. Moreover, her neighbours told the police that she supported herself with hard work. This information—together with the fact of her sex, no doubt—encouraged the magistrate to release her without penalty.[60]

[60] These cases are documented in *ADN* 2, U 155, *Pièces* 517, 518, 519, 521, 527, 'Dossiers criminels, Lille: cris séditeux en faveur de l'anarchie'.

In addition to police records, a rich source of local gossip was the local popular press. Some highlights taken from these papers reveal the varied nature of this information, as well as the sorts of activities which occasioned community comment or, perhaps, censure.

Without blurring the infinite variety or complex texture of this local gossip, it is possible to place items into five loosely defined categories. These include tales of local misery, designed to solicit community help, protests against outrages committed by supervisors in the textile mills, anti-clerical stories, mocking the local clergy, tales condemning immorality, and, finally, individual statements of opinion on some public issue.

Tales of their neighbours' misfortune always brought a response from the warm-hearted Flemings. Monetary aid was likely to come from better-paid men, while women offered personal help, including assuming domestic tasks for sick neighbours, and so on. One writer remarked in *Le Cri du forçat* in 1884, 'happily the women of the people . . . have a heart which beats in their breasts; they do not wish that one of their sisters should go under, so that which the *Bureau de bienfaisance* does not do, they do willingly.'[61]

Once the story circulated in a neighbourhood, then, people in trouble got help. One example concerned a local man, raising his four children alone after his wife's death. A letter detailing his plight came to the local paper explaining that he had been rejected from the bureau because he was not a practising Catholic. (This was in 1882, a decade before the socialists took control of the bureaux in both Roubaix and Lille.) Thus, when he was laid off, he was forced to send his oldest child, a 12-year-old girl, to work in a textile mill. Three months later, she was 'seduced' (a euphemism in the case of a 12-year-old) by a supervisor, leaving her pregnant. Because her pregnancy forced her to quit work, her family found itself with no means of support.[62] As was customary in such cases, the paper established a fund for this family's support, to which local readers subscribed—usualy 5 centimes each.

A second example came from Lille, where an abandoned mother of nine had for some time been feeding her children by selling, piece by piece, every item of household furnishings. When

[61] 'Bureau de bienfaisance', *CdF* (18 May 1884).
[62] See *LF* (29 July 1882).

nothing was left to sell, she went in despair to a local order of
nuns, who gave her help until they discovered that she was not a
baptized Catholic. They then sent her away.[63] This woman, too,
became the object of a fund, set up by the local paper.

The most harrowing story of all, however, appeared in *Le Cri de
l'ouvrier* in 1885. A father, discovering that his small daughter had
been raped, took her to the police station in Moulins-Lille to
report the incident. A doctor examined her and reported that she
had been raped '7 or 8 times'. But although the rapist was
arrested, he was allowed to go free after only three days in prison
because, according to the paper, he was 'under the protection of
the clerical 'farderie Moulinoise'. In the name of the working
people of Moulins-Lille, the paper sent a demand for redress to
the procurer of the Republic, and to the local police commis-
sioner.[64]

In addition to such woeful stories, the local papers constantly
reported the suicides of workers who did not get the help they
required. Each story of a suicide included a request for help for the
survivors, along with an explanation of the suicide—usually long-
term unemployment, homelessness, or a degree of poverty which
prevented a parent from feeding his or her children.[65]

Among the most hated forms of oppression in the mills was
sexual harassment, mostly aimed at women. Throughout the 1880s
and 1890s, numerous reports of incidents, varying from immoral
talk and propositions to physical abuse and even rape, appeared in
the local socialist press. One story, for example, denounced the
behaviour of several factory foremen in an article entitled 'les
grossièretés des contremaîtres', in *Le Réveil du forçat* in the
autumn of 1985.[66] Another local paper criticized one supervisor at
the LeBlan factory who was notorious for 'favouring certain pretty
workers'. 'Everyone knows', the reporter added, 'at what price a
girl gains his favour.' One day, his jealous wife turned up at the
mill to see what was going on. She decided that her husband was
over-fond of one young girl, an orphan who had worked at LeBlan
for five years. She forced her husband to fire the girl. 'We leave it
to our readers to figure out why,' the paper concluded.[67]

[63] *CdF* (4 May 1884).
[64] 'Viol à Lille', *Cdl'O* (4–11 Jan. 1885).
[65] See *Égalité de R-T* (1897–1905).
[66] *RdF* (18 Oct. 1885).
[67] *LF* (17 Dec. 1882).

The local press condemned another shop-floor supervisor for beating women workers at the Lemaire spinning mills in Tourcoing. The beatings had become so frequent that the women had finally risked their jobs by complaining formally to the local police.[68]

Not all reporters of work problems involved sexual harassment, of course. Fines (exacted for every breach of strict factory rules) were a common source of anger and frustration for workers, and occasioned repeated complaints. One report told of an *ouvrière* who was fired for an offence without being given her fifteen-day notice as required by law. She refused to leave the factory without her fifteen days, so the factory directors called the police, who joined them in trying to evict her. She continued to hold out for her rights in spite of this pressure, and finally won her legal notice—though the foreman added a stiff fine as a parting shot. The paper added, 'We offer our congratulations to the courageous *ouvrière* who has kept her head against the pretensions of her exploiter. We present her as an example to the over-large number of *ouvrières* who let themselves be "skinned" too easily.'[69]

Many briefer reports of fines and other penalties dotted the pages of the local journals—serving both as protest and warning against certain employers. Such reports allowed workers to vent some of the anger and frustration stored up during long days of tight discipline in the mills.

The third type of local gossip was aimed at the local clergy. Socialist newspaper editors fell with special glee upon any story which cast a bad light upon the hated priests or nuns. They were particularly pleased when critical stories tied the clergy to the local *patronat*, thus attacking two birds with the same stone.

Typical of this *genre* was a story run by *Le Cri de l'ouvrier* in 1884. It told of two girls, 'demoiselles Delplanque et Thierry', who were going from door to door in the workers' district of Esquermes, collecting funds to build a new church. The paper's reporter pointed out that, although begging was illegal, these girls were exempt from police attention because both were daughters of mill owners. This story aroused the wrath of at least one reader, who, in the following week, sent a contribution to the paper's charity fund with the accompanying note: 'With the hope that all

[68] 'Un surveillant qui bat les ouvrières', *Égalité de R-T* (8 Jan. 1897).
[69] 'Rue de Wazemmes', *Cdl'O* (1–8 Feb. 1885).

the crows who descend upon Esquermes will be put in cages.'[70] ('Crows' was the popular name for priests and nuns who, of course, wore black.)

In Tourcoing, where the Church continued to attract a substantial number of workers throughout our period, newspapers often condemned what their editors saw as the Church's efforts to lure working-class children into clerical orders. One story written in highly sentimental prose told of a young woman who had 'abandoned her home and her aged parents, in the early hours before dawn' to sneak off to join the *Petites sœurs de l'ouvrier*. 'Religious fanaticism', the writer opined, 'had withered her heart.' 'It is only surprising' he concluded, 'that this sort of thing does not happen more often in a clerical city like Tourcoing.'[71]

Stories aimed at controlling local morality took many forms. One series of stories condemned a woman called Mme Delannoy who caused constant trouble in her neighbourhood in Croix by falsely reporting her neighbours to the police, by sending anonymous letters around the *courée*, and so on. Several successive issues of *Le Cri du travailleur* warned the woman to cease her destructive behaviour, outlining her neighbours' accusations against her in great detail.[72]

Another report criticized Marie Stricanne, a *cabaretière*, who was arrested for 'inciting minors to debauchery'. The paper claimed that she had lured girls as young as 12 to work in her café-bar. The authorities had only caught on to the situation when one of Mme Stricanne's 'girls' was admitted to the local hospice suffering from syphilis. The writers of this story warned local parents that *cabarets* and *maisons de tolérance* (brothels) often worked together to entrap young girls into prostitution.[73]

Finally, two brief tales of breaches of public morality appeared in the official journal of Tourcoing's yellow (anti-socialist) unions, *Le Petit Jaune*. In May 1901 the paper reported two 'scandalous incidents': firstly a wedding-party brawl in an *estaminet*, during which a pregnant woman, 35, was 'gravely injured'; and, secondly, an incident wherein a man bit off the nose of a woman with whom

---

[70] *Cdl'O* (14–21 Dec. 1884, and 21–28 Dec. 1884).

[71] *RdF* (20 Sept. 1885).

[72] Mme Delannoy's transgressions are described in 'Croix. Les Agissements de Mme Delannoy', *CdT* (13–20 Nov. 1887).

[73] 'Armentières. Affaire de mœurs', *CdT* (24–31 July 1887).

he had been living because she wanted to marry someone else![74]

Such stories of course not only imposed community pressure on miscreants, but also offered some amusement, a bit of titillation for people whose lives offered very little of either.

Lastly, the local press provided a forum where local people could voice their political opinions. Each time a worker, or group of workers, sent in a contribution to various collections, an epithet was appended which served the same function as a badge or car sticker serves today. These collection columns were, therefore, an informal gauge of local political opinion. The earliest socialist newspapers were a particularly rich source for these epithets. *Le Cri de l'ouvrier*, published in the early 1880s in Lille, included these examples:

One who deserves prison, but who believes himself to be more honest than Ferry;
A group of imbeciles;
One citizen of St-Éloi who would like to hold Ferry and his acolytes under an anvil;
In order that the priests and their minions may all be dead before tomorrow![75]

One writer's purposes are lost, but his or her feelings remain perfectly clear:

I wish that the municipal council of Tourcoing would go to the devil![76]

As time went on, more and more of these contributors expressed identifiably socialist sympathies. Their declarations ranged from the simple such as 'Une femme socialiste', to self-deprecating statements such as 'A blind person who begins to peceive the abuses of the bourgeoisie', and 'I have a hard head, but I begin to understand the revolutionary programme'. Some suggested the degree to which the socialist party had penetrated local households, including one which read, 'A wife who keeps a good house since her husband became a socialist'.[77]

---

[74] *PJ* (14 May 1901).
[75] See *Cdl'O* (30 Nov.–7 Dec. 1884, and 7–14 Dec. 1884).
[76] Ibid. (21–28 Dec. 1884).
[77] *LT* (18 Oct. 1893) and *Cdl'O* (28 Dec.–4 Jan. 1884–5, 4–11, Jan. 1885, and 15–22 Mar. 1885, respectively).

It was in these newspaper columns, then, that local people found a voice, however modest. The fact that contributors rarely let an opportunity for an epithet slip by suggests the pleasure they bought with their small donation to the papers' charitable causes.

The willingness of local workers to share their opinions—both on public issues and on each other—highlighted the extent to which life in the workers' *quartiers* of Lille, Roubaix, and Tourcoing was lived in public. In the case of Flemish life among the popular classes, the phrase 'la vie intime' is little more than a euphemism. Indeed, if life was private at all it was only private to a particular street or *courée*. Few activities in these areas escaped the vigilance of relatives, friends, and neighbours. Anxious to share the rare joys of life as well as willing to share the miseries, workers paid close attention to the smallest details of community life. Given the extent of textile workers' problems during the *belle époque*, the supportive character of the traditional Flemish community proved altogether crucial in maintaining a life that was not altogether unbearable.

3

THE TEXTILE MILLS

i

ALTHOUGH the textile industry was in decline throughout France in the last third of the nineteenth century, the picture from the Nord department was not altogether bleak. In fact, for most large mill owners, the thirty-four years before the Great War were characterized both by increased production and expanding factories, as well as by constant industrial crises.

For workers, however, conditions worsened, and relations with mill owners deteriorated. Moreover, most small producers, unable to ride out periodic crises, gradually vanished from the industrial scene in Lille, Roubaix, and Tourcoing in our period.

For big mill owners, several elements combined to offer opportunities for expansion in these years. The most important of these was the accessibility of the two main raw materials necessary for steam production: coal (which came from the coalfields south of Lille and from Belgium), and water (piped into all three cities from the river Lys). Furthermore, transport was readily available. Beginning in the 1850s, railway lines linked the three cities with one another, with the coalfields, and with the all-important ports of Dunkerque, Le Havre, and Anvers, through which passed both raw materials (primarily wool and cotton) and finished products for export. In this period, exports included combed and carded wool, cotton, linen, jute, plus wool thread and yarn, hemp rope, and finished fabrics of all kinds. Local canals, as we have seen, also tied the three cities together, carrying partially processed materials from one mill to another. Finally, a massive increase in available workers, particularly that resulting from a steady influx of work-hungry Belgians, allowed the textile *patronat* great latitude in the utilization of their work-force. During increasing periods of labour unrest the Belgians were especially valued as they commonly returned home, leaving the French workers to demonstrate alone. Furthermore, low wages in Belgium's textile mills helped dampen any incipient volatility in the face of increasingly onerous French conditions and dropping wages.

These factors, coupled with the mechanization of the last major handwork task—wool preparation—made it possible for efficient, well-capitalized producers to grow throughout our period. Furthermore, those *industriels* who processed wool were suddenly inundated by a greatly increased supply of raw materials. Once imported only from Britain and Holland, wool began to flow into France from the Middle East, from Argentina, and from Australia.

Like most other changes, however, the emergence of new suppliers of wool proved a mixed blessing. Many small mill owners, who had stockpiled raw material at a higher price, were unable to take quick advantage of new, cheaper supplies. In addition, many mill owners lacked the capital to invest in new factories or to increase their production in order to benefit from the sudden increase in supplies of unprocessed wool. As a result, many small owners went under, to the ultimate benefit of the large textile families, who tightened their grip on the production of thread, yarn, and cloth in Lille, Roubaix, and Tourcoing.

On the other hand, too much enthusiasm on the part of larger producers occasionally pushed them across the fine line between growth and over-production. Many manufacturers quickly found themselves with a large stock of unwanted goods. The changing whims of fashion further exacerbated the problem, as did growing competition from the industrializing countries, including Germany, Belgium, and, toward the later years of our period, Russia and Japan.

The industry was also attacked by external factors. The long-term effects of two occurrences of the 1860s—the American Civil War and unfavourable trade treaties with Great Britain and Belgium—were worsened by the 1890 McKinley tariff, which protected American textiles by imposing staggering duties on foreign imports. The immediate results were, firstly, a flurry of mill closures, and secondly, a series of product shifts by those mill owners backed by sufficient capital. Because cotton was particularly hard hit by the combination of events, cotton producers in Roubaix and Tourcoing turned to producing wool. Lille owners stayed with cotton, but increased the spinning of flax and wool, and added the production of jute and hemp products (including rope).

Combined with these factors was the long-term economic depression which wracked all of France from the 1880s onwards.

The effects of this depression on Lille area textiles were long lived: not until the winter of 1908–9 did the local textile industry begin to stabilize.

Understandably, relations between the *patronat* and the workers soured during this rocky period. Worsening conditions outside the mills produced worsening conditions in them. These, in turn, brought workers out into the streets of Lille, Roubaix, and Tourcoing both in small, spontaneous demonstrations and in massive general strikes, which broke out at least once every decade. Increased worker militancy further complicated the fluid state of the Nord's major industry.

The constant clash of employers and employed throughout the early decades of the Third Republic troubled the social history of the textile industry. The *patronat* on their side and the workers on theirs found themselves enmeshed in a long struggle which worked itself out against a dark backdrop of severe economic problems. Before discussing the textile workers' collective resistance to changing conditions, it is necessary to detail those economic, social, and cultural factors which together formed the daily experiences of textile workers in the *belle époque*.

ii

As textile production in the Lille region fell into the hands of a few extended families toward the end of the nineteenth century, information about the industry was increasingly scarce. An exaggerated secrecy about production figures, profits, and working conditions, long characteristic of the great northern textile families, worsened in the *belle époque*. Officials of the Third Republic, therefore, faced growing frustration as they attempted to gather accurate data. Ironically, perhaps, their mandate came from a newly centralized government run by bureaucrats with an insatiable thirst for industrial data. Their enthusiasm produced a plethora of governmental inquiries in the 1880s. Sent to factory owners throughout France, these solicited data about numbers, ages, and sexes of workers, about wages, about factory processes and housing conditions, and so on. But northern mill owners were unforthcoming. Nearly all replies to these *enquêtes* from Lille's *industriels* were, at best, cryptic. A typical reply, sent by one Lille mill owner to the Nord's prefect in 1886, read, 'Flax spinning—

critical. Many workers unemployed. Manufacture of tulle—restrained.'[1]

Given such vagueness, it is not surprising to find that official documents throughout our period recorded a series of contradictions.[2] Even the 1904 parliamentary commission, determined to sort out the constant stream of misinformation issuing from propagandists of both sides of the textile battleground, encountered a totally obstinate and uncooperative textile *patronat* in French Flanders. Lille mill owners, for example, told the frustrated committee that their total exports for 1904 had been 'about 10% for spun flax, no cotton thread, and a little cotton cloth'. Their *roubaisien* counterparts were even less helpful: they reported that they could give no prices or changes in prices for the preceding twenty-year period because the situation was 'all too variable'.[3] Thus, for the commission (as well as for subsequent historians), the task of painting any but a very general picture of the textile industry of Lille, Roubaix, and Tourcoing in the *belle époque* was virtually impossible.

Nevertheless, some generalizations—however vulnerable—must be made. Between 1880 and 1914, four major elements dominated textile production in the three cities. Firstly, most small factories vanished, swallowed up by the giants of the local industry. The number of owners and factories, along with the sociological and political heterogeneity of the *patronat*, declined markedly. Secondly, changes in the work processes occurred as manufacturers met growing international competition and the crisis of over-production both by specializing (e.g. in a very fine cloth of unusual colours) and by lowering wages, speeding up work, tightening factory discipline, extending factory workdays during the high season, and laying off vast numbers of workers, willy-nilly, during low periods. Furthermore, most mill owners chose not to invest in new machinery or new techniques—either of which might have improved working conditions. Instead, the Nord's textile *patronat*

[1] *ADN* M 572 8, 'Régime industriel: rapports sur la situation de l'industrie, 1886, avril, Lille'. David Landes argues that this behaviour was typical of most French entrepreneurs in the nineteenth century. See 'Religion and Enterprise' in Edward Carter, *et al.*, eds., *Enterprise and Entrepreneurs in 19th and 20th Century France* (Baltimore, 1976), p. 42.
[2] See, e.g. *ADN* 581 148, 'Usines: renseignements statistiques 1891'.
[3] *Enquête sur l'industrie, 1904*, 'dépositions, chambre de commerce de Lille', p. 242; 'chambre de commerce de Roubaix', p. 154.

(like many other French men and women in the period) invested their profits abroad.[4]

Thirdly, these giant owners, mindful of the workers' increased discontent, began to draw more tightly together to pursue their collective interests. This consortial growth, with its accompanying secrecy and paranoia, was reflected in the deliberately vague information allowed beyond factory office doors. It also shaped the *patronat*'s relations with the central government and with the prefecture, both in the hands of republicans with little sympathy for the Catholic, conservative mill owners. Of course, these relations were not entirely hostile. Because local manufacturers were forced to turn to the central government for help against stiff foreign competition, and to the prefect for troops to quell the increasingly organized strikes of the period, their religious, conservative ideals constantly clashed with their practical needs. The politics of the employers, therefore, rarely followed a coherent strategy, but instead developed and changed according to the exigencies of the moment.

Taken together, these elements added up to a confusing industrial picture in the *belle époque*. For workers, it meant constant uncertainty. Even the *patronat* probably did not know from month to month or year to year what the demand might be for their products and, concomitantly, what their demand for workers might be. Prices—for finished products as well as for raw materials—fluctuated wildly. Overall, it is fair to say that the coherence that began to characterize capitalist enterprises during these years in other countries remained a stranger to textile production in the Nord.

A similar lack of coherence afflicted the work process itself. While production in the United States, for example, was rapidly undergoing 'Taylorization' in the *belle époque*, leading to the rationalization and increased efficiency of the production process, work routines in the Lille area remained very similar to those followed much earlier in the nineteenth century. More confusingly still, these varied from city to city and even from mill to mill.

[4] Ibid., 'déposition, chambre de commerce de Roubaix', p. 153. This report documents the absence of any new combing or carding machinery in the area since the 1860s. See also Jean Jaurès's indictment of those who failed to reinvest profits in France in 'Le Témoignage extraordinaire sur le patronat', in Jacques Dumortier, *Le Syndicat patronal textile de Roubaix-Tourcoing de 1942–1972* (Lille, 1975), appendix ii, and Jaurès, 'Les Grèves d'Armentières', *RS* (July–Dec. 1903), p. 578.

Moreover, wages were nowhere uniform. Even in the same factory, wages were commonly divided by gender, with women earning considerably less than men, whatever their tasks. Nor could workers count on steady employment throughout a year. Fashion changes threw one group of workers out of work at the same time as they offered suddenly increased work to their neighbours in another mill. Furthermore, long 'dead' seasons were often followed by frenzied over-activity, as the industry attempted to match the pace set in Paris.

Amidst all this confusion, however, one must attempt to discern at least a very general outline in order to understand the rise and fall of workers' responses to their conditions.

During the 1880s, the situation in all spinning mills of Lille, Roubaix, and Tourcoing, except those where wool was processed, was grave. *Weavers* of cotton and linen, however, remained employed. (Cotton weavers continued to benefit from the earlier loss of Alsace and, with it, the great cotton industry of Mulhouse.) Because Lille workers produced most of the cotton thread and yarn of the area, this decline resulted in widespread unemployment in that city. On the other hand, most workers in the neighbouring wool cities of Roubaix and Tourcoing had steady work throughout the 1880s.[5]

But the relative good fortune enjoyed by most textile workers in Roubaix and Tourcoing was short-lived. In 1890, wool joined the other textile products in a long downward plunge. In 1891, prices paid for wool, as well as for processed cotton, flax, hemp, and jute, fell—in a long downward spiral slowed only occasionally by brief upturns in the market. This general trend was briefly broken in 1896 by a shift upward in the price paid for combed wool and in 1897 in the prices of other fibres. But this improvement quickly disappeared. By 1898 prices were again falling.

Concurrently, textile exports dropped in the Nord, as well as throughout the French textile industry. The total value of France's textile exports fell from 180 million francs in 1890 to 128 million in 1897, 93 million in 1900, and finally to 72 million in 1902.[6]

[5] *ADN* M 572 8, 'Régime industriel'.

[6] *Enquête sur l'industrie, 1904*, vol. ii, Tables I, IV, 'Cours moyens annuels du coton, lin, chauvre, jute de 1890 à 1904', and 'Cours moyens des laines peignées, 1891 à 1903, Roubaix et Tourcoing'. See also *ADN* M 625 1–3, and France, *Bulletin de l'Office du travail 1896* (Paris, 1897).

By the end of the nineteenth century, moreover, wool exports, which had remained fairly stable throughout the preceding decade in spite of the McKinley tariff, began to drop as the American market closed its doors.[7] Worse still, the internal market for wool shrank in the face of French fashion, which prescribed lighter fabrics more suited to the 'sportive' life favoured by the *fin de siècle* bourgeoisie. Particularly fashionable were fabrics which combined wool and cotton—in a process widespread in the British industry but beyond the technical scope of French manufacturers.[8]

Nineteen hundred was a black year in the textile cities. Prices of processed cotton, flax, and wool plunged further, and raw materials were scarce and of poor quality. Desperation led the mill owners of Lille to lay off all their workers for one full day each week, in an effort to forestall vast over-production.[9] For the textile proletariat, 1900 to 1907 were a biblical seven years of misery and hardship, broken only by sporadic employment for wool-combers and carders and, to a lesser extent, for wool-spinners. Both prepared and spun wool found a market in the infant textile industries of Belgium and Germany. But it was a market which would quickly disappear as manufacturers in those countries became more sophisticated. One spokesman for the Tourcoing *patronat* commented that the more carded and combed wool was sent abroad, the less wool yarn was needed, and the more yarn, the less cloth.[10] Nevertheless, in the short term, workers in these

[7] Jacques Toulemonde, *Naissance d'une métropole: Roubaix et Tourcoing au XIXᵉ siècle* (Tourcoing, n.d.), p. 64.

[8] The reasons for fashion changes included feminism, which opposed restrictive clothing, as well as new leisure activities, such as bicycling, which demanded lighter fabrics. Furthermore, the increasing numbers of bourgeois women who began to fill the thousands of new white-collar jobs opening up at the turn of the century began to demand more practical clothing. The most thoroughgoing discussion of the local wool industry's problems is Georges Franchomme, 'L'Évolution démographique et économique de Roubaix dans le dernier tiers du XIXᵉ siècle', *RdN* (Apr.–June 1969), pp. 201 ff.

[9] *AN* F⁷ 12767, 'Industrie textile: renseignements généraux, questions ouvrières 1900–1910'.

[10] See *Enquête sur l'industrie, 1904*, 'déposition, chambre de commerce de Tourcoing', pp. 370 ff. See also 'dépositions, chambre de commerce de Roubaix', pp. 153 ff. and chambre de commerce de Lille', pp. 242 ff. These show that exports of combed and carded wool from Tourcoing and Roubaix grew from 12,156,939 kg. and 15,252,197 kg. in 1882 to 31,539,464 kg. and 33,631,589 kg. in 1904 (in Tourcoing and Roubaix respectively). These exports amounted to more than one third of the total production in these cities during this period.

industries enjoyed at least some earnings in the otherwise bleak years. However, the bulk of wool-carders and combers were women, whose wages were always lower than those of men workers. This meant that the overall wages supporting many local textile families were extremely low despite the steady employment of many female family members.

Of course, the great textile mill-owning families suffered these economic crises with a good deal less misery than was experienced by their workers. Many, in fact, managed to keep abreast of competition by adding specialized products to their usual line. These included double-twisted thread and yarn, chained yarn, and yarn dyed in special processes. Such changes warded off disaster for several years, at least, while the Belgians and Germans continued to concentrate on weaving French yarns. But gradually, and inevitably, Belgian and German manufacturers began to prepare and spin their own yarns, and the market for French yarn shrank. One local mill owner reported the loss of 70,000 of Roubaix's 325,000 spindles in 1904.[11] This signalled, of course, a concomitant loss of jobs in the local spinning mills.

The vicious cycle of depression and unemployment broke at last in 1908. The years 1908–12, in fact, saw a rapid increase in the export of wool yarn—particularly good news for workers in Roubaix and Tourcoing, but also important to Lille's remaining wool-spinners. The growth of wool yarn exports in all three cities rose from 8,543,000 kilograms, worth 47,628,000 francs, in 1908, to 13,528,000 kg., worth over 86,000,000 fr., in 1912.[12] Of course, workers were understandably cautious about becoming too optimistic too quickly, but by 1913 even union leaders were ready to predict a bright future in the industry. A euphoric Victor Renard, head of the national socialist textile union, proclaimed the long dark period at an end.[13] Unfortunately, the industry's rebirth lasted only one more year; the German invasion in the autumn of 1914 threw textile production into chaos once again.

These years between 1880 and 1914, then, were years of decline and crises in Lille, Roubaix, and Tourcoing. But they were

---

[11] Ibid., 'déposition, Syndicat des peigneurs de laine, filtiers de laine et de coton, Roubaix-Croix et Tourcoing', pp. 200, 204.

[12] France, Ministère du travail, Enquête sur la réduction de la durée du travail le samedi (Paris, 1913).

[13] Renard, 'La Vie confédérale', *VdP* (7–14 Sept. 1913).

experienced very differently by the workers and the *patronat*. As the numbers of mill owners diminished, they drew increasingly into a tighter defensive circle, defying both the state—represented by factory work inspectors sent to enforce protective labour legislation—and the workers, who mobilized against their misery with continual strikes and mass demonstrations, as well as by electing socialist deputies and socialist municipal councils. Before turning to workers' collective reaction to their circumstances in the *belle époque*, we shall examine the structure and character of the *patronat*, as well as the ways in which it attempted to control the work-force and their allies in the Republic.

iii

The great founding families of the Nord's textile industry consistently ran against the French tide by refusing to sell shares in their enterprises to the public. Thus the production of textiles stayed in the hands of relatively few owners, most of whom belonged either by birth or by marriage to one or more of the largest families. These families expanded their numbers and their wealth by building new mills for each new generation. 'For each son', it was said, 'his own factory'. Daughters, on the other hand, were assigned a feudal role. They married—or were married—into other textile families, thus effectively tying businesses together. Because this process went on simultaneously with the failure of small competitors during the *belle époque*, control of the local industry fell into fewer and fewer hands.

A few examples illustrate the extent of the wealth and power of the mill owners in Roubaix, Tourcoing, and Lille in this period. The grandest textile family of them all were the Roubaix Mottes. In 1914, one of the smallest of the family's enterprises, Alfred Motte *et cie* (founded in 1879) employed 7,000 workers in nine Roubaix cotton mills. This firm also owned works in three other cities, all in the Nord department, as well as factories in Belgium, Russian Poland, and Moscow. Its total worth was said to be five million gold francs. Another side of the prolific Motte family owned vast mills producing virtually every type of wool yarn and woollen fabric. Wool production attracted the young Eugène Motte, future deputy from Roubaix, when his father gave him the choice of a wool mill or a cotton factory. His cousin Fernand, on the other hand, found himself unable to make the required decision at the customary age of 16½. His family sent him to England and to the United States to view other countries' industries as he tried to make up his mind. Finally, a visit to the cotton mills of Georgia, in 1907, decided him to choose cotton, and he, too, was given a mill.[14]

In neighbouring Tourcoing at the close of the nineteenth century, Tiberghien *et fils*, which produced combed and carded wool, wool yarn, and woollen cloth, employed 2,300 workers. The firm owned 50,000 spindles for spinning and twisting wool yarn, and 1,050 power looms. Fifty tons of wool were processed in the Tiberghien mill each week; the annual turnover was worth 16 million francs. A smaller wool firm in the city was owned by a Motte cousin, François Masurel, who employed 900 workers on 66,500 spindles. His annual turnover amounted to over 14 million francs.[15]

In Lille in the 1880s, despite the depression, one firm, J. Thiriez *père et fils*, was highly profitable. The family's factories sprawled over twenty hectares, and included a spinning mill, a thread-twisting mill, a bleaching factory, several machine repair workshops, and a building workshop. Thiriez employed 1,535 workers, including 672 women.[16]

Loud protestations to the contrary notwithstanding, then, many of the largest textile mill owners prospered throughout the *belle époque*. As personal fortunes grew, the families threw themselves enthusiastically into all the activities associated with the era.[17] They built elaborate homes, and maintained equally magnificent 'résidences secondaires'. They travelled abroad frequently, and many spent the 'season' in Paris.

On the other hand, their private lives remained highly traditional. Centred on church and family, the experiences of most textile

---

[14] See Codaccioni, *et al.*, *Histoire d'une métropole*, pp. 350–1; *VdP* (10–17 Apr. 1904); Fernand Motte, *Souvenirs personnels d'un demi-siècle de vie et de pensée, 1886–1942* (n.p., n.d).

[15] Jacques Toulemonde, *Naissance d'une métropole*, p. 63.

[16] Codaccioni, *et al.*, *Histoire d'une métropole*, p. 386.

[17] See: F. Motte, *Souvenirs personnels*; Gaston Motte, *Roubaix à travers les âges* (Roubaix, 1946), esp. p. 97; Paul Catrice, *Roubaix au delà des mers* (Roubaix, 1969), pp. 67–9; J.-E. Van den Driessche, *Histoire de Tourcoing* (Tourcoing, 1928), pp. x, 205; *Enquête sur l'industrie, 1904*, 'rapport. l'inspecteur départemental de Roubaix, M. Bellon', pp. 230–1; and 'Patronat et prolétariat textiles', *VdP* (22–29 May 1904).

magnates were constrained by long custom. For example, the two great events in the lives of many Motte children in our period were First Communion, which for boys clearly marked a transition from childhood to adult status, and marriage (at which point most sons were given their factories, and most daughters their *dot*). At the birth of every child, a Motte father customarily marked off two sections of his wine cellar, in preparation for these two important events.

While in residence in Lille, Roubaix, or Tourcoing, the textile families gathered frequently to share lavish meals. The contrast between their meals and the near-starvation of their workers was striking. A typical menu for one day in Fernand Motte's household at the turn of the century included a midday dinner of soup, followed by two meat dishes and potatoes, and ending with cheeses and dessert. Evening supper involved more meat and potatoes, plus vegetables, cheeses, and another dessert. Both meals, needless to say, were accompanied by several wines. Recalling these meals of his childhood, Fernand Motte claimed that they were unusually frugal and abstemious.

Most children of textile families attended Catholic schools, where they were taught by nuns and priests. Virtually all the boys joined Catholic youth organizations, at meetings of which they spent their leisure time. (As we shall see in chapter 4, these groups frequently entertained themselves by rioting whenever socialist speakers arrived at the local train stations.) The girls, of course, were confined to convents or to private instruction within the family home until they married.

During holidays, the families often motored to fashionable resorts, including Trouville or Vichy. While Fernand Motte's parents 'took the cure' at Vichy each year, their Roubaix house was entirely redecorated. Occasionally, the sons of the families travelled apart from their parents—often abroad. At 13, for example, Eugène took his younger cousin Fernand to Stuttgart for several weeks. There, Fernand was struck by the efficiency of the German police—who, he recalled, 'had already begun to register both bicycles and Jews'. Visiting Leicester a few years later, Fernand discovered that the feeling of inferiority aroused by the Germans was matched by feelings of superiority, provoked by the English.[18]

[18] F. Motte, *Souvenirs personnels*. Motte was an enthusiastic Vichy-ite during the war.

The ease with which Fernand Motte drew conclusions about national character suggests the ease with which he and other textile mill owners assigned workers to a category separate from the one they and their families inhabited. From within their safe superiority, they found it easy to ignore the plight of those whose work made their luxurious lives possible. Ernest Labrousse has remarked that the vast gap between these rich families and their workers made him think of the French title of Arthur Koestler's best-known book: *Le Zéro et l'infini*.[19] From their lofty social position the textile owners gazed down upon the narrow, confined world of their workers, in which almost nothing was possible. Still, their collective reaction was not only one of indifference. Instead, they exhibited a mixture of paternalistic concern (mostly provoked by what they thought of as workers' poor morals) and scorn.

A few of the more paternalistic mill owners assumed some responsibility for their workers, providing housing, a few crèches, some mutual aid societies, and so on. Some—but, alas, only a few—became social Catholics after the appearance of the Pope's 1891 encyclical, *Rerum Novarum*, which instructed Catholics to try to ameliorate the harsh conditions in which industrial workers lived. Their work is examined in a subsequent section. But the bulk of the textile *patronat* remained true to the model offered by America's Robber Barons in the Gilded Age. Most agreed that any problems were due strictly to the workers' own lack of providence—a characteristic of 'lesser' human beings. A few among the 'deserving poor' got help, but only of the most minimal kind, lest they develop lavish habits or laziness. Like many other French industrialists of the period, textile owners customarily described their workers as rather dim children, constantly in need of supervision and restriction.[20]

Such attitudes bolstered the isolation of owners from workers in the *belle époque*. The great mill-owning families lived out their lives behind high walls, in houses whose grandeur was exaggerated by a constant visual comparison with the *courées* and slums surrounding their mills.

---

[19] Labrousse, 'Préface', in Félix-Paul Codaccioni, *De l'inégalité sociale dans une grande ville industrielle: le drame de Lille de 1850 à 1914* (Lille, 1976), p.v.

[20] See Alberto Melucci, 'Idéologies et pratiques patronales pendant l'industrialisation capitaliste: le cas de France' (3e cycle, École Pratique des Hautes Études, Paris, 1974), esp. pp. 277 and 322.

These were the habits and attitudes which underlay the behaviour of the mill owners in Lille, Roubaix, and Tourcoing around the turn of the century. There are three recent studies of their collective conduct toward their workers in this period.[21] One focuses on the role of the Catholic Church in shaping or prescribing such behaviour. A second details the part many female members of the great textile families played in dealing with the workers. The third more general study concerns the attitudes of the industrial *patronat* throughout France in the nineteenth century, but depends substantially on the writings of textile owners in French Flanders.

The three studies, though quite different in method and emphasis, reach similar conclusions: firstly, that the more human aspects of Catholic belief rarely interfered with the capitalistic drive to increase profits—at whatever cost to the workers—and, secondly, that the efforts made to enforce religious belief and practice among workers were basically motivated by cynicism, providing little more than a means of disciplining and controlling the work-force.

Before turning to this issue of the Church's role in the interaction between classes in Lille, Roubaix, and Tourcoing in the *belle époque*, it is instructive to examine the attitudes of the *patronat* in some detail—though with the caveat in mind that this overview is just that: painted on a broad canvas with little attempt made to identify subtler variations among the many mill-owning families of the region.

The attitudes of employers in our period had two focuses: women of the textile proletariat and workers in general. Attitudes—and consequent behaviour—toward women in the mills were constructed of prevalent nineteenth-century stereotypes about the 'weaker sex' and the need to rationalize the widespread employment of women and girls at low wages in exhausting jobs.

The prevalent view of women (of all classes) in France in the late Victorian period differed only slightly from that held

---

[21] M. l'abbé R. Talmy, *L'Association catholique des patrons du Nord, 1884–95: une forme hybride de catholicisme social en France* (Lille, 1962); Bonnie Sullivan Smith, 'The Women of the Lille Bourgeoisie, 1850–1914 (Ph.D., University of Rochester, 1975); Melucci, 'Idéologies'. (Smith's recent book, *Ladies of the Leisure Class: the Bourgeoises of Northern France in the Nineteenth Century* (Princeton, 1981), makes many of the same points as does her dissertation.)

throughout the industrialized world. Bourgeois women had but two paths in life: that exemplified by the life of the Virgin Mother (or, in Anglican England, by the Queen), or the downward path of the Magdalene.[22] The lives and activities of the women of mill-owning families, and particularly their work among female textile workers, reflected their efforts to follow the upward path of domesticity, which occasionally they extended into the homes of their labouring sisters.

It had not always been so; among the founders of many textile businesses earlier in the century were several powerful, independent women. Gaston Motte's history of the local industry cautions, 'One must not underestimate the role that the women played in the origins of the *roubaisien* industry,' and cites as evidence the considerable careers of his grandmother and great grandmother. Another local writer recalled Mme Pierre Motte (born a Motte and married to a cousin) who had, in mid-century, brought to the area three orders of nuns—the Little Sisters of the Poor, the Daughters of Charity, and the Sisters of Saint-Sauveur—whose activities including helping the mill owners to control and discipline the workers, particularly the female workers.[23] Whatever their inheritance, however, the women of the early Third Republic found themselves almost totally isolated from the 'man's world' of business.

Local bourgeois women's childhoods were passed in convents or, if they were slightly poorer, in local *pensions* much like that described in Charlotte Brontë's *Villette*. The results were predictable. Fernand Motte, writing in the 1940s, recalled: 'In that era girls enjoyed none of the liberties which they presently have.' Until they made their formal débuts into society, the only men girls were allowed to see were family members. When they met strange men on the street—on those rare trips away from the convent or home—they were expected to lower their eyes. (It is not surprising that so many among them ended by marrying their

---

[22] Discussions of this ideology are found in Viola Klein, *The Feminine Character: History of an Ideology* (New York, 1946); Françoise Basch, *Relative Creatures* (New York, 1974), esp. pp. 3–15; Madeleine Guilbert, *Les Fonctions des femmes dans l'industrie* (Paris, 1966), pp. 55 ff.; Françoise Mayeur, *L'Enseignement secondaire des jeunes filles sous la Troisième République* (Paris, 1977).
[23] G. Motte, *Roubaix à travers*, pp. 46–7; Paul Catrice, *Roubaix au delà*, p. 67; Pierre Pierrard, *La Vie ouvrière à Lille sous le Second Empire* (Paris, 1965), p. 186.

cousins!) The end result of this sort of isolation from the world was sometimes extreme piety. Sometimes, on the other hand, it was childlike frivolity. Fernand's mother was of the latter type: 'My mother, still strikingly young and pretty, had very refined tastes; she adored her 'toilette', pretty furniture, and mother-of-pearl dinner service. She was totally ignorant of the *value* of money, though in no time she mastered the art of spending vast pots of it'.[24] Whether pious or childlike, however, women of the local textile bourgeoisie were restricted to their lives as wives and mothers. They occupied a narrow, if luxurious, world, cocooned against the evils of the outside world. Their duty was to the family—for whose physical and spiritual needs they provided. The strict sanctions of the Catholic Church ensured that few strayed from the prescribed path; it is not surprising that no local Mme Bovary troubled the still waters of bourgeois life in the *belle époque.*

Women's sole outlet came in the form of charitable work among the deserving poor of the three cities. Literally their only unsupervised outings were those taken to the workers' *quartiers* where they visited *ouvrières'* homes, sometimes carrying food, clothing, or money, more often seeking to identify deserving families who were then eligible for help.[25]

In a word, these late nineteenth-century women were 'ladies'. 'Grace and poetry incarnate, the flowers of creation', in the words of Jules and Gustave Simon.[26]

In the world of Lille, Roubaix, and Tourcoing at the turn of the century, however, the conditions of the majority of local women was considerably less sublime. Most were *ouvrières*—creatures of industrial capitalism who had provoked Michelet's horror early in the century. '*L'ouvrière*', he had exclaimed, 'mot impie, sordide, qu'aucune langue n'eût jamais, qu'aucun temps n'aurait compris avant cet âge de fer . . .'.[27] Like most bourgeois observers, of

---

[24] F. Motte, *Souvenirs personnels*, p. 19. The education of northern French girls is discussed in Robert Gildea, *Education in Provincial France, 1800–1914: a Study of Three Departments* (Oxford, 1983), pp. 119, 123–4.

[25] See Smith, 'Women of the Lille Bourgeoisie', and Marie-Hélène Zylberberg-Hocquard, 'L'Ouvrière dans les romans populaires du dix-neuvième siècle', *RdN, numéro spécial*, 'Histoire des femmes du Nord' (July–Sept. 1981), pp. 603–36.

[26] Gustave and Jules Simon, *La Femme du vingtième siècle* (Paris, 1982), p. 109.

[27] Jules Michelet, *La Femme* (Paris, n.d.), p. 22. Michelet added, 'Woman is no longer made for love, for men's happiness, still less for maternity . . .

course, Michelet identified the factory as the seat of women's degradation. It was work in the mills that had brought women into cities, dragged them from their *foyers*, and thrown them into labour cheek by jowl with men.[28]

Though the coming of the factory, Michelet to the contrary notwithstanding, did not suddenly signal the beginning of women's work, or even women's waged work, it did mean that women's work was more public, more visible to a bourgeoisie which cherished notions of 'women's place' near the familial hearth. For the local bourgeoisie, the visibility of their own female work-force served to highlight the vast difference between *ouvrières'* lives and the lives of bourgeois women. Furthermore, *ouvrières'* daily experiences directly contradicted stereotypes resting on beliefs about women's weakness, their need to be shielded from the harsh realities of industrial life. This contradiction contained a further irony, too. In the textile cities, it was the labour of proletarian women which, to a very considerable extent, made it possible for male factory owners to protect their wives, mothers, and daughters from the awful realities lurking in the cities' mills.

This contradiction posed a problem for mill owners. They had at the same time to maintain two views of women, one which said that women were weak, spiritual, and domestically inclined, in need of constant male protection, and one which allowed them to underpay and overwork thousands of working-class mothers, wives, and daughters.

The three tactics with which the textile *patronat* accommodated the realities of working women's lives to their stereotypes of women in general were similar to those employed elsewhere in the industrial world. Firstly, they adopted the view that working-class people—of both sexes—were different from them, altogether inferior beings, in fact. Thus they described workers as wayward and improvident folk who might be saved for their true reward in the afterlife only by dint of strict controls in the present.[29]

---

[28] Michelet's view that working women were peculiar to industry would have surprised most of the several million peasant women in nineteenth-century France. One book which describes their labour is Martine Segalen's *Love and Power in the Peasant Family: Rural France in the Nineteenth Century*, trans. Sarah Matthews (Oxford, 1983).

[29] See Jacques Dumortier, *Le Syndicat patronal textile de Roubaix-Tourcoing de 1942 à 1972* (Lille, 1975), appendix ii, and Melucci, '*Idéologies*', n. 40, pp. 323 and 277.

Secondly, the *patronat* claimed to share a special concern for working women's weaknesses—though they saw these only as spiritual, never as physical. This concern supported strenuous attempts to impose rigid religious controls upon working women. Because these controls were imposed within the factories themselves, they included a practical corollary beneficial to the mill owners: they provided a special means of disciplining and controlling a substantial minority of the textile work-force.

A third attitude of the *patronat* was less complicated by religious ideology or by beliefs about the special nature of women. This was an attitude of indifference. If the more detached among the textile *patronat* thought of workers at all, it was because of mass protests which workers continually launched against their conditions in these years. Even then, however, many mill owners could not be bothered to contemplate their workers' grievances. Instead, they explained such events as the result of 'outside agitators', who had duped the childlike workers. One smug Roubaix mill owner explained to the prefect that 'there was always perfect harmony between *patronat* and workers until now, when it is diminishing daily because of a *unique cause* [emphasis his]—the International and revolutionary socialist doctrines which are spreading alarmingly among workers.' He added that as a result of this interference, *roubaisien* workers had become 'immoral and drunk'. Furthermore, while it was true, as this owner pointed out, that their 'very low level of education' made them particularly susceptible to these outsiders, he thought nothing could alter that fact because they refused the education available to them in both lay and Catholic schools. These latter, he added, even provided workers with libraries for their self-improvement. Of course, children were prevented from going to school by 'avaricious' parents, who sent them into the factories as soon as they could. Lest the prefect conclude from this that higher wages would be a solution, the owner pointed out that more money would only encourage 'debauchery'.[30]

The disdain which most of the mill owners expressed surprised some of the bourgeois reformers who were drawn to the Nord's cities by the presence of widespread misery, as well as by the

[30] *AN* C 'Enquête des situations ouvrières 1872–85'. and Melucci, 'Idéologies', n. 44, p. 325.

presence among the professional classes of the three cities of like-minded people. In 1909, for example, Dr René Potelet concluded his visit by suggesting that mill owners build crèches within their factories, so that nursing mothers could feed their infants during the working day. The reaction surprised him. None among the *patronat* was interested in such a reform. Nor was their hostility lessened when he suggested that such crèches need not be large, or even staffed with additional workers. Women who worked near the crèches, he said, could keep an eye on the babies during the hours when they were not being fed. Furthermore, those women who left their machines to feed infants could leave those machines in the care of their sister workers.

But all his efforts bore no fruit. Most textile mill owners told him that their mills were already overcrowded. And they repeated for him their often-expressed view that high infant mortality had nothing to do with a lack of breast-feeding, but rather was due to the 'indifference' of working women.[31]

Official messengers of the republican state, especially work inspectors (who, after 1892, monitored observance of factory legislation), likewise attracted the hostility of the employers. They were unanimous in their complaints that mill owners rarely even deigned to respond to criticisms of mill practices—let alone act to improve them.[32]

While most of the textile *patronat* remained indifferent to the plight of their workers, a few members of the textile families ventured into charitable work aimed at relieving some of the wretchedness of life in *courées* or slums. The primary institution through which they worked was the *bureau de bienfaisance* (founded during the Napoleonic period), one of which existed in each city. These bureaux were directed by a relief committee chosen from among local notables. It was to this committee that indigent workers applied for help throughout the nineteenth and

[31] Dr R. Potelet, 'Les Crèches d'usines dans le département du Nord', France, *Bulletin de l'Office du travail*, 1909 (Paris, 1910), pp. 429–31.

[32] *Enquête sur l'industrie, 1904*, 'dépositions, juge de paix de Roubaix, canton nord', p. 218; juge de paix de Roubaix, canton ouest-est', p. 221; 'juges de paix, trois cantons, Tourcoing', p. 450; 'M. Boulisset, l'inspecteur divisionnel, et MM Herbo et Gillet, inspecteurs de travail à Lille', p. 326. See also J.-B. Knockaert, 'La Lutte contre le patronat textile à Tourcoing', *BS* (13 Oct. 1913).

early twentieth centuries. Unfortunately, in the years before the socialists gained control of the municipalities of Lille and Roubaix in the nineties, these bureaux had relatively little impact. In Lille in 1895, for example, there were 32,000 indigents (classed as 'deserving poor' by the bureau) enrolled on the welfare lists. The city's budget for the bureau in that year was 280,000 francs, or an average of only 8.75 fr. per person for the whole year.[33] In especially hard years, local donations sometimes swelled a bureau's budget—and, in our period, many of these contributions came from the textile *patronat*. In the bleak winter of 1891, when Tourcoing's municipal council was only able to add 10,000 fr. for food for the deserving poor, local donations, mostly from textile families, doubled the figure.[34]

In addition to these relief committees, each city had a few hospices—staffed by nuns as well as lay people. In Lille, in 1895, there were seven hospices, with 700 beds for the sick and wounded, and a further 2,090 beds for the old, the incurable, or for orphans. In Roubaix, a civic hospice, built in 1865 by M. and Mme Joseph Pollet-Motte, offered beds for 350 patients of both sexes. The city added the *Hospice de Barbieux* in 1890 (with room for 500 aged or terminally ill patients), and the *Hôpital de la fraternité* in 1902, which had 700 beds and 38 cradles.[35] Given the vast and growing populations of the three cities, the number of beds was very small. Tourcoing was similarly underequipped to meet even the most minimal health needs of its citizens. It is not surprising, then, that throughout our period hospital care was a great rarity to most workers.

Each city also ran a few night refuges for the homeless, but these were opened only when winter was at its worst. A few crèches also dotted the urban landscape in Lille, Roubaix, and Tourcoing in our period. In Tourcoing in 1892 there were six municipal crèches, some of which offered free lunches to children in their care. Lille had crèches run by nuns, which charged parents a few centimes a day. In these crèches, as in most others in Tourcoing and Roubaix

---

[33] Henri Ghesquière, 'L'Action des municipalités socialistes: assistance communale à Lille', *MS* (Jan.–June 1899), p. 117.

[34] Ibid., and Jules Watteeuw, *Tourcoing au XIXe siècle* (Tourcoing, 1904), p. 444, and *VdP* (10–17 Apr. 1904).

[35] Gaston Motte, *Roubaix à travers*, pp. 77–8.

in the early nineties, only 'deserving' children were welcomed. No illegitimate boys or girls found places.[36]

The wives and daughters of the textile *patronat* played a special role in the cities' charities. They established and ran several groups aimed at working women's needs. Among the largest of these was the *Société de charité maternelle*, in Lille, which offered money, a midwife, and a modest layette to new mothers. Of course, the recipient had to prove her moral fitness in order to benefit from the society's funds. Probity was established by a visit from the committee, who sought evidence that potential recipients met three requirements. Firstly, they had to possess a certificate from the local police attesting to their good character and morality. Secondly, they had to have at least three living children under 14, two if they were unable to work, or one if the father was either totally disabled or dead. Thirdly, they had to show a church marriage certificate. These rigorous requirements doubtless help explain why this charity gave aid to only 1400 women in the entire decade of the 1880s, and only 1100 the following decade.[37]

Another organization headed by the local bourgeoises was *Mutualité maternelle*, with groups in Lille and Roubaix. Women workers were encouraged to join this maternity insurance scheme, to which they regularly paid small sums. When they gave birth, they received money and a layette. These groups too were unpopular: in 1908 there were only 334 members in Lille and 402 in Roubaix.[38]

When one contemplates the minimal social efforts made by the local textile *patronat*, one must agree with M. l'abbé Talmy who concluded that most employer reactions to Leo XIII's encyclical, *Rerum novarum*, amounted to little more than window-dressing. Collectively, most mill owners carried on after the 1891 encyclical in their traditional way, firm in their view that they owed their workers nothing in this life. They were, however, willing to assume responsibility for workers' fate in the next life. The

[36] For Tourcoing, see Van den Driessche, *Histoire de Tourcoing*, p. 202. For Lille, see Smith, 'Women of the Lille Bourgeoisie'. See also Yvonne Knibielher and Cathérine Fouquet, *Histoire des mères du Moyen Âge à nos jours* (Paris, 1977), pp. 236–7.

[37] Smith, 'Women of the Lille Bourgeoisie' and A. Vallin, *La Femme salariée et la maternité* (Paris, 1911), pp. 183–4.

[38] Vallin, *La Femme salariée*.

sanctimonious rhetoric of the 1878 charter of the *Association des patrons chrétiens* exemplified this latter attitude: 'The worker is not a force that one utilizes or rejects according only to the needs of production. He is our brother in Jesus Christ, given by God to the *patrons* who remain obligated to place him in the proper conditions to facilitate his *eternal* life.'[39] When Ardouin-Dumazet visited Roubaix in 1903 he discovered little change in this attitude. He concluded that charities run by the *patronat* constituted little more than false façades behind which the mill owners hoped to impose their conservative religious views onto the textile workforce. He wrote, 'in exchange for charity [they] demand the sacrifice of opinions or religious demonstrations.'[40]

Although an indictment of the wealthy *patronat* is justified by the abundant evidence of their indifference to the local workers, it must be said that a few among the mill owners demonstrated greater kindness in their dealings with their workers. Two families, the Masurels of Tourcoing and the Crépys of Lille, treated their workers with the paternalism characteristic of textile producers in Alsace, notably, of course, at Mulhouse. In the massive red-brick wool mill founded by François-Joseph Masurel-Pollett with his three sons in 1877, workers were offered a mutual aid society and savings society. The owners also built nursing-rooms and crèches near the factory work-rooms. Furthermore, they offered new mothers a short, but paid, maternity leave following childbirth. The Masurels also sponsored a *Goutte du lait* for their workers, whose infants received free—and more importantly sterile—milk throughout infancy.[41]

In Lille, the cotton-spinning mill of Lucien Crépy offered another good place to work. The Crépy family built crèches for workers' young children, and founded a maternity insurance scheme, which paid for medical care during childbirth as well as for maternity leave. Outside the factory, Lucien Crépy sponsored several night refuges for Lille's homeless as well as free soup-kitchens for the hungry.[42]

---

[39] Quoted in Talmy, *L'Association*, p. 384. *Rerum Novarum* instructed Catholics to ease the burdens of workers in industrial society.
[40] Ardouin-Dumazet, *Voyage en France, région du Nord* (Paris, 1903), p. 25.
[41] See *Dictionnaire biographique illustré* (2nd edn., Paris, n.d.), pp. 754–6.
[42] Ibid., p. 259.

Both families were equally unusual in their politics. Unlike the majority of the local textile *patronat*, the Masurels and Crépys held republican views, and both had children who became involved in local republican politics. Their republicanism set them apart from their neighbours, most of whom were strictly conservative and deeply religious. In fact, one historian of the Lille area in the *belle époque* has argued that, just as politics animated the workers, so religion animated the mill owners.[43]

Speaking very generally, it was true that most textile mill owners in the area were politically conservative and deeply religious. Nevertheless, certain key differences separated the *patronats* of each city, differences which helped shape the ways in which organized workers responded to their situation during the *belle époque*.

In Lille, because of an historically more varied economic infrastructure, the politics of the bourgeoisie were less homogeneous than in the one-industry cities of Roubaix and Tourcoing. Alongside the Catholic conservatism of most textile families ran the republicanism and even radical republicanism of many of the professional classes of Lille. Doctors, lawyers, teachers, journalists, printers, and even manufacturers in industries other than textiles supported republican and anti-clerical politics in our period. A few among Lille's textile families belong to this group as well. In addition to the sons of the Crépy family, Alfred Thiriez, of a local cotton-spinning family, and Charles Delasalle, from linen-spinners, were active in local republican politics. Throughout our period, the commitment of such local notables to social reform and to anti-clericalism helped weaken the local socialists' more revolutionary message from time to time.[44]

The picture in Roubaix was altogether less muddled. Throughout our period, the city was clearly divided in two, each half symbolized by one of the two statues which still stand in the city: Jules Guesde, leader of the socialist party and Roubaix's deputy from 1893 to 1899, and Eugène Motte, 'the prototype of the *patron roubaisien*' in the words of his cousin, who succeeded Guesde as Roubaix's deputy.[45] Roubaix was a city divided, the socialist

---

[43] Codaccioni, *De l'inégalité sociale*, p. 65.
[44] Pierre Pierrard, *Lille et les Lillois* (Paris, 1967), p. 207.
[45] G. Motte, *Roubaix à travers*, p. 70.

workers lined up on one side against the conservative Catholic *patrons*. Ardouin-Dumazet described the abyss which separated one group from the other: 'No point of contact', he wrote, '. . . none of the venues where the French bourgeoisie customarily meets the proletariat: no public libraries, no public race courses.'[46] Instead, each group existed apart from the other. Not even minimal respect cloaked the relations between the leaders of the two opposing groups. Fernand Motte recalled that the Roubaix of his youth was 'the invisible citadel of socialism', led by a mayor, Henri Carrette, 'le rouge'. He described the leader of the socialist party, Jules Guesde, as 'the apostle of the long hair and of the black, but shorter, beard'. To those who doubted the accuracy of his portrait, he recommended a visit to the Carrette memorial in Roubaix's cemetery. 'On the pedestal supporting his effigy', he wrote, 'a hateful, uncontrolled fury seems to hurl itself on the end of the sword formed by these words cut into the stone: "Arise ye wretched of the earth".'[47] (Motte apparently did not recognize the first line of the Internationale.)

Motte shared this antagonism with other members of his family. When Eugène Motte managed to unseat Guesde, in 1899, after a long and vicious (and many said corrupt) campaign, in which numbers of textile workers were manipulated into voting for Motte, he was asked how 'a world of workers' had elected a *patron* as their representative. He replied disdainfully, 'I did not realize that it was necessary to be a tramp in order to be a deputy.'[48]

Roubaix's close neighbour, Tourcoing, was a very different place through most of our period. It was, in Ardouin-Dumazet's words, 'a city of sedate good sense'.[49] There, both political extremes, socialism as well as ultra-royalist Catholicism, found fewer adherents. Thus, through the 1880s and 1890s, while both Lille and Roubaix turned to socialism, Tourcoing chose a moderate republican path, led by the deputy and mayor, Gustave Dron. At the same time, religion found more adherents among workers, as well as owners, though it was a Catholicism which rarely took political form. Instead, religion permeated the two

---

[46] Ardouin-Dumazet, *Voyage*, pp. 9, 22.
[47] F. Motte, *Souvenirs personnels*, p. 12.
[48] Ibid.
[49] Ardouin-Dumazet, *Voyage*, p. 9.

focuses of *tourquenois* attentions, the family and the work-place.[50] This shared religious base tended to lessen the effects of industrial confrontation. As we shall see, in the early period at least, most Tourcoing industrial disputes were settled rapidly, and left fewer scars than those in neighbouring Roubaix and Lille. The prefect of the Nord reported in 1880 that the Tourcoing *patronat* was, on the whole, 'more conciliatory' than owners in Lille and Roubaix. They rarely reacted to industrial crises by lowering wages and, when times were bad, they made more effort to help their workers. Witnesses before the parliamentary commission in 1904, moreover, reported better relations between mill owners and workers in Tourcoing during the general strike of that year.[51]

On the other hand, a growing current of distrust ran beneath this apparently untroubled surface. Records of Tourcoing's *conseil des prud'hommes* suggest that the years around the turn of the century were less peaceful than most public pronouncements suggested. Even Ardouin-Dumazet added a caveat to his otherwise sanguine view of industrial relations in Tourcoing in 1903. 'Class relations', he warned, 'are beginning to lose their cordiality' with the 'approach of dangerous and destructive ideas'.[52]

Moreover, the rhetoric of representatives of Tourcoing's *patronat*, testifying in 1904, was scarcely less disdainful than that employed by their fellows in Lille and Roubaix. One Tourcoing witness told the parliamentary committee president, Jean Jaurès, that French textile workers were 'greatly inferior' to English workers, as they lacked what he called 'the English will to work'. When Jaurès interrupted him to say, 'Are not the English workers better fed?', he responded airily, 'Oh, just a little better . . . and even the Belgians are better workers than the French.'[53]

Thus although the textile *patronat* in Lille, Roubaix, and Tourcoing was not a homogeneous mass, they did share certain attitudes which coloured their reaction to workers' attempts to

[50] Van den Driessche, *Histoire de Tourcoing*, p. x.

[51] *ADN* M 151 7, 'Partis politiques, dossiers individuels, 1878'; *ADN* M 572 8, 'Régime industriel. Rapports sur la situation de l'industrie 1886'; *Enquête sur l'industrie, 1904*, pp. 347 ff.

[52] *ADN* 1 U 79, 'Conseils des prud'hommes, Tourcoing'; Ardouin-Dumazet, *Voyage*, pp. 39–40.

[53] *Enquête sur l'industrie, 1904*, 'déposition, Chambre de commerce de Tourcoing', p. 347.

alter their work conditions. Before turning to the public clash between workers and employers, however, it is important to understand what those working conditions were in this period in the great textile mills of the three cities.

When Léon Bocquet visited one textile factory in Lille just after the First World War, he remarked: 'At first contact, it exudes an impression of organized force, of imposing power, but force and power that are tyrannical and brutal.'[54] Indeed, tyranny and brutality characterized the experiences of most textile workers in our period. From the day when a child first entered a mill—that 'douloureux calvaire des femmes du peuple', in the words of a contemporary—to the day when ill health, or, less frequently, a surplus of children freed her, a textile worker's life was rigidly circumscribed by the demands of factory routine.[55] For both male and female mill workers, the daily monotony of life was broken only by strikes, lay-offs, and the occasional fête. So pervasive were these factory routines that a new worker 'quickly became little more than a machine, which ran another machine', according to one writer. 'But', she added, 'she is a living machine, who feels pain, who suffers, who overworks, who becomes anaemic from overwork.'[56]

A worker's day began with the sound of a steam whistle summoning her from a *courée* bed before dawn. By 6 a.m. most workers were inside the great iron gates of the mills, making their way to their work-rooms and to their machines. Generally, the ground-floor work-rooms, regardless of the fibre being processed, were reserved for the various stages of preparation. In cotton mills these included the opening and beating of cotton bales, followed by washing, which prepared the raw cotton for carding machines. These machines pulled the cotton into long, flat shanks, ready for spinning. In some factories, this prepared cotton was packaged and sent to spinning mills elsewhere, but in most it was sent on to winding rooms, usually upstairs in the same building. Wool fleeces, on the other hand, underwent a more involved preparation. Incoming fleeces went first to skilled wool-sorters (*trieurs*), who had served long apprenticeships. These workers (usually men),

---

[54] Léon Bocquet, *Villes meurtries de France. Villes du Nord: Lille, Douai, Cambrai, Valenciennes, Bergues, Dunkerque* (Brussels and Paris, 1918), p. 6.
[55] Alice Delucheux, 'L'Émancipation de la femme', *BS* (1 Dec. 1911).
[56] Ibid.

sorted each fleece into categories depending on thickness, regularity, length of the wool, and so on. The work-room where this process of 'triage' took place provided the best conditions in wool mills. Well lit and well ventilated, sorting rooms were altogether more salubrious than other work-rooms in the mills. The good conditions were testimony to the value employers placed on *trieurs*' work. Following the sorting process, wool was washed, carded, and/or combed, and sent on to be wound on bobbins, then spun and woven in processes similar to those employed for other fibres.

Mills varied according to whether they included the entire process, from raw material to finished cloth, or limited the work to various stages. The largest and most elaborate mills often combined several functions, including scouring, dyeing and bleaching rooms, as well as rooms for 'finishing' ('fulling') the end products.

Almost every stage of this production process employed a combination of men, women, and children of both sexes. Traditionally, northern textile production rarely separated work into 'men's' or 'women's' work. Villermé had noted this unusual situation even in the 1830s. He wrote that most textile jobs in the Nord were performed 'indifferently by workers of both sexes'.[57] This remained the situation well into our period. Only in bleaching, dyeing, and wool-sorting, where men tended to predominate, and in some stages of preparation (especially in flax mills) where women tended to predominate were there identifiable patterns of sex-segregated work. And, even in these jobs, workers rarely worked in sex-segregated work-rooms. Thus, although women usually tended carding machines, men worked nearby, transporting rollers of carded materials, and so on. On the whole, the men and women workers of French Flanders usually laboured together, not infrequently at identical tasks.[58]

---

[57] Dr L.-R. Villermé, *État physique et moral des ouvriers des manufactures de coton, laine . . .* (Paris, 1840), vol. i, pp. 4–5.

[58] Documentary evidence of the lack of a clear-cut sexual division of labour is found in: *ADN* M 597 18 11, 'Livrets délivrés, 1881, Tourcoing, Lille, Roubaix'; France. *Résultats statistiques du recensement des industries et professions, 29 mars 1896* (Paris, 1897); *Enquête sur l'industrie, 1904*, pp. 271–9, 280–92, 293–303, 484, 486; Léon de Seilhac, *La Grève du tissage de Lille* (Paris, 1910); France, *Statistique des grèves 1896, 1902, 1906, 1911*; Charles Poisson, *Le Salaire des femmes* (Paris, 1906), pp. 21–2, 30–4.

However unproblematic this statement might first appear, recent histories of working women have rendered it less so. Frequently, the sexual division of factory labour, which did occur elsewhere in France as well as in England—has bolstered explanations for women's putative lack of political participation. It has been argued that because women were separated from male workers in the work-place, on top of being burdened with ;all domestic responsibilities after work, they proved unable to develop class-consciousness. Some historians have gone so far as to suggest that women's separation from their male colleagues exacerbated their natural timidity in the company of men, making it impossible for most *ouvrières* to confront men in unions or in political organizations. In the northern textile industry, however, such explanations find no support. On the contrary, more than one observer noted—often with contempt—the familiarity between men and women at work in the mills. Flemish women were, in fact, far from fearful or timorous in the presence of their male co-workers. In fact, quite the contrary: they drank along with the men, and—to the detriment of their safety— they took part in the speed competitions that frequently broke out in weaving and spinning rooms near the end of the day.[59]

Although textile jobs were rarely segregated by sex, however, wages were. Women consistently earned from one-half to two-thirds as much as their male co-workers who themselves earned very low wages. In fact, the pay of all workers in Lille, Roubaix, and Tourcoing in our period failed to rise throughout the thirty-four years before the war. Given the rapid, and sometimes precipitate rise in the cost of living over these decades, textile workers faced a continual drop in real wages.

Of course, the secrecy of the Nord's textile families extended to this issue of wages as well as to all others concerning the conditions of workers in the industry. This means that all generalizations about wages must be viewed with scepticism. One must concur with the view expressed by a frustrated parliamentary committee, which concluded its detailed investigation of wages in Lille, Roubaix, and Tourcoing with these words: 'It is, in reality, nearly

---

[59] M. Boulin, 'Les Accidents évitables dans les filatures et dans les peignages', France, *Bulletin de l'inspection du travail, 1913* (Paris, 1914), p. 348.

impossible to draw any general conclusion from the numbers obtained.'[60]

That said, however, Tables 1 and 2 show a very general picture of wages for adult men and women during our period, based on figures available.

Table 1

Average daily wages in Lille, Roubaix, and Tourcoing in 1885 (all occupations)

	Men (fr.)	Women (fr.)
Lille	2.72–5.00	2.00–2.50
Roubaix	2.75–5.00	2.50–3.50
Tourcoing	2.75–5.00	2.20

(Source: ANC 3019 'Enquête des situations ouvrières, 1872–1885)

Table 2

Average daily wages (in francs) for the period 1896–1911 (Lille, Roubaix, and Tourcoing combined)

Occupation	1896		1902		1906		1911	
	m.	f.	m.	f.	m.	f.	m.	f.
Rattacheur	3.90	2.80	3.00	3.00	3.40	3.40	?	?
Fileur	5.00	2.15/ 2.25	?	?	6.60	2.75	4.50	2.50/ 3.00
Tisseur	3.67	2.98	3.63	2.80	3.50	2.75	5.00	3.00
All Occup.	3.47	2.89	4.50	2.60	4.45	2.77	4.31	2.48

(Source: France, *Statistique des grèves*, 1896, 1902, 1906, 1911)

[60] *Enquête sur l'industrie, 1904*, p. 279. See also pp. 274, 286, 290, 297, and: *LT* (12 Feb. 1893); Aline Valette, 'La Femme dans l'usine', *LT* (3 Feb. 1894; *ADN* M 594 6, 'Travail des enfants dans l'industrie, 1897–99'; France, *Salaires et coût de l'existence, 1906* (Paris, 1907), p. 165.

These tables suggest three conclusions. Firstly, wages were, on the whole, dropping slightly in our period. Secondly, women's wages as a percentage of men's were dropping more rapidly in some occupations, though holding steady in others. Thirdly, women who worked in mixed-sex jobs—with the exception of *rattacheuses* (tiers of broken threads)—earned on the average only slightly more than women working in occupations usually assigned to women only.

Lower real wages reflected the overall decline in textiles in our period. The textile workers' plight appears even worse by comparison with miners' wages, which rose by 46.3 per cent between 1880 and 1914. Whereas a 'good' miner in the Nord coal industry in 1901 earned an average of 10 francs a day, a woman textile worker earned between 2 and 3 francs. Furthermore a miner's company housing was cheap, his coal free.[61]

The problems accompanying this decline in workers' real wages in the *belle époque* were exacerbated by extended and usually unpredictable periods of unemployment. Smaller factories continually failed. When prices fell (often quite suddenly) or foreign demand dropped, large factories cut hours, or even laid some workers off. Textile workers in Lille, Roubaix, and Tourcoing lived therefore with a constant and often harrowing insecurity.[62]

In the first decade of our period, workers had recourse during these protracted periods of unemployment to two traditional remedies. Some found work in agriculture—which still existed nearby in the eighties—and some took in work in the domestic out-putting system, remnants of which continued to survive in that decade. But both alternatives had disappeared by the end of the decade. When one local mayor sent a distress signal to the Nord

[61] B.R. Mitchell, *European Historical Statistics 1750–1970* (New York, 1978), p. 72. A coal miner's view of wages in his industry is found in M. Carémiaux, untitled article, *PJ* (1 June 1901). My estimates err on the side of optimism. Many contemporaries described sharply falling textile wages. *VdP*, for example, reported on 19 February 1900 that a weaver who had earned 35–38 fr. a week in 1880, only averaged from 10–18 fr. a week in 1900. One socialist union reported that textile wages had fallen by 25 per cent in twenty-five years. Weavers, they said, had dropped from 28–30 fr. a week in 1885 to 15–16 fr. a week in 1910, and spinners from 40 fr. a week to 30 fr. See *ADN* M 625 1–3, 'Rapports'. These were male wages.

[62] Textile workers' despair culminated in a mass march of the unemployed from Roubaix to Paris in 1901. See *ADN* M 616 13, 'Les Sans-Travail, voyage à Paris, 1901'.

prefect requesting aid for the masses of unemployed textile workers in his commune, he noted that fewer and fewer were able to find agricultural jobs or bits of wool-carding, spinning, or weaving which they could do at home. Even among these latter home workers, moreover, income was derisory. Though they worked from six in the morning to eleven at night, few earned enough even to subsist. In this commune of 4,324 (of whom 3,752 were textile workers or families of textile workers), 571 people in 117 households were totally indigent, and thus dependent on the commune for their existence. Faced with so much poverty, the commune needed help from the department just to keep its citizens alive.[63]

As both rural jobs and domestic out-putting vanished, problems of unemployment increased. On top of unemployment occasioned by over-production and dropping prices, workers suffered long 'dead' seasons when little work was available. One census which counted unemployment in the Nord department in 1896, 1901, and 1906 showed that workers in the department as a whole suffered considerably more unemployment than workers elsewhere in France—at a rate nearly 1½ times greater.[64]

Workers survived this sporadic, chronic unemployment through a variety of tactics. First among these was credit, which they obtained in one of four places. Firstly, the ubiquitous *monts-de-piété* offered workers a place where they might pawn whatever goods they owned. In times of near-destitution, these goods included every scrap of household linen, of cookware, of clothing, as well as most furniture. For many in the *courées* of Lille, Roubaix, and Tourcoing, these humble pawnshops were nearly as familiar as the local *estaminet*—and, for the most part, they

---

[63] *ADN* M 581 141, 'Industrie textile, ouvriers tisseurs du département, enquête sur leur situation'.

[64] France, *Résultats statistiques du recensement général de la population, 4 mars 1906* (Paris, 1907), vol. i. For 1904 figures see *Enquête sur l'industrie, 1904*, pp. 148, 162, 328. The Roubaix *patronat* claimed that there were two dead seasons a year, each two months long, one in spring and one in autumn. A socialist union agreed that workers suffered about four months unemployment a year, but argued that it was irregular. Furthermore, the pattern varied from factory to factory. Lille's work inspector, M. Boulisset, agreed with the workers' view. He added that long periods of unemployment were usually broken by intense overwork; in wool the work lasted from February to August or September.

retained the affection of workers forced to use them with such frequency.

Secondly, a very few among the textile employers offered workers *économats*, or company stores. These, so common a feature of mining towns throughout the industrialized world,[65] were both uncommon and unpopular in French Flanders. Workers resented being forced to shop at such stores—where credit was backed by their wages, from which deductions were made by the employer each month. Furthermore, such shops prevented workers from buying food and other commodities at their own co-operative stores, several of which were thriving in the cities by the end of the century. Finally, many workers complained that company *économats* charged higher prices than other shops. At both Tiberghien *frères* (Tourcoing) and Thiriez *père et fils* (Lille) workers found prices to be at least 10 per cent higher than elsewhere.[66]

The third source of credit was the *estaminet*. In 1885, one Roubaix mill owner complained that his workers' imprudence at *cabarets* forced them into almost constant debt to the bar owners. A Tourcoing spinning-mill owner agreed, complaining that his workers were 'always' in debt.[67] Many witnesses before the 1904 board of inquiry corroborated this earlier view, citing heavy indebtedness among most textile families. In fact, some witnesses claimed that many pay packets arrived empty at the end of the week, having been attached by impatient creditors (a practice that was legal in France throughout our period). The Tourcoing chamber of commerce estimated that, in 1904, the normal cost of such credit was 27.25 fr. for a 20 fr. debt, an interest rate of 36.25 per cent.[68]

To the loss of wages to creditors, some women textile workers added a second loss—to husbands. How widespread this abuse was is impossible to ascertain. But in 1904 a women's section of the local yellow union complained to the parliamentary committee that their employers often paid their wages directly to their husbands when the latter worked in the same mill. They demanded that the commission put a stop to this practice, ensuring

[65] See *PJ* (1 June 1901).

[66] *Enquête sur l'industrie, 1904*, 'déposition. Fédération nationale des ouvriers en textile', p. 270; *CdT* (19–26 Jan. 1899).

[67] *AN* C 3019 36, 51, 'Enquête des situations ouvrières, 1872–1885'.

[68] *Enquête sur l'industrie, 1904*, p. 260, 359, 397.

that their wages belonged solely to them. Clearly the married women's property act, passed in the *Chambre* in the 1890s but blocked by the senate until 1907, was needed by working women in the Nord.[69]

Textile workers' pay-packets had to stretch further and further after 1880, as the cost of living in the area rose steadily. Even at the best of times, moreover, and even using the most optimistic criteria as a basis for estimates, the yearly incomes of textile workers were extremely low.

Most textile workers probably worked between seven and eight full months a year. Assuming that two adult incomes supported most textile families, and assuming that each worker worked at least 200 days a year, the best combined yearly averages were:

1885: 1,320 francs
1893: 1,420 francs
1896: 1,272 francs
1902: 1,420 francs
1906: 1,444 francs
1911: 1,358 francs

If one adds between 1 fr. and 1.50 fr. a day for each child, also working 200 days a year, the total can be increased by 200 to 300 francs per child working.[70]

How far did these wages stretch in Lille, Roubaix, and Tourcoing in the *belle époque*? One government study estimated that one provincial male manual labourer, living alone, and eating 'normally' (which meant he ate meat and fresh fruit along with the more mundane staples like potatoes), needed the following yearly wage: (francs)

1885: 1,635
1893: 1,491
1896: 1,397
1906: 1,181
1909: 1,234[71]

[69] Ibid. The married women's property act passed by the *Chambre* in 1896 read, in part, '. . . women have a right to their own earnings and to the use of them'. See *Proposition de loi: adoptée par la Chambre des députés, no. 47*, (2 Mar. 1896).

[70] Wages are estimated from Tables 1 and 2 as well as from *Enquête sur l'industrie, 1904*, pp. 162, 328, and Léon and Maurice Bonneff, *Vie tragique*, pp. 37–9. The Bonneffs estimated child textile workers' earnings at 50 c. to 1.75 fr. per day.

[71] France, Ministère du travail, *Salaires et coût de l'existence à diverses époques jusqu'en 1910* (Paris, 1911).

According to the government's own estimate, then, a textile family never earned enough for its members—or even one of them—to 'eat normally'. This fact aroused little concern from most mill owners. When one *bobineuse* told a factory director that her 1888 wage—10 fr. a week—did not allow her to 'butter her bread' he replied, 'Use lard. It's cheaper and good enough for an *ouvrière*.'[72]

In spite of these problems, textile families did manage to survive from year to year. A typical workers' budget shows how one family managed in 1880. The father, a flax-comber, earned 15.15 fr. a week or about 500 fr. a year, assuming a work year of 200 days. Two of the family's young sons also worked in textiles, and together earned 13.20 fr. a week (440 fr. a year). The mother was unemployed, and lived at home with the family's four younger children. The family subsisted on the wage-earners' 28.35 fr. a week. The local *bureau de bienfaisance* added three kilograms of bread a week. Their weekly budget included:

rent	2.75 fr.
bread	11.50
coal	2.20
coffee/chicory	1.20
butter/lard	3.50
gas (lighting)	.75
salt/pepper	.30
vegetables	1.75
potatoes	1.40
soap	.60
milk	.70
faggots, matches	.50
Total	27.15

Each week, they tried to find money to replace one pair of sabots, or to buy a few clothes. (Wooden sabots cost about 1.80 fr. a pair.) The family's staples, then, were bread and about one half pound of potatoes per person, per day. Thus they made do on their 940 fr. a year.[73]

A rise in the cost of living over the subsequent decades meant

---

[72] *CdT* (18–25 Feb. 1888).
[73] *ADN* M 591 1–10, 'Industrie linière, 1880, Lille'.

greater frugality was required if textile workers were going to stretch their earnings from week to week. In 1904, a Tourcoing textile workers' union representative said that the normal weekly budget for a family with only two children (though the average family had four) was 20.50 fr. a week or 1,066 fr. a year. This budget included only the bare necessities of life: no entertainment, clothes, new sabots, alcohol, meat, butter—and certainly no money for newspaper subscriptions or union dues. Like their counterparts in 1880, this family lived mainly on bread (10 kilos a week), and potatoes (20 kilos a week). After rent and bread, their largest single expense was a credit payment of 3 francs—which suggests that they could not, in reality, manage on their income.[74]

Such budgets highlight the difficulties of most textile workers' lives. But if the situation was bleak for families of textile workers, how much more difficult it was for single women or single mothers! Working women averaged at best only 2.70 fr. a day which amounted to a mere 541 fr. a year, assuming a 200-day working year. For those who lived alone, or worse, for those supporting children or an unemployed husband, this income was not enough. Thus they were forced to depend either on public and private charity (if they were 'deserving') or on other work, including prostitution. So prevalent was this latter source of additional income that one visitor to the area called it the *ouvrières*' 'pain amer'. Another added, 'Now we can understand the painful truth of the phrase a little *ouvrière* let slip in our hearing: "It is hard to die when one is still young, but all the same, it is harder still to live!" '[75]

In addition to their 'bitter bread', women workers lived on 'some beer, . . . some salted butter, some buttermilk, sometimes some vegetables, but almost never any meat', in the words of one *ouvrière*.[76]

Many contemporaries remarked the sorrowful plight of women textile workers. One factory inspector, Caroline Milhaud, wrote that the hardships she had witnessed among women textile workers helped to explain the increase in women's suicides in the

---

[74] *Enquête sur l'industrie, 1904*, 'rapport, fédération textile, "La Solidarité ouvrière", Tourcoing', p. 427.

[75] Poisson, *Salaire des femmes*, pp. 109, 201.

[76] P. Brisson, *Histoire du travail et des travailleurs* (Paris, 1906), p. 439.

first decade of the twentieth century.[77] Another observer, watching some *ouvrières* leaving a Lille mill at the end of the day, wrote that the women were so thin that 'their sabots looked like boats'.[78] Some 16-year-old girls, she added, looked more like 12-year-olds, with skin yellowed by malnutrition. Their lunch consisted of a thin soup, some potatoes, and bits of bread washed down with beer which they bought at an *estaminet* near their mill. For supper, they had only bread with some coffee and chicory.[79]

Clearly, then, suffering was endemic among the textile workers of Lille, Roubaix, and Tourcoing in the *belle époque*. Only by accepting some charitable help and by depending on credit did the textile workers scrape by from day to day. Furthermore, women alone, particularly those with children, barely subsisted. Looking at workers' incomes, one can only concur with Paul Brisson's conclusion after his visit to the textile cities of the Nord: 'One has now', he wrote, 'a clear idea of the distress that lies at the heart of a working woman's existence, though she sometimes tries to hide her misery behind a few flowers and ribbons.'[80]

To earn this meagre existence, textile workers laboured long hours in the mills of the three cities. Before 1892 factory legislation shortened their hours, women worked the same hours as men, limited only by production demands. Both men and women, moreover, frequently exceeded the twelve-hour limit set by an 1848 law. In the eighties, all the workers commonly worked twelve to fourteen-hour days.[81] Breaks, moreover, were usually spent at the machines—either cleaning them (always the duty of workers, and always unpaid) or continuing to tend them. Machine stoppages during the day were virtually unknown; such stoppages were costly both to the *patronat* and to workers, trying to make their piece-rate each hour.

In 1892, the Third Republic passed a law limiting the legal working day. Children, proscribed from entering the mills before 12 or 13 (depending on whether or not they had obtained a school

---

[77] Caroline Milhaud, *L'Ouvrière en France* (Paris, 1907), pp. 35–6.

[78] Marcelle Capy, 'Midi à la porte d'une filature', *BS* (3 Apr. 1914).

[79] Capy, 'Filature de coton, Lille', *BS* (6 Apr. 1914), and 'Industrie textile. Mal logés, mal nourris', *BS* (16 Apr. 1914), 'Filature au mouillé, *BS* (26 Mar. 1914).

[80] Brisson, *Histoire du travail*, p. 439.

[81] *ADN* M 572 6–7, 'Situation industrielle, 1885'; M 594 2, 'Travail de l'industrie. Inspection, 1891'.

leavers' certificate) were limited to ten hours until they turned 16. Then they, together with women, were allowed a maximum of eleven hours a day. The law further required that the mills close down at least one day a week—usually Sundays.

Work inspectors were appointed to enforce the new law. Their influence, however, was negligible. When a 1900 law further limited hours to 10½ (including in its provisions all male workers in mixed-sex work-rooms) the sparsely distributed work inspectors found their work-load increased while at the same time sanctions remained weak or non-existent. Moreover, the textile *patronat* responded to protective labour legislation by developing a variety of ways to flout the laws. And even when inspectors managed to discover infractions, magistrates typically levied only the most derisory fines—usually only a few francs.[82] (In fact, the average fine levied against all French industrialists in 1897 was a mere 4 francs)

Tiny fines, of no consequence to the rich textile *patronat*, remained the rule throughout our period. In 1906, the court in Lille fined the hugh Vandenburghe spinning mill for two safety violations. For each infraction, the mill's owners paid a fine of 5 francs. (In comparison, small employers were far more likely to be heavily fined for breaking the law. One woman who ran a small sweat-shop in Lille was fined 100 francs in the same year—for repeatedly keeping her workers overtime.[83])

Not only did the local *patronat* ignore the laws with relative impunity, but it occasionally managed to turn them to its advantage. Thus, for example, in 1900, in one Tourcoing wool mill, the bosses met a strike threat by raising men's wages to an eleven-hour scale, though they, like their female co-workers, worked only 10½ hours. By dividing wages by gender, the *patronat* effectively split the workers, thus forcing the women to strike by themselves, an action which failed.[84]

---

[82] M. Max-Albert, 'Législation ouvrière: l'inspecteur du travail en 1897', *MS* (Jan.–June 1899), p. 38. Total fines for all France had dropped from 58,545 fr. in 1896 to 39,500 fr. in 1897. See also France, *Bulletin de l'inspection du travail 1906* (Paris, 1907).

[83] In France, *Bulletin de l'inspection du travail 1906*.

[84] *VdP* (20–27 Apr. 1900). See also: *ADN* M 594 27, 'Travail de l'industrie. Inspection' and *L'Ouvrier des deux mondes* (1 Apr. 1897, 1 June 1897, 1 Oct. 1897).

Among the most common tactics by which the *patronat* avoided obeying the laws were flimsy barriers, erected to 'separate' male and female workers into separate work-rooms, thus side-stepping the law which shortened men's hours. But more important than such subterfuges was the efficient warning system developed by the closely-knit textile mill owners of Lille, Roubaix, and Tourcoing. Word of the approach of a work inspector spread rapidly among the mills, and illegal workers, along with safety violations, were hidden before the inspector appeared at the factory gates.

Some owners, moreover, forced women workers to carry additional work home at the end of their shortened days. To refuse was to lose a job. The onus of this unpaid overtime fell most heavily on older women who retained the necessary skills of hand washing, combing, carding, and winding from an earlier era.

Another means of countering the shortened hours was to speed up the work process, which, in turn, necessitated tighter factory discipline. Rest periods became increasingly scarce. Moreover, if any time was lost during a working day—through machine breakdowns or accidents—it was made up during an unpaid period of obligatory overtime at the end of the day. Though making up lost time was allowed by law, workers complained that such stoppages never signalled a break from work. Instead, during periods of stoppage, directors and supervisors made sure that workers stayed busy—cleaning machines or tidying the work-rooms.[85]

Work inspectors assigned to the Nord department found their tasks constantly frustrating. Caroline Milhaud, for one, thought her efforts fruitless. She knew, for example, that women in Roubaix's and Tourcoing's mills were working up to nineteen hours at a stretch in 1906, but she constantly failed to catch them at it. Finally, in desperation, she plotted a midnight raid. 'By happy accident', she wrote, 'I was able to reach the factory without a signal being given. But my arrival had been anticipated. Male

---

[85] *Enquête sur l'industrie, 1904*, 'déposition. Chambre syndicale des ouvrières de l'industrie textile', p. 162. These socialist unionists also complained that protective hour legislation was costing women their jobs, as owners preferred to employ men who could work long hours without inviting the attentions of work inspectors. See also 'dépositions, M. Boulisset, MM Herbo et Gillet', pp. 322–7.

workers, under orders, guarded all the doors. Lights were immediately extinguished so that the 250 workers could flee.' Failing the success of even the most carefully planned inspection, then, inspectors were forced to depend on the testimony of workers. But many found that workers were reluctant to risk their jobs, and likely blacklisting, by complaining. Women workers, Milhaud discovered, were even less likely than men to report infractions to inspectors. 'The fear of being fired, which I can read in their faces, nails their tongues.' If Milhaud pressed them, 'a half-blindness strikes them'.[86]

The Third Republic's factory laws of 1892, 1900, and 1904 were not limited to setting hours, but included further provisions for protecting the health and safety of workers. Several provisions specifically attacked problems in the textile industry. Among the most important of these was the requirement that mill work-rooms be ventilated, so that steamy air was cooled and circulated, and some of the dangerous textile fibre dust evacuated from the work-rooms. Further, the new laws required changing-rooms where workers' street clothes could remain dry during the day. Toilets, wash-basins, and supplies of 'good quality' drinking-water were prescribed as well.

In addition to these health measures, the laws required increased safety provisions. The dangerous moving parts of machines, especially lethal gears, were to be covered. Owners were told to widen spaces between machines so that workers whose jobs required them to move among machines—or worse, under them—would be less likely to get caught. (Most of these mobile workers were children, whose duties entailed crawling about on the floors beneath the machines, tying broken threads or dragging heavy bobbins and reels between machines.) Space was also crucial in case of fire—a constant threat in work-rooms coated with flammable dust and oils and lit (in the early decades of the Third Republic) by gas. Lighting was supposed to be adequate to prevent accidents, particularly during night shifts. Further, the law absolutely forbade the dangerous, but ubiquitous, practice of cleaning or oiling machines in motion. Finally, workers were

---

[86] Milhaud, *L'Ouvrière*, p. 189. See also Max-Albert, 'Législation ouvrière', pp. 3–43.

allotted three rest breaks during the day—during which they were supposed to leave their machines, to sit down, and to relax.[87]

On the whole, these laws were ignored in the textile mills of Lille, Roubaix, and Tourcoing throughout our period. And this neglect took its toll. Relatively young men and women, dying of tuberculosis, chronic bronchitis, or 'brown lung' (which was only beginning to be understood in this period) crowded the slums, unemployable because of badly impaired breathing. More obviously horrific victims were also found in the workers' *quartiers*. These included workers with missing fingers, hands, and even arms, or, more commonly, those with limbs deformed by factory accidents. The most appalling group of all were the women who had been 'scalped' when their long hair got caught in the moving gears of the textile machines.[88]

Poor conditions in the mills, therefore, complemented conditions in the wretched *courées* and slums of the workers' *quartiers*. At work, workers constantly inhaled bits of cotton, jute, hemp, flax, and wool. The dust, moreover, clung to their skin, hair, and clothes, which in turn remained soaked by the constant steam present in most work-rooms. This humidity was accompanied by staggeringly high temperatures which were required in most textile processes. Heat in what many called 'hellish' work-rooms ranged from 77 to 104° Fahrenheit, accompanied, in most mills, by 90 per cent humidity. Seconds after entering these hot, steamy rooms, workers were coated with dust, drenched, and sweating. After only a few minutes at work, most shed as much of their clothing as possible (thus adding to their reputation for loose morals). Men

[87] Workers' drinking-water is described in M. Albert-Levy, 'L'Eau de boisson dans les ateliers', France, *Bulletin de l'inspection du travail 1906* (Paris, 1907), p. 55. Lack of general hygiene is described in *Enquête sur l'industrie, 1904*, 'rapport de l'inspecteur départemental de Roubaix', pp. 227–9, dépositions, chambre de commerce de Lille', p. 248; 'M. Broquart, juge de paix de Tourcoing', p. 447; M. Leclerc Puligny, 'Les Conditions d'hygiène dans les filatures de lin', France, *Bulletin de l'inspection du travail 1903* (Paris, 1904); p. 230, M. Bellon, 'Le Dépoussièrage des carderies de coton', and 'Conférence internationale pour la protection ouvrière à Bern, 8–17 mai 1905', in *Bulletin 1906*, p. 432 and *Bulletin 1912*, p. 212, respectively. See also: J.P. Langlois, 'Étude physiologique expérimentale sur le travail aux milieux chauds et humides', *Bulletin 1914*, p. 263.

[88] Marcelle Capy' 'Drames du travail', *BS* (17 Apr. 1914). Capy reports that scalpings most often happened at the end of the day, when women paused in their work to comb some of the dust and débris from their long hair without waiting for the machines to stop.

worked bare-chested, women in their *chemises*. Street clothes hung on nails on nearby walls—and quickly became covered with dust and saturated with water. After an exhausting, noisy, hot day, the workers put these clothes back on, and set out for home in the usually cold, foggy evenings of French Flanders. In winter, workers traded steaming factory work-rooms for outside temperatures which ranged between 35 and 37° Fahrenheit. Not surprisingly, the quick temperature changes left them particularly susceptible to disease. Women workers, moreover, were vulnerable to the 'anaemia' noted by so many bourgeois reformers, as well as to miscarriages and still births.[89]

Simple sanitation measures also proved too troublesome for most mill owners. Open-air latrines were common. Where indoor lavatories were provided, they were often located in cubicles just to the side of factory work-rooms. One worker described the lavatories at Barrois *frères* in Lille as 'black holes without air'. 'You can imagine', he added, 'the odour one breathes in the summer in such factories.'[90]

As we have seen, the workers' universal palliative for these conditions was drink. But although drinking temporarily alleviated some of their misery, it also contributed to the harrowing accidents that broke the monotony of working days in Lille, Roubaix, and Tourcoing.

Before describing these accidents, however, it is important to note that textile mills were not anywhere near as dangerous as other industrial work in this period. More textile workers died or were disabled by the long-term effects of dust, noise, heat, and humidity than were struck by serious accidents. None the less, accidents did occur at a steady rate throughout our period.

Moreover, accidents were doubtless more numerous than official reports suggest. All reports of accidents depended on the co-operation of the textile *patronat*, who were no more forthcoming

---

[89] See *Enquête sur l'industrie, 1904*, p. 227, p. 449. The Bonneffs, in *Vie tragique*, reported 1,745 anaemics for every 4,166 women working in wet spinning mills. They also estimated that 14.3 per cent of all women textile workers in the Nord had chronic respiratory problems—a percentage which rose to 54.5 per cent among linen and cotton preparation workers. See pp. 34–6. Maternity problems are described by A. Vallin, *La Femme salariée*, p. 32.

[90] *Enquête sur l'industrie, 1904*, 'déposition, Fédération nationale des ouvriers en textile', p. 267. See also testimony of M. Prouvost, a Roubaix work inspector, in 'Peigneurs de laine à Roubaix', *AN* F[12] 4938, 'Hygiène et sanitation'.

about these figures than they were about any others. In addition, owners were required to list only the 'most serious accidents', and they decided which events fell into this category. Lille mill owners earned the worst reputation among work inspectors for their truculent reactions when queried about such accidents.[91]

Secondly, workers were reluctant to report accidents, lest they lose their jobs. Even grievous injuries to hands and arms went unreported. In 1900, in fact, work inspectors were instructed to examine the hands and arms of women workers, because most women tried to hide their injuries under their aprons.[92]

Even assuming that official figures are low, however, they do show an increase in accidents between 1880 and 1914. It was not a per capita increase, however, but rather reflected two changes. Firstly, the work-force grew during the *belle époque*. Secondly, increased numbers of work inspectors began to discover accidents which were previously unreported by the *patronat*.

Accidents most commonly affected hands and arms. In 1885, for example, in Tourcoing, there were four reported accidents. Two men, 32 and 40, were 'heavily wounded'. One lost the fingers of his right hand. In that same year, two women were reported injured. One mashed her fingers, the other her right hand. (The reporting mill owners cited two reasons for these four accidents: imprudence and carelessness.)

Once work inspectors began to report accidents, figures grew dramatically. During a single month in 1899, thirty-four women workers were reported injured in the three cities. Most of them had caught their hands in weaving machines. A few had fallen into the gears of machines.

---

[91] Ibid., 'rapport de M. le ministère du commerce et de l'industrie', p. 47, lists the most dangerous French industries. In 1904, 24.9 per thousand textile workers were involved in reported accidents, compared to 186.6 per thousand metal-workers. Causes of accidents in textiles are discussed in ibid., p. 450, and 'Note sur les accidents occasionnés par le nettoyage et le graissage en marche dans les ateliers de préparation de fils de laine peigné', France, *Bulletin de l'Office du travail 1910* (Paris, 1911), p. 188. See also 'Tribunal correctionnel de Lille, juin 1904', in France, *Bulletin de l'inspection du travail 1904* (Paris, 1905), p. 219. This documents an accident in which a 12-year-old girl, assigned to clean a running machine, caught and crushed her right hand. The mill owner received a relatively stiff fine of 115 fr.

[92] M. Boulin, 'Les Accidents évitables dans les filatures et dans les peignages', France, *Bulletin de l'inspection du travail 1913* (Paris, 1914), p. 339.

A few years later, in 1902, a Roubaix work inspector recorded 2,133 *'reported'* (emphasis his) accidents, which resulted in 5 deaths and 59 permanent disabilities. Two thousand and sixty-six of the injuries were serious enough to require at least four days away from work. Of the injured, 240 were boys under 18, 123 girls, 284 women, and 1,486 men.

By 1911–12, much larger figures attested to the increased vigilance of factory work inspectors. In the three cities of Roubaix, Tourcoing, and nearby Wattrelos in that year, inspectors reported a combined total of 12,980 injuries. Among these were 1,948 boys, 1,069 girls, 9,733 men, and only 230 women. Women's extremely low rate in these cities was a result of the fact that they tended to work in fairly safe occupations in most wool mills—particularly in preparation rooms where washing, combing, and carding took place. On the other hand, in Lille, where women were employed in most jobs in cotton, flax, and jute mills, there were many more women injured in a single year. In 1911–12, for example, 5,375 women workers were injured, along with 18,675 men. In the majority of cases, hands and arms sustained the injuries.[93]

On the whole, then, textile mills were safer for women and girls than they were for men and boys. As we have seen, many adult women worked in less hazardous jobs, where there was less risk of accidental injury. For example, the improperly called 'fileuses' who worked in wet spinning (a process necessary for processing flax, hemp, and jute) spent long days feeding thread through tubs of very hot water. Each worker stood between two tubs, one hand in each, pulling the heavy material through and passing it out to nearby spinners. The floors ran with water, and many women stood bare-footed, in order to preserve their wooden sabots a bit longer. Clouds of dust and steam whirled round their heads, and stuck to their hair, creating the impression that they wore turbans. Most observers agreed that theirs was the most miserable work of all. One wrote, 'Anaemic, pale, riddled with TB, these are the most sorrowful victims of textiles.'[94] Nevertheless, they contended with no exposed gears, no heavy pressing machinery, no whirling

---

[93] Figures found in *ADN* M 572 6–7, 'Situation industrielle, 1885, accidents, août 1885', M 614 14, 'Accidents du travail, procès-verbaux des accidents survenus, juin, 1899', *Enquête sur l'industrie, 1904*, 'rapport de l'inspecteur départemental, Roubaix', p. 26 and Boulin, 'Accidents évitables', p. 348.

[94] Marcelle Capy, 'Filature au mouillé', *BS* (26 Mar. 1914).

bobbins or flying mechanical shuttles. The likelihood of chronic disease was high; the likelihood of accident fairly small.

But many women, as has been noted before, worked in the same occupations as men in textile production in our period. They were spinners and weavers, as well as *rattacheuses*. Men's higher accident rate in these occupations has a different explanation. Men, more than the women, had a dangerous tendency to 'show off' at work. Taking pride in exhibiting speed and dexterity to their fellow workers, men frequently fell victim to their machine's appetite for workers' hands and arms. And, of course, men drank more than women. Free of child-care responsibilities, which prevented many women from spending their breaks drinking, men often got very drunk as the day progressed. This drunkenness inevitably led to carelessness, particularly toward the end of the working day.[95]

Thirdly, many observers argued that women workers were, on the whole, more careful workers than the men. Most inspectors remarked on women's 'womanly habits', which made them more cautious, as well as more dextrous. On the other hand, however, these habits had their negative consequences. One work inspector wrote:

It is easy to understand that by instinct, by habits learned in the family, an *ouvrière* is trained to use a dust-cloth or brush as though it were an extension of her hand. Thus, when her work requires only that she watch a machine, she too easily, unthinkingly, reaches out to clean or adjust something in the machine, and thus catches her hand.[96]

The *patronat* was generally quite unmoved by textile workers' accidents. True to form, they blamed workers' carelessness on poor work habits. In the early years, owners' propensity to explain away such accidents was understandable. If accidents were the fault of the mill owners' management, compensation was paid to the wounded workers. But, after 1898, such explanations were gratuitous, as the law required compensation whatever the cause of the accident. Nevertheless, most owners continued to blame their workers for accidents in their mills.

Moreover, even when workers received compensation, it was minimal, and in no way made up for the loss of a job. In the case of

[95] Boulin condemned this showing off in 'Accidents évitables', pp. 348–9.
[96] Ibid., p. 349.

permanent, total disability, for example, workers had the right to free medical care and drugs, and to two-thirds of their annual wage. In case of death—and death had to follow immediately after the injury—the *patron* paid for the funeral (up to 100 francs) and paid the following indemnities: 20 per cent of the dead worker's annual wage to the surviving spouse; 15 per cent of that wage for one surviving child under the age of 16 if both her parents were dead, 25 per cent for two surviving children, 35 per cent for three, and 40 per cent for four or more.[97]

The combination of accidents and ill health joined all the other factors which together made life miserable for workers in the *belle époque*. They did not, however, remain quiescent in the face of increasing misery. Rather, mass protest, as well as organized political resistance, shattered the industrial calm in all three cities during our period. But before turning to these forms of worker resistance, it is important to delineate the ways in which mill owners attempted to prevent such explosions by imposing their will on workers.

Unlike the officials of the Third Republic, the textile *patronat* put no faith in reform as a useful means of curbing worker militancy. Instead, they relied on a combination of economic, religious, and political sanctions to control their work-forces. The Catholic Church willingly collaborated in such efforts—both by providing surveillance on the shop-floors and by keeping close watch on the workers' private lives.

Mill owners applied three kinds of economic pressure in their often futile campaign to keep their unruly workers in line. Firstly, the hiring system was increasingly meticulous, and full of pitfalls for unwary or rashly militant workers. Secondly, a straightforward system of fines and bonuses enforced factory rules, and helped foremen and women and supervisors to separate 'good' (i.e. obedient) workers from the rest. Thirdly, a sophisticated system of factory surveillance and intimidation—which included the sexual harassment of female workers—strengthened the workers' ever-present fear of unemployment, which was, needless to say, the ultimate sanction applied to those who deviated from prescribed behaviour.

Hiring occurred only at the factory gates. There were no

[97] Ibid., p. 343, and *PJ* (7 Nov. 1902).

placement bureaux (or *bourses du travail*) in the three cities until late in our period. Prospective workers simply turned up at mill gates—occasionally accompanied by a friend willing to act as a character witness. There, they were asked for their *livrets*—their identification booklets—which were reviewed with care. These *livrets* included their work history, and thus provided an effective means of blacklisting uncooperative or politically active workers. Although *livrets* were abolished by the Third Republic in 1890, this law, like other reform legislation, was ignored by the *patronat* of French Flanders. A clean *livret*, in fact, continued to be a condition of employment in the textile mills well into the twentieth century.[98] The more cautious employers further required that prospective workers submit recommendations from their parish priest, or evidence of membership in one or more approved workers' organizations.[99]

Those who successfully jumped these hurdles were hired. Before starting work, however, they were forced to sign a contract stating their willingness to abide by all factory rules. These rules were strict, and rigidly enforced by stiff fines. A typical set of 1882 rules forbade lateness, absence without an approved medical certificate (i.e., the doctor had to be on the *patronat*'s approved list), leaving the mill without written permission, allowing any strangers inside the factory, touching any machine without permission from a supervisor, smoking, drinking, or damaging anything in the factory. All workers were responsible for keeping their work areas clean. Furthermore, they were expected to be 'honest, respectful, and obedient'. 'Horseplay' inside the work-rooms was strictly forbidden. Children were specifically cautioned against throwing bobbins or playing during work hours. The rules further stipulated that anything broken because of a worker's carelessness had to be paid for out of wages, and anything stolen brought immediate firing plus a fine equal to double the value of the stolen item. Workers were forbidden to allow any machine parts to touch the floors (which ran with water and filth), nor could they enter or leave the work-room by any door other than that

[98] Bonneffs, *Vie tragique*, p. 42, and *Enquête sur l'industrie, 1904*, 'déposition, Fédération nationale des ouvriers textiles', p. 288; 'rapport, Chambre de commerce, Tourcoing', p. 359; 'déposition, Chambre de commerce, Roubaix', p. 160.

[99] Ibid., 'déposition, Syndicat de la filature, Tourcoing', p. 347.

designated (and guarded by a 'concierge'). This latter rule ensured that only one worker left the work-room at a time—a tactic aimed at preventing collusion and subsequent walk-outs or protests, as well as at preventing meetings between male and female workers. To this latter end, men and women were further forbidden to use the outdoor lavatories at the same time, even in those rare instances when men's and women's facilities were separate. Finally, workers were adjured not to leave any machine untended, nor to leave any machines dirty at the end of the day.[100]

In addition to fines for breaking the rules, workers were fined for producing 'inferior' work. This made the distribution of raw materials crucial. If a foreman or woman disliked any worker, for any reason, that worker received inferior raw materials, which in turn produced lower quality work, and thus a fine. Furthermore, poor raw materials slowed the work rate—thus lowering the unlucky worker's piece-rate.[101] The fear of incurring a supervisor's wrath, and thus becoming an unfavoured worker, was naturally rife in the textile mills—especially among the lowest-paid workers, who were almost always women.

Fines varied from about 20 centimes (the usual fine for talking), to several francs. And the workers' fear of these fines was completely justified, as they were freely applied. One writer noted in 1914 that one Lille mill, employing 250 workers, collected 1,000 francs in fines every fifteen days. This amounted to 1.6 fr. per six-day week per worker. In a neighbouring mill, the most frequent fines were those levied for lateness (25 centimes), for talking (25–50 centimes), and for missing a day without an approved doctor's excuse (1 franc). The hypocrisy of the latter fine was especially galling, as employers benefited from such absences. No substitute workers were supplied; instead, workers doubled up to run the absent worker's machine. For this doubled work, they were paid a 1-franc bonus. Because medical care was not free—and especially because women were more often absent because of a child's illness than because of their own—most workers forfeited the 1-franc

---

[100] *AN* F[12] 4660, March 1882. See also Roubaix factory rules quoted in Georges Duveau, *La Vie ouvrière en France sous le Second Empire* (Paris, 1946), pp. 260–1. A list of rules for *employés*, in Dumortier, *Syndicat patronal*, appendix viii, p. 233, shows that their rules were equally strict.

[101] This 'favoured worker' system is described in *Enquête sur l'industrie, 1904*, p. 288.

fine, thus neatly compensating the employer for his 'bonus' payment. The absent worker's wages—normally between 2 fr. and 4.5 fr.—were thus saved without any loss in production.[102]

Not surprisingly, workers hated the fines. In their view, fines were both humiliating and impossible to avoid. A local paper told of a Lille *ouvrière* who was fined 1 franc for falling while dragging a heavy case of bobbins. When she responded angrily with 'violent words', the foreman retaliated by pulling the drive belt on her machine. Then he fined her an additional 2 francs—for breaking her machine. Indulging her anger thus cost this *ouvrière* 3 francs— the equivalent of 1½ days' work.[103]

Occasionally, workers' frustration at this system produced ironic humour. One widely told story concerned an *ouvrière* at *Filature* Wallaert who became ill, stayed home from work one day, and died that night. The *patron*, it was said, withheld 20 sous (1 franc) from her final pay packet as a fine, on the grounds that she had failed to get the proper medical certificate before she died![104]

Nevertheless, such humour did nothing to alter the onerous system, against which few workers could afford to protest. Most, indeed, accepted their fines with resignation—a resignation said to be especially typical of women workers' attitudes. The Lille workers' *syndicat*, for example, testifying before the parliamentary commission of 1904, echoed many factory inspectors' laments that women's greater fear of unemployment often reduced them to silence in the face of various outrages in the mills.[105] This judgement may indeed have been accurate. Nevertheless, most women had no choice but to accede to owners' demands. As a group of flax-spinners told Marcelle Capy in 1914, 'If the men spend their pay in the *estaminets*, don't we have to feed the kids?'[106]

Women workers endured one further penalty in the mills. Constant sexual harassment clouded their days—either directed at them, or at younger women or girls. To object to the advances of male supervisors was to risk instant *chômage*, or the lesser penalty

[102] Marcelle Capy, 'Filature de lin: dernières manipulations', *BS* (29 Mar. 1914), 'Filature du coton', *BS* (6 Apr. 1914), 'Filature au mouillé', *BS* (26 Mar. 1914).
[103] *LT* (8 Feb. 1893).
[104] Capy, 'Filature du coton'.
[105] *Enquête sur l'industrie, 1904*, p. 270.
[106] Capy, 'Filature au mouillé'.

of classification as a 'difficult' worker. Resistance also provoked extra fines—a variety of pretexts was always available. So ubiquitous was this harassment that the local socialist paper, *Le Cri du travailleur*, launched a protest campaign in 1887. The campaign had at least one success: one 'brutal' foreman became so notorious that owners finally fired him for continually abusing a young girl.[107]

A few years later, the *Parti ouvrier* paper *Le Travailleur* cited one instance of sexual harrassment to mock the religious pretensions of the *patronat*. In 1894 the paper reported with disingenuous indignation that in one Motte factory, 'there exists something that we believe should be submitted to public opinion. There, the *soigneuses* must endure all the vexations that spring up in the imagination of a young idiot who is only 17 years old. Not one day passes when these *ouvrières* are not insulted by his brutalities. This young torturer makes a habit of taking the women by the shoulders in order to "help" them, in an abominable manner.' The director of this mill, nicknamed 'l'oiseau parfumé' by the workers, supported this boy, even going so far as to menace those who objected to his behaviour. 'If it is true', the story concluded, 'that M. Motte expects to reconcile his workers with the Christ who said "love one another", this is a strange way to propagate that doctrine!'[108]

Such opportunities to mock the paternalistic Catholicism of the textile *patronat* were rare, however. The Catholic Church of Lille, Roubaix, and Tourcoing was solidly in league with the *patronat* during the *belle époque*; in fact, Church personnel provided some of the most severe pressures with which workers and worker organizations had to contend.

The heavily conservative, Catholic mill-owning families of the area employed several tactics in their struggle to impose religious controls on their work-force. Firstly, they established and supported their religious organizations, into which they made valiant attempts to lure workers, with promises of jobs, with extra money, with aid from local employer-run charities, and occasionally with food and drink. Secondly, they used nuns and priests as spies, in and out of the mills. Thirdly, they imposed a variety of religious obligations within the factories themselves.

---

[107] See *CdT* (31 July–Aug. 1887) for opening story of this campaign.
[108] *LT* (16 May 1894).

The earliest of the workers' groups run by employers in our period were Catholic *cercles*. These were the creation of paternalistic employers committed to the Nord's special form of social Catholicism. In 1887, Abbé Fichaux, the leader of the first such group in Tourcoing, outlined their goals: 'The duties of the *patronat*', he wrote, 'are not limited to paying the workers an equitable, living wage. In the special name of charity, he owes them aid and protection. In the name of justice, he must do nothing, and allow nothing to be done—within the limits of his authority—that would injure either their morals or their faith.'[109]

Evidence shows that this obligation rarely, if ever, extended to the corporeal health of workers, as virtually no efforts were made by the textile *patronat* to alleviate the misery of workers' daily existence. Nor did the *patronat* trouble themselves with paying 'living wages', as we have seen. Instead, they concentrated on the spiritual health of their workers.

At first, until the Third Republic's initial wave of anti-clericalism produced effective anti-Church legislation, many *patrons* established religious groups within their factories. For women, there were the 'groupes du vingt'—usually several in each participating mill. For men, there were *cercles catholiques*. Both groups existed to 'guard the morals' of members. Women's groups, for example, collected fines of 20 centimes each time a member 'sinned'. Sinners were identified either by their own confessions, or by fellow members. Funds collected in this manner paid for an annual banquet. By the end of the 1880s, such groups were found in many of the largest textile mills, including those of the Tiberghien brothers, Duprés-Lepers, Barrois-Lepers, Bayart-Parent, Sion, and, of course, the Mottes. According to workers in those mills, not to join these groups was to risk losing 'favoured worker' status, or even a job.[110]

After the 1884 law on *syndicats* prohibited organizers from mixing politics or religion with workers' organizations (which were legal only if they remained strictly economic), the *patronat* abolished these overtly religious groups. In their place they founded 'mixed' *syndicats*—composed of both workers and owners. The members of these 'unions' were encouraged, but not required,

---

[109] Quoted in Talmy, *L'Association*, p. 21.
[110] *CdT* (3 July–6 Aug. 1887 and 2–9 Feb. 1888).

to affiliate with Catholic organizations, which ostensibly existed outside the factory and thus beyond the reach of union legislation. The umbrella group for many of these *syndicats mixtes* was *Notre Dame de l'Usine*, which had a men's section—*St Joseph*—and a women's *Conception Immaculée*. Rules for joining *Notre Dame* were similar to those for other Catholic worker groups. Members were at least 18, practising Catholics, and of 'good reputation' (established by the recommendation of a local priest). Further, they promised to say, every day, three *Ave Marias*, and 'Our Lady of the Factory, pray for us'.[111]

Though technically illegal, these men's and women's groups were organized in many textile factories. They were led either by the *patron* himself (or, in rare cases, herself), or by female family members. Further sub-groups of ten—the *dizaines*—were created, led by a *dizainier* or *dizainière* chosen by the *patron*. These group leaders were responsible for the behaviour and well-being of their members. Once a month, they met with the *patron* to report on their groups, and to solicit aid—in the form of charitable visits by the wives of *patrons* or by nuns—for ill or incapacitated members.

Although those manufacturers who participated in such groups may have regarded them as an adequate means of discharging the obligations laid down by their religious principles (and detailed in *Rerum Novarum* in 1891), most workers viewed the groups with suspicion. To them, such organizations were little more than another means for creating a docile work-force. Join and one was transformed into a favoured worker. Refuse and one risked fines and even unemployment. Furthermore, anti-clerical workers (who were not necessarily anti-religious) viewed these groups as none-too-subtle vehicles for religious coercion. Continued complaints about such coercion appeared in the popular press throughout the eighties and nineties. In 1887, *Le Cri du travailleur* declared that more and more 'religion' was being imposed on workers in the factories. At Tiberghien *frères* in Tourcoing, for example, workers were subjected to sermons and religious teachings almost every day. Furthermore, those supposedly independent Catholic groups which met outside the factories were closely watched by the *patronat*, who hired spies to check attendance and to reward loyal workers with free food and drink.[112]

[111] *CdT* (18–25 Feb. 1888).
[112] *CdT* (2–9 Oct. 1887 and 1–8 Jan., 18–25 Feb. 1888).

Mill owners relied on economic pressures to lure workers into such groups. Recruiting was done in the mills themselves, usually by a priest invited to speak to the assembled workers. Both owners and most of the mill's supervisory personnel were present at such meetings, checking attendance and watching for visible signs of reluctance or hostility. A meeting at a Tourcoing factory in 1887 was typical. At eight o'clock, at the end of the Saturday workday, all the work-force was assembled in one factory work-room—men on one side, women on the other. A priest extolled the virtues of joining *Notre Dame de l'Usine*. Then new members were regis-tered. Those who were not convinced, and who refused to join, were duly noted by the factory staff.[113]

In addition to mixed *syndicats* and Catholic *cercles*, textile owners sponsored 'yellow unions', called *jaunes*. Although these claimed independence from the *patronat*, most workers saw a close link between them and the mill owners.[114] Certainly qualifications for membership in the *jaunes* closely resembled those for membership in openly Catholic *cercles*. For example, all pros-pective members were carefully vetted, and admitted only if they could show good moral character. And, though the leaders of the *jaunes* constantly protested their independence, some occasionally let slip the real nature of the relationship between these unions and the *patronat*. One woman leader of a Tourcoing *jaune* admitted, 'in the beginning, some wives of the *patronat* were involved with our group because the working women who were trying to organize had asked for their advice.' 'Now', she added, 'it is purely a workers' group.'[115]

Moreover, the yellow unions normally favoured the owners' side of most industrial disputes. The journal of Tourcoing *jaunes*, *Le Petit Jaune*, proselytized continually for industrial peace, for an end to strikes, and for an end to all protective labour legislation (especially that limiting children's hours, and setting a minimum age for their entrance into the mills). An end to labour legislation

---

[113] *CdT* (2–9 Oct. 1887).

[114] *ADN* M 596 68, 'Syndicats professionnels, Tourcoing', M 596 2, 'Syndicats professionnels 1899', M 596 66, 'Syndicats professionnels 1903', *ADN* 596 69, 'Syndicats professionnels 1908', *AN* F⁷ 12793, 'Syndicats jaunes'. See also Maurice Petitcollot, *Les Syndicats ouvriers de l'industrie textile dans l'arrondissement de Lille* (Paris, 1907), and *PJ* from 1901 to 1911.

[115] *PJ* (14 May 1901).

would, in turn, see an end to work inspectors, whom the journal's editors claimed to despise. In one story serialized in *Le Petit Jaune*, a worker complained to his neighbours that he had no sooner succeeded in getting his boy a job, than 'the door opened and a great dry fellow with glasses and a grey beard came in, saying, "I am the work inspector" '. This inspector then proceeded to attack the *patron*, whom the writer portrayed as a humble and self-effacing fellow in contrast to the brutal work inspector.[116]

Women's yellow unions were more restrictive than were the men's. Only women workers of the highest character were allowed to join, or to participate in union benefits. For example, those who wished to join the *jaune*-sponsored maternity and illness insurance scheme, the *Jeanne d'Arc* (founded in Tourcoing in 1902), had to prove themselves worthy via recommendations from local clerics. Furthermore, members whose illness resulted from 'debauchery' or 'intemperance' got no help, whatever the level of their previous contributions. Those injured in 'riots' were also excluded from benefits. New mothers, in turn, received their 10-franc indemnity only if they were legally married (by the Church) for at least eight months preceding their child's birth. Marriage 'livrets' were the only evidence accepted. Finally, any member was immediately expelled—forfeiting her dues—for 'scandalous behaviour'.[117]

Despite widespread recruiting efforts, and despite the threat of economic sanctions, neither yellow nor mixed unions enjoyed much success among the textile workers of Lille or Roubaix in the *belle époque*. By the end of the 1890s, mixed unions were on the wane. Of 139 factories in Tourcoing, only 15 continued to offer mixed *syndicats*. Of the 6,500 workers employed in these mills, moreover, fewer than half (43 per cent) belonged to mixed unions, or only 13 per cent of the total Tourcoing textile work-force. Similarly in Roubaix, in 1899, 5,488 workers (16 per cent) out of the total work-force in that city belonged to a *syndicat mixte*. Of these, moreover, only 1,606 participated in affiliated Catholic groups attached to *Notre Dame de l'Usine*.[118] No figures remain for Lille's mixed unions, but there is no reason to assume that they enjoyed any greater success there.

As for the *jaunes*, which increased after the turn of the century,

---

[116] 'Dans un ménage ouvrier', *PJ* (1 Nov. 1901).

[117] *PJ* (9 Jan. 1902).

[118] Talmy, *L'Association*, p. 110.

they were no more successful in attracting textile workers than the mixed unions had been. Moreover, whenever class loyalties were tested in major strikes or large-scale industrial confrontations, members of the *jaunes* were more than likely to side with their fellow workers against the *patronat*. This curious combination of yellows and members of socialist-controlled unions, called 'reds', produced what one observer called a vast *'syndicat vert'*, a hybrid union which appeared during each general strike in the industry after 1900.[119]

Naturally the republican prefect was delighted at the failure of the politically conservative textile *patronat*'s efforts to organize the mill workers. Contented reports of workers' indifference in the face of employers' blandishments and pressures flowed steadily from the prefecture to the *Office du travail* in Paris. Even when mill owners resorted to 'free cabarets, concerts, and theatricals' the prefect noted, workers remained indifferent.[120]

Thus, membership in the *jaunes* remained small. In Lille, in 1906, the three *jaunes* together counted only 1500 members of both sexes. In Roubaix in that year, the two yellow unions claimed a membership of 400 women and 1300 men. The larger of these Roubaix *jaunes*, moreover, included supervisory personnel and 'employés' as well as workers properly so-called.[121]

In Tourcoing, the *jaunes* enjoyed more support. There, the yellow unions' umbrella organization, the *Union fédérale du tissage*, established a headquarters in 1901. By 1906, this group claimed to represent 100 small *syndicats*, each limited to 30 members (a number which facilitated the moral surveillance required for membership). These copied many of the activities of the earlier *cercles du vingt* and *dizaines*. Of the 3,000 members claimed by the *Union*, 60 per cent were women. It is important to note, however, that these claims were disputed by the prefect, who reported only 145 women members in Tourcoing's *jaunes* in the first decade of this century.[122]

---

[119] Ibid., p. 106, and Léon de Seilhac, *La Grève du tissage de Lille* (Paris, 1910), pp. 43–4.

[120] *ADN* M 596 2, 'Rapport, 16 mars 1893, au ministère du commerce et de l'industrie'.

[121] *AN* F⁷ 12793, 'Syndicats jaunes'; France, Ministère du commerce, *Les Associations professionnelles ouvrières*, vol. ii (Paris, 1901), pp. 375–404, *ADN* M 596 68, 'Syndicats professionnels, Tourcoing'.

[122] See *AN* F⁷ 12793 and *ADN* 596 66, 69, 'États des syndicats'.

On the whole, then, neither mixed nor yellow unions succeeded in luring most textile workers into the circle of influence of the *patronat*. Thus mill owners were forced to resort to other, more obvious ploys in their efforts to control their workers in these difficult years.

The most important of the tactics employed by the textile manufacturers was the system of religious obligations which was designed to press workers into submission. The special objects of most religious discipline were, moreover, the women workers, who came in for a large dose of religious surveillance in the mills of Lille, Roubaix, and Tourcoing throughout our period.

The reasons for this greater attention were not far to seek. Women, more than men, were victims of the traditional moral double standard. In the eyes of the Church, their primary duty was maternity. As mothers, or potential mothers, their private lives were the focus of clerical attentions. Many Catholic mill owners, moreover, thought it their duty to nurture and protect the moral sanctity of these mothers—though most cared little for the health or living conditions of these same women, as we have seen. A widespread belief in the special holiness of mothers—even working-mothers—was reflected in the symbols of Catholicism with which owners chose to decorate their work-rooms. Images of *Notre Dame de l'Usine*, holding a Christ-child, stood everywhere in the mills; most hovered just above entrances to dank and noisome factory work-rooms. Beneath these images of the Virgin were engraved the words: 'Notre Dame de l'Usine, priez pour nous'. In addition to such visual reminders of the sanctity of Catholic motherhood, the *patronat* employed verbal reminders, naming their women's groups 'Immaculate conception', 'Christian mothers', and so on, and requiring daily prayers addressed to Mary.

Of course, the intensity of such religious controls varied from factory to factory. Some owners, including those few with republican sympathies, expressed little interest in the religious lives of their workers. Others flung themselves with enthusiasm into religious activities in their mills, utilizing the willing local clergy as concierges, forewomen, and spies.

The collaboration of Church personnel with the *patronat* included every kind of activity, from the initial recommendation (or condemnation) of potential workers to the certification of Church marriages. Furthermore, priests kept careful records of attendance at mass, and the performance of various sacraments, which they made available to the *patronat*. They ferreted out unmarried pregnant girls from among the 'innocent' workers—and their information often cost these unfortunate girls their jobs.

So close were relations between the Church and the *patronat* that, until the Third Republic succeeded in disbanding most congregations, many nuns worked openly in the textile mills as supervisors. As we have seen, it was Mme Pierre Motte who originally brought three orders to Lille earlier in the century specifically to work among the textile workers.[123]

And work they did. Even after their orders were disbanded the workers complained that the nuns merely removed their identifying habits, donned 'civvies', called themselves 'lay sisters', and remained at their posts in the mills.[124]

The rule of one of the largest of these orders, the Little Sisters of the Poor (also known as the Little Sisters of the Worker), suggests the variety of pressures they applied to the workers. Each new nun promised to 'provide the religious instruction of young *ouvrières*', to guard the morals of women workers, to visit the homes of sick workers—whether or not they belonged to Catholic groups—and to keep male and female workers strictly separate during working hours, especially during the rare rest breaks.[125]

Among the mill owners who participated most enthusiastically in this programme of clerical industrial surveillance were Feron-Vrau in Lille, and the Tiberghien brothers in Tourcoing. In both mills in the 1880s women workers were supervised by members of the *Petites Sœurs*, who acted as *contre-dames* on the shop-floor. Women workers in both mills were required to attend confession once a week, as a condition of their employment. Their behaviour, furthermore, was closely watched outside the factory as well as inside. *Le Cri du travailleur* complained in 1888 that any girl or woman working at Tiberghien who was seen keeping company with a man was expected to marry him 'soon after' being spotted. If she did not, she risked losing her job.[126]

---

[123] Paul Catrice, *Roubaix au delà des mers* (Roubaix, 1969), p. 65.

[124] Talmy, *L'Association*, p. 33, and *Enquête sur l'industrie, 1904,* p. 173.

[125] Talmy, *L'Association*, and France, Ministère du commerce, *Associations professionnelles*, pp. 375–404.

[126] Pierre Pierrard, *La Vie ouvrière à Lille sous le Second Empire*, p. 412, and *CdT* (18–25 Feb. 1888).

The situation changed little over time. In 1904, the socialist workers' *syndicat* of Roubaix, testifying before the parliamentary commission, strongly protested against the nuns' continued presence on the shop-floor, where they harassed the *ouvrières*. In the words of one witness: 'One sees these little sisters, going from one machine to another, questioning the women thus: "How many children do you have? What school [Catholic or lay] do they attend? Do you go to mass?" ' (Presumably, talking to nuns during working hours was not prohibited.) These 'lay sisters' also distributed rosaries and religious images among favoured *ouvrières*. 'You might think', added the witness, 'that any woman of spirit would rebel at this and leave such factories, but if she does, she is choosing to go without work, and without bread.'[127]

Representatives of Lille's socialist *syndicat* corroborated this testimony from Roubaix. They described the particularly close regime of surveillance at Thiriez, in Lille. In that factory, girls or women who were pregnant and unmarried were immediately fired: married women were fired if their babies were born sooner than nine months after the legal ceremony. (Given the high risk of premature births among these desperately weak and anaemic women, this stricture must have been especially frightening.) Watchful nuns willingly provided information about the morals of their female charges to the *patronat* at Thiriez—as well as to other Catholic factory owners in Lille.[128] In 1914, the Bonneff brothers' catalogue of textile workers' miseries in French Flanders included 'a domination by the employers which extends both outside the factories and within, which demands the most tyrannical religious servitude'.[129]

In addition to supervision on the factory floor, workers were expected to participate regularly in Church sacraments. To this end, many of the owners of the largest factories built chapels adjacent to the work-rooms themselves. Workers in these mills were forced to begin and end their days with prayers. In some factories, this obligation extended only to the women workers, in others it included everyone. In factories without chapels, workers were often forced to kneel on the work-room floors. In 1906, the

---

[127] *Enquête sur l'industrie, 1904*, p. 173.
[128] Ibid., p. 272.
[129] Bonneffs, *Vie tragique*, pp. 41–2.

official journal of the *Confédération générale du travail* (*CGT*) complained that in Roubaix textile mills, workers were forced to kneel on the stone floor twice a day to repeat: 'Je vous salue Marie, pleine de grâce. Le Seigneur est avec vous.'[130]

Most Flemish workers, however privately religious, resented such pressures. Worse than the small indignities imposed by required prayer or by group confession was the constant surveillance. Any moment of frivolity, any transgression, might result in unemployment for workers employed by the more religiously fanatical among the *patronat*. It was not surprising that the omnipresent images of Mary and Jesus perched above work-room doors provided a common focus of workers' hostility. One group of strikers—including both socialists and *jaunes*—painted 'Condamé à mort!' [*sic*] beneath one such statue during a general strike.[131] Marcelle Capy thought the many statues exemplified the hypocrisy of employers who attempted to use religion to pacify and discipline a sick and miserable work-force. She suggested that the rallying cry for *ouvrières* in French Flanders ought to be 'Sus! à Notre Dame de l'Usine'.[132]

Catholic employers also tried to control the reading matter of the textile work-force—though in the case of most women workers, this would seem to have been gratuitous given their low literacy levels throughout our period. Catholic newspapers—notably *La Croix*—were distributed in the mills, sometimes given away, more often sold for a few centimes. Supervisors kept records of who bought them and who did not. Such purchases, therefore, became an investment in better working conditions. On the other hand, those workers who bought *workers'* newspapers risked losing many factory privileges. More than one worker blamed fines or even loss of a job on the fact that he or she had been discovered carrying a socialist paper. So extensive was the employers' attention to the reading matter of their work-forces that one worker remarked that only certain 'safe' *cabarets* offered freedom from this surveillance. Thus certain local *estaminets* acquired reputations as 'safe houses', where both the distribution and spread of socialist propaganda were possible.[133]

---

[130] 'La Religion, aide à l'exploitation', *VdP* (4–11 Nov. 1906).
[131] Marcelle Capy, 'Quelques réflexions', *BS* (20 Apr. 1914).
[132] Quoted in Talmy, *L'Association*, p. 106.
[133] Marcelle Capy, 'Quelques réflexions', *BS* (20 Apr. 1914).

Although it is clear that both male and female textile workers suffered from coercion by religious orders working in conjunction with the *patronat*, women suffered more. The security of their employment depended much more heavily upon their observance of imposed moral norms and required religious duties. Then, too, their moral transgressions were quickly obvious to alert spies, whereas male immorality was both more easily hidden and more widely tolerated. Thus, from their earliest years women textile workers were forced to guard their private lives, lest they be branded 'immoral'—and thus prevented both from working and from receiving employer-controlled charity.

Of course it must be said that enforced religious practices amongst *ouvrières* did not necessarily erase their private religious beliefs. In so far as belief is a private matter, it is less easily identified and certainly impossible for the historian to measure. Moreover, given the destruction by fire of the relevant diocesan archives (of the diocese of Cambrai) on the eve of the Great War, not even accurate records of the extent of women and men's actual religious practice remain from which one might infer the existence or absence of widespread religious convictions.

Whatever the condition of workers' personal religious beliefs, however, it is clear that coerced religious practice, taken together with the web of other constraints within which women textile workers lived during the *belle époque*, help to explain women's lesser political militancy. Poverty, poor health, work accidents, economic pressures, plus religious obligations together set the boundaries within which *ouvrières* functioned during our period.

4

WOMEN WORKERS, THE TEXTILE UNIONS, AND MASS PROTEST, 1880–1914

i

THERE are two distinct ways of writing the history of relations between women industrial workers and the organized French left. One is to tell the story as a subsection of the history of labour and socialism in France, with allowance made for the peculiarities of region and community. The second is to write the history in terms of how it was experienced by its constituency, in this case the women textile workers of the Lille conurbation. This latter is itself part of a quite different history, with a different chronology, different referents, and so on.

Choosing between the two ways provides one means of avoiding a complex tangle of histories. But this solution skirts the real problem which is to show how and why both tales are part of the same story.

The price of bringing the two together while retaining a degree of clarity is that one must separate—quite artificially—a complex narrative from an analytical framework. And this is how the argument proceeds from here on. Narratives of both union and party politics are followed by more properly analytical discussions of women workers' politics in the Nord department during the *belle époque*.

Although necessary for coherence, separation of union from party activities in the Lille area after 1880 is artificial. At no time during our period was it easy to distinguish between socialist party and socialist textile union activities. So closely intertwined were these two movements that even strike meetings often merged into party meetings, and vice versa. Nevertheless, we must take the two strands separately, in order adequately to disaggregate key elements in our story.

ii

Union organizing among the textile workers of Lille, Roubaix, and

Tourcoing falls into two distinct periods. In the first decade and a half after 1880, most textile unions tended to be small, evanescent groups, often founded during a strike, only to die shortly thereafter. The base of such unions was usually a single factory or group of factories located near one another, though occasionally a strike grew to include textile workers throughout one of the three cities.

During the 1890s, however, concurrent with the gradual centralization of unions all over France, the largest and best organized of the local textile unions began to dominate the scene. Their leaders' organizational *savoir-faire*, plus their numerical strength—and thus their eventual victory over other local unions— came from their close ties to the *Parti ouvrier français* (after 1905 the *Parti socialiste*, or *SFIO*). Like the *POF* itself, these unions gradually centralized into a national textile federation, head- quartered in Roubaix throughout the pre-war period. Further- more, despite formal ties with the national syndicalist movement (organized into the *Confédération générale du travail*, or *CGT*, in 1895) the national textile federation was, by the turn of the century, effectively an auxiliary group to a political party, the *POF*. Thus, unlike many other unionized French workers, members of the national textile federation were either socialists themselves or willing to accede to socialist party decisions regarding union politics. Furthermore, relations between the socialist party and women workers clearly coloured the national union's treatment of its female constituency.

Before narrating the tangled history of textile union politics between 1880 and 1914, a caution: throughout the first thirty years of the Third Republic, relatively few among France's industrialized workers of either sex joined unions—and textile workers proved no exception to this rule. Even after years of intensive organiza- tional work, only 9 per cent of all textile workers in France belonged to a union in 1901, compared with 60 per cent of miners, 31 per cent of printers, 21 per cent of metal-workers, 19 per cent of leather-workers, and 11 per cent of construction workers.[1] (That these latter, who were mostly men, were nearly as unorganized as the textile workers suggests that gender had less to do with the

---

[1] Georges Lefranc, *Le Mouvement syndical sous la Troisième République* (Paris, 1967), p. 106.

success of union efforts than has sometimes been thought.) Locally, the situation was similar in those years, though exact figures for union membership are lacking. On the other hand, one need not assume that low membership figures meant that union politics were only of peripheral importance in the everyday lives of textile workers in the region. Indeed, the situation was quite the opposite. After 1895, textile union politics touched the lives of virtually every textile worker in Lille, Roubaix, and Tourcoing.

In the early years, organizational attempts, whether internal—a local response to particular industrial crises—or external— stemming from nationally based movements of owners and workers—were sporadic. In the 1880s, groups emerged, often in the heat of a strike, flourished for a time, and died away. During this fluid period, however, leaders began to learn how to build a union, and how to plan and control a strike. They were aided in their initial efforts by a growing crisis in the local textile industry, which resulted in the gradual drawing of clear class-lines in the three cities. This process in turn provided local socialist leaders with a constituency, with whose interests they quickly identified themselves.

The first successful textile union in the Lille *arrondissement* was born in Roubaix, in 1872. The *Chambre syndicale ouvrière de Roubaix*, founded by Henri Carrette and Achille Lepers, gradually collected around it several other small unions, which eventually formed the nucleus of the national textile federation. When Carrette and Lepers founded the local section of Jules Guesde's *Parti ouvrier* in 1881, they joined their union to the party. Initially, at least, the move proved popular. In just one year, at least eleven more socialist textile unions joined the original group.

Of course, unions, as such, were still illegal in 1882. Thus union members hid their activities behind the smoke-screen of social study groups, modelled on the religious *cercles* through which mill owners attempted to co-opt worker-led union initiatives. This ruse discouraged police attention at the same time as it attracted a growing number of groups. When unions were legalized in 1884, thirty-seven textile workers' groups emerged from everywhere in textile workers' districts. Sixteen declared themselves in Lille, fifteen in Roubaix, and six in Tourcoing. At this time, the activities of the study groups became public knowledge. Generally speaking, these consisted of weekly meetings where topics of concern to socialist workers were discussed, including in 1884 'property', 'capitalism', 'religion', and 'the family'.[2] In the last years of the eighties, many of these groups disappeared. Those remaining, however, united at the beginning of the next decade to form the Roubaix-based socialist *Fédération nationale textile*, headed by a loyal *POF* member, Victor Renard. At the same time, several of the smaller local unions joined together to form yet another new union with a cumbersome name: the *Chambre syndicale de l'industrie textile de Roubaix, Tourcoing, Mouveaux, Wattrelos, et environs*. (Obviously, no group wanted to be left out!) Both the size and consequent visibility of this new union quickly aroused police interest. The *commissariat central* in Roubaix informed the prefect in 1891 that this group included 'at least 5,000 members', all firmly committed to the *POF*, and all working to elect socialist candidates in the upcoming municipal elections.[3] This information quickly proved to be correct: a socialist municipal council was elected in Roubaix in 1892, headed by the textile union leader Henri Carrette. Achille Lepers was also elected to the council.

Lille's largest textile union—similarly burdened with a long name, the *Chambre syndicale ouvrière de l'industrie textile à Lille et environs*—also joined the socialists during the course of the 1880s. In the early nineties, it claimed 1,200 members, and by 1900, a total of 6,500.

These two large unions did not tell the whole story of local union activity. In each of the three cities, many smaller socialist textile unions existed, which for one reason or another were reluctant to merge with the larger groups. Most of these belonged to the national textile federation.

When the national workers' movement unified in 1895—'pell-mell', in Georges Lefranc's words[4]—the socialist textile unions of the Lille area, led by the umbrella *fédération*, joined the new *Confédération générale du travail*, though their simultaneous

---

[2] Maurice Petitcollot, *Les Syndicats ouvriers de l'industrie textile dans l'arrondissement de Lille* (Paris, 1907); France, Ministère du commerce, *Les Associations professionnelles ouvrières*, vol. ii (Paris, 1901), pp. 375–404; and A. Compère-Morel, *et al.*, *Encyclopédie socialiste, syndicale et coopérative de l'Internationale ouvrière*, vol. ii (Paris, 1913), pp. 399–400.

[3] *ADN* M 596 2, 'Syndicats professionnels. Janvier 1891'.

[4] Lefranc, *Mouvement syndical*, p. 104.

adherence to the socialist Second International, as well as to the *Parti ouvrier*, clearly flouted the apolitical stance of the syndicalist movement. Despite this contradiction, the socialist unions remained inside the *CGT* until the First World War—though an uneasy truce was declared between their openly socialist politics and the wider movement's militant anti-parliamentarism at the Amiens *CGT* congress in 1906.[5]

The extent of women workers' participation in socialist *syndicats* in these earlier years is impossible to assess accurately, as few membership records were broken down by sex. Only after 1900 did estimates of the number of women members appear. The numbers were small. In 1900, the *Chambre syndicale ouvrière textile de Roubaix et Tourcoing* claimed 6,000 members, of whom only 200 were women. After the 1904 general strike in the industry, which shut down textile mills throughout the Nord department, the number of women members in this union grew to 800, while the number of male members remained stable. And after that year women continued to provide the fastest growing constituency. By 1909, the union had 1,250 women members out of a total of 6,250.[6]

In Lille, on the other hand, total textile union membership was lower but the proportion of women higher. The *Chambre syndicale* of Lille reported in 1905 that it had 245 women amongst its 887 members. A second Lille union, which represented spinners of flax, hemp, and jute (where women workers were heavily concentrated) reported 400 members in 1906, 266 (or 67 per cent) of them women.[7]

Most of Tourcoing's textile unions merged with those in Roubaix in the 1890s. But among those that did not was the *Chambre syndicale textile unitaire de Tourcoing et environs*. In 1909 that union claimed 900 members, only 50 of whom were women.[8]

Clearly, then, women textile workers were far less likely to join

[5] Ibid., p. 137, and Renard's view in 'Après le congrès d'Amiens', *L'Ouvrier textile* (1 Nov. 1906).

[6] See Madeleine Guilbert, *Les Femmes et l'organisation syndicale avant 1914* (Paris, 1966); France, *Associations professionnelles*; Petitcollot, *Les Syndicats*, pp. 66–7; *AN* F⁷ 13820, 'Syndicats'.

[7] Petitcollot, *Les Syndicats*, p. 65.

[8] *ADN* M 596, 68, 'Syndicats professionnels. Tourcoing'.

a socialist union in these years than were their male co-workers. But what of the competitor unions? Did the mixed unions, or *jaunes*, or even those that claimed to be neither, find greater success in attracting women textile workers?

Mixed *syndicats* (i.e. unions of both owners and workers) were, in fact, remarkably unsuccessful in organizing women workers anywhere in France. In January 1908 mixed unions claimed only 12,028 women members in France as a whole, compared with 116,652 women in other types of unions. By 1911, that figure had dropped to 7,372.[9]

Yellow unions found slightly more success among women and men workers. In the Lille area, the *jaunes* included three types: those which were genuinely independent of both owners and socialists, a few that were independent Catholic women's unions, and some which were little more than 'fronts' for the textile *patronat*.

Independent unions attracted members who preferred not to ally themselves with the *Parti ouvrier* which, by the mid-nineties, controlled most textile unions in the area. Among these independents were workers hostile to the socialists' constant anti-clerical rhetoric as well as to their political activities. However, the independents modelled most of their activities on those of the socialist unions. They offered similar benefits to members, including an office of welfare information, a free job-placement bureau, free legal advice, a savings society (including one which allowed women workers to save dowries), an insurance scheme for potential conscripts, health and unemployment insurance, a low-cost housing society, two consumer co-operatives (*Indépendante* and *Grande Brasserie*) and a full range of leisure activities similar to those offered by the socialists, including lectures, dances, musical evenings, and so on.[10]

In addition to these mixed-sex independent unions, a few women's textile unions appeared in the area. These unions belonged to the national umbrella group, the *Assemblée générale des syndicats des femmes*, a Christian syndical organization (which joined the *Confédération français des travailleurs chrétiens* after

[9] Auguste Pawlowski, *Les Syndicats féminins et les syndicats mixtes en France* (Paris, 1912), p. 8.
[10] Léon de Seilhac, *La Grève du tissage de Lille* (Paris, 1910), p. 41.

1919). This national organization was founded in 1903 by Marie-Louise Rochebillard in Lyon, to group together those working women who wanted to organize their union efforts around the goals prescribed in *Rerum Novarum*.[11]

The statutes of one Lille women's union show it to have been carefully organized and tightly controlled. Members were warned to avoid using strikes as a means to settle industrial disputes whenever possible. When conflicts were unavoidable, however, after arbitration had failed, members were expected to behave with perfect solidarity. The statutes announced: 'Any unionized *ouvrière* who does not stop work or does the work of a striking comrade will forfeit all rights to strike pay; she will immediately be expelled from the union and will be considered as a traitor to the cause of *travailleuses*.' Furthermore, 'unionized women who take jobs from striking *ouvrières* will be pitilessly chased out of the union.'[12]

Both the genuinely independent mixed-sex unions and the Christian women's unions attracted some members in the Lille area, though neither lasted very long. One writer observed that by 1912 most of the women's unions, including 'numerous unions of Tourcoing spinners and Lille preparation workers', had vanished in the previous five years.[13]

The only *jaunes* that continued to enjoy steady success in the pre-war years were those linked to the Tourcoing-based *Union fédérale du tissage*. These unions were in no way independent of employer influence, but reflected, instead, an attempt by the employers to organize workers fearful of joining openly mixed unions (and thus incurring the wrath of their co-workers). These *jaunes* were organized into single-sex groups, with women's sections subordinate to men's. Not only were no women allowed on the administrative council of the *jaune* federation, but their meeting agendas, like all their activities, were decided solely by male union leaders. Doubtless this male domination explained the *jaunes*' stand against protective labour legislation for women

---

[11] See: *Le Petit Jaune*, Sept., Oct. 1903 and 15 Aug. 1904; AN F^7 12793, 'Syndicats jaunes', *Rapport du congrès des indépendents des femmes, Lyon, juillet 1906*; Jean Maitron, ed., *Dictionnaire biographique du mouvement ouvrier français*, vol. xv (Paris, 1977), p. 74.
[12] *AN* F^7 12793, 'Syndicats jaunes'.
[13] Pawlowski, *Syndicats féminins*, p. 17.

workers—a position which directly contradicted that taken by both socialist textile unions and independent women's unions.[14] (The latter, in fact, not only supported shorter hours for women workers, but also campaigned vigorously against a consequent lowering of women's wages.)

Given their strict relegation to the margins of yellow union activity, it was not surprising that women were rarely mentioned in *jaune* union meetings. And, when they were mentioned, the terms were less than flattering. In 1895, at one meeting, a male delegate enquired whether 'women and foreigners' would be allowed to vote in the *Chambre du travail* then being formed. There was no discussion on the question of women's participation. Foreigners— defined as 'greedy German Jews'—were restricted from voting.[15]

Then, too, these *jaunes* were rarely interested in women's conditions in the mills. Instead, male leaders focused on women members' domestic lives. Most yellow union propaganda instructed women members to be dutiful wives, mothers, daughters, and sisters. Above all, male union leaders cautioned, women must not become socialists, lest they turn into what one Tourcoing speaker called 'liberated wives'. If they did descend to that level, he warned, life for male *jaunes* would become intolerable. 'In the evening after an exhausting day, when we go home, the *foyer* will be deserted,' he predicted. 'We will no longer find our dear little children, whom we love more than ourselves. Maybe we will find a wife who tomorrow will abandon us if her caprices demand it.'[16]

Neither this home-centred propaganda nor the male-dominated union structure attracted many women workers to the *jaunes*. Even the most optimistic figures available show that female membership never totalled more than 2,500 in the period from 1901 to 1914. When one recalls that there were nearly 70,000 women textile workers in the three cities in these years, the lack of widespread appeal of these unions is clear.[17]

Socialist unions, on the other hand, did succeed in attracting relatively more women members, although, as we have seen,

[14] Ibid., and Louise-Marie Compain, *Le Femme dans les organisations ouvrières* (Paris, 1910), p. 62.
[15] *AN* F⁷ 12793.
[16] *ADN* M 154 39, 'Partis politiques, deuxième conférence ouvrière. Tourcoing, 25 février 1894'; *ADN* 154 37, 38, 'Partis politiques socialistes'.
[17] *AN* F⁷ 12793.

women did not swarm into red unions in anywhere near the numbers of their male colleagues. Several factors shaped women's decisions to join socialist textile unions in our period, some negative, some positive.

Among the latter were a series of straightforward economic benefits. These included consumer co-operatives (which grew massively in the *belle époque*, backed by the *POF* as well as by newly arrived Belgian textile workers), free legal counselling, libraries, maternity benefits, and insurance against illness, unemployment, and conscription. In addition, at least one group, the giant *Chambre syndicale ouvrière textile de Roubaix et environs* (with 6,000 members in 1906, 800 of whom were women), provided funds for lobbying the *Chambre* to enact safety measures in the textile mills.[18]

Unlike the mixed or yellow unions, these socialist unions acknowledged workers' right to strike by collecting strike funds. Strike benefits varied from union to union, though all workers organized into socialist unions in the 1909 general strike received a standard 12 francs a week. (Non-unionized workers received 2.50 fr. a week from the common funds of both *rouges* and *jaunes*, who united for the purposes of the strike.[19]) During many strikes, moreover, socialist co-operatives provided free food, and organized the ubiquitous *soupes communistes* characteristic of French Flanders.

Socialist unions, moreover, did not discriminate against women in paying benefits, except in some cases where women workers paid lower dues. The largest Lille union, for example, collected 50 centimes a month from men and only 30 centimes from women. Commensurately, they paid men 1.50 fr. a day during strikes, and women 1 fr. On the other hand, the Roubaix textile union charged everyone 25 centimes a week and paid identical benefits. (It is the low dues, of course, which in part attracted the Lille union's large female membership.) A third union, the *Chambre syndicale ouvrière de l'industrie textile de Lille et environs* charged men 1 fr. a month and women 60 centimes, but paid out identical benefits.[20]

The various *syndicats rouges* supported protective labour

[18] Petitcollot, *Les Syndicats*, pp. 66–7.
[19] Seilhac, *La Grève*, p. 40.
[20] Compain, *La Femme*, p. 63 and Petitcollot, *Les Syndicats*, pp. 66–7.

legislation, though they added two additional demands: first, that the legislation should not discriminate by sex, and second, that it should shorten all workers' hours to eight rather than ten.[21]

In spite of these positive benefits, however, potential women members encountered discrimination in many of the red unions. Statutes in at least three of the earliest unions included rules limiting women's participation, which did not begin to disappear until the late 1890s. A typical provision was this one from the giant Roubaix textile union: 'women . . . are admitted to the benefits of the union. But they may address observations or propositions to the union only in writing and by the intermediation of two male members.'[22] This type of discriminatory statute remained part of most red union rules until the *Parti ouvrier*'s campaign on behalf of women's equality succeeded in abolishing them.

On the other hand, such discrimination was countered, at least in part, by the constantly expressed commitment of the local *POF* to women's equality in the work-place. *Le Forçat*, Roubaix's socialist party paper in 1882 and 1883, addressed all union announcements and invitations to meetings to both men and women. Furthermore, the *POF*'s uncompromising stand against sex discrimination (embodied in the paper's motto which read 'considérant que l'émancipation de la classe productive est celle de tous les êtres humains sans distinction de sexe ni de race') coloured most socialist union activities and concerns, even though discriminatory statutes remained on the unions' books.[23]

Thus, by the 1890s, the socialists had succeeded in eliminating most blatant hostility toward women from union discourse. In 1900, most local *syndicats rouges* adopted a goal specifically aimed at including all workers. That of Tourcoing's *Chambre syndicale ouvrière textile* was typical. It read: 'To represent, defend, and protect all textile workers in particular, and all workers in general, without distinction by sex, race, or nationality.'[24] One contemporary observer, visiting the area in 1909, confirmed the

---

[21] *Enquête sur l'industrie, 1904*, pp. 274, 297–8, 286, 290.

[22] France, *Associations professionnelles*, p. 383, and *ADN* M 595 10 i, 'Syndicats—généralites'; *ADN* M 595 10 ii, 'Chambres syndicales, dossiers par commune, 1880s'.

[23] The wording appeared first in *Le Forçat* (4 Mar. 1883). See also Jules Guesde and Paul Lafargue, *Le Programme du Parti ouvrier* (Lille, 1902).

[24] *ADN* M 596, 68, 'Syndicats professionnels de Tourcoing'.

prevalence of this attitude. 'Among the collectivists', she wrote, 'is no unwholesome hostility against working women.'[25]

Consistent with their stand against sex discrimination was the socialists' practice of addressing all union propaganda to *ouvrières*, rather than to wives, mothers, and so on.[26] Furthermore, during the early organizational years, from 1880 to 1899, local organizers made it a policy to include numerous women speakers at their public meetings. Most women speakers, moreover, specifically addressed what they called the 'double exploitation' of *ouvrières* who, they said, were enslaved both to the *patronat* and to their male relations.[27] Not surprisingly, this kind of attention to women's special difficulties attracted more women to the *syndicats rouges* than to alternative unions.

Unfortunately, however, socialist union leaders gradually changed their essentially progressive attitudes toward women workers. In the years after the turn of the century, as the textile federation attempted to tighten its control over its member unions, women as a potential union constituency began to disappear from national view. At the same time, in their anxiety to recruit more male union members, many leaders gave up what they saw as a potentially controversial stand in favour of women's equality, adopting instead a more traditional position in favour of working women's return to the home.

This process was exacerbated by the disappearance from both the national and the regional scene of those women militants whose presence among socialist activists had successfully dis-

---

[25] Compain, *La Femme*, p. 63.

[26] Only in 1912, during a strike of male wool-sorters against the hiring of women, did the socialists lapse into open hostility to women's work. But the absence of most such hostility was unique to the area. Elsewhere negative attitudes toward working women flourished, particularly in areas where women workers were increasingly being hired to replace men at much lower wages. The Couriau affair of 1913 brought this quarrel to a head. See the heated discussion of women in printing trades in the two national syndicalist papers, *La Voix du peuple* and *La Bataille syndicaliste*, and in the SFIO's *L'Humanité* in 1913–14.

[27] See *Conférence du Syndicat ouvrier des peigneurs de lin, cotonniers, tisserands et filtiers, Roubaix, 15 mai 1882, compte rendu*, and *ADN* M 154 61, 'Commissariat de police. Lille, 15 mai 1882'. Throughout 1882, feminists spoke to crowded meetings of textile workers in the three cities. See reports of Rouzade's other appearances in *Le Forçat* (29 July and 10 Sept. 1882), Louise Michel's talk on working women's problems in *LF* (29 Oct. 1882), and Paule Minck's talk, discussed in *LF* (26 Nov. 1882).

couraged such a tactic in the earlier years. Paule Minck gave her last speech in Lille in 1899, and died in 1901. Léonie Rouzade turned away from socialist activities and buried herself in Parisian feminism. Louise Michel died in 1905. After 1905 few women appeared on union platforms in the Nord, and none as a union leader.

This change in union attitudes towards working women was reflected in the pages of the national textile union's journal, *L'Ouvrier textile*. From its first issue in 1903 until 1911, reporters and editors, led by the federation secretary-general Victor Renard, rarely mentioned women's presence in the industry. And even on those occasions when they did take notice of women workers, it was on back pages, in marginal columns. Moreover, women had to go a long way to get even this limited attention. Only those *ouvrières* who organized their own unions and asked to join the socialist federation found themselves mentioned in the journal's pages. (In these years, such militant women's unions emerged in the Isère, the Gard, and the Rhône, as well as in a few other isolated areas in the south-west.[28])

Even more symbolic of the national union's indifference to women textile workers was the fact that only once did a woman appear in the annual May Day cartoon which appeared on *L'Ouvrier textile*'s front page each year. On the single occasion when a woman was portrayed, moreover, she was accompanied by two male token figures—one Asian and one black.[29]

Textile union leaders marginalized women workers in their rhetoric as well, neglecting to include 'ouvrières' in most of their speeches, or in their written propaganda. One particularly revealing omission occurred in 1904, in the published minutes of the annual textile congress. *L'Ouvrier textile* admitted that one key resolution had 'inadvertently' been left out of the official

---

[28] The history of women textile workers' unions in the Lyon area, in the Isère, the Gard, the Cevennes, makes it clear that the virtual disappearance of women from Nord textile union activities was a purely local phenomenon. Some of the activities of women textile union leaders, including Lucie Baud and Louise Chaboseau-Napias of the Isère, Edith Agulhon of the Cevennes, and Marie Bonnafoux of the Gard, can be traced in *L'Ouvrier textile* (1903–1914). See also Raymond Jonas, 'From Radical Republic to the Social Republic: the example of the Isère' (unpub. Ph.D., University of California, Berkeley, 1984).

[29] *OT* (1 May 1910).

publication—that was the resolution supporting women worker's eligibility to stand, and to vote for *conseils des prud'hommes*.[30] A few months later, Victor Renard let slip his private attitude toward women workers when he described a strike of organized silk-workers (who were predominantly women) in these words: 'At Vizille, at Voiron, and at Lyon, workers—especially *their* wives or *their* daughters—are struggling against having to run two machines' (emphasis mine).[31]

During the textile unions' campaign for a 5½ day working week (popularly known as the 'semaine anglaise'), the union's negative attitude toward women's waged work became even more apparent. This campaign, launched in 1911, constantly reiterated the importance and 'naturalness' of women's role within the home. The national textile federation's resolution in favour of the *semaine anglaise*, passed at its congress in 1911, stated: 'there is thus the possibility for industrialized women to see to the housework a little more, to the profit of their health and that of their family.'[32] One union leader, V. Vandeputte, warned that without the *semaine anglaise* the working-class family would vanish. Men would be driven from home if their wives and daughters lacked the time to make their *foyers* 'homely and appealing'.[33]

Attitudes like these did nothing to attract women members into the socialist textile unions. Indeed, in all the years after 1911, even the militant and vocal women's silk-workers' unions dropped out of the national federation. But the leadership never suspected that misogyny lay at the heart of the union's failure. Instead, Renard explained, 'It must be remembered that in the textile industry, propaganda and recruitment are less effective than the 900,000 workers employed there might suggest, because among them are more than 400,000 women and children. From this fact arises the necessity, indeed the obligation, to proceed with prudence and method.'[34] And what was Renard's suggestion for recruiting these

---

[30] 'Rectification et omission', *OT* (1 Oct. 1905).

[31] 'Dans le tissage–La Question des deux métiers', *OT* (1 Jan. 1907).

[32] 'Compte-rendu du XIIᵉ congrès', *OT* (1 Oct. 1911).

[33] V. Vandeputte, 'La Semaine anglaise: subterfuges des patrons pour le combattre', *OT* (1 July 1914).

[34] 'Comment on fait de la propagande', *OT* (1 Sept. 1911).

large numbers of women? 'There are many localities where no leisure activities exist', he told male union members, 'and where there is a great opportunity for militants to meet with the wife [*sic*], girls, young men, and children, and to spend an evening as educational as it is recreational.'[35] Presumably, neither 'the wife' nor 'girls' were able to take a full evening of union politics unless it was mixed with lighter recreation.

iii

Although the numbers of women members in textile unions remained low, most observers noted the striking visibility of textile *ouvrières* in collective activities in Lille, Roubaix, and Tourcoing, most of which remained outside official union control throughout the *belle époque*. Like many others, Marie-Louise Compain was perplexed by this combination of women's absence from formal organizations and their apparently equal participation in working-class life. After visiting the Lille area in 1910, she wrote:

One has no clear sense of politically militant, nor even furious women emerging from this army of women, constrained to hard labour in the unhealthy combing rooms and overheated spinning mills . . . But it may be that, in this homeland of labour and struggle, where working men and women live and suffer side by side, the organization of women's labour will yet achieve its greatest success. In these smoky cities, drawn into the economic mêlée, the working woman is not subject to a thousand distractions, unlike the *modiste* or the working girl of Paris. She is truly the companion of her male comrades, not having learned to be ashamed of her work-shirt or her calloused hands, nor tempted to dream of the student or clerk whose passing passion might make her a 'lady'.[36]

Indeed, Compain's view that women textile workers were potentially an important constituency for unions was echoed by many observers of unorganized worker activities in the area. More than one suggested that women were more militant than their male co-workers. One police report from 1909 observed, 'In strikes, women generally distinguish themselves by their aggressive ardour with regard to the *patronat*, and encourage, by their attitude, their husbands to resistance. In important movements, in serious

---

[35] See ibid., and 'Notre premier mai', *TO* (1 Apr. 1913).
[36] Compain, *La Femme*, p. 64.

conflicts, one often sees them going down to the public streets to join the demonstrators . . . In general, they are animated by a spirit of struggle against capital, and show themselves very ardent in their demands.'[37]

These, then, were the working women whom the union neglected in the years after the turn of the century. The extent of male union leaders' misjudgement of women's potential strength becomes clear when one looks at strikes and spontaneous mass demonstrations, in both of which women workers were visible and militant.

Within the general pattern of women's participation in strikes and other mass activities, however, two key elements must be kept in mind. Firstly, however militant women strikers showed themselves to be, they were never present in the same numbers as male textile workers. On the whole, working women were less likely to strike or to take to the streets in spontaneous rebellion against their conditions throughout the *belle époque*. Secondly, the peception of women in strikes—both among union leaders as well as among other observers—did not remain static, but rather changed over time. This meant that evidence of women's activities in collective efforts was distorted. Increasingly, over time, women were portrayed as passive victims. Thus, when they did strike or demonstrate, most observers reacted as though their behaviour constituted either a surprising anomaly or a 'sudden awakening'. In general, most male observers wore blinkers which effectively isolated any mass movement of women from the broader flow of collective working-class resistance.[38]

Even allowing for the distortion of historical evidence, however, it is clear that fewer women joined mass protests of various kinds. Several practical constraints shaped their behaviour. Firstly, women were among the lowest-paid workers in the textile mills of Lille, Roubaix, and Tourcoing. This meant that they never managed to save any money which might have helped them to

---

[37] *AN* F[7] 13820, 'Commissariat spécial. Lille. 31 janvier 1909'.

[38] This practice is still common. In the Paris–Paris exhibit, centre Georges Pompidou, 28 May–2 Nov. 1981, one photograph of a women's strike meeting at Renault during the popular front bore the caption 'Ouvriers en grève'. See also Jacques Borgé and Nicolas Viasnoff, eds., *Archives du Nord* (Paris, 1979), pp. 150–1. Huguette Bouchardeau has explored this phenomenon in *Pas d'histoire, les femmes . . .* , (Paris, 1977).

sustain a strike. Moreover, many women supported families. For both single mothers and women whose husbands were employed, their tiny wages meant survival for several people. Concomitantly, the textile unions' greater neglect of women workers increased the risks they incurred by protesting against their conditions, just as it left most women workers without the practice or skills necessary for organizing effective mass resistance. Finally, as we have seen, women workers bore the brunt of mill owners' efforts to discipline the textile work-force. Not only was their behaviour more closely studied on the shop-floor, but their private lives were the objects of scrutiny, either from the *patronat* and their families, or from local clerics, working in tandem with the mill owners.

These factors taken together help explain the greater absence of *ouvrières* from strikes in our period. At the same time, however, women were by no means entirely absent from collective mass behaviour at any time during our period. A brief look at the most important strikes in Lille, Roubaix, and Tourcoing from 1880 to 1914 makes it clear that virtually all textile *ouvrières* at one time or another joined the struggles of their class.

In the 3½ decades before the war, textile strikes in the Lille area fell into a pattern shaped by the development and growth of unions. In the 1880s and 1890s, most strikes (often little more than brief walk-outs) were small, short-lived, and ineffective. The two exceptions to this rule were the mass general strikes which opened each decade, in 1880 and 1890. These two strikes had more in common with two later general strikes, in 1903–4 and 1909, than with the more frequent, smaller strikes of the *fin de siècle*.

After the turn of the century, most textile strikes remained fairly small and generally unsuccessful, but they were increasingly backed by the growing resources of unions and the local socialist party. This support allowed them a longer life, although it contributed little to the overall success rate.

In addition to the growing presence of unions in most strikes, three other elements characterized textile strikes in the Lille area in this period. Firstly, most were mixed, and included men and women workers together. Secondly, in both mixed and single-sex strikes, male and female workers voiced similar demands. Except for two flurries of all-women strikes, occasioned by the effects of protective labour legislation, and for three strikes of male wool-sorters protesting against employers' attempts to replace them with lower-paid women workers (in 1899, 1906, and 1912) no identifiably 'male' or 'female' strike demands or behaviour emerged. Thirdly, the formal responses of socialist unions to women strikers changed over the years. Between 1880 and 1895, local union organizers treated *ouvrières* as an integral part of the workers' movement. In later years, however, women gradually dropped from sight.[39]

iv

The first general textile strike began quietly in the spring of 1880. A handful of Roubaix weavers at MM Delattre *père et fils* stopped work, demanding a higher wage. Their modest venture quickly grew into a mass strike. By April, twelve Roubaix mills were closed, and 25,000 workers on strike. A second demand was added to the first: for a ten-hour working day. Throughout the month of April, and well into May, the movement spread—down the roads and along the tramlines leading out of Roubaix into Lille, Houplines, Armentières, and even, finally, to Tourcoing. By June, textile production in the Nord department was at a standstill.

Why 1880? The prefect blamed the economic crisis of 1876, which had produced widespread unemployment and ghastly conditions on the shop-floor.[40] Attempting to minimize the worst effects of the crisis, the textile *patronat* bought cheap, poor quality raw materials which both made work harder and slower and increased fines levied for bad work. As demand for textile products continued to drop in 1877, Lille area manufacturers further exacerbated the workers' frustrations by adopting a slow-down policy, which left workers waiting before empty machines. As most workers were paid on the piece-rate system, this situation naturally increased friction between workers and supervisors (who controlled the distribution of raw materials). In an effort to

---

[39] See Marie-Hélène Zylberberg-Hocquart, *Femmes et féminisme dans le movement ouvrier français* (Paris, 1981), and Madeleine Guilbert, *Les Femmes et l'organisation syndicale avant 1914* (Paris, 1966). One male worker expressed this widely held view in *OT* (1 Jan. 1905). He wrote, 'the place of woman is not in a factory. She must be returned to the family home in order to raise our children and prepare our meals. Obliged to eat hastily, we have no rest, no joy.'

[40] *AN* F[12] 4660, 'Grèves et coalitions. 1880–1'.

forestall likely explosions between the work-force and supervisory personnel, owners tightened discipline. They increased fines for unruly behaviour, added new and more restrictive rules, and hired more foremen and forewomen to enforce them.

As the economic crisis lifted slightly in 1879, workers' hopes for a return to pre-crisis conditions (and wages) rose. Collectively, they began to think about ways to force an end to the unemployment, low wages, and harsh regime in the mills. They found support for these ideas in the growing workers' movement of the period, which began to mobilize around three national congresses held in 1876, 1878, and 1879. This movement sowed the first seeds of organized resistance among the textile workers of Lille, Roubaix, and Tourcoing, as locally chosen delegates returned from the meetings carrying a new message of collective resistance to industrial problems.

To local *ouvrières*, these delegates brought an additional message. Working women, they promised, would henceforth form an equal half of the new industrial working class. Efforts to free the working class from the strictures of industrial capitalism, moreover, would at the same time include efforts to ensure women's civil, political, economic, and even social equality.

Despite this revolutionary rhetoric (an amalgam of ideas long present among the popular classes and new Marxist ideas of proletarian revolution) the leaders of the movement in the Lille area were not initially fiery revolutionaries, committed to the immediate overthrow of capitalism.[41] Indeed, the earliest delegates argued forcefully for peaceful, gradual change. But, as local employers imposed increasingly harsh discipline in the mills, in reaction to the growing industrial crisis, most workers hardened their opinions. Hostility to the visibly rich textile *patronat* increased from 1876 to 1879, and in 1880 the most militant of the local workers adopted a firm stand in favour of revolutionary change. When the crisis began in the opening months of 1880, then, many workers were prepared to demand immediate changes based on a more equal sharing of profits which their labour produced.

True to form, the *patronat* turned a blind eye to the militant

---

[41] See Robert Vandenbussche, 'Aspects de l'histoire politique du radicalisme dans le département du Nord (1870–1905)', *RdN* (Apr.–June 1965), pp. 223–68.

stirrings in the workers' *quartiers* of the three cities. Anxious to recoup the losses they had suffered during the previous four years, they even ignored several sporadic acts of violence in January and February of 1880, acts which proved to be warning signs of the first general strike in the area's textile industry. When the strike began, therefore, they—along with virtually everyone else, including most workers—were taken completely by surprise.[42]

As the strike spread from Delattre to other mills in Roubaix in April, mass strike meetings began to occur, initially in fields just across the Belgian border at Ballon, where strikers were safely beyond the reach of the French police. No doubt partly because of the spring weather, most of the early meetings were really little more than family picnics. But the continuing hostility of the employers to workers' demands quickly turned the festive atmosphere sour. Bands of workers began to return from these mass meetings in a militant mood. Not only did crowds of strikers organize at the gates of non-striking mills in an attempt to convince their co-workers to join the strike, but they also guarded closed mills against possible scabs. Any workers who tried to cross their lines were subjected to violent intimidation. Finally, such intimidation stimulated local police into action. They began arresting strikers who harassed scabbing workers. At one mill, they arrested Coralie Lesage, 22, for threatening to beat up a potential scab when she emerged from the mill.[43]

By the fifth of May, tension ran high. The prefect, fearing violence, sent a warning to the central government in Paris. He described a 'certain frightening of the bourgeoisie' which he hoped to calm with a small show of force. To that end, he called up nine brigades of gendarmes, together with mounted troops from the Lille garrison.[44]

Not surprisingly, the presence of troops did little to calm the situation. At first, however, the workers reacted peacefully. In Roubaix, on the seventh of May, organized groups of between 100 and 500 workers marched in relays to the *Hôtel de Ville*. Upon arrival, each group sent men and women delegates to present their demands to the mayor. All told, their day-long parade included

[42] *Le Temps* (23 May 1880).
[43] *AN* F[12] 4660, 'Grève à Roubaix–Lille, 29 avril 1880'.
[44] Ibid., 'Télégramme au ministère des postes et télégraphes, Lille, 5 mai 1880'.

6,000 men, women, and children, marching slowly and in disciplined fashion through the streets of the city. There was no violence; while the delegates spoke to the mayor or his representatives, the crowds waited quietly outside.[45]

The peace of these early days was short-lived, however. The increasing visibility of troops, concentrated in Roubaix in early May, together with the silence of the *patronat* altered the workers' mood. By the thirteenth of May, more than 12,000 Roubaix strikers massed on the *boulevard de Paris* near the city's centre, and prepared to march again on the town hall. Rather than gathering in small groups, however, they formed a single unbroken column, led by children and young people, and set out for the *Hôtel de Ville*. More menacing than earlier crowds, they chanted 'Si on ne veut pas nous renchérir, nous allons tout démolir.' Alerted by the threat, the troops positioned themselves between the strikers and the town hall. As the strikers drew near, mounted troops charged. No serious injuries resulted from the ensuing panic. Nevertheless, that act was a match for the dry kindling of workers' frustrations. That night, bands of women and men roamed the streets of Roubaix, breaking factory windows and menacing any scabs who ventured outside their homes. From that night on, troops took up permanent stations guarding both the mills and the homes of mill owners from the collective wrath of the strikers.[46]

The story of this strike in both Lille and Tourcoing was quite different. Lille's workers showed none of the organized solidarity of their *roubaisien* neighbours. In the first place, many fewer *Lillois* participated in the strike. At the end of the second week in May, when most Roubaix textile mills were closed by the strike, only 1,954 Lille workers were officially out, with a further 475 in two neighbouring towns. Fewer strikers did not mean smaller crowds in Lille's streets, however. Instead, many workers from other industries, as well as many from among the area's unemployed population, quickly joined the strike activities. Among these latter were crowds of casual labourers, vagabonds, and smugglers, whose presence turned the Lille crowds into something much more potentially menacing than those in Roubaix. Marches

---

[45] Ibid., 'Rapport de l'armée au ministère de guerre', 7 May 1880.
[46] Ibid., 'Cabinet du Préfet du Nord. Lille, 1 juin 1880. Histoire de la grève'.

and mass demonstrations, then, included many thousands of people with no interest in the textile strike as such, but a good deal of interest in stirring up trouble. Up to 40,000 people appeared in one mass march and, because of their heterogeneity, they were far less organized than the crowds of *roubaisien* textile strikers. With good reason, the local forces of order viewed them with much more suspicion. Troops—both mounted and unmounted—as well as armed police were deployed in Lille in an effort to prevent random violence. Police spies were also sent to infiltrate the crowds to provide local officials with a warning of any mob action. These latter warned their superiors that the 'Lille working class', was 'far less disciplined than in Roubaix'.[47]

This obvious lack of discipline gave the Lille *patronat* the opening they desired to strengthen the mounted troop presence in the city. Throughout May, confrontations between the troops and crowds of strikers and others broke out nearly every day. At each troop appearance, angry crowds filled the streets. The bigger the crowd, the more mounted troops arrived on the scene. By the twenty-fourth of May the situation was so potentially explosive that the prefect decided to intervene. He offered to arbitrate the dispute if the workers would return to work in the process. But although the workers quickly agreed to this offer, the *patronat* refused point-blank. Confident that misery would ultimately drive the workers back into the mills, they held out. And by early June their certainty was proved right; one by one the Lille workers drifted back into the mills, having won nothing.

In Tourcoing, the strike took still a third form. In early May, 5,820 workers in the city were officially on strike, with an additional 897 in the city's suburbs. Together these 6,717 strikers chose delegates to present their demands to the *patronat*. The mill owners responded calmly. They agreed to offer a wage increase to all workers whose mills had made a profit in the early months of 1880. This meant, effectively, that all workers in Tourcoing got a pay rise except for those few working in cotton-spinning mills. Sweet reason thus prevailed in Tourcoing; by mid-May, normal work had resumed.

While it was doubtless the *patronat*'s rapid agreement to meet workers' just demands which ended the strike, the prefect

---

[47] Ibid.

suggested an ancillary explanation. He wrote that workers in Tourcoing were 'more elegant and better turned out' than those in Roubaix. Furthermore, he added, 'the women workers particularly evince a certain coquetry in their appearance which is unknown to their female neighbours.'[48] In the prefect's view, then, it was the style of the textile workers which carried the day in Tourcoing.

Once the strikes in Lille and Tourcoing ended, *roubaisien* solidarity broke. Roubaix workers had little hope of holding out against a firmly hostile *patronat*. In spite of their collective solidarity, they were backed by no organizations which could counter the group resources of the mill owners. And, as they returned to work, many kept this important lesson in mind. They now saw the potential of collective, mass activity—which, they had discovered, could provoke fear and over-reaction from the local bourgeoisie. Secondly, they had learned that solidarity and unity of tactics and strategies must extend throughout the local industry, lest the tactics of one group of owners succeed in breaking the strike in one city at the expense of those in its neighbour's mills.

In addition to learning these lessons, strike leaders for the first time began to visit workers' *quartiers* outside their own. As they carried news of the strike's varying progress in each of the cities, they exchanged ideas about more successful tactics, as well as broader ideas about collective, class-based resistance to their conditions. As a consequence, the workers of Lille, Roubaix, and Tourcoing began to grow together. Almost immediately following the end of the strike, sections of the *Parti ouvrier* were formed in various workers' *quartiers*, first in Roubaix, then in Lille, and finally Tourcoing. By 1881, several *POF* sections were in full swing, with new ones added monthly.

As these new political groups emerged, so local leaders began to identify themselves. And as these new leaders began to organize amongst themselves, they began the long, important process of determining the forms of mass behaviour most likely to mobilize the textile workers of French Flanders. The first thing they saw was the extent to which the 1880 strike had been a community event, encompassing parents and children, old people and non-textile worker neighbours. In Lille, the strike had drawn huge numbers of the local poor, whose presence, if disciplined, could

[48] Ibid.

bolster the strength of future political or economic demonstrations.

The basic form of the textile community's spontaneous protest was the mass meeting or parade—the latter organized along the lines prescribed by the centuries-old Flemish fêtes. People marched in groups—organized around the mill, social club, or *quartier*. Bugles kept order among the festively dressed marchers, who carried banners and flags identifying their group.[49]

In addition to mass meetings and parades, these textile workers also added new forms appropriate to their strikes. 'Communist soup kitchens', a feature of working-class behaviour elsewhere in France, appeared on the local scene during the strike. Local workers' food co-operatives offered both a venue for these collective meals as well as a source of raw materials. Moreover, the whole community provided the labour for these communal meals, which offered an ideal occasion for the spread of union propaganda amongst all the workers and their families.

Of course, the most important lesson the workers learned from the 1880 strike was that misery accompanied long periods without wages or supporting strike funds. So difficult did most workers find the relatively short strike in that spring that enthusiasm for such activities disappeared from the area for the next several years. Only a few small strikes broke the industrial calm of the 1880s, even as industrial conditions grew increasingly worse. Particularly hard hit were the cotton and flax mills of Lille, though most local mills laid off a substantial percentage of the work-force. Unemployment became so common in fact that even the hint of a walk-out brought thousands of willing scabs to factory gates. Moreover, employers, aware of the vast reserve army of scabs, readily handed rebellious workers their *livrets*, dismissing them on the spot.

In fact, throughout the decade, only one strike was large enough to draw much attention from the press or local officials. It happened in the autumn of 1882, when 200 *fileuses* at the LeBlan cotton mill sent a letter to the employer demanding higher wages. M. LeBlan replied that although he would not answer an anonymous letter, he would receive a delegation. The women refused his offer, pointing out that they did not want any among

---

[49] *Le Gaulois* (20 May 1880), quoted in Michèle Perrot, *Les Ouvriers en grève*, vol. 1 (Paris, 1974), p. 550, and *Le Temps* (23 May 1880).

their number singled out for punishment. Instead, they walked out together. Other women working at LeBlan, including those in combing, carding, and other spinning rooms, joined them. Together, the LeBlan strikers approached the local socialist newspaper, *Le Forçat*, for advice and help. The editors obliged, collecting strike funds and encouraging other textile workers to strike in solidarity with the LeBlan *ouvrières*. These pleas brought the rest of the LeBlan workers (who were mostly men) out as well. At its peak, the strike included 870 workers.

After two weeks, M LeBlan released a statement to the local press announcing an end of the strike. He hoped that this tactic would fool some of his workers into returning to work, thus breaking the strike. And it did. Eventually 800 men and women returned to work, thinking the strike over. Only 70, most of them from the original *fileuses*, stayed out. Dismayed by LeBlan's success, *Le Forçat*'s editors sought outside help to prevent the remaining women from giving up their effort. Aware that Louise Michel was then on a speaking tour in nearby Belgium, they invited her to hold a strike benefit meeting in Lille's *Hippodrome*. She quickly accepted the invitation, and boarded a train for France.

The appearance of the famous ex-*communarde* provoked widespread concern among the local bourgeoisie. Catholic youths, most of whom were drunk, packed the *Hippodrome*, preventing many workers from getting in to the meeting. While they heckled Michel—finally preventing her from speaking altogether—their comrades crowded the streets outside, threatening those who hoped to catch a glimpse of the popular leader as she returned to the Lille train station after the meeting. In the end, both groups were disappointed. The meeting's leaders smuggled Michel out by a back entrance in order to avoid confronting the drunken young men.

Nevertheless, the meeting raised 500 francs for the LeBlan *fileuses*—most of it ironically from the pockets of the sons of the local bourgeoisie. But the violence of the affair proved the final straw for the women strikers. Completely demoralized, they gradually returned to work.

The legacy of the event, however, lingered. For the first time, the local bourgeoisie was open about its hostility to working-class leaders. Newspaper reporters castigated Louse Michel, hinting at her dark past and her unwomanly activities. One local reporter described the popular heroine of the Commune in typically vitriolic terms: 'Louise Michel was dressed in black and enveloped in a magnificent and scarcely democratic fur mantle. Everyone knows the truly repulsive face of the neo-Caledonian virago—the bald forehead, the thin lips, the bilious and murky compexion, the short hair, flung back from her face . . .'[50] Such negative opinions contrasted sharply with the affection which met Michel in the workers' *quartiers* of Lille, Roubaix, and Tourcoing throughout the years before her death in 1905. Their virulence, moreover, suggested both the widespread fear such a militant woman engendered in the breasts of the local bourgeoisie and the gap between the views held by opposing classes in these industrial cities.

A few other strikes marred the local calm during the eighties, but they invariably lasted only a few hours. In most such walk-outs, workers abandoned their machines over some grievance, were handed their *livrets*, and quickly replaced. Such was the fate, for example, of forty women bobbin-winders at Motte-Bossut in Roubaix when they tried collectively to protest against the firing of a co-worker. Their protest lasted only long enough for their employer to find and hire forty new *bobineuses*.[51]

Despite the surface calm of the local industrial scene, however, the 1880s supported an active underground working-class move-ment. In the ten years following the general strike, the socialists spread their message into every workers' *quartier* in the region. Socialist unions grew, slowly but inexorably penetrating every large mill. And, in this early period, the *patronat* seemed unable to mount any effective campaign against what they perceived to be a growing threat to the status quo. Except for encouraging Catholic workers' groups and mixed *syndicats*, and imposing increasingly restrictive behaviour on their female workers, most employers avoided confronting the growing militancy of their workers unless it became absolutely necessary to do so. In general, employers reacted rather than acted. Their reactions included firing workers who spread the socialist message in the mills, abusing socialist

[50] See *LF* (15 Oct., 22 Oct., 5 Nov., 1882). *Progrès du Nord* is quoted in the latter.
[51] *AN* F[12] 4660.

speakers, and occasionally calling out police or troops to threaten reprisals for any mass action. But these tactics only served to amplify socialists' criticism of the industrial system as workers experienced it in the textile mills.

V

Given the various subliminal political rumblings of the 1880s, a perceptive observer should not have been surprised when the second great general strike in the industry exploded in May 1890. But most local people, including socialist leaders, were again taken utterly unaware by the events of that spring.

The action which provoked the strike was called by the local socialists to celebrate the first May Day, on 1 May 1890, in compliance with the decision of the socialist second International taken at its 1889 congress. The day's plans included demonstrations and meetings in the afternnon, followed by a dance in the evening. But the socialists were at least as shocked as the *patronat* when those deliberately limited events turned overnight into an uncontrolled, undisciplined general strike, which spread throughout Lille, Roubaix, and Tourcoing.[52]

Although it looked similar to its predecessor ten years before, this general strike had one key difference. By 1890, socialist unions had circulated their influence throughout the three cities. Leaders and militants not only expected to lead meetings and marches, but were trained to do so. Many of that May Day's leaders, moreover, came from outside the area. Indeed, the original May Day planning committee included leaders from outside the Nord department itself. And, more importantly for women textile workers, all of these leaders were men.

The character of this recently formed socialist infrastructure had both positive and negative consequences for the strikers. Because organized unions could deploy financial resources collected over a period of time, strikers knew they could count on enough help to sustain a fairly long strike. Furthermore, the fact that the strike had been initiated by the May Day call of the *Parti ouvrier* meant that strikers' actions were to some extent legitimated by their connection (however tenuous it was in fact) with that national

[52] Details in France, *Associations professionnelles*, pp. 375–404.

movement. In the Lille area, this strike thus became the first mass demonstration which to some extent measured local socialist sympathies.

On the other hand, the structure of union leadership had deleterious effects on the participation of women workers. The long-standing socialist union's restrictions on women members' participation meant that there were no women leaders, even at the local level; nor were there any women who had been identified by the union as possible militants, and trained as organizers. Thus, there was no one among the strike leaders to encourage women's front-line participation in the strike. These problems affected the way in which the strike unfolded, as well as the way socialist leaders perceived strikers' activities.

The first workers' May Day was called in Lille for the afernoon and evening of 1 May 1890. It was not merely a workers' holiday in that year but instead included a demand for the ten-hour day. Because this event was to be the first public test of *Parti ouvrier* strength in the area, local politicians threw themselves enthusiastically into the effort to mobilize the textile workers. They printed thousands of handbills announcing the May Day. Meetings blossomed in every sympathetic *estaminet*. Militants in nearly every mill enthused about the importance of the planned demonstration. In addition, local *syndicats* and socialist groups organized petitions supporting the workers' demand throughout the workers' *quartiers*. Furthermore, every organized group planned marches, meetings, and so on.[53]

Pre-May Day agitation did not go unnoticed by the increasingly vigilant *patronat*, nor by the prefect. Many mill owners planned to foil the midday walk-out on 1 May by locking workers in after the start of the day. Others hired armed guards to stand outside their mill gates as further insurance against a work stoppage. One writer described one group of local mills on May Day morning as 'armed fortresses, where all communication with the outside world was cut off'.[54]

Even the most cautious owners, however, allowed their workers a lunch-break, and some mistakenly opened the factory gates. The

[53] See Aline Valette, 'Une Journée historique—le 1ᵉ mai 1890 en France', *RS* (July—Dec. 1890), pp. 129–55, 433–48.
[54] Ibid., p. 444.

sound of the noon whistle thus became the signal for a mass exit from the mills, overwhelming the scattered guards. Mobs of workers poured into the streets of all three cities in a celebratory mood. Once outside the mill gates, however, they quickly discovered armed and mounted troops stationed at every cross-roads, and blocking all roads out of town. Even the tramlines between Lille, Roubaix, and Tourcoing were blocked to all except workers returning home. Thus had the prefect hoped to isolate each of the three cities' workers from their neighbours, thus keeping the crowds down to a manageable size. But the actions of both the *patronat* and the prefect had a more negative effect than they had anticipated. They changed a happy crowd into a hostile mob, and effectively ensured that subsequent events would unfold amidst tension and hostility.

May Day developed similarly in all three cities. In Lille, workers met to elect a delegation (which included both men and women) to carry their ten-hour day petitions to the prefecture. On their first attempt, the 54 delegates were accompanied by 10,000 strikers. But they were turned away before they reached their goal by strategically placed troops. They regrouped, 'undiscouraged', in the words of one socialist leader.[55] This time, they selected a smaller delegation, hoping that it could get past the troops massed before the prefecture. Nine men thus set out for a second attempt. This time, however, the accompanying crowd had doubled. The crowd marched toward the prefecture, singing and waving May Day banners. But this time the troops let them through, and the prefect received their petitions. Having successfully delivered their demands, the delegates and the crowd returned to Lille's city centre where a further 4,000 people awaited them.

In both Roubaix and Tourcoing workers followed a similar pattern, though their delegates' goals were the *mairies* of both cities rather than the prefecture. Both mayors received the petitions without incident.

The total number of people involved in this 1890 May Day in all three cities was considerable, though exact figures are unknown. Contemporary estimates of crowd size varied wildly. The socialist militant Aline Valette counted 6,000 workers in Lille, drawn from 26 textile mills and one chicory-processing plant. She added a

[55] Ibid., p. 152.

further 100,000 workers from 22 Roubaix mills and 14 in Tourcoing. Claude Willard, on the other hand, estimated that 24,007 (*sic!*) workers from Roubaix alone were on strike on the second of May.[56]

Whatever the exact figures, however, it is clear that a majority of the textile work-force in Lille, Roubaix, and Tourcoing walked out on the first of May, in response to the *Parti ouvrier*'s call. But what was intended to be only a one-day strike quickly got out of socialist hands. On 2 May, *POF* leaders declared with dismay that 'a spontaneous strike' was in progress. By the third, 35,000 workers thronged Roubaix's streets, fending off all attempts to get them back to work. A further 40,000 strikers from Tourcoing and neighbouring suburbs joined crowds in Roubaix.[57]

As the days passed, numbers continued to grow. By 11 May, more than 80,000 workers were absent from the mills and factories of Lille and Roubaix, most of them spending their days in the streets and squares of the cities. The size of the crowds frightened mounted troops into charging, willy-nilly, scattering groups of workers which included, in the words of the outraged local socialists, 'even women and children'.[58]

The continuing confrontation between workers and the local bourgeoisie culminated with the arrest of two local socialist leaders, Henri Carrette (the founder of the original Roubaix socialist union in the 1870s) and Gustave Delory (leader of Lille's *Parti ouvrier*). Together, the two men were charged with incitement to violence. Though quickly released, they provided useful martyrs to the local textile workers' cause.[59] Not surprisingly, the troops' violence provoked matching violence from the workers, who broke numerous factory windows. During the nights, mobs massed outside the mill owners' homes, yelling threats to occupants. On the night of 6 May, more than 2,000 people climbed the fence around the home of M. Cordonnier, in Roubaix, and

---

[56] Ibid., p. 441 and Willard, *Les Guesdistes: le mouvement socialiste en France, 1893–1905* (Paris, 1965), p. 45.

[57] *CdT* (4 May 1890), and Perrot, *Les Ouvriers*, p. 99.

[58] *CdT* (11 May 1890).

[59] Ibid., and Robert Baker, 'A Regional Study of Working Class Organisation in France: socialism in the Nord, 1870–1924' (Ph.D., Stanford University, 1967), pp. 58–9.

demolished a garden pavilion, menacing household staff who tried to intervene.[60]

Despite the high level of tension, however, the strike died with a whimper rather than a bang. By mid-May, workers began drifting back to work, having obtained no change in their wages or working conditions. Whatever the strength of the workers' initial collective anger and frustration, such a spontaneous strike without any articulate demands beyond the ten-hour day was doomed to fail.

Although in this general strike socialist union leaders had shown themselves to be powerless to control events after 1 May, they did gain some benefits. Not least of these was a substantial increase in union membership. The Roubaix section of the textile union claimed 9,000 dues-paying members by the end of May, each of whom represented, in the leaders' view, an entire family of textile workers. (Most of the officially enrolled members, of course, were heads of families and thus mostly men. Nevertheless, a substantial number of women 'belonged' to the socialist union, though informally. Thus the union paid out strike benefits to a total of 14,000 adults.)

In Lille as well, union leaders claimed that this strike had 'doubled the numerical strength of the socialist section'. And the usually more cautious government figures supported such claims by showing a significant increase in membership in all *syndicats rouges*, including those in Tourcoing.[61]

A second, more subtle benefit arose from the clarity with which class confronted class in all three cities during the strike. From this time on, few on either side of the class divide assumed the likelihood of harmonious relations between mill owners and workers. Confrontation became the order of the day in all negotiations between manufacturers and the local working class. This stark class configuration transformed the political scene in each of the great textile cities in the years which followed.

From the point of view of most workers, however, the May strike had had few positive effects. For women, in fact, the strike

---

[60] Perrot, *Les Ouvriers*, p. 581. Perrot argues that attacks on employers' houses were remnants of similar attacks on seigneurial estates.

[61] Valette, 'Une Journée', p. 446, and France, *Associations professionnalles*, p. 380.

produced negative results. With increasing union organization, bolstered by an enlarged membership that was substantially male (whatever women's unofficial relationship with such unions), women workers began to drop into a secondary place. This disappearance from the view of many local union leaders was, moreover, hastened by the *POF*'s decision to focus its efforts on election politics. Women, who could not vote, were thus further marginalized from the centre of the struggle.

vi

In the final decade of the nineteenth century, two series of events underscored this growing gap between socialist union and party leaders and women textile workers in the area. These were two groups of strikes, one in 1893 and the second in 1899. In 1893, several groups of women workers struck to protest against the fall in their wages which inevitably accompanied the shorter hours prescribed by the Millerand–Colliard Act of 1892, which cut women's and children's hours to eleven. The second set of strikes, at the end of the decade, involved male wool-sorters, who struck to protest against the sexual integration of their occupation. In both cases, the reactions of union and party leaders reflected their apparent inability to deal with the presence of a large, vocal female proletariat in their midst.[62]

The largest of the 1893 women's strikes broke out at the Rémy mill at Yon, just outside Lille, in January. *Ouvrières* at that mill called a meeting to discuss ways of keeping their previous levels of pay despite shorter hours. At that meeting, they elected a committee to voice their concerns to the mill owner. At the same time, they sent a delegation to Paul Lafargue, Lille's newly elected socialist deputy, from whom they hoped to get help and advice in case a strike became necessary. Lafargue agreed to help them and, when the mill owner refused to negotiate with the committee, the local socialist party swung into action.

Male socialist union leaders called a general meeting of all women workers at Rémy, to draft the women's demands. With their demands in hand the strike committee, accompanied by M.

---

[62] See *Enquête sur l'industrie, 1904*, 'Extraits du rapport de juge de paix au canton Roubaix-Nord', p. 218 and *LT* (3 Dec. 1892, 11 Jan., 18 Oct. 1893).

Lambert, the treasurer of the local *syndicat rouge*, called on the *patron* on the following day. He offered the women a small pay rise, of 5 centimes a day for those few paid by the day, and 1 centime per kilo for piece-workers. But, because this rise came nowhere near to maintaining the women's earlier wage levels, the workers rejected it and voted to strike. They added one new demand to their earlier one: that their employer recognize their new union and negotiate solely with its elected representatives. Although their boss acceded to this second demand, he refused any increase in his wage offer, and a strike began.

Although the *Parti ouvrier* was officially opposed to strikes in the 1890s (on the grounds that they drained energy needed for the coming class struggle), local leaders threw themselves behind the Rémy women once the strike became inevitable. But their support took a curious turn. Because the strikers were women, Lafargue and other male leaders handed them over to the local socialist women's groups, led by the *Comité des femmes de Lille*, founded in the previous year. (This group is discussed in detail in the next chapter.)

Initially their tactic proved beneficial to the strikers. The *Comité des femmes* held a meeting to raise strike funds on 12 January.[63] But, shortly thereafter, the two groups of women found themselves at cross purposes. The *Comité* regarded the Rémy strikers as potential recruits to their ongoing campaign for free school meals for local poor children. The strikers, on the other hand, saw themselves as newly unionized workers on strike in defence of their wages. Because the *Comité des femmes* backed by the local *POF* controlled the content of subsequent meetings, the strikers' interests were quickly overwhelmed in the series of meetings organized to support the *Comité*'s goals.[64] As a consequence, the Rémy *ouvrières*' new union vanished into the *Comité*'s embrace. Without proper union support, the strike died—a victim of the male union leader's misperceptions as well as the local socialist women's enthusiasm for a quite different goal.[65]

---

[63] *LT* (11 Jan. 1893).

[64] See *LT* throughout January 1893; in February and March, the *Comité*'s meetings had ceased to mention the Rémy women.

[65] This was not the first time that women strikers were used by the socialists for their own ends. See Claire Auzias and Annik Houel, *La Grève des ovalistes, Lyon, juin–juillet 1869* (Paris, 1982).

Although this Rémy strike symbolized local male leaders' growing misapprehension of working women's primary goals (a misapprehension fortified by the more traditional 'women's goals' of the *Comité des femmes*), relations between men and women workers in the textile mills themselves remained as they always had been throughout the 1890s. These relations were remarkably amicable. In fact, contrary to the pattern elsewhere in industrial France, few men showed hostility to women working. Only three strikes against women's employment in local textile mills broke out in the area, in direct contrast to the increasing number of such strikes elsewhere.[66] These men's strikes, moreover, involved skilled workers—the *trieurs* of Tourcoing and Roubaix—who were unique among the area's textile workers in possessing an ancient skill, traditionally handed down from father to son, which required a long apprenticeship. Theirs was the last work in the production of textiles which could not be done by machine, and they took pride in this fact. Indeed, even long training could not teach every potential *trieur* the skills necessary to sort fleeces into as many as ten different types of raw wool. For those who did attain these skills, moreover, the rewards in both pay and status were high. Thus, these local *trieurs* formed a proud aristocracy of labour. Like others before them, they scorned unions—particularly those which mixed machine-tenders with more skilled workers. When a few did form a few unions in the 1890s, they included only *trieurs* among their members.

By the end of the century, however, wool-sorters' specialized skills were gradually becoming obsolete. New combing and carding machines and a shift from the manufacture of fine, luxury wool yarn and cloth to more heavy-duty, coarser products combined to reduce the need for so many differentiated categories of raw wool. As a result, many mill owners began contemplating adding cheaper women to their sorting rooms—women who could be quickly trained to sort wool fleeces into the few types needed. As early as the mid-eighties, in fact, one mill owner, M. Morel, had tried to hire *trieuses*—provoking the wrath of one local socialist journalist, who condemned them as mere 'demoiselles à

[66] France, Ministère du commerce, *Statistiques des grèves 1896* (Paris, 1897). Strikes against women were so common that they were coded—'k'—in official strike reports.

jolis minois'. Of course what attracted Morel as well as subsequent employers was neither women's marital status, nor their 'pretty faces'. Rather it was the practicality of hiring workers who would work for 2.50 fr. a day compared with the 6 fr. a day paid to most *trieurs*.[67]

Morel's early attempts came to nothing, as his male sorters refused absolutely to countenance women in the sorting room. But, as the economic crisis deepened, the introduction of lower-paid women wool-sorters became inevitable. Thus, in 1899, several Tourcoing mill owners grouped together and agreed simultaneously to hire women as *trieuses*. But, as soon as the new women workers appeared, the men walked out. Following local custom, they gathered outside the gates of the struck mills, harassing and threatening any women who attempted to go to work. Most of the newly hired *trieuses* were very young, and particularly susceptible to such abuse at the mill gates. Moreover, police reported that many girls and young women were chased home by striking *trieurs*, who promised them physical abuse if they returned to work the following day.

In addition to this constant intimidation, the women became the subject of a widely sung strike song, written by the Tourcoing *POF* leader (and police spy), Victor Capart. The song, written in patois, revealed a misogyny that went well beyond a traditional hostility to scabs. It read in part:

> Ah! qu'in va êtes heureux tout d'mêmes
> Avant deux tro'innées d'ichis
> Car tous les filles ainsi q'les femmes
> Vont rimplachi l'ouvritrieur
> Si l'patron préfère la Cocotte
> Pou' rimplachi l'ouvritrieur
> J'les plains si un jour in s'revolte
> Y d'mand 'ront pardon j'in sus seur.
>
> Tous ces bons patrons catholiques
> Ces semblants d'rin mingeux d'ragôut
> Y pourront trier din se l'Clique
> De ces Cocottes, pour tchangi gôut
> Cha s'ra tout bénéfice pour eusses

---

[67] 'A Travers les bagnes', *RdF* (13 Sept. 1885), and 'L'Intelligent Jules Morel', *RdF* (11 Oct. 1885).

Des belles y n'devront pus paihi
Pour eusses avoir des bonnes ploteusses
Y les f'ront apprinte a trihi.[68]

(A 'cocotte' is a tart. Capart's words played on the double meaning of prostitute.)

Although Victor Capart's song was the sole reaction from the local socialists to this *trieurs'* strike, the level of its hostility did not bode well for the local socialists' efforts to support working women's rights along with those of working men. On the other hand, however, the song did not signal any change in day-to-day relations between *ouvrières* and *ouvriers* on the shop-floor. Indeed, a strike in 1902 suggested that solidarity—regardless of gender—often carried the day. In this strike, at the Binet wool mill in Tourcoing, workers were protesting against the drop in wages occasioned by the shorter hours legislation which applied to all women and children, and to men who worked in mixed-sex workrooms. When the mill owner complied with the law and dropped hours to 10½, he also effectively lowered wages, as most workers affected were paid by the piece-rate system. The workers struck. After several days, the mill owner offered to settle the strike by raising male workers' pay back to its previous level, a tactic he hoped would break the strike. But, as *La Voix du peuple* reported, 'The men workers have rejected that solution and joined together in solidarity with the women to continue the strike.'[69] Alas, however, the strikers could not sustain that solidarity. After a few weeks, the work-force returned, accepting the owner's conditions.

vii

The third general strike in the region's textile industry began in the autumn of 1903, surprising everyone except the workers themselves. It began in Armentières mills, but quickly spread throughout the textile cities of the Nord. It was a genuine wildcat strike, without clear demands, planning, or leaders. Victor Renard announced angrily that it was little more than a 'jacquerie industrielle'.[70]

---

[68] *ADN* M 625 106, 'Chansons nouvelles. Les Trieuses', by V. Capart.
[69] 'Dans le Nord', *VdP* (13–20 Apr. 1902).
[70] V. Renard, 'Les Grèves du Nord', *OT* (1 Nov. 1903).

And so it proved to be. So chaotic did the workers' behaviour appear to most local eyes that all the various arms of the forces of Third Republican order rapidly appeared on the scene in an effort to halt the spontaneous mobilization of virtually all the textile workers throughout the department. Mounted troops and armed police turned cities into armed camps; in October, one paper declared Lille, Roubaix, and Tourcoing to be in 'a state of siege'.[71] Bolstered by this heavy presence of troops, most mill owners refused even to talk with the workers. The leaders of the socialist unions, however, could not so easily ignore this spontaneous mass demonstration of workers' rebellion. They tried instead to take over the strike. In strident tones, socialist leaders warned the workers to organize behind them, lest the strike collapse in defeat. At the same time, they threw the considerable resources of the union and socialist party behind the strike, supplying strike pay and food from the giant socialist food co-operatives, organizing soup-kitchens, and holding benefit meetings.

Although the strikers accepted the help of socialist unions, they rejected union leaders' attempts to direct their behaviour. Instead, the strike continued as it had begun—as *politique de la rue*. Following the pattern established in the general strikes of 1880 and 1890, workers formed processions and celebrated mass *fêtes familiales* in the streets of the industrial cities. Youths spent their evenings menacing bourgeois homes and mill windows. Informal meetings were organized in every workers' *estaminet*. During the days, crowds of workers massed outside factory gates, preventing any possibility of scabbing workers breaking the strike. In short, nothing about the events of the general strike of 1903–4 suggested a significant change in the ways workers mobilized to demonstrate their grievances, despite the efforts of both red and yellow unions to channel that rebellion into organized forms.

But the activities of the strike itself do not tell the whole story. In contrast to the workers' own perceptions of their grievances and the ways in which they expressed their anger and frustration, there were several different views of their collective activities articulated by those outside the strike. And these reports, more than those concerned with the two previous mass strikes in the area, showed that outsiders' perceptions of workers' behaviour had changed

[71] 'L'État de siège dans le Nord', *VdP* (11–18 Oct. 1903).

significantly. The focus of this change was the women textile workers of French Flanders.

Among the most interesting of the reactions to the strike were those which appeared in the socialist and syndicalist press, written by reporters who claimed a close affinity with the workers. Their reports suggested a marked change in the way union leaders saw the activities of women workers within the larger workers' movement.

Both *La Voix du peuple* and *L'Ouvrier textile*, for example, singled out women's participation in communal soup-kitchens, in reports which suggested the total absence of male efforts in this 'women's work'. *La Voix's* reporter wrote that the cooks in these soup-kitchens were 'naturally women strikers or the wives of strikers'. In patronizing tones, he remarked that the women 'cooked with spirit, and performed their tasks with the absolute devotion which merited the thanks of all the strikers'. *L'Ouvrier textile*, on the other hand, chose another tack. That journal's reporter applauded the male strikers who overcame their natural antipathy to domestic 'women's work' and helped the women in these soup-kitchens. In Roubaix and Tourcoing, *L'Ouvrier textile* reported, men helped the women by cutting wood, drawing water, washing vegetables, and even, on occasion, serving the soups and stews—which amounted to 4,812 bowls of soup and 4,950 portions of stew every day in one city alone. Moreover, in Tourcoing, the running of the soup-kitchen was entirely in the hands of a male union leader, who himself served thousands of strikers and their families every day.[72]

Two other reports of the general strike focused on women's involvement in order to generate sympathy for the workers and hostility to the bourgeoise. *L'Humanité* reported widespread group begging, in which groups of strikers walked the streets banging wooden spoons on soup-bowls in order to solicit contributions from passers-by. The writer of this report was shocked that these itinerant groups included 'numerous women'.[73] *L'Ouvrier textile* highlighted a much more harrowing incident. That journal's reporter described the plight of Maria Lefebvre, 28, who was

[72] 'Les Soupes communistes', *VdP* (24 Apr.–1 May 1904), 'Les Repas communistes', *OT* (1 May 1904).
[73] A. Thomas, 'La Grève textile—Lille', *H* (19 Apr. 1904). See also *VdP* (25 Oct.—1 Nov. 1903).

wounded by a cavalry charge whilst she was on her way home after a strike meeting in April 1904. The paper's reporter detailed Lefebvre's 'bruised body and torn clothes' with care. The wounds of the three male strikers, attacked alongside her, by contrast received no mention at all. In fact, the reporter was so aggrieved by the wounding of a women that he did not even bother to record the injured men's names.[74]

These reports suggest the extent to which leaders' perceptions of working women were changing. Whereas women had once been accepted as an integral (albeit secondary) part of the local working class, now they were seen primarily as 'women', with natural proclivities for selfless domestic work. Moreover, they, more than working-class men, were the special victims of bourgeois attacks. The injury of a woman (or a child) was an event with which male socialists expected to arouse particular shock.

On the other hand, the events of the strike itself showed that such a change in thinking at the upper level of the workers' movement had effected no analogous change at the grass roots. Instead, groups of strikers elected strike committees which included women along with men. Lille strikers, moreover, chose as their spokesperson the articulate socialist and feminist Mme Sorgue. She, along with four male strikers from the textile mills of Roubaix and Tourcoing, was chosen to carry the strikers' demands to Paris.[75] Mme Sorgue reflected none of the leaders' stereotypes of the womanly woman, preoccupied with home and family. In fact, quite the contrary: she was vocal on behalf of women's claims for legal, economic, and personal equality with men. Thus the fact that Lille strikers elected her to represent them suggests that they, unlike their leaders, continued to see women's place as at the front of their movement, as well as in the soup-kitchens.

In the end, the massive general strike of the winter of 1903–4 produced only a few changes in the textile mills of the Lille area.

---

[74] 'Le Réveil du prolétariat textile', *OT* (1 May 1904).
[75] See ibid., and 'Dans le Nord—Lille. Délégation au ministère', *OT* (1 May 1904). Mme Sorgue remains a little-known figure. 'Dossier Mme Sorgue', in *Bibliothèque Marguerite Durand*, Paris, contains a few newspaper clippings describing her activities among women workers outside the Nord department. A short reference to her, along with a photograph, are found in A. Compère-Morel, *et al.*, *Encyclopédie socialiste, syndicale et coopérative de l'internationale ouvrière* (Paris, 1913), p. 145.

Four thousand Lille linen-weavers gained an 8 per cent pay-rise. Furthermore, many owners joined together to promise workers that a commission would be set up to determine future wages, a body composed of both workers and owners. Armentières workers, however, made the most significant gain. They won a uniform wage system throughout the linen industry of that city.[76] (Their achievement remained a source of frustration for Lille area workers, a frustration which finally erupted in the next general strike in 1909.)

viii

In the years between 1904 and the next general work stoppage in 1909, only one series of strikes stood out from the mass of small, spontaneous, and short-lived walk-outs in the textile mills. These 1906 strikes, again involving wool-sorters opposed to the hiring of *trieuses*, brought to the fore the increasing hostility of many male textile leaders toward working women—hostility most had kept hidden from public view in previous years.

Trieurs in both Roubaix and Tourcoing once again walked out when their employers attempted to mix their numbers with lower-paid women. Although most of the striking *trieurs* were not union members (or even active socialists) the socialist textile union leapt to their defence. Victor Renard called a strike meeting where he advised them to organize to defend their jobs. 'Remain at your sorting frames', he told them, 'and send your wives back to their housekeeping. The family budget will be higher and misery less great in your homes.'[77]

Although the *trieurs* once again prevented some local employers from mixing their wool-sorting work-rooms, their efforts were doomed in the long run. In many local mills, women already worked side by side with men in the sorting rooms, apparently without friction. In fact, in July of 1906, one Roubaix group of male and female wool-sorters together called a strike, to demand an end to the piece-rate system and higher wages. They did not demand equal pay for men and women, however. Instead, they

---

[76] *OT* (1 June 1904).

[77] See France, *Statistique des grèves 1906*, and 'Reims. La Fête syndicale des trieurs de Laines', *OT* (1 May 1906).

wanted women's wages set at 17 fr. a week, and men's at 22 fr. This meant, in effect, a wage rise only for the women, who averaged only 13.75 fr. a week on the piece-rate. Men's average wage, of 4 fr. a day, would remain the same under the new weekly pay system.[78]

Of course this strike did not necessarily mean widespread altruism among the *trieurs*. Some, no doubt, hoped that if women were paid at a rate closer to that paid to men, fewer employers would decide to hire them. In addition, many of the *trieurs* depended upon the wages of wives and daughters, as well as their own, for the support of their families. Thus, for those with female relatives working as wool-sorters, higher women's pay was an immediate benefit. None the less, the solidarity of these strikers did underline the gap between workers' perceptions of their common cause and the perceptions of male leaders such as Victor Renard, who hoped to win men's favour by pandering to more reactionary ideas of wives' domestic duties.

This division between union leaders and the mass of textile workers over this issue was only one among many such problems which continued to grow. For example, although the leadership railed against unplanned, spontaneous strikes, workers continued to use them as their primary means of expressing their views. Endless small wildcat strikes broke out between 1904 and 1909—typically over low pay, the firing of a co-worker, or efforts to speed up, or 'Taylorize' the work process. All such strikes were unorganized and unplanned. And most of them involved men and women striking together. That the union leadership continually failed to prevent such strikes—or even to shape them after they had begun—underlined a growing loss of contact between the levels of the workers' movement in the Lille area. Thus it is not surprising that the fourth general strike in the industry, which broke out in the fall of 1909, once again caught the union leaders unawares.

ix

The fact that the Armentières workers had won a uniform wage structure in 1904 continued to rankle among Lille, Roubaix, and

---

[78] See France, *Statistique des grèves 1906.*

Tourcoing workers. Moreover, the Armentières workers, fearful that their wage system might be taken away by employers under pressure from Lille area mill owners, fed the Lille workers' discontent with a constant barrage of propaganda in favour of uniform wages. When the 1909 strike finally came, therefore, it was accompanied by an unusual degree of coherence, backed by firm commitment to a single demand. One observer remarked that the entire textile community of the Lille *arrondissement* was 'hypnotized by the word "unification" '.[79] In every street workers mobilized singing this song:

> Ouverriers d'tissache
> Et d'preparation
> Luttons avec coroche
> Pou' l'Unification.
>
> Ch' est eun affaire bien légitime
> Qu' not'grève et nos r'vindications;
> On veur qu'i n'y euche pus eun'centime
> De diffirence su' les façons.
> On vodort qu'chez Pierre, Paul, ou Jacques
> L'même toile souch'payée au même prix;
> De faim, faut point qu'l'ouverrier claque
> Nou' mouv'mint n'est point *politique*
> Ni en faveur d'eun' *réligion*.
> Si y a des tisserands *catholiques*.
> Y in a aussi des *protestants*.
>
> L'toile, solide, légère, et coquette,
> Qui sort de nos mains d'ouverriers
> N'porte point marque su' l'etiquette
> L'couleur de ch' ti qui l'a tissée.[80]

Thus, the workers declared that unification of wages overrode all local divisions—between Catholics and non-Catholics, between socialists and non-socialists, between red unions and yellow unions. It was this solidarity which sustained them through the seventy-two winter days of the ensuing strike.

Throughout the strike, both yellow and red unions paid benefits

---

[79] See France, *Statistique des grèves 1906* and *1907*; and V. Renard, 'Dans l'industrie textile—les trucs patronaux', *H* (26 Jan. 1907); *AN* F⁷ 13819, 'Textile—1908'.

[80] Quoted in Léon de Seilhac, *La Grève du tissage de Lille* (Paris, 1910), p. 63.

to their own members as well as to non-unionized workers. *Jaunes* received 15 fr. a week, *rouges*, 12 fr. Socialists also received free food every week, amounting to two-thirds of a family's average weekly needs. All the unions together paid non-unionized workers—of both sexes—2.50 fr. a week. Some free food, particularly in the soup-kitchens, was also available to all strikers regardless of political or union affiliation.[81]

The strike, like every other general strike in the area's textile industry, followed a customary course.[82] Parades, mass meetings, *soupes communistes*, as well as family fêtes and endless *estaminet* discussions, marked the progress of the strike. Women strikers were at least as militant as the men, and in some cases were more so. Two photographs of strike processions, one in *Progrès du Nord* and the second in *Petite République*, showed more women than men among crowds of strikers.[83]

But, as was the case in 1903–4, women's equal militancy was in no way reflected in outsiders' reports of the strike. Instead, reporters continued to patronize working women's collective efforts by suggesting that such behaviour was very un-usual. One reporter, describing a strike parade, was moved to maudlin eloquence by the presence of women. They were, he wrote, 'the objects of lively curiosity'. Moreover, the younger *ouvrières* 'showed much merit, because they had got themselves out of bed at an early hour in order to be on time at the meeting-place. Furthermore, since their arrival at the *Place de la République*, they have walked more than 16 kilo-metres.'[84]

Given these same women's daily early rising as well as the considerable energy they expended in the mills, this reporter's words revealed his astounding ignorance, whch would have struck the women strikers themselves as ludicrous. Equal ignorance, however, was expressed by a second reporter who viewed women's appearance with exaggerated pity. Describing one group of young *rattacheuses*, grouped together in a procession, he noted their 'pale faces and sorrowful expressions'. He went on: 'These

[81] Ibid., pp. 66, 79. See also: *AN* F⁷ 13820, 'Textiles—Presse. 1090'; *H* (1Nov. 1909).
[82] 'Nos Grèves—Lille', *OT* (1 Nov. 1909).
[83] *AN* F⁷ 13820.
[84] Ibid.

are young girls made anaemic by the harassing labour of the factory.'[85]

As was the case in 1903–4, women's behaviour belied the accuracy of such outsiders' views. Once again, local workers chose a militant feminist as a spokeswoman. This woman, Gabrielle Petit, was an ardent neo-Malthusian as well as a feminist. In one mass meeting, in Lille, she shocked male *syndicalistes* by climbing onto a table and demanding a separate meeting of women strikers, where they could discuss 'birth control, women's health, and an end to corsets'. Her words were greeted with 'good-natured laughter', according to one witness. Many of the women in the audience responded to her mention of birth control by holding their infants above their heads and crying: 'We knew what we were doing.'[86]

Although the radical feminism of Gabrielle Petit clearly fell on mostly deaf ears, it provoked no hostility. Quite the contrary, in fact. Like Mme Sorgue before her, she remained a popular speaker in the textile cities in the years before the First World War.

Despite the strength of the workers' intentions, despite the length of the strike, a unified wage structure remained beyond their collective grasp. The strike ended with few tangible gains: a few among the more sympathetic mill owners granted their workers a small pay-rise, but most got nothing. A 2½ month effort, then, came to naught.

X

The textile strikes of the *belle époque*, particularly those which spread throughout the mills of the three cities, showed that women and men tended to participate equally, and in very similar ways. At the same time, reports of the strikes, from both the socialist press and the bourgeois press, reflected the ways in which leaders' perceptions of women's roles changed over time. As the years went on, many male leaders increasingly saw women in their biological identity—which in turn shaped popular stereotypes of 'women's weaker nature' and women's special victimization in industry.

---

[85] Ibid.
[86] Seilhac, *La Grève*, p. 72.

In most cases, these observations found no evidence in fact. Nothing in women's collective strike behaviour showed either their weakness or their perceptions of their special nature. But industrial strikes were not the only form of mass behaviour in which women indulged in the *belle époque*. We have mentioned the organized socialist women's campaigns for free school lunches of the 1890s, which had been led by women in Lille and Roubaix. In addition to that campaign, the women of the Nord department launched a second mass effort, in this case aimed to bring down rising food prices. This effort became the great food riots of 1911.

These food 'riots'—the term was used by officials to denigrate the organized and sometimes violent efforts of women—were important for two reasons. Firstly, they were organized and led by working-class women. The tactics and strategies employed by these women, moreover, demonstrated the level of organizational sophistication achieved in the workers' movement of the area by 1911. Secondly, the working women of the area sought and obtained the co-operation of their bourgeois sisters in their mass demonstrations. These food riots thus became the only events in the *belle époque* which defied the stark class divisions which shaped every other mass protest throughout the period.[87]

The 'riots' began in August 1911, when women textile workers, together with miners' wives, joined together to parade through the streets and roads of most northern towns and cities, protesting against the intolerably high prices of milk, butter, and especially eggs. Their marches continued, day after day. As time went on, tempers flared; many protesters began waylaying food wagons, turning them over, spilling milk and breaking eggs. As a result of these activities, troops were posted along most routes to ensure the safe passage of food vehicles in and out of the Nord's towns and cities. Women reacted to the arrival of troops by organizing meetings to plan further strategy. They elected leaders, and voted to continue their parades, this time avoiding violence, spreading their message instead via huge banners.

---

[87] Women's demonstrations against high food prices had a long history in France, and the behaviour of the Nord women had much in common with earlier mass riots. See Olwen Hufton, 'Women in Revolution, 1789–1796', *Past and Present*, liii (1971), pp. 90–108, and Louise Tilly, 'The Food Riot as a form of political conflict in France', *Journal of Interdisciplinary History*, ii (1971), pp. 23–58.

In Valenciennes, the women protesters added one further tactic. They reasoned that the troops would not hesitate to charge a working-class women's march. So they decided to recruit women of the local bourgeoisie—readily identifiable by their distinct hats—to walk in front of the parades in order to deter the troops. Their parade began early in the morning, when the movement's leaders went from door to door in bourgeois districts asking women to don their hats and gloves and to march at the head of their lines. Many *bourgeoises* agreed willingly, and took up positions at the front of the parade. Together, the women marched into the Valenciennes town centre, singing the Internationale. As the organizers had hoped, the presence of bourgeois women effectively prevented any openly hostile reaction from the troops massed along the way.[88]

Other groups of women, however, lacking the support of bourgeois women, found the forces of order ready and willing to break up their demonstrations. At Fourmies, 4,000 women crowded the streets, singing the Internationale and waving red banners. Local police reacted harshly, charging the crowd and arresting many participants for 'threatening behaviour'.[89]

Given male union leaders' claims to support the organization of women workers into unions, one might have expected that they would greet the food protests with joy—especially as the protesters organized a department-wide *syndicat* during the strike. But no such positive reactions were forthcoming. Instead, some male leaders in the region met the food protests with patronizing instructions to the women as to how they ought to leave such demonstrations to the men who knew better than they did now to run such public events. Other men, particularly those from outside the Nord department, attempted to explain women's collective protest against high food prices as a natural outgrowth of their biological role. Georges Yvetot, a syndicalist militant, seems to have thought women carried a genetic proclivity for food economies. He wrote, 'with their economical sense of things, women have found that it is time to put an end to the insane height

[88] 'Échos—Belles Mesdames', *BS* (6–12 Sept. 1911).
[89] B. Broutchoux, 'Quelques détails', *BS* (6–12 Sept. 1911). See also Émile Pouget, 'L'Émeute de la faim', Ibid., and 'Les Ménagères du Nord luttent contre la vie chère', *BS* (28 Aug. 1911).

of prices for necessary produce.' He lamented men's absence from the movement. 'Women, without us,' he told his male readers, 'have felt the need to react against this scandalous increase.' Moreover, men should see that 'the woman, the *éternelle sacrifiée*, seems finally to want to take her place at the banquet of life'. People were in for a surprise, he added, because 'a revolutionary movement into which women throw themselves is always special'.[90] A second writer joined his applause to Yvetot's: 'Brave women', he wrote, 'are acting like men.' Among the movement's leaders, he added, were 'even some *femmes cyclistes!*'[91]

Victor Renard typified the reaction of Nord department union leaders to the mass protest in their midst. He had two primary concerns. Firstly he worried that the women's activities—carried on in the name of the socialist movement—would compromise socialist promises to small shopkeepers and male peasants to guard their interests in exchange for their votes. Secondly, he feared that women could not carry out an organized protest without men. He wrote in *L'Ouvrier textile*, 'I can understand the anger of housewives—wives of proletarians in metal-work and textiles, whose men suffer daily in the capitalist hell . . . but I am concerned that the little people will get caught in the women's anger. . . . I deplore the fact that poor little people, with their few kilos of butter and their few quarters of eggs, are victims of the crowd's demands . . .' The only way to prevent such errors was for women to put themselves into his hands. 'I have said that this awakening of consciousness among the *femmes ouvrières* augurs well. I view these demonstrations with satisfaction. Only, it is necessary that they be organized, methodical, and well directed. To that end, it is necessary that workers' organizations—unions, co-operatives, *Parti socialiste*—take over the direction of the movement, and that they stimulate the actions of these leagues of consumers who can agree with the producers to establish contractual prices.' Only thus, Renard concluded, could 'tumultuous, chaotic demonstrations be avoided; regrettable scenes of pillage, of shop-window breaking, assault and battery, and other violent things that will change nothing'.[92]

[90] 'La Révolte des affamés', *VdP* (10–17 Sept. 1911).
[91] Broutchoux, 'Quelques détails,' *BS* (6–12 Sept. 1911).
[92] V. Renard, 'La Cherté de la vie', *OT* (1 Nov. 1911).

Not surprisingly, the women paid him no attention. But his rhetoric underlines the extent to which the national textile union of 1911 was a completely male organization. Even the women textile workers who joined the food price protest were, in Renard's eyes, not *workers*, but *wives* of workers. In that role they formed no constituency for his union, but only potential background for the men. This attitude, of course, is a primary factor in the reasons for the absence of the vast majority of women textile workers in Renard's national textile federation.

In 1912, Renard altogether ceased attempting to hide his hostility to women in the workers' movement. During the last of the wool-sorters' strikes, in 1912, he threw the full support of the socialist textile union behind the *trieurs*' efforts to prevent women from taking jobs as sorters. He declared that his union was solidly against the employment of women in 'a man's occupation'.[93] As for equality, as for the earlier socialist rhetoric about women's right to work for their economic independence, well, those ideas had never had a prominent place in textile union propaganda, and now they had gone for good.

This brief overview of changing relations between women textile workers and the organized union movement is, of course, only a fragment of a much larger picture of relations between *ouvrières* and the socialist political movement. It is to the latter story that we now turn our attention in order to examine the ways in which women's politics during the *belle époque* grew increasingly separate from the politics of the party which claimed to represent them.

The narrative falls into two parts. First, between 1880 and 1896, relations between women and socialists were generally good. Chapter 5 examines those relations in detail. After 1896, however, a gap developed between women textile workers and leaders of the socialist party, which mirrored that increasingly apparent in the union movement. Chapter 6 narrates the unhappy history of these declining relations—to the point where working women virtually disappeared from the view of socialist leaders on the eve of the Great War.

[93] *AN* F⁷ 13820, 'Textile—1910–1914'.

5

WOMEN IN GUESDIST POLITICS,
1880–1897

i

THE story of the relations between women textile workers in the Lille *arrondissement* and the local socialist party is even more complex than that describing relations between women workers and textile unions. Four elements underlay these relations as they developed in the years between 1880 and 1914. Firstly, practical political problems—particularly that posed by an exclusively male suffrage—persistently reshaped the ways in which the local party addressed their female constituents. Secondly, and more importantly, ideological issues—unique to Marxian socialism—confronted leaders who formed policy and chose tactics and strategies. And whereas the industrial proletariat played a straightforward role in Marxist analyses of capitalist society, women proletarians—*qua* women—did not. Instead, they presented a constant theoretical irritant to party ideologues in our period. Thirdly, the period after 1880 was one of national and international socialist organization, and decisions at both levels necessarily affected the behaviour of local socialist leaders in Lille, Roubaix, and Tourcoing. Finally, leadership was a key issue in the formation of socialist policies *vis-à-vis* their female constituency. Both the presence or absence of women socialist leaders and the attitudes of male leaders toward women coloured the ways in which socialist organizations in the Nord department regarded the mobilization of working women.

At every turn of events, therefore, an interplay of forces was at work, shaping the local party's actions toward women. Not least among these forces were the women themselves, who voted with their feet if not with ballots. This chapter takes up the early years of socialist growth, from 1880 to the mid-1890s, and follows a chronological pattern which focuses on the rise of local working women's socialist politics in these years. It begins, however, with a brief overview of local socialist developments, the background against which the more particular politics of textile *ouvrières* evolved.

ii

Socialist politics, properly so-called, in Lille, Roubaix, and, latterly, Tourcoing, began in the latter half of the 1870s, when the first post-Commune stirrings of workers' organizations were felt locally. These culminated in the organization, in 1879, of a *comité d'initiative*, the purpose of which was to select delegates and issues for the Marseilles workers' congress held in the autumn of that year. The first delegates chosen from Lille were not committed to any particular socialist movement or system of ideas. But, quite soon after the close of the 1879 congress, most of them began to swing toward the most clearly Marxist of the various *tendances* represented in the workers' movement of that day. This *tendance* was led by Jules Guesde, whose ideas rapidly won over socialist workers in the Nord.[1]

These early militants returned from Marseilles prepared to immerse themselves in local politics. In 1880, one Marseilles delegate, Gustave Jonquet, became the first socialist candidate for local office, standing for election in the south-east canton of Lille, where he won a surprising 21.6 per cent of the vote. Simultaneously, a number of small, *quartier*-based socialist study groups emerged in the area, organized to learn the new vocabulary of Marxism, transmitted in brochures and in the socialist newspaper edited by Jules Guesde, *L'Égalité*.

These several small local groups, as we have seen, were the core of the first local section of Jules Guesde's *Parti ouvrier français*, founded in 1881 in Roubaix by Henri Carrette and Achille Lepers. The Roubaix section was quickly joined by one in Lille, headed by Gustave Jonquet and Gustave Delory, and one in Tourcoing, led by the popular song-writer (and later police informer) Victor Capart.

The electoral programme of these Guesdists was that written the year before in London by Jules Guesde and Paul Lafargue, with the advice of Marx and Engels. Basically, the programme had two goals: firstly, to organize the French working class into a force

---

[1] Details are found in Claude Willard, *Les Guesdistes: le mouvement socialiste en France (1893–1905)* (Paris, 1965), and Robert Baker, 'A Regional study of working-class organization in France: Socialism in the Nord 1870–1924' Ph.D. Stanford University, 1967. See also *ADN* 154 79, 'Organisation du Parti ouvrier. Congrès de Marseille, de Roubaix et de Lille'.

which would, eventually, launch the proletarian revolution in the name of its own liberation from capitalist economic structures; and, secondly, to elect socialists to office who would institute immediate reforms in workers' conditions.[2]

In addition, this programme offered several promises attractive to the textile workers in the Lille area. Among immediate ameliorative reforms were the establishment of free—or low-cost—school meals for workers' children, as well as a twice-yearly distribution of clothing and shoes for the poorest children. In addition, the party promised reforms which would allow workers more control over their lives. These included factory work inspectors chosen by the workers themselves and including workers (both male and female) among them. The programme also pledged support for an elected area commission, comprising both local workers and members of the *patronat*, which would regulate work practices, fix bread and milk prices, establish rent controls, oversee the repair of substandard housing, and offer free public services for the poor including medical care (with maternity care for all women, whether married or not), drugs, and baths in municipal bath houses.[3]

Throughout the 1880s, these promises formed the heart of the local *POF* message. In addition to spreading these socialist party promises, local *POF* leaders launched a massive effort to transform the cultural and social lives of the Flemish workers into what ultimately became a genuinely socialist subculture. The largely communitarian traditions of local sociability lent themselves perfectly to the socialists' ends. In the 1880s, socialists gradually absorbed most of the cultural traditions of French Flanders. The May lace-makers' fête of *Broquelet* was the first to assume a distinctly political air early in the decade, but other local festivals rapidly followed suit. In addition, socialists used marionette shows, amateur theatricals, and music to spread their message throughout the workers' *quartiers*. Worker puppets fought greedy capitalists; proletarian girls fell victim to bourgeois seducers in countless popular melodramas. And both poets and composers increasingly contributed their talents to the party, which took

---

[2] Quoted in Adéodat Compère-Morel, *Jules Guesde, le socialisme fait homme, 1845–1922* (Paris, 1937).
[3] See 'Élections municipales de Lille', *CdT* (11–14 Apr. 1888).

special pains to recruit them. The best known of local songs was, in fact, the Internationale, written by the local poet Eugène Pottier and set to music by a Lille textile worker, Pierre de Geyter, at the behest of Gustave Delory. First sung in Lille in 1888, the Internationale soon became the hymn of the workers' movement throughout the industrialized world.

By far the most important vehicles for the spread of the local socialist message were the ubiquitous *estaminets* of Lille, Roubaix, and Tourcoing. Because every worker—of either sex and all ages—used his or her 'local' as a second home, the oral dissemination of political ideas—fortified by a vast consumption of beer and gin—was rapid.

As soon as the *patronat* became aware of the growing importance of these political *estaminets*, they sponsored some of their own—sweetening their efforts to lure workers to their side with free food and drink. In addition, other local interest groups joined the war of the *cabarets*. By 1890, no *estaminet* was without a political identity. Socialists, anarchists, republicans, and conservative Catholics vied for the loyalties of working-class customers. Among textile workers, however, it was no contest. The great majority of their café-bars remained socialist centres throughout the *belle époque*.

By the end of the 1880s, socialists had a large enough constituency to justify starting their own printing-press to produce the vast quantities of brochures, broadsheets, songs, posters, and so on without government interference. Gustave Delory (blacklisted by the textile *patronat*) was put in charge of the new socialist press in Lille. Pages and pages of socialist propaganda began to pour from its presses into socialist *estaminets* where they were read aloud and passed from hand to hand among local workers.

The local *POF* also took over long-established food co-operatives, including the two largest, the *Union* of Lille and *Paix* in Roubaix. After 1880, membership in a socialist co-op effectively constituted informal membership in the *POF*. The party used the vast public halls of both co-ops for mass recruiting meetings as well as for fund-raising benefits. Moreover, the importance of these centres of food distribution to the spread of socialist influence in the area became instantly obvious during the general strike of 1880, when co-op members received free food and were welcomed to the strikers' soup-kitchens set up in the co-ops' premises. In the event, the edible benefits of joining the *POF* co-ops were instantly apparent.

Finally, as we have seen, socialist politicians wasted no time in creating socialist textile unions, led by loyal party members. The activities of these unions, particularly during strikes, provided effective agitprop for the local party. After only ten years of work, then, the local *POF* had succeeded in politicizing popular culture as well as in organizing many workers into more formal socialist groups, including study groups and food co-operatives. As Jules Guesde quickly recognized, the next step was to mould these disparate and fragmented groups into an organized political party. To that end, he assigned to Gustave Delory the task of reorganizing this amalgam of socialist clubs into proper party sections in 1889. Most local study groups quickly became official party sections. (These, in turn, formed the nucleus of what became, later in the 1890s, a more centralized, nationally based political party.) By the close of 1889, Delory reported to Guesde that the new local *POF* organization had succeeded in mobilizing 'entire *quartiers*' of Lille and Roubaix.[4] (Tourcoing's *quartiers* remained aloof from the charmed circle, as the majority of that city's voters—whether worker or *patron*—stayed loyal to the progressive radical, Gustave Dron, who held office as mayor and as deputy well into the twentieth century.)

The first major socialist victory followed rapidly. In 1891, Lille voters sent Paul Lafargue to the *Chambre*. His victory owed something to the careful reorganization of local *POF* forces. But it is doubtful that it would have occurred without the Fourmies massacre of May Day, 1891, when charging troops wounded or killed thirty-nine local workers, demonstrating in support of an eight-hour day. The result of that well-publicized blood-letting was that hundreds of French workers lost their faith in the still new republic. When state officials compounded their error by flinging Paul Lafargue and a local Fourmies Guesdist, Hippolyte Culine, into prison for inciting the riot leading to the deaths, they handed the socialists a massive propaganda tool. The campaign to free Lafargue from prison became at the same time an election campaign. His win, moreover, showed how rapidly the Fourmies massacre had increased the local vote. Lafargue won 5,005 votes in

---

[4] IISH, 'Dossier Jules Guesde', Delory to Guesde (26 Apr. 1889).

the first round—nearly 30 per cent of the vote—in a district where Delory had won only 1,406 votes (about 7 per cent) one year earlier.[5]

Following Lafargue's election, socialist victories in Lille and Roubaix multiplied. In 1892, Roubaix's voters returned a socialist municipal council, headed by Henri Carrette (who remained mayor until 1902). In the following year, Roubaix elected Jules Guesde its deputy, thereby earning two popular appellations— 'la ville sainte de socialisme' and 'Roubaix rouge'—by which it came to be known throughout Europe.

In Lille, voters followed Roubaix's lead, electing a socialist municipal council in 1895, headed by Gustave Delory. (His tenure as mayor lasted until 1904 when, like Henri Carrette, he fell victim to voters' annoyance with what they saw as constant socialist wrangling in the area.)

The picture in Tourcoing was bleaker for local socialist hopes. Although the *POF* was not without support among the textile workers of that city, it remained a minority party until a few years before the Great War. Part of the socialists' failure was due to Tourcoing's *POF* leader, Victor Capart, whose commitment to socialism was, as we have seen, less than firm. But more important still was the harmony between classes which characterized the population. A traditional loyalty to Tourcoing, bolstered by the ready paternalism of the textile *patronat*, dampened the effects of socialist agitation throughout the years before the turn of the century. Better treated than their neighbours, Tourcoing's workers offered a frustratingly unenthusiastic constituency for socialist efforts.

By 1895, then, fifteen years of socialist organization had produced both electoral and cultural successes for the *POF* in Lille and Roubaix—and some cultural successes, at least, in recalcitrant Tourcoing. On the other hand, it must be remembered that the bones of the *POF*—disciplined cadres, dues-paying members— comprised only a minority of the textile workers of the three cities in that year. Men and women who willingly joined campaigns and marched in socialist parades—who, moreover, filled their leisure hours with socialist activities of every variety—as well as men who

[5] Details of the election are found in Félix-Paul Codaccioni, 'L'Élection de Paul Lafargue 1891', *RdN*, vol. ccxx (Jan.–Mar. 1974), pp. 43–7.

consistently voted for socialist candidates, rarely brought themselves to the point of paying dues to the official party. Unwaveringly loyal to what they perceived as their class interests—a loyalty tested in countless demonstrations and strikes—most workers saw little reason to prove that loyalty by spending a part of their small wages on official party membership. Nevertheless, despite small membership figures, most textile workers' politics were clearly socialist. Moreover, the language with which they described their situation was increasingly the language of Marxist discourse: class struggle, rebellion against exploitation of labour by capitalists, and so on.

The trajectory of socialist fortunes in the Lille area during these first fifteen years quickly split into two parts after 1880. On one side was the public socialism of the local working class, expressed in popular culture and in political discourse. On the other was the official party itself, increasingly organized into a disciplined hierarchy—a form deeply antithetical to Flemish tradition. In 1895, however, only the most percipient observer might have noted the problems such a division would provoke in the ensuing years. Most were blinded by the speed of the socialist take-over in the area and believed that the *POF* was solidly entrenched in Roubaix and Lille, and well on its way to conquering neighbouring Tourcoing.

iii

Throughout the early years of Guesdist organizing in the Lille area, *ouvrières* joined with local men in virtually all aspects of socialist activity. The party responded to their presence and enthusiasm by including them equally in most party debates. Moreover, considerable propaganda efforts were directed at *ouvrières*—both as women and as workers. In fact, among the most frequently discussed problems in the workers' *quartiers* in these years was women's right to equality with men—both in the work-place and in the domestic *foyer*.

In the 1880s party leaders spread the *POF* position on this issue throughout the area via vast public meetings which featured four key socialist speakers: Jules Guesde himself, along with Paule Minck, Léonie Rouzade, and Louise Michel. All four were tireless, appearing on countless platforms in Lille and Roubaix—

and, more rarely, Tourcoing—throughout the years 1880 and 1895.

The outlines of what became the official Guesdist line on women's equality were first promulgated by Jules Guesde in an 1876 pamphlet, 'The Rights of Man'. In that essay, Guesde took a remarkably progressive stand on the issue. Unlike many other socialist leaders of the period, he made no attempt to straddle a safe line between widespread traditional ideas of women's place in the home and their obvious, growing presence in the industrial work-force. Instead, he argued that 'women's place' was within the socialist movement where, together with their male co-workers, they could liberate themselves both from the exploitative grip of industrial capitalism and from confining domestic relations. Furthermore, he embraced women's waged work as the single means by which they might free themselves from that economic dependence which kept them enslaved to men. He also argued that women needed to work in order to become fully human—to discover the extent of their individual capacities, and to enjoy the freedom to fulfill these capacities. In Guesde's words: '. . . woman's place is no longer in the home. She is everywhere her activity can, and wishes to deploy itself. Why, by what right, lock her up in the cage of her sex which thus is transformed, whether she wishes it or not, into a profession, or even into a business?'

Guesde added, moreover, 'man also has functions related to his sex. But these do not prevent him from being a doctor, an artist, a manual or mental worker!' Thus, he concluded, a woman must be similarly free from the dictates of her biology in order 'to manifest herself socially in the form which best suits her'.[6]

Guesde was not unaware of the unpopularity of his position among many male workers of the period. In an attempt to defuse men's hostility to women's equality, he wrote an article in *Égalité* in 1878 which argued gently against widespread male prejudices.[7] He began by agreeing that women's presence in the waged labour force did present special problems. Firstly, in the context of the prevailing economic conditions of the late 1870s few working women could subsist on their wages alone. This fact collapsed the

---

[6] Quoted in Compère-Morel, *Jules Guesde*, pp. 110–11.
[7] Guesde, 'Le Travail des femmes', *É* (27 Jan. 1878).

Marxist principle that workers' wages could not fall below the level necessary for the reproduction of the labour force. Why? 'Because', Guesde wrote, 'an *ouvrière* can find in her sex, transformed into merchandise, the resources which she otherwise lacks. The remuneration for her work, therefore, need not be so high as to allow her to subsist.' And once capitalists became aware of women's option, they paid women less than men. This, in turn, meant serious competition for male workers. It was this fact, Guesde noted, which explained the cry of so many male workers: 'woman's place is in the home.' He cautioned, however, that such a position was both 'unrealistic and unethical'. If women's work in the present system constituted an evil, it must be transformed by the workers' movement into a good, as women would never against exist solely within the home. Moreover, women must not be confined within the domestic sphere because of their sex—lest that existence become 'at one time both the sole reason for her being as well as the sole means of her being'. Given Marx's dictum that work is the essential characteristic of humanness, as well as the means through which each individual attains fulfilment, women who existed only by virtue of a domestic or sexual relation with a man would necessarily enjoy only a 'conditional existence'. Thus, Guesde concluded, Proudhon's pronouncement, 'housewife or courtesan' was 'entirely contrary to socialism'. In fact, a socialist analysis of women's circumstances revealed no difference between the two roles: a housewife unable to exist outside her domestic relationship had merely sold herself to a husband just as a prostitute sold herself to a customer. Only socialism would break the market relations of this sexual economy by ensuring that women could work for their own independence, owing nothing to anyone.

However attractive to working women, or however consistent with Marxist principles, these ideas left Guesde, and with him his movement, wide open to accusations that socialism disdained the family—as sacrosanct an entity then as it remains today. In these early years Guesde answered such attacks by pointing out that economically emancipated women were at the same time intellectually emancipated human beings, who could become the equal partners, rather than the ignorant slaves, of their husbands. Families, Guesde argued, would cease forming solely around economic relations; instead they would be grounded in 'common interests, reciprocal satisfaction, and love'. These factors together safeguarded 'the dignity of all parties'.[8]

Far from remaining in the ideological ether, far above the heads of the masses of textile workers, these radical new ideas found a large and enthusiastic audience in the workers' *quartiers* of the Lille area in the 1880s and early 1890s. There they were promulgated in mass meetings, held after working hours, often in the meeting-halls of food co-operatives, in Lille's large *Hippodrome*, or in some of the bigger *estaminets*. One typical meeting, held in the Roubaix suburb of Fontenoy in the autumn of 1881, was described by Guesde's friend and biographer, Adéodat Compère-Morel. It is worth quoting in detail:

In the midst of complete silence . . . Guesde was able to speak about how woman, both as woman and as worker, was the *grande sacrifiée* of the present social order. He demonstrated that in the civic order, subordinated to man, to whom she owes obedience as father and husband, and without whose formal consent she can make no move, woman can accomplish nothing. In the political realm it is worse still: there, the woman does not exist!

National sovereignty is the sovereignty of the nation's masculine party. The rights of the male citizen have been proclaimed but the rights of the female citizen have never been discussed, and the bourgeois order does not wish to speak of them. Prostitute, housewife, or factory machine, such is the triple role, or more specifically the triple prison, into which it intends to enclose the woman—become a being in an under order, something like a lap-dog or a cart-horse.

. . . .

The *Parti ouvrier* . . . intends to end this triple civil, political, and economic exploitation of woman—that is to say, of half of humanity. Alone among all the existing political parties, socialists proclaim the equality of woman and man. Alone, in the transformed society, they call for the enjoyment of the same rights and the sharing of the same duties. . . .

We demand, moreover, that no distinction be made between girls and boys and that all children of both sexes find in society, until the age of work, the double guarantee of a complete scientific and professional education, and the satisfaction of their physiological needs.

[8] 'De la famille', *É* (16 June 1878).

Personally, Guesde concluded, you would not benefit from this last reform, but it would benefit your children. . . .

The women applauded his speech so warmly that Guesde ended the evening saying, 'You are convinced, are you not, *citoyennes*? Your applause proves it to me.'[9]

Local working women's enthusiasm did not go unnoticed by local party leaders. Militants were quick to comprehend the importance of the women's energy in their organizational work. Thus, after 1881, virtually every socialist meeting focused on recruiting women to the party. To this end, socialists included women speakers and organizers in most party-sponsored events. Fortunately, three national women leaders made themselves available to the Lille and Roubaix Guesdists throughout the organizational period of the 1880s.

iv

Of the three, the most popular was undoubtedly Paule Minck. Although she—along with most other women activists of the late nineteenth century—awaits a biographer, several recent historians have retrieved at least the outlines of her active life.[10] Born in Clermont-Ferrand, the daughter of Polish *émigrés*, Minck first became active in radical politics during the Second Empire. From the first, she was committed to the struggle for women's equality, which she saw as integral to the struggle of all oppressed groups in French society. Working within the political clubs of the 1860s, Minck helped shape the politics which exploded into the Commune. Forced into exile after the fall of the Commune, she met Jules Guesde with whom she remained in close contact throughout her period in Switzerland. Convinced by his brand of Marxian socialism, she joined the Guesdist movement upon her return to France after the amnesty.

Minck enjoyed enormous popularity among Lille area textile workers. Even police spies, normally hostile and sarcastic about the socialists' various women speakers, admitted that she was a

---

[9] Compère-Morel, *Jules Guesde*, pp. 218–19.

[10] See Alain Dalôtel, ed., *Paule Minck: communarde et féministe, 1839–1901* (Paris, 1981); Marilyn Boxer and Jean Quataert, eds., *Socialist Women: European Socialist Feminism in the Nineteenth and Twentieth Centuries* (New York, 1978).

compelling personality. One police informer wrote in 1881 that Minck's local audiences were 'completely taken in by her charms'. Another agreed that 'her imposing figure commands respect'.[11]

Among her most frequent lecture topics in this decade was one titled 'Women's Work'. In this lecture, Minck argued that idealizing woman's role as wife and mother was wrong. Criticizing the excessive burdens of waged women was not the same as saying that woman should not work at all outside her home. 'Work', Minck told her audiences, 'does not destroy beauty and grace but rather brings health by using the body, and moral beauty by developing the brain.' As for remarks such as 'women are the weaker sex', Minck said, 'we have had enough of these ringing banalities, which are recognized by nearly everyone as inane; we want to live and to bloom in the sunshine of liberty, and not continue to vegetate and yearn without voice, without strength, and nearly without thoughts!'

Minck's lecture also included a message to the men in her audience. She told them, 'Woman is neither a slave, nor a queen, nor an idol; she is a human being like you, having the same right to autonomy. She is the friend, the companion of her husband and not his saint. . . . Take away her right to work and you do it only for masculine pleasure. Work alone gives independence—without it, no dignity is possible.'[12]

The two other women who visited the Nord repeatedly in these years, Louise Michel and Léonie Rouzade, shared Minck's ideas. Rouzade's grasp of the socialist principles which underlay Minck's ideas was, however, rather feeble. Instead of theoretical coherence, Rouzade relied on her gifts as a forceful and enthusiastic speaker as well as on her deep commitment to feminism. During one lengthy and typically confused speech at Lille's *Hippodrome* in 1882 (which attracted 1500 local people, among them about 500 women), Rouzade attacked popular beliefs in men's superiority— an attack which drew both applause and sympathetic laughter from the crowd, according to eyewitnesses. She pointed out that the Catholic Church blamed women's original sin for all the wrongs of the world. But in her eyes, Eve's desire to have knowledge of good and evil 'provided sufficient evidence of her

[11] APP, Ba 1178, 'Dossier Paule Minck'.
[12] Quoted in Dalôtel, *Minck*, p. 122.

intelligence'. She claimed that ideas of male superiority were bourgeois ideas, spread by bourgeois writers in an effort 'to prove that two plus two equal six'. According to one reporter present, these assertions drew more enthusiastic cries from her audience.[13]

Like Rouzade, Michel held views that were far from the strict Marxism of Jules Guesde or his party. Michel's 'revolution', to which she referred constantly, had more in common with the revolution espoused in that period by French anarchists (who, incidentally, claimed her as one of their heroines). This event would come about by the spontaneous uprising of all the wretched of the earth (and not just the proletariat). Because (in Michel's eyes) women—all women—were among these wretched, whether or not they worked for wages, they were an essential constituency for revolution.

Michel was beloved by the workers of the Lille *arrondissement* in the *belle époque* and they turned out to hear her in large numbers. In addition, however, many were attracted to her meetings out of curiosity, provoked by the loathing in which the bourgeoisie held her.[14] The bourgeois press castigated every appearance of the 'red virgin' of the Commune, the putative leader of the feared, and mostly apocryphal, *pétroleuses* of Paris. Such rhetoric aroused hostile crowds who frequently turned her local appearances into riots.

Most of Michel's speeches mixed socialist rhetoric—'proletarians, work for the revolution'—and moral outrage. Before one audience of 2500 textile workers (again, the reporter estimated that a third of them were women) gathered in Lille in 1882, Michel spoke in fiery tones. 'Women are revolting against the tyranny of capital', she told her audience, 'and this augurs well for the social revolution. . . . Woman cannot live from her work, but no longer wishes to sell herself. She disdains the turpitude of the bourgeois order!' 'Warm applause', in the words of one witness, 'greeted her words.'[15]

Rouzade, Minck, Jules Guesde, and Michel, together these four national figures articulated the *POF*'s message of women's

---

[13] *ADN* M 154 61, 'Compte-rendu de la conférence faite par la citoyenne Léonie Rouzade et le citoyen John Labusquière, 15 mai 1882'.
[14] See Édith Thomas, *Louise Michel*, trans. by Penelope Williams (Montreal, 1980), and Michel, *Mémoires* (Paris, 1977).
[15] Reported in 'La Presse bourgeoise et le Parti ouvrier à Lille', *LF* (5 Nov. 1882).

liberation from countless socialist platforms in the 1880s. Frequently, they were joined at the speaker's rostrum by local Guesdist leaders, including Gustave Delory and Henri Ghesquière, who shared a commitment to recruiting local women into the party. The frequency of such meetings, moreover, underlined the extent to which the issues concerning women's equality were integral to the Lille socialists' efforts in these early, formative years.

But these socialist politics were not merely empty words. To a large extent, practice mirrored theory (though unfortunately it was a practice not unmarred by competing theories of women's place and nature). The party approached women workers in three ways. Firstly, they addressed women as members of working-class families, whose collective interests, they promised, were served by membership in various socialist enterprises (including food co-ops, savings and insurance schemes, and so on) as well as by the election of socialists to public office. Socialist candidates promised 'fathers and mothers' a range of municipal reforms which would improve the lives of their children. Secondly, socialists talked to women as workers, whose class interests were identical with those of their male co-workers. Thirdly, local militants acted on a generally unformulated understanding that women comprised a special group among the proletariat. To that end, they promoted several meetings restricted to women only—on the occasionally articulated grounds that women would feel freer to join the party without pressure from male family members. At such women-only meetings, agendas included women's emancipation from their 'double slavery', as well as the party's commitment to women's right to stand and to vote for *conseils des prud'hommes*, and for factory work inspectors.

Women workers in the area heard the socialist message in such meetings, as well as in the *estaminets* which they frequented after work and at weekends. In addition, printed party propaganda reached them, as it did others in the textile community. Posters, pamphlets, brochures, leaflets, printed party programmes, and so on flooded the workers' *quartiers*, and were handed round surreptitiously in the mills during work breaks. Most were also read aloud in the *estaminets* for those many workers of both sexes who could not read. Many socialist ideas also found their way into popular songs, which, in their turn, brought them into popular discourse.

Most of the party's official records, moreover, highlighted women's emancipation. Among the first of these documents was the original invitation to an organizational meeting of the *comité d'initiative* of Lille, Roubaix, and Tourcoing, held at the beginning of 1879. The meeting's purpose was to formulate an agenda and choose delegates for the Marseilles workers' congress to be held later that year. The invitation was addressed '*citoyennes et citoyens*', and contained a specific invitation to women to offer their suggestions for the agenda. In a further effort to encourage women's participation, the organizers suggested that one possible agenda item might concern the ways in which the workers' movement could help ameliorate the peculiarly hard conditions suffered by women working in industry.[16]

At the Marseilles congress, the Lille area delegates supported a strongly worded resolution supporting women's equality which committed the workers' movement to a wide range of activities which today would together constitute a programme of affirmative action. This resolution committed the movement to include women in every activity—including study groups, election committees, and all meetings. Indeed, it was a gesture of 'breadth and profundity', as Charles Sowerwine has noted.[17]

It should be observed, however, that there was a worm in this apple. The resolution owed most of its breadth to the tireless activities of the bourgeois feminists led by Hubertine Auclert, who had formed what proved to be only a temporary alliance with the workers' movement. The resolution was, therefore, essentially the product of a short-lived and artificial alliance between groups whose interests diverged on virtually every other important issue.[18]

Nevertheless, Jules Guesde's own views, as we have seen, did not vary significantly from those contained in the 1879 resolution. And because of this, the feminist message found its way into the workers' movement as it took shape in the *quartiers* of Lille, Roubaix, and Tourcoing in the ensuing years.

[16] *ADN* M 154 79, 'Organisation du Parti ouvrier. Congrès de Marseille, de Roubaix et de Lille (1879–1890).

[17] Charles Sowerwine, *Sisters or Citizens? Women and Socialism in France Since 1876* (Cambridge, 1982), p. 26.

[18] Sowerwine details the influence of the bourgeois feminist Hubertine Auclert at this conference in *Sisters*. See also Edith Taïeb, *Hubertine Auclert. La Citoyenne, 1848–1914* (Paris, 1982).

V

The *comité*'s early commitment to local working women did not disappear after its leaders founded local sections of Guesde's *Parti ouvrier* in 1881. Every mass meeting held in the three cities in 1882 (at least once a month) attracted large numbers of women as well as men. Audiences varied in size from a low of 500 to a high of nearly 4000 (this latter for a Roubaix meeting featuring Jules Guesde and Louise Michel). At each meeting, moreover, speakers addressed themselves equally to men and women, either as 'citoyennes et citoyens', or as 'ouvriers et ouvrières'. The only distinction drawn between the sexes in this period was drawn at the ticket-booth, where higher-paid men were customarily charged more for their tickets. (A typical ticket cost men 40 centimes and women 20.)[19]

This commitment to sex equality culminated in the adoption of the official party slogan in the autumn of 1882: 'Everything for the people and by the people, without distinction by sex or by race.'[20]

The women textile workers, together with their men comrades in Lille, Roubaix, and Tourcoing, responded quickly to these early socialist initiatives, though the precise extent of that response cannot be known with any accuracy. Reports in the local press, as well as those from increasingly worried local officials and police informers, show that socialist meetings, demonstrations, and study groups attracted many thousands of local workers between 1881 and 1882. Occasionally, the documents record a few voices, rising from among the mass of workers, whose words suggested the extent to which socialist language had penetrated the mills and *quartiers*. These voices were heard in the local socialist newspaper, to which women and men workers addressed complaints about work conditions, poor housing, and so on. One such letter appeared at the offices of *Le Forçat* in October 1882, sent by a Lille *ouvrière*. Clearly assured of a sympathetic ear, she detailed the problems she and her co-workers encountered every day in their mill. She signed the letter, 'To you, and to the revolution, from a woman reader desiring the suppression of private property'.[21]

[19] *LF* (24 Dec. 1882 and 26 Nov. 1882).
[20] Ibid. (22 Oct. 1882).
[21] Ibid. (29 Apr. 1883).

In May of 1882, the *POF* joined *Broquelet* for the first time by holding a series of public meetings featuring Paule Minck speaking on women's liberation under socialism. Her lectures proved so popular that she was asked to extend her stay through to the end of the month, which she did, speaking nightly in one of the three cities.[22]

In that year, too, socialists began to absorb all the various local workers' groups, including both those with a political content and those organized around various leisure activities. Among the most important of these groups were the Free Thinkers, who fell rapidly in line behind the Guesdist banner. By the end of the 1880s, in fact, all local groups of *Libre-Penseurs* were safely in the socialist fold. They were particularly important additions to the *Parti ouvrier* because most included a substantial number of workers in their membership. Among these, moreover, were 'a great number of women', according to one observer.[23]

In addition to taking over existing groups, local socialists founded many new ones. Among these was one whose precise date of birth has been lost. This was a women's group which first appeared in Roubaix shortly before the national *POF* congress was held in that city in the spring of 1884. This group, along with a sister socialist women's group in Roanne, sent delegates to the national party congress. These women became the first women's representatives at a *POF* congress. In the course of the meetings, moreover, a second Roubaix socialist women's group was organized (with the backing of Paule Minck), at the home of Mme Henri Carrette.[24]

Both these local women's groups joined the pleiad of small, informally organized groups which together comprised the *Parti ouvrier* in 1884. In these early days, the lack of formal party structure allowed great latitude in the choice of goals, of venues, and of group names; most local groups chose colourful names which expressed their militancy, including 'Equality', 'Emancipation', 'Revolt', 'Solidarity', 'Resistance', and so on. The first two women's groups called themselves 'Women's Equality' and 'Women's Rights'. They were later joined by 'Women's Emanci-

---

[22] Ibid. (13 May 1883).
[23] Ibid. (1 Apr. 1883).
[24] See *ADN* M154 62, 'Commissariat de police. 4 Avril 1884', and *7ᵉ congrès national du PO, Roubaix 29 mars–7 avril 1884, compte rendu* (Paris, 1884).

pation' and 'Women's Revenge'. (In retrospect, it seems a great pity that the imposition of a formal party structure subsumed this particular form of workers' expression into party sections, listed only by *quartier* or district.)

Although all this local activity supported a generally optimistic view of socialists' progress in the area, most workers remained outside the *Parti ouvrier* itself, just as most failed to join the socialist textile union. Socialist support was growing, but it was growing slowly. Moreover, electoral support rose and fell capriciously in the early years. For example, in Roubaix—the *POF*'s most loyal city—494 votes were cast for socialist candidates in the general legislative elections of 1881. This vote increased to 1,925 in the municipal elections of 1882, but then dropped slightly, to 1,390, in the *conseils des prud'hommes* election in 1883.[25] Clearly, voting support was rising, but not in a reassuringly clear-cut pattern.

These election vote gains were, however, sufficient to frighten the *patronat* into reaction. And, in their efforts to stifle the nascent party, they deployed all the formidable weapons in their arsenal, including those willingly lent by the Church (particularly cleric-controlled local charities). The most useful weapon was withholding charitable funds from suspicious workers and their families. In the 1880s, when the long industrial depression first began to be felt, mass unemployment spread poverty throughout in the textile districts of the area. In addition, the *patronat* began to blacklist socialist workers. Among these were several local *POF* leaders, including Gustave Delory and Henri Ghesquière, whose wives' wages supported them and their families as they continued their political work. The local bourgeois press also directed its ire at socialist speakers from outside. (These were the notorious 'outside agitators from the Second International', whose presence was adduced to explain the sudden increase in textile strikes in this decade.) Paule Minck especially came in for attack by the employers. Mill owners feared her pernicious influence particularly on women workers. One socialist reporter remarked that 'in the eyes of the great capitalists and industrialists of the Nord', Minck was 'a Medusa'.[26]

---

[25] See *7e congrès national du PO, compte rendu*.
[26] *CdF* (8 June 1884 and 22 June 1884).

Sadly, but not surprisingly, these efforts by the employers began to take their toll. By the early months of 1885, open socialist support in the area had declined sharply. The various militantly named groups, including the two women's groups, disappeared from public view. In reaction to this decline, local socialist rhetoric turned plaintive. One speaker, addressing an audience of women in the autumn of 1887, begged them 'to concern themselves with politics if they wanted their situation to change for the better'. 'Abandon your prejudices', he told them, 'enter the lists, help your husbands in the struggle against capitalist rapacity.' Alas, the 'vigourous applause' that greeted his words signalled no immediate upswing in socialist party fortunes in the area.[27] Economic hardship, coupled with stringent efforts to control workers' political expression, effectively prevented most textile workers from openly joining the party—whatever their private views. And for women, already at the bottom of the wage scale and without alternative job possibilities (save prostitution), the choice to join the *Parti ouvrier* or one of its groups was even harder.

In response to the decline in their support, the local socialists began to mix the message they sent out to women workers in the second half of the 1880s. Abandoning their unequivocal position in favour of women's complete equality, the *POF* began to court men's allegiance by arguing against women's equal employment. Some leaders told local men that it was 'women's competition for men's jobs' that was the root cause of the mass unemployment of the late 1880s. One socialist writer—addressing himself only to male readers—complained that industrialization had created competition for men from 'your wives, your sisters, your daughters'.[28] Although the writer noted that the *POF* official position supported 'equal pay for equal work', he pointed out that it did so on the grounds that such a policy would destroy female competition, since no employer would hire a woman unless he could pay her less.

This attitude, articulated in the local socialist press, was not openly supported by official party policy during the second half of the eighties. Instead, the party's policy toward women became ambiguous. Potential male party members could interpret such

---

[27] *CdT* (13–20 Nov. 1887).
[28] Ibid. (1–4 May 1888). '

policies variously. One article which appeared in *Le Cri du travailleur* in February 1888 was typically vague. It began, 'The woman worker, that flower of bourgeois civilization, was only invented in order to increase employers' profits and to make the male worker starve.' (Echoes of Michelet, echoes, even, of Proudhon.) But the writer went on to say that the easy solution of forbidding women's waged work (already adopted by the printers) was not possible in the textile industry, or in most other French industry where 'too many French women' were already working for wages by the end of the 1880s. Efforts to push several million women out of the labour market would be futile. Instead, this writer offered a contradictory solution, which mixed Guesde's progressive rhetoric with Proudhonian prescriptions. Echoing Guesde, he argued that socialism would 'transform women's work into a good', thereby bringing an end to women's economic dependence and permitting them to live 'by and for themselves'. Furthermore, 'in order that the woman become her own master, in order that she recover the freedom of her body, without which there is only prostitution, whatever the equality of relations she might have with the opposite sex, it is necessary that the woman find in herself, independent of the man, her means of existence.'

This was, of course, the straight Guesdist line on the material conditions of women's emancipation. But this writer then offered the precisely contrary view. 'Higher wages for fathers', he wrote, would preserve children's health by 'reconstituting workers' homes . . . returning the wife to the husband and the mother to the child.' Apparently, he was unaware of the impossibility of achieving both goals at the same time.[29]

This sort of theoretical muddle was not unusual in these early years when workers were faced with assimilating new, complex ideas about class and (among the Guesdists at least) gender relations in industrial society. It is therefore not surprising to discover such confusion muddying the waters of such a difficult issue as that concerning working women's place in the socialist project. Nevertheless, the introduction of traditional ideas about women's place into the rhetoric of local Guesdist propaganda augured badly for the long-term policies of the party.

[29] 'Étude sur le programme du Parti ouvrier', *CdT* (12–16 May 1888).

Jules Guesde was sufficiently concerned about this mixed message to attempt clarification of the official Guesdist position in the next issue of *Le Cri du travailleur*. He told readers that 'among the most important decisions of the last workers' congress in Lille [was] one upon which we must insist'. This was the resolution which supported the demand that women have the right to stand for and elect *conseils des prud'hommes*, which would have the effect of 'proclaiming the equality of the sexes before corporative justice'. 'In doing this', Guesde continued, 'the workers of Lille, of Roubaix, of Armentières, of Calais, of St Quentin, and so on, are mending, in so far as they are able, one of the greatest crimes of a society full of crimes.' He went on,

Poor women . . . have been assigned industrial work by the bourgeois capitalist order, on top of the work they are assigned by nature. They already had children to rear, a household to care for, but that was not enough. Speculating employers added machines to their burdens. Thus in addition . . . to maternity, and the servitude of the domestic *foyer*, women must submit to the servitude of the mill . . .

'Without political rights', he continued, 'the woman worker is denied her professional rights. More wronged, and more susceptible to wrongs, than the male worker . . . It is not only her wage that is at the mercy of the employer, but also her body—and thus also her dignity as a woman.'

He concluded,

In rising against such a state of things and in reclaiming for their sisters in exploitation the right to elect and to be elected, the proletarians of the Nord have shown the new order, the truly human order, that socialist society will bring. It was Mme Roland who said: 'Women have the same right to mount the tribunal as they have to mount the scaffold.' We add: to the duty to work must be added, for the woman worker, the right, all the rights, which have been acquired by the man worker.[30]

Rousing words. And, on the surface, generally consistent with Guesde's earlier position on women's equal role in the class struggle. But Guesde's words held two subliminal messages for women workers wishing to take an equal place in the *POF*. Firstly, Guesde's view of women's past included the popular, Proudhonist view of an idyllic pre-industrial time when women spent their lives

---

[30] 'Les Droits de l'ouvrière', *CdT* (30 May–2 June 1888).

fulfilling 'nature's' prescription. In his view, not only child-bearing was women's natural work, but also rearing the children and 'caring for the household'. Industrialization added 'unnatural' work to the women's domestic duties. Of course, Guesde did not draw the same conclusions drawn by many of his contemporaries—that men must return women to their natural place in the home. But what he did suggest was nearly as problematic for socialist efforts to organize women. That is, he instructed the males of the *POF*, the 'proletarians' to 'reclaim for their sisters' women's rights. Thus, although women of the proletariat would be beneficiaries of the socialist struggle, they had no equal place in it—even in that part of the movement specifically aimed at gaining them their rights.

In fact, Guesde's 1888 restatement of the *POF*'s position on women's rights reflected a wider problem within the party itself. The problem came to the fore at the end of the 1880s during local party reorganization, which was designed to tighten control and to transform an amorphous collection of many small groups into a proper political party. In the process of this reorganization, local leaders were forced to consider the problem of separate autonomous women's groups, like those that continued to exist—though barely—in Roubaix. Should women, like members of other socialist groups, be forced to join regular party sections? Or could they remain in their own groups? When Guesde asked advice from women within the party, he got contradictory advice.

Paule Minck, for one, had long struggled with the problem, both before becoming a Guesdist and after. In the mid-1880s, she had demonstrated her commitment to women working *within* the party by refusing to stand as an election candidate for the *Fédération socialiste des femmes* (a group independent of any of the French socialist groups of the decade). In her refusal, she made it clear that she believed it important for women to stay within official party structures, rather than to wage a separate struggle on the periphery, without regard to prevailing class relations. She sent a copy of her refusal to Guesde at the same time as she sent it to the leaders of the *Fédération*.[31]

But Guesde received contrary advice from his friend, Clara Zetkin, leader of the massive German socialist women's movement.

---

[31] Dalôtel, *Minck*, p. 16.

Zetkin wrote to Guesde that she favoured separate women's groups, federated into the party structure. She suggested that the French socialists should follow the German model by founding such women's groups and holding separate women's congresses. The principle underlying Zetkin's position was one which argued that women needed a forum in which they felt free of men's domination, and in which they could develop political skills needed for the larger class struggle.[32] (Of course it must be remembered that the German women were organized in this manner because German law forbade women from joining in any organized political activity.)

In the end, the Lille area *POF* took no position on the matter of organizing women in this last year of the decade. But the reorganized party of 1890 had no place within the party structure for women's groups, a *de facto* policy decision of considerable importance.[33] Roubaix's two groups may well have continued to exist outside the party (of course, alongside other informally structured socialist activities). Into the vacuum created by the local party's failure to formulate a policy on women's groups came three new personalities, each of whom held strong views on the subject of organizing working women. These were Paul Lafargue, Henri Ghesquière, and Aline Valette. Because each affected the party's policies toward working women in this decade, it is instructive to compare the views of each with those promulgated by Guesde himself throughout the previous ten years.

Paul Lafargue rose suddenly to local prominence when he became the first socialist elected to national office from the Lille area, in 1891. Elected, as we have seen, on the flood-tide of sentiment following the Fourmies massacre, he remained deputy of Lille from 1892 until his death in 1911. During his tenure in the *Chambre*, Lafargue's influence on the local politics of his constituents was sporadic, but important. Unfortunately, his attitudes toward working women were altogether different from

---

[32] IISH, 'Dossier Jules Guesde', 195/1, Clara Zetkin to Jules Guesde. Most of this letter is damaged and therefore illegible. I have dated this letter from its presence in Guesde's file at the end of the 1880s.

[33] Ibid. 177/3, Delory to Guesde (Lille, 26 Apr. 1889). Not only did Delory claim that the reorganization of the *POF* was complete in his area, but he added that some worker's *quartiers* were entirely socialist. Moulins–Lille was among these.

those of his colleague, Jules Guesde, for all that Lafargue co-authored the official electoral programme of the *POF* which set out such a radical view of women's right to equal treatment.

His views had their root in his often expressed disdain for bourgeois women, whom he saw not as a group of individuals but rather as an abstract category called 'woman'. This disdain spilled over into his attitude toward working-class women, however hard he tried to pose them as the ideal against which bourgeois women were doomed to fall short. Working-class women became 'woman' in Lafargue's eyes—embodying virtues accruing to them solely by virtue of their sex and to a lesser extent their class.

Lafargue's ideal woman was a selfless earth mother, whose fulfilment came not from the unfettered exercise of her faculties, nor from her ability to live independent from men, but rather from her devoted, untiring service to her family.

The first expression of Lafargue's views to appear locally came in an article on the family, published in *Le Cri du travailleur* in 1890.[34] In this piece, Lafargue made two points: firstly, that capitalism had destroyed the working-class family's 'natural' unity (characteristic, in his view, of pre-industrial artisan families), and, secondly, that capitalism had reduced the bourgeois family to a meaningless set of purely monetary relations. In the first case, women of the popular classes had been 'torn' from their homes, and thus prevented from accomplishing their maternal duties. (Lafargue's constant use of the passive voice when speaking of 'woman' underlined the extent to which he was unable to see women as agents of their own past.) In the second case, bourgeois women had become 'bored, overly sensitive, weak, and idle creatures', whose natural function, maternity, had ceased to have any interest for them. In Lafargue's opinion, the fact that they could afford to hire other women to do their 'natural' duties meant that bourgeois women could neglect their children, choosing instead a life of adulterous love affairs.

Lafargue described these idle, bourgeois women with vicious sarcasm. When she is pregnant, he wrote, 'a *bourgeoise*'s stomach is distended, her waist disappears, and she often becomes ugly; women already deformed and degraded by civilization are terribly shaken up by maternity.'

[34] *CdT* (9 Feb. 1890).

After giving birth, these women refused to care for their children. Thus, in Lafargue's critical view, bourgeois children played but a small part in family life. No 'intimate feelings' held the family together. Instead, he wrote, 'bored wives cuckolded their husbands'.

Against these reprehensible creatures, Lafargue juxtaposed his ideal women—those of the popular classes during the pre-industrial period. These women were not forced by capitalism to compete for 'men's jobs', nor prevented from doing their duties by overwork in factories or workshops. Instead, Lafargue wrote, 'as members of an artisan's family, wives were true *ménagères*'. They 'spun the wool and jute, knitted stockings, cut and sewed the family's clothing, baked the household's bread', and so on. Aided by their daughters, these women 'provided for all the needs of the household'. But, in the industrial present, Lafargue complained, 'what remained of this work that had once been the *raison d'être* of the housewife? Nothing.'

Lafargue's Pre-Raphaelite earth mother, busy at her spinning-wheel, her loom, her oven, may have been a figment of Lafargue's romantic urban imagination, but she shaped his behaviour toward women of the Lille proletariat, as we saw during the LeBlan strike of *ouvrières* in 1892. Unable to see women as workers struggling to change their working conditions in the mills, he saw them rather as misplaced housewives, whose real frustration arose from the fact that they had insuffient time or energy to fulfil their domestic 'duties'.

Fortunately, Lafargue's reactionary views formed only part of prevailing Guesdist attitudes toward women workers in the 1890s. Counter to his views ran a more properly Marxist account of women's place in the class struggle, summarized by the local Lille Guesdist Henri Ghesquière in *Le Cri du travailleur* in 1890, in an article entitled 'Women's Rights'.[35] Ghesquière's essay was prompted by the massive and visible presence of textile *ouvrières* in the May Day demonstration and subsequent general strike of that year. Women's militancy in those events reminded the Guesdists of their debt to their female constituency—and of the importance of mobilizing that enthusiasm to their own ends. Thus local leaders reassessed the role of local women in the party, and one result was Ghesquière's position paper.

[35] Ibid. (1 June 1890).

Ghesquière addressed himself to women readers, telling them that although all previous party discussions of 'the rights of man' had employed the term 'man' generically 'this practice left some people unaware of women's inclusion. Thus women's rights should sometimes be discussed separately', as he intended to do in this piece.

His argument rested on three premises. Firstly, just as men possessed certain rights—e.g. the rights to existence and to happiness—which they 'earned' by producing, so women producers necessarily had these same rights. Secondly, if men only attained full humanity by exercising their rights, so women who lacked them were blocked from achieving a similar humanity. Thirdly, because women were, in Ghesquière's view, everywhere the slaves of men—in the family, in the nation, and in society at large—they could not exercise even those few rights they had. Thus they were effectively deprived of life. Women must, therefore, be emancipated in all spheres of life—from the domestic to the political and economic.

The implications of Ghesquière's argument were less clear than a first reading suggested. Firstly, if only a productive relationship to society earned a person his or her 'rights', then how might an unwaged housewife earn those same rights in a society formed by the production relations of industrial capitalism? Worse still, how could an unwaged housewife, dependent for her economic existence on her male relations, exercise her 'free and equal' existence? It would seem that she could not. Thus unwaged women were effectively excluded from the class struggle.

Finally, Ghesquière's words contained within them the most vexing problem of all: how could women be liberated from their onerous domestic slavery unless men voluntarily agreed to share all domestic tasks equally? This was, of course, not a theoretical problem, but it was a massive practical one. Aware of the probable extent of male hostility to demands that they assume domestic duties, neither Ghesquière nor before him Jules Guesde ventured to address the problem head on. Instead, they contented themselves with deliberately vague references to women's liberation from their private slavery.

This difficulty was equally a problem for those French feminists of the period who influenced the Guesdists. However, because they were unconcerned with losing a male constituency, they had no similar difficulty in solving it. Hubertine Auclert declared, 'In order for a woman to have the possibility of doing productive work, it is necessary that the man share with her all unproductive work.' Furthermore, she added, 'it cannot be argued that those functions are women's tasks . . . All those unproductive tasks that are assigned to women in the home are, in society, done by men for money. For money, men sweep, clean, brush shoes and clothes; for money, men sew, for money, men cook, lay and clear tables, and wash dishes. For money, men care for young children.'[36] But to this length socialist men were unwilling to go.

Ghesquière, then, embodied one side of the local Guesdist position on working women, and Lafargue the other. The gap between their views may be explained in part by their private relations with women. Lafargue's wife Laura Marx was herself something of an earth mother. Without waged occupation, she enjoyed no private life of her own outside her family. Her primary activities consisted of serving her family, particularly Lafargue himself, whose interests she apparently never contradicted. Throughout our period, her role in the socialist community consisted almost entirely of appearing on party platforms, where she graciously received bouquets usually presented by the socialist women of various localities. Her political identity stemmed from her relationship with two men: her father and her husband.

Of course, anyone acquainted with Paul Lafargue's political views before his marriage might have expected that he would marry such a domestically oriented woman. As Claude Willard notes, Lafargue began his political life as a Proudhonist—and even after meeting Marx and marrying his daughter he retained a basically Proudhonist view of women.[37]

Ghesquière, on the other hand, was born the son of Lille textile workers. Like virtually every other working-class child born in the area in the Second Empire, he went early into the mills, where he remained until his socialist activities earned him a place on the employers' black list. Fortunately, the earnings of his wife, a street merchant, were sufficient to allow him to continue his activism— and even sufficient to support their numerous children. Moreover, Anna Ghesquière had political views of her own, which no doubt

---

[36] Taïeb, *Hubertine Auclert*, pp. 73–7.
[37] Willard, *Les Guesdistes*, p. 27.

influenced those of her husband. She, along with Maria Delory Devernay and others, helped to found and lead the Lille women's groups which began to emerge in the 1890s. It is likely that her position as family wage-earner (which she shared with more than one other local socialist wife in this early period), as well as her strong views in favour of women's emancipation, made the Ghesquières' domestic relations more equal than was usual in that area in that period. But, like so many other women, Anna Ghesquière left no records, and thus such conclusions remain speculative.

The expressed views of these two socialist men represented the two strains of male socialist opinion about working women which existed side by side throughout the 1890's. The two approaches, moreover, vied for dominance within the French socialist movement until 1905, when the new *SFIO* settled the question in favour of the more reactionary view.

But what of socialist *women's* views? There was, in the last decade of the nineteenth century, only one woman who consistently had the ear of socialist leaders in the Nord department, and that was Aline Valette, who joined the national council of the *POF* in 1893 and remained on it until her death in 1899. Although Jules Guesde once declared that Valette was 'the only woman who really understood Marxism',[38] her writings on the subject of women suggest that this was hardly the case. Her views on women's emancipation within the class struggle were a curious, uneasy mixture of Lafargue's traditionalism and Guesde's more progressive ideas. Perhaps nowhere was this problematic conceptual mix more apparent than in the *Cahier des doléances féminines*, which she prepared for the May Day celebration of 1893 in her capacity as secretary of the *Fédération française des sociétés féministes*. Valette also presented these women's grievances to the national *POF* congress, held in the autumn of the same year—a presentation which, among other things, won her a place on the national council.[39]

---

[38] Quoted in Willard, *Les Guesdistes*, p. 648 (This is perhaps more than a little hard on, *inter alia*, Rosa Luxemburg . . . !).

[39] See Valette, *Cahier des doléances féminines, 1er mai 1893* (Paris, 1893). See also *APP* Ba 1290, 'Dossier Aline Valette, rapport de police' (9 Apr. 1896), which reports that Valette was chosen for the administrative committee because she was Guesde's mistress, who 'sapped his vital energies'. No corroborating evidence for this relationship exists.

Valette's list of women's grievances rested on two contradictory ideas. Firstly, she argued that women were men's equal in every way. Thus they should enjoy equal social, political, and economic rights. Secondly, she proposed that women were both different from, and not infrequently superior to, men, particularly in those areas long assigned to them by tradition. For example, Valette claimed that jobs 'requiring tact and self-sacrifice, such as public assistance officers, infant teachers, and so on' fell 'more naturally upon women'.[40]

This unhappy marriage of equality and biologically determined difference was devastating to organized women's demands for equal rights. Women's claim that they were morally superior only served to mirror many men's traditional claim that *their* superior logic, rationality, and strength suited them to run the world, just as women's superior morality placed her squarely, and justly, inside the home.[41]

Valette's views elicited no criticism from socialist quarters, not least because they fitted neatly into views already promulgated by Paul Lafargue, as well as by Engels, and, to some extent, by August Bebel, both of whose recent books on women's place in the class struggle had foundered on similar logical shoals. Worse still, Valette began spreading her views throughout the workers' *quartiers* of Lille, Roubaix, and Tourcoing immediately following her appointment to the national party council. In a speech to a group of Lille workers in the spring of 1894, Valette argued that women practised a superior morality—based on the special qualities natural to mothers. Moreover, she said, women's morality only highlighted the hypocritical foundations of men's morals, which prescribed monogamy for women but adultery for men. What was needed, she concluded, was a society like that

---

[40] This change in ideas occurred everywhere in the feminist movement of the period. Rebecca West complained that some British feminists were changing 'a march toward freedom into a romp towards voluptuous servitude'. See 'The Sin of Self-Sacrifice', quoted in Jane Marcus, ed., *The Young Rebecca: The Writings of Rebecca West 1911–1917* (London, 1982), p. 235.

[41] The American suffrage agitators replied to similar male assertions with satire. Alice Duer Miller wrote a poster called 'Why We Oppose Votes for Men' which read, in part, 'Because no really manly man wants to settle any question otherwise than by fighting about it . . . Because men are too emotional to vote. Their conduct at baseball games and political conventions shows this . . .'

described by Engels—in which women ruled and female goddesses reigned in the original collective society of 'primitive communism'.[42]

The logical problems inherent in a socialist claim that women possessed a special, superior morality which in turn underlay their claims for equal rights never troubled Valette. Instead, she continued to assert the primacy of gender over class, although she managed to borrow Marxian vocabulary to support her case. She told more than 2,000 people gathered in the Lille *Hippodrome* in 1894: 'Even more than this word "proletarian" applied to men is a synonym for labour and for suffering, applied to women it is a synonym for double labour, double suffering, without even that demarcation which, for men, exists between proletarians and men of other classes. Women, all women, are proletarians.'[43]

Her ideas elicited 'wild applause and prolonged acclamations' from the crowd, who repeatedly interrupted her talk to express their agreement. None the less, her words embodied a key conflict which deformed all subsequent socialist attempts to formulate a Marxist doctrine of women's emancipation under socialism. 'All women' were not members of the revolutionary Marxist class—and saying would not make it so. Furthermore, on a practical level this confusion led straight to organizational problems. Should women be organized around their different biological roles? Were their peculiar moral gifts to be deployed in some special way in the class struggle? Or were they primarily workers, who should be organized as proletarians, on the assumption that their place in the working class overrode their gender? If the socialist response was to choose to organize women around their moral gifts, rather than around their role in production relations, then women would necessarily assume a marginal, supporting role, detached from their lives in the factories of industrial capitalism. Such women would logically be unable to develop class-consciousness.[44]

[42] Friedrich Engels's *Origins of the Family, Private Property and the State* appeared in 1884 and August Bebel's *Women Under Socialism* in German in 1883. Valette's speech is reported in 'La Réunion de l'Hippodrome à Lille', LT (16 May 1894).

[43] Ibid.

[44] A clear discussion of this unfolding theoretical dilemma is found in Alfred Meyer, 'Marxism and the women's movement', in Dorothy Atkinson, *et al.*, eds., *Women in Russia* (Brighton, 1978), pp. 85–114.

vi

This theoretical conflict between two organizing principles—women as waged workers or women as wives and mothers—was unfortunately replicated in the practical politics of the Guesdists in the Lille area in the 1890s. During this decade as we have seen, socialist women added several new groups to those already established in Roubaix. Several new, *quartier*-based groups emerged in Lille and Roubaix, and perhaps in Tourcoing, though the documents show only vague references to 'the socialist women of Tourcoing'. Although little is known about these groups beyond the fact of their existence their names suggest that their members thought of themselves as militants, in favour both of class and of gender liberation. Thus local groups included *Revanche des femmes, Droits des femmes, Émancipation des femmes*, and so on. A few followed the practice of socialist party sections and identified themselves merely by *quartier*—for example the *Femmes socialistes de l'Épeule*. Together these groups were loosely linked to an umbrella group called the *Comité des femmes de Lille*.

However militant these various women's groups, however, male socialist leaders left little doubt that they saw them strictly as auxiliary to the main socialist struggle in the area—support troops for the male front-line infantry of the *POF*. The resulting conflict between women's goals and men's view of their collective role in the party left the women's groups flailing helplessly between single-issue 'women's' campaigns (including the campaign for free school lunches) on the one hand and a wider participation in the class struggle on the other. It was this conflict that more than anything else ensured the disappearance of the women's groups by the end of the decade.

The rise and fall of these groups was rapid. They arrived on the scene suddenly following the appearance of the 1891 *POF* electoral programme, which gave prominence to socialist demands for women's equal civil, political, and economic rights.[45] During the campaign which ensued, launched to free Paul Lafargue from prison following the Fourmies massacre, women played a vocal, active role. In October of that year a group of textile workers and

---

[45] This was also the year when the Second Socialist International passed a strong resolution supporting women's equal rights following motions from Germany's Louise Kautsky and Italy's Dr Anna Kulischioff. Guesde kept a copy of this motion among his private papers, IISH, 'Dossier Jules Guesde', 205/9.

housewives from Fourmies and a neighbouring town, Wignehies, published an appeal to their Lille sisters to join what they called 'their' campaign on behalf of Lafargue's candidacy. They addressed their neighbours in words which showed that they, unlike many male socialists, found no problem in accepting a mixture of women's roles: 'Workers like you,' they wrote, 'like you mothers, wives, and daughters of workers.' The appeal was signed by over fifty women, some fo whom listed occupations, and some of whom did not.[46]

The Lille *POF* reacted swiftly. The day after local male leaders received the appeal they issued a second one, addressed to 'Women, working women, and sisters in work and in misery . . .'. It read, in part,

the *Parti ouvrier*, which demands equal rights and equal wages for women and for men, invites you to an election meeting which will take place on Thursday evening. . . . Join us with confidence. There is a work of deliverance to accomplish; it is to prepare the enfranchisement of workers without distinction by sex, in freeing from prison Lafargue and Culine, condemned for their devotion to the working class.[47]

The election campaign which followed drew the enthusiastic support of textile workers throughout the area. Doubtless the Fourmies massacre had helped dissipate any lingering hopes for harmonious class relations. Furthermore, the vast unemployment among textile workers in the area in 1891 meant that many had little to lose and everything to gain by showing their true colours and electing Lafargue to represent them.

The *Parti ouvrier* was naturally ecstatic at the result. And women's participation in the victory did not go unnoticed. At the Lyon party congress just after the election, a unanimous resolution was passed in favour of 'the complete equality of both sexes'. It instructed 'all workers to demand for women the same political and civil rights men have, and an end to all laws that keep women outside communal and public life'. The distance still to be travelled by these workers (clearly all male) before these goals would be reached was, however, symbolized by the absence of women delegates at the congress itself.[48]

[46] 'Les Femmes de Wignehies et de Fourmies font appel aux femmes de Lille', *LT* (22 Oct. 1891).
[47] *LT* (23 Oct. 1891).
[48] *9ᵉ Congrès national du Parti ouvrier, Lyon 26–28 novembre 1891, compte rendu* (Lille, 1891).

Early in 1892, however, things began to move swiftly. In that spring, Roubaix voters returned a socialist municipal council, headed by Henri Carrette, whose wife was a leading member of the original socialist women's group. Not surprisingly, the campaign featured the issue of women's emancipation, though it was often couched in curious terms. Lafargue, for one, demonstrated a perplexing volte-face during one election meeting where the topic was 'the evolution of the family'. In his speech, Lafargue argued in favour of what he called Engels's notion that women should be liberated from bourgeois monogamy. Thus, he said, whereas they were presently miserable in 'factories, mines, offices', soon they would find that machines had taken over their hard jobs, leaving them free to find less onerous work. This, in turn, would pay them enough so that they could be economically independent. At that point, these women of the future would be 'mistresses of all . . . truly free to be polygamous [*sic*] or monogamous'.

It is, of course, tempting to cast one's imagination back to that cold night in Lille in 1892 to try to envisage the reactions which Lafargue's words evoked from his audience of Flemish workers. One reporter noted that his words were greeted with 'widespread shock'. But, he added, the talk ended in 'warm applause' none the less.[49]

However revolutionary Lafargue's ideas may have seemed, however, they were in fact only slightly less reactionary than his earlier views. What he was offering working women was not liberation from the strictures of industrial capitalism via the collective ownership of the means of production, nor even liberation from the restrictive laws of bourgeois society. Instead, Lafargue proposed a sort of biological socialism—a liberation of women's sexuality from the restraints imposed in the monogamous family. (And this, needless to say, without any form of reliable birth control!) Despite the Flemish workers' tolerance of illegitimate babies and relationships established outside the Church it is doubtful whether they had much enthusiasm for free love or for 'polygamy'. The latter idea may well have aroused horror from local working women, who certainly did not need to double or triple their domestic burdens.

Whatever the reactions to speeches of that sort, however, local women did begin to organize and join socialist women's groups

[49] 'Conférence sur l'évolution de la famille', *LT* (28 Feb. 1892).

during this 1892 election. Each of these small groups in turn joined the umbrella group, the *Comité des femmes de Lille*, led by Anna Ghesquière, Mme Carrette, Citoyenne Delory, and three other women.[50]

Throughout the summer and autumn of 1892 these new groups continued to meet. More formed whenever one group got too big. They met weekly, either in a local *estaminet* or in members' homes. By January of 1893 the groups' increasing visibility attracted the attention of local authorities. *Le Travailleur*, Lille's socialist newspaper, reported with scarcely disguised glee that the mayor, Gery Legrand, was so fearful of local women's groups that he banned all public demonstrations. 'One would think', gloated the reporter, 'that the women had sticks of dynamite under their skirts to blow up the *Hôtel de Ville*.' Legrand's ban proved counter-productive, however. A second report described 'hundreds of women' at mass meetings called to protest against the ban.[51]

Such occurrences to the contrary notwithstanding, the focus for most women's groups' efforts in 1893 was far from a provocative one. Rather, their campaign for free school dinners slotted smoothly into prevailing assumptions about women's familial preoccupations. What made local officials uneasy, however, was not the women's goal, but rather their militant tactics on behalf of that goal.

The campaign, conceived and led entirely by women, originated in Roubaix following the election of the socialist municipal council at the end of 1892. In December of that year Roubaix's women leaders organized a meeting in Lille to persuade that city's women to join their efforts. Doubtless because posters announced that the meeting was closed to men, crowds of youths turned up, intending to make trouble. Nevertheless, the chairwoman, Mme Carrette, prevented their entrance into the hall and the meeting went off without a hitch.[52]

More meetings ensued, provoking greater hostility from the local male bourgeoisie. *Progrès du Nord* issued an appeal to local men to prevent their wives from attending such meetings. 'What kind of a man allows his wife to leave home to go to LaFargue's [*sic*] meetings?' the paper asked rhetorically. The male editors of

[50] This committee is described in 'Les Cantines scolaires', *LT* (21 Jan. 1893).
[51] See *LT* (21 Jan. 1893 and 11 Jan. 1893).
[52] Ibid. (3 Dec. 1892).

Le Travailleur quickly rose to their own defence, 'Yes, we lead our wives, daughters, and sisters to socialist meetings', they wrote, 'in order to improve the lot of women and children and to emancipate the better part of humanity.'[53] Both sides in this dispute obviously found the autonomy of this women's campaign distressing, however much they attempted to claim control of 'their' women's behaviour.

Men's publicly voiced worries did not dissipate over time, especially as the number of women involved grew as the campaign began to enjoy considerable success. In the first few months of 1893, four new school meal programmes were begun in Roubaix— and, in some cases, these were staffed by male municipal councillors! When Maria Delory Devernay visited one of the scholars' canteens she was startled to see 'a municipal councillor in sabots, armed with an enormous spoon, serving the *plats du jour*'. In all, there were 1,794 Roubaix families enrolled in the programme by early 1893.[54]

Because Lille women did not enjoy the support of a socialist municipal council, their work was harder. Their first tactic was to petition the mayor, Legrand, presenting him with as many signatures as they could gather in the last few weeks of January 1893. They carried their first petition to the *Hôtel de Ville* at 2 p.m. on a Sunday, a day and time chosen so that women would not have to miss work to attend. Legrand received the first petition graciously, and Maria Devernay predicted happily, 'the united will of the women of Lille will prove irresistible'.[55]

A second petition, however, met hostility. At the *mairie*, leaders were met not by the mayor, but instead by one of his assistants, M. Gavelle. To their disgust, Gavelle attempted to patronize them, telling them: 'These school lunch canteens are surely not meant for you ladies; your hats and your *toilette* are too pretty.' The women replied that they had naturally worn their best clothes to present themselves to the mayor, and one woman added defensively, 'my pay is never more than 28 sous (1.40 fr.) a day'.[56]

Given their hostile second reception, the Lille women decided

---

[53] This debate is described by 'J. V.' in 'Les Femmes de Lille et les cantines scolaires', ibid.

[54] Devernay, 'Visite aux cantines scolaires de Roubaix', *LT* (15 Jan. 1893).

[55] 'Aux Femmes de Lille', *LT* (11 Jan. 1893).

[56] 'A l'Insolent Gavelle', *LT* (18 Jan. 1893).

to call a public demonstration—which the mayor immediately prohibited under the banning order then in effect. This prohibition occasioned a series of meetings in Lille, led by Citoyenne Collignon. Among the speakers at these meetings were Paul Lafargue and several local women, including Citoyennes Bonduel and Dernelle. Each of these meetings stimulated the founding of another women's group; by the end of February that year, every workers' *quartier* in Lille had at least one such group.[57]

However hopeful these signs, the fact that women were organizing around a single issue, particularly one which did not directly address their place within the class struggle, limited the groups' influence, both among other working women and among male socialist leaders. Thus, as we have seen, when the Rémy strikers asked male leaders for party support in their strike, they were shunted aside into the hands of the *Comité des femmes*. The *Comité*, lacking any tactical experience beyond that aimed at achieving their single goal, could offer women strikers only a place within their struggle. That the women strikers quickly rejected the *Comité*'s efforts—and thereby rejected organized socialists—was not surprising.

Moreover, the school dinner campaign was a 'women's issue', which posed no ideological threat to socialist members unwilling to allow women an equal place in the more central political struggle. For the most misogynistic among male socialist leaders, such a 'women's campaign' provided a useful means for siphoning off the energies of women who might actually have demanded their 'revenge', their 'emancipation', or their equal rights. Women busy gathering signatures for school lunch petitions or holding campaign meetings were unlikely to trouble the consciences of male leaders unwilling to rock the electoral boat by bringing women into the more important heart of the socialist party where they might have called in the debt long owed them.

Thus, this women's campaign freed the men to concentrate on winning more elections in the area; and this they did. The first election successes whetted appetites, and in 1893 the *POF* doubled its efforts to win workers' votes, regardless of whether they could at the same time win their dues. In fact, formal party membership

---

[57] These women remain anonymous but for notices in *LT* (21 Jan. 1893) and 'De l'attitude du comité des femmes de Lille', *LT* (25 Jan. 1893).

took a back seat to votes—a development which Guesde supported, as he began to envisage a more carefully selected, tighter, disciplined 'vanguard' party (to use an anachronism) which would then lead the class it represented without the problems presented by a genuinely mass party.

Both these factors, an increasing emphasis upon winning elections accompanied by a decreasing emphasis upon recruiting a mass membership, worked against women's interests. First and foremost, their disfranchisement placed them solidly beyond the attention of electioneering politicians. Secondly, once the *Parti ouvrier* ceased trying to recruit all workers in the Lille area into the party structure, women—always harder to organize—were more than likely to be ignored altogether. This, in turn, meant that the party ceased its early, fairly tentative efforts to encourage some women to become militants within the party, whose work it was to attract more women to its ranks. That no local women rose out of the rank and file of women workers to become party militants in the generation following that of Anna Ghesquière, Maria Delory Devernay, and Mme Carrette, owes its explanation to this change in party policy in the early 1890s.

These problems and developments did not entirely escape the notice of some of the women leaders. By late spring, 1893, many had begun to attempt to broaden their base beyond single-issue campaigns on behalf of 'women's' concerns. They held a series of meetings—again restricted to women—in the various workers' *quartiers* of Lille, Roubaix, and Tourcoing, to discuss the role working women ought to play in the socialist movement. Mme Carrette and Citoyenne Vermeulen chaired most of these meetings, and occasionally they invited Paul Lafargue as guest speaker. Unfortunately, the usual disregard of women's ideas by local officials (including socialist party reporters) means that the speeches of Carrette and Vermeulen, along with those of other women, are lost. Only Paul Lafargue's talks received detailed attention; it is thus from those reports that we must draw information about the content of these discussions.

When Lafargue spoke to these women's meetings he did not repeat his ideas about sexual liberation and polygamy but concentrated instead on a broad analysis of women's working conditions in the mills. His detailed description of women's experiences in the textile factories of the area stimulated great enthusiasm from his audiences. Occasionally they corrected his facts. When he told one group that most women 'earned only 20 francs a week', his listeners cried, 'No! only 15'. The answer to their problems of low wages and poor conditions, Lafargue said, was to organize themselves. To that end, they must begin spreading socialist propaganda among all their female co-workers. They must tell working women of socialism's promises to increase their derisory wages and to provide them with free maternity care.[58]

The content of these talks suggested that Lafargue had changed his views of women's place and women's duties. But, alas, he had not. As the meetings continued, he threw caution to the winds, abandoning this strictly socialist message in favour of his older views. At one meeting of 300 Roubaix women he spoke about 'women's correct place', at home, where they could care for their children properly. He admitted that the present state of affairs precluded this ideal situation. So they must 'spend their energies' organizing—in order to persuade the municipality to provide better public child care. But, he promised them, these public reforms were only stopgap; once socialism had come, they would be returned to their homes. (As usual, he spoke of socialism as the vehicle, and women as its passive objects.) He added that the women's groups' efforts to broaden their goals were laudable: he suggested they add demands for crèches and 'écoles maternelles' to their school meal programmes. 'Join the socialist party' he added, 'and make your husbands vote socialist.' He concluded this instruction patronizingly. 'Husbands are sometimes a bit brutal with their wives, are they not?' he asked. 'But you know how to act like the calm before the storm and then to raise your head when the storm is passed. You bend in the moment of the storm, but when calm returns, you are not changed.' (In effect, close your eyes and think of socialism.)

One witness noted that Lafargue's version of relations between husband and wife in the workers' *quartiers* met with 'laughter', but recorded no other reaction.

At this meeting, however, a second male speaker followed Lafargue and, because of his gender, a reporter wrote down the details of his talk. M. Wattel, a municipal councillor in Roubaix,

---

[58] *LT* (5 Feb. 1893, 12 Feb. 1893).

appealed directly to his audience in their capacity as industrial workers as well as constituents. He encouraged them to join their local socialist sections—not as surrogates or pace-setters for their husbands but for themselves. At the same time, he told them that he recognized the special problems faced by working women who made the decision to join the party. More closely watched by the *patronat*, they risked immediate blacklisting. The solution, Wattel concluded, was to keep their party membership secret. To that end, he told them, the party promised to keep membership lists away from public scrutiny.

Wattel's talk provoked 'enthusiastic cries'. The women ended their meeting by passing a resolution to organize further meetings 'in every *quartier* of Roubaix'. And this they proceeded to do. From mid-summer to the national party congress in October 1893, local women organized weekly meetings throughout the area.[59]

In addition to regular women's meetings, all public events continued to draw crowds of local working women. The by now customary socialist May Day parade attracted many thousands of women in Lille and Roubaix in 1893. In Lille, women and men marched together, led by Anna Ghesquière and Citoyenne Collignon as well as by local male socialist leaders. In Roubaix, the parade was organized around various socialist groups. Several of the women's groups marched together, carrying their banners proclaiming their identity. At the parade's end, 20,000 *Roubaisiens* gathered to hear speeches from local leaders, including a leader of the women's groups. In Tourcoing, the parade was much smaller and attracted only 4,000 marchers. Among these were women— but no women's groups or women leaders appeared in the reports of the event.[60].

For local socialist women in both Lille and Roubaix—and even, to some extent, in Tourcoing—1893 proved a golden year. Throughout the year, women's groups formed an articulate, visible presence in the local *Parti ouvrier* milieu. But, despite this achievement, trouble was brewing at the national level, and ultimately spilled over into local politics. The consequence was the slow strangulation of the women's groups of the *Comité des femmes*.

---

[59] 'Roubaix. La Réunion des femmes', ibid., (14 Feb. 1893); other meetings are reported in *LT* (8 Mar., 18 Apr., 2 Aug., 12 Aug. 1893).
[60] 'Le Premier mai a Lille', *LT* (6 May 1893).

vii

While the local women in these early years tended to take socialist words at face value, and to assume that repeated expressions of the party's commitment to women's equality were genuine, more politically sophisticated Paris women were less sanguine about male socialists' sincerity. In 1892, therefore, the *Solidarité des femmes*, led by Eugénie Potonié-Pierre, decided to test the various organized socialist groups in France, including the *Parti ouvrier*, by demanding that all socialist parties select women candidates to stand at the next election. The demand met with universal silence: none of the national socialist party leaders even deigned to reply to Potonié-Pierre's letter. Jules Guesde placed Pontonié-Pierre's letter in his personal files, but there it remained, unanswered.[61]

Local socialists did choose, however, to express their congratulations to women who refused to stand as *Solidarité* candidates. *Le Travailleur* applauded the decision of one woman, Angèle Duc-Quercy, not to stand. Duc-Quercy earned the approbation of the local *Parti ouvrier* by stating in her refusal her view that to stand for office would, in effect, place the feminist struggle above the more important class struggle.[62]

At the same time, one of the staunchest defenders of Guesdism, Paule Minck, decided that the time had come to change her earlier opposition to such feminist-backed candidacies. Like Potonié-Pierre, Minck thought it was time to demand that Guesdists back their words with action. Thus she accepted *Solidarité*'s invitation to stand for office, 'as a disciplined soldier of the *Parti ouvrier*', a role she had played tirelessly for twelve years. Moreover, she stated that she was standing as a candidate both for *Solidarité* and for the *Parti ouvrier*.

Minck immediately informed her long-time friend, Jules Guesde, of her decision, sending him a copy of her acceptance letter. She left no room for doubt about the reasons for her decision. 'I believe it is my duty', she told Guesde, 'to put into practice the decisions of our congresses which, every one, have affirmed the equality of women from all points of view—economic, civil, and political.'

---

[61] This 1892–3 strategy is described in Sowerwine, *Sisters*, pp. 70 ff. The letter is found in IISH, 'Dossier Jules Guesde', Eugénie Pontonié-Pierre to Guesde (Paris, 19 Oct. 1892).

[62] *LT* (8 Feb. 1893).

On the other hand, Minck's letter to Guesde reflected a sea-change in her view of women's place in the class struggle. She had abandoned her earlier views, which placed women squarely within the proletariat on an equal plane with men of the revolutionary class, in favour of a view closer to Lafargue's. She wrote, 'the presence of women in all elective functions, especially on municipal councils, will render a great service to the nation. . . . The sad, corrupt affairs of the *bureau de bienfaisance* of the Seine, . . . plus various public scandals, prove that it is time for a new element in public affairs.' This new element, in Minck's view, must be women, because they were, in her words, 'more penetrating, tender, and more economical because they manage households'. Furthermore, as they were 'before everything, mothers', they were natural teachers of the young. Thus she offered her candidacy as 'mother, socialist, republican', in order 'to defend the party programme of the *Parti ouvrier français*.'[63] For Minck, this was a volte-face. However, her action provoked no response and no publicity from the party to which she had declared her unwavering loyalty, and for which she had worked hard for so many years.

Thus, the Guesdists demonstrated publicly that they had no real collective commitment to affirmative action, whatever the heat of their words. On the other hand, they had no aversion to continuing to pay lip-service to women's emancipation. Thus they invited a group of socialist feminists to present their *Cahiers des doléances* to the party congress of October 1893 where, as we have seen, they appointed the women's leader Aline Valette to the national party council.

Despite the fact that many socialist women recognized the tokenism which Valette's appointment represented, they did not leave the party in protest. Many, including a disillusioned Paule Minck, found that they had nowhere else to go. At least the Guesdists offered *words* about women's rights, and a forum for their expression.

After the congress, then, Minck threw herself into women's politics in Lille, Roubaix, and Tourcoing. She helped to organize several women-only meetings in the area, held for the purpose of expressing solidarity with the wives of miners, involved in a

---

[63] IISH, 'Dossier Guesde', 564/12, I–III 1893.

difficult and prolonged strike in the Nord in that year. (It should be noted, too, that many of these miners' wives were also striking workers, employed at the pit-head cleaning and preparing lamps.)

Lille's *Comité des femmes*, led by Anna Ghesquière and Mme Collignon, were quick to join Minck's efforts. They called a series of benefits for the miners' wives. In Roubaix, similar events were organized by the largest women's group, Women's Emancipation. A tireless Paule Minck travelled between the cities, explaining the miners' strike and encouraging women to join the *Parti ouvrier* which supported the strikers. Occasionally Minck was joined on a platform by Henri Ghesquière, who added his voice to Minck's, inviting women to join the *POF* and to organize still more socialist women's groups. At least one new group emerged from these meetings.[64]

Local authorities were even more worried by these meetings than they had been by women's demonstrations and petitions for school lunches earlier in the year. On this occasion, however, local officials directed their attack against the 'outside agitator' rather than at the organized women. As a result, Paule Minck was arrested at the beginning of November, charged with 'outrages against the agents of authority'. She was sentenced to six days in prison by the correctional tribunal in Lille.[65]

Minck's efforts, however, had proved so fruitful that by the close of 1893 organized women in the area were able to publish their own pamphlets, including Henri Ghesquière's brochure entitled *La Femme et le socialisme*.[66] These booklets were distributed widely, and brought the women's groups into even greater local prominence.

Taken together, the women's efforts of 1893 provoked wild self-congratulation among male socialist leaders at the end of the year. Henri Carrette waxed eloquent when describing Roubaix's women's groups to a female audience in Calais. The Roubaix Free Thinkers also congratulated themselves on local women's new militancy. They pointed out that women had begun to join their ranks, providing the largest group of new members. 'This conquest of

---

[64] 'Le Meeting', *LT* (25 Oct. 1893 and 11, 13, 18 Oct. 1893).

[65] *APP* Ba 1178, 'Dossier Paule Minck'. Clipping from *Le Radical* (16 Nov. 1893).

[66] Lille, 1893.

women' they announced, 'is at the same time the conquest of their husbands and children . . .'[67]

viii

Eighteen ninety-four opened with a significant addition to the ranks of local women's groups: the first Tourcoing women's group was organized following a series of public meetings featuring Paule Minck in January of that year.[68] Though details of the Tourcoing group's activities are lost, they had sufficient local impact to provoke hostility from the vigilant male Catholic workers' movement. At that group's second local congress in February 1894, several speakers railed against women's liberation which, they said, had been brought into their midst by socialist leaders. One speaker warned that women's emancipation as the socialists envisaged it would mean that 'wives would cease looking after us and our [sic] children'. Furthermore, he warned, socialists would lure women strikers into the larger movement for women's emancipation, a development he claimed had already occurred during a recent textile strike at Amiens.[69]

But, once more, the progress which the new Tourcoing group seemed to symbolize was compromised within the *Parti ouvrier* itself, this time by the increasingly influential views of the party's token woman, Aline Valette. Her ideas began to shape all local *POF* propaganda directed at women in 1894. Valette's views appeared in a series of articles which appeared in the local socialist press early in the year. Her message to women was, characteristically, a curious mix of socialism with what might be called 'separate-but-equal' feminism.

Valette's analysis rested on two basic ideas. Firstly, she pointed to the indisputable fact that working women played a key role in the waged labour force of France in the 1890s. Valette's figures showed 3,875,000 waged women in France in 1894. But, secondly, she argued that these women were different from male proletarians because nature had given them a special moral superiority. Thus,

---

[67] *LT* (28 Jan. 1893), and 'Libres Penseurs de Roubaix', *LT* (11 Jan. 1893).
[68] 'Tourcoing Conférence Paule Minck', *LT* (27 Jan. 1894 and 24 Jan. 1894).
[69] *LT* (6 Feb. 1894).

when they were organized into the *Parti ouvrier*, they would inevitably raise its moral tone along with its income.[70]

The practical corollary of her position was a neglect of women's interests as workers, and an overemphasis on their traditional roles. Thus, she promised one group of local women that if they, whom she called 'wives and mothers', joined the socialist party, their hours would be shortened and their wages raised so that they could 'do their duty' and 'protect the lives of your children and your nephews'. 'My poor working sisters', she said, 'support your husbands, fathers, and brothers' when they marched or demonstrated. 'Do your duty!' she entreated them, 'Enough misery and tears in your household.'[71]

In another speech, she again conflated women with the proletariat. She told an audience that the emancipation of women necessarily crossed class lines, as all women were proletarians, and some women double proletarians. This speech, according to one writer, brought 'rich applause' and 'prolonged acclamations'.[72]

Local women, however, interpreted the socialist message in their own—and more clearly socialist—way. Women's Revenge of Roubaix, for example, described socialism's promise to women in an appeal sent to their unorganized sisters:

Citoyennes, at the hour when powerful capitalist reaction concentrates all its power to barricade the route to social progress, to murder in the egg the embryo of a better society, one which is being proposed in order to eliminate not only inequalities and social evils but also the inequality of the sexes; at this hour, we say to you, women must freely enter into the struggle for their own emancipation.

To this ringing appeal, the writers added some Flemish humour: 'As women have the reputation for being chatterers, so let us chatter: but of things that interest us in the highest degree, and in order to bring about our social well-being.'[73]

Although the gap between Valette's opinions and those held by working women at the local level was not in the least unique in the young *POF*, it did have more unfortunate consequences than other such disagreements between party leaders and constituents.

---

[70] A. Valette, 'La Femme et la loi morale', ibid. (7 Apr. 1894).
[71] Valette, 'Appel aux ouvrières', *LT* (28 Apr. 1894).
[72] 'La Réunion de l'Hippodrome à Lille', *LT* (16 May 1894).
[73] 'Roubaix Groupe la Revanche des femmes socialistes', *LT* (15 Sept. 1894).

Working women comprised more than just another interest group within the French working class. They were, as we have seen, harder to organize, given both their greater poverty and their extraordinarily busy lives. The effort necessary for an *ouvrière* to continue, month after month, a commitment to a women's political group meant that that group had to hold some real attraction, beyond merely providing a social base. And, whereas many local women willingly mobilized around the early Guesdist message, which promised to work for women's complete equality and which, moreover, accepted women's equal status within the waged work-force of Lille, Roubaix, and Tourcoing, they proved considerably less willing to organize around a party determined to marginalize their place within the working-class community. Increasing propaganda which glorified their domestic duties soon sent them away from the party.

The first sign of women's disappearance came at the third regional *POF* congress of the Nord federation, in February 1894. Only the oldest of the local women's groups—Roubaix's *Émancipation des femmes*—sent delegates to the meeting. Worse still, the congress voted a resolution which effectively pushed even that last vestige of autonomous women's organizations to the periphery of the party. As part of the Guesdists' larger organizational strategy, aimed at tightening control of party structures as well as party cadres, they decided to eliminate all non-official party groups from the central party structure. Thus women's groups were no longer allowed to belong to the *POF* as official sections: rather they, like youth groups and groups of Free Thinkers, were relegated to a special category called 'cultural groups'. Such groups, needless to say, played little role in the increasingly election-oriented activities of the Nord *POF*.[74]

Given the Guesdist leaders' growing assumption that women were in fact caretakers of workers' 'cultural' lives—at least in so far as those existed within private families, or in the cultural affairs of the larger community—this new policy was perfectly logical. But it did not suit working women who, as we have seen, balanced several roles in their own self-perceptions, including not only their domestic functions but also their place in the waged work-force.

---

[74] See 'Troisième congrès régional. Fédération du Nord du Parti ouvrier français', *LT* (21 Feb. 1894); *12ᵉ congrès nationale du PO, Nantes, 14–16 septembre 1894, compte rendu* (Lille, 1894); and Willard, *Les Guesdistes*, pp. 106 ff.

Of course, many party leaders had two basic reasons for pushing aside their earlier commitment to women's liberation. Firstly, women's disfranchisement made them far less important to socialist hopes. Thus, in the quest for votes, the vexed issue of women's equal rights was increasingly seen as divisive. Secondly, as the Guesdists grew stronger, the Marxist analysis which underlay their politics grew increasingly more important as the primary legitimizing tool. And, of course, as more leaders became familiar with Marxist theories of proletarian revolution, women's separate demands began to pose logical problems. If they were merely part of the industrial proletariat, then they would be liberated with the socialist revolution. If, on the other hand, they were 'double proletarians'—or worse, if women of all classes were proletarians regardless of their relationship to industrial capitalism—then their liberation was only partly achieved by a Marxist revolution. Organizing women into gender-defined groups, then, however practically successful, ran counter to a properly Marxist politics, in which there was no necessary connection between working women's liberation from industrial capitalist exploitation and the liberation of all women from the exploitation they suffered at the hands of men.

Given the apparent enormity of the problem posed by organized socialist women's groups, it may appear surprising that male leaders ever supported such efforts. But, in the 1880s and early nineties, there were several reasons for male leaders' commitment to this kind of organization at the local level. Firstly, even the most obdurate man could not fail to see the attraction which women's politics held for local *ouvrières*. It was quickly apparent, for example, that strike meetings restricted to women drew substantial crowds of local working women. Moreover, meetings which featured women speakers were more likely to lure local women than were those which did not concern them directly.

Secondly, many male socialists felt a genuine commitment to overthrowing the injustices of women's domestic conditions. Just as many leaders, including Jules Guesde, had initially been impelled toward Marxism because of their deep moral revulsion against the conditions brought by industrial capitalism, so were they drawn toward feminist ideas which promised to end the day-to-day 'double' burdens of proletarian women. Thus, when local leaders, including Guesde, Delory, Carrette, and Ghesquière, supported local women's groups, they were not motivated simply by opportunistic considerations.

Thirdly, in at least some areas of France, socialist leaders voiced concern that women's opposition to the socialist politics of their husbands would serve to weaken men's commitment to political organizing. A family united behind socialist party efforts was always preferable to one divided by political disagreements.

Finally, most local leaders, cognizant of the community base of all local politics, were aware of the importance of mobilizing women behind socialist reform campaigns. The aptness of this judgement was quickly demonstrated by the success of the *Comité des femmes*' campaign for school meals and crèches. In the day-to-day politics of municipal socialists, then, women were essential to success.

But the basic problems of including women—*qua* women—in a politics of proletarian revolution did not disappear over time, but rather grew increasingly more visible, ironically as more and more women joined autonomous women's groups, aimed at transforming the domestic status quo. The more local women shouted 'Long live the rights of women!' the more difficult socialist men's response.[75] In other words, the more local women appeared to lean toward putting feminist demands at the top of their collective agenda, the less socialist they became.

ix

Of course this web of practical and theoretical contradictions never found its way to the centre of socialist attentions in the early years, but rather lived just below the surface. And nowhere was it more crucial than in the developing electoral politics of the *POF*. By the mid-1890s, winning elections had become the Guesdists' primary goal. The more elections they won, the more they wanted to win. And the more leaders focused on broadening their voting base, the less important—indeed, in many constituencies, the more dangerous—became the party's long-standing commitment to the increasingly peripheral goal of liberating women.

---

[75] This was the rallying cry of the *Comité des femmes de Lille* during the May Day parade in 1894. 'Lille Manifestation du 1er mai. Appel aux ouvrières', *LT* (28 Apr. 1894).

As the *Parti ouvrier* broadened its electoral base in the 1890s, it reached out to hitherto neglected groups of potential voters. These included small shopkeepers and peasants, as well as workers in industries beyond mining, textiles, and othes where they had found earlier successes. In the process of designing party programmes aimed at attracting such new groups to the party, socialist leaders encountered the stolid misogyny shared by many working men in France in the *belle époque*. Some of the hostility toward working women was, of course, a realistic reaction to the growing practice in some industries of replacing men with cheaper women. This problem the socialists could, and did, address, by promising equal pay for equal work which, they argued, would effectively block the employers' tactic. But the more widespread, often visceral hostility to women—bolstered in many regions by a traditional separation of the sexes in all aspects of social and economic life, proved more of a problem. Then, too, some occupations, especially printing, had long traditions of male exclusivity. The addition of women to such occupational groups was feared less because of the competition to men's wages than because of women's expected alteration of working men's cultural lives. When men's self-respect depended upon their belief that their jobs required virtues long attributed to manliness—including strength, endurance, and competitive aggression—the mere idea of women's presence was threatening.

As the *POF* extended its hand toward such new groups of potential voters, leaders understandably became considerably less enthusiastic about spreading the socialist message on behalf of women's liberation. They did not drop such propaganda entirely, however, but they did increasingly begin to restrict it to those areas where it was acceptable, including the textile cities of the Nord. Thus, in that department, despite the developing loss of socialist women's groups from the textile cities, the Guesdists' commitment to women's emancipation continued to shape practical politics, though it did so under an increasingly equivocal theoretical banner.

An example of the Guesdists' recognition of the importance of women in *practical* politics came after a series of successful women-only strike meetings in Roanne, in January 1895, when Guesde wrote home to women's groups in the Lille area. 'Women of Roubaix, of Lille, of Calais', he wrote, 'who have so valiantly fought for the *Parti ouvrier*, you have, in your Roanne sisters, companions worthy of you!'[76] He encouraged them to continue their efforts on behalf of Guesdists, which they did, throwing themselves into the successful municipal election campaign which returned a socialist municipal council in Lille in 1895.

But the theoretical message grew increasingly muddled. More and more, local audiences heard the Lafarguian version of women's eventual liberation under socialism. It was this line which Aline Valette articulated at the national party congress in the autumn of 1895. In a typically confused speech, Valette decried industrialization on the grounds that it had pulled women and children from their homes. If the process continued, she warned, the working-class family would cease to exist. Mechanization had, moreover, put the wife to work beside the husband in industry, so that the family, which she called a 'domestic refuge', now existed in name only. 'Women', she added, 'are far from their children, far from their kitchens, far from their households.' Organizing women into unions was merely a temporary solution. Only the revolution could provide the ultimate solution by returning women to their domestic roles.[77] Following Valette's speech, the congress voted its customary resolution supporting women's liberation. But, on this occasion, the words of the resolution were considerably less radical than they had been in previous years. It read:

Considering that woman today is as industrialized as man, that this industrialization has given birth to a feminine proletariat which from this hour constitutes an increasing force . . . it is important, and in the interests of woman, that is to say of the species, and of socialism to organize that force. Thus the 13th national congress invites all delegates present to put all their efforts toward the union and federative organization of women workers.[78]

This disappointing resolution represented two shifts in the party's emphasis. Firstly, the Guesdists no longer promised to work toward women's equal rights at work or in society, but limited themselves to a vague commitment to union organizing.

---

[76] Guesde, 'La Grève de Roanne', *LT* (2 Jan. 1895).

[77] 'Roubaix Groupe la Revanche des femmes socialistes', *LT* (15 Sept. 1894).

[78] *13ᵉ congrès national du Parti ouvrier Romilly, 8–11 septembre 1895, compte rendu* (Lille, 1895). See also *Lyon Républicain* (12 Sept. 1895), clipping in *Musée Social*, dossier '13ᵉ congrès national du *POF*'.

Secondly, and more importantly, the resolution suggested that party leaders had ceased to view women as agents of their own destiny. Women were not invited to struggle for their own liberation, or even to organize themselves into unions or into the party. Instead, men were instructed to organize them—on behalf not only of the women themselves, but also of the 'species'.

Local working women reacted negatively to the changing party view of their place in the class struggle. Over the next few years, all traces of socialist women's groups in Lille, Roubaix, and Tourcoing vanished from sight, as women voted with their feet. It was not an easy death however; between 1895 and 1900 the issue of women's place in the socialist movement continued to rear its troublesome head, but, after the mid-1890s, it never found a clear-cut home within the increasingly fractured socialist political movement.

Thus did relations between working women and the national *Parti ouvrier* wither after 1895. But what of the Guesdist leaders themselves? Had Guesde, for example, changed his earlier radical views in favour of women's rights? As Roubaix's deputy through the decade of the nineties, Guesde naturally helped to shape local socialist politics—including those directed at organizing working women. Thus, it is instructive to review Guesde's changing position on the vexed issue as it developed through this period, especially as it helped to change day-to-day relations between the *POF* and local women.

Guesde's behaviour in these years suggested the extent to which he was increasingly perplexed by the issue of women's liberation. He did, for example, talk constantly in public about women's equality, though he did nothing to encourage the party to act in order to achieve it. Moreover, he maintained a close friendship with many socialist feminists throughout the nineties. Much of his private correspondence showed a continuing—if secondary—interest in problems encountered in the feminist struggle. Finally, he actively involved himself in those limited struggles demanded by the 1895 congress resolution, including efforts to bring women into existing socialist unions.

At the same time it must be remembered that Guesde's activities were hampered in these years by two factors. Firstly, his precarious health kept him out of many local party battles and away from various local activities. Secondly, what energy he could muster went increasingly toward the national battle being fought for dominance within the French socialist movement. His main rival for leadership of the many warring *tendances* of the era was Jean Jaurès. Much younger, and considerably healthier, Jaurès was always willing to participate in public debates which further sapped Guesde's strength.[79] These debates, moreover, were often counter-productive at the grass-roots level, as many workers became increasingly disenchanted with their constantly bickering leaders.

Nevertheless, the women's issue remained at least at the back of Guesde's mind, in spite of his other preoccupations. Throughout 1896 he corresponded with several national feminist leaders, occasionally agreeing to appear in their activities, though he was never able to fulfil those promises. One letter written to Guesde by Pauline Spony, a Guesdist feminist in Paris, suggested the extent of his contact with grass-roots socialist feminists in 1896. Spony wrote to him, 'If your health had permitted you to take part in the electoral struggle in our *quartier*, you would have seen with satisfaction that even more than the women of the Nord, the *Parisiennes* are interested in politics.'[80] Guesde also kept a second document among private papers sent to him by delegates at the 1896 feminist congress held in Paris. They wrote to Guesde explaining their position on protective labour legislation for women. In contrast to the *POF* stand, these women opposed such legislation, on the grounds that it would throw many women out of work. Further, they foresaw that the expected prohibition of night-work for women would effectively prevent women from breaking into some of the higher-paying night jobs, including typesetting.[81]

Guesde's correspondence makes it clear that women—both socialists and non-socialists—saw in Guesde a sympathetic ally in the mid-nineties. Guesde's continuing interest in such feminist activities, moreover, shows that he had not shifted altogether away from his earlier commitment to women's interests. Nevertheless, in Guesde's mind, as in other *POF* leaders' minds, the problem of women's emancipation was on a back burner. Clara Zetkin, the

[79] See *Les Débats* (12 Sept. 1895).
[80] IISH, 'Dosier Guesde', 262/4 Spony to Guesde (Paris, 16 May 1896).
[81] In ibid., 263/4 (Paris, 14 June 1896).

German socialist women's leader, summed up her view of the situation in France at the London meeting of the Second International in the summer of 1896. She told an interviewer that 'there is no socialist women's movement in France'. She explained that, instead, women in all the French socialist parties (there were four in that year) worked side by side with men, demanding 'the complete enfranchisement of both sexes'. At the same time, Zetkin said, 'there are no interesting women leaders connected with the French movement', except for Louise Michel, Paule Minck (whom she identified as a 'blanquiste'), and Valette.[82]

However common Zetkin's view, it was both right and wrong. It was true that by 1896 women's groups were disappearing from the public view. Optimists might explain this development by arguing that women were working side by side with men, especially as they were rarely seen anywhere else. But Zetkin was wrong to suggest that only three women leaders existed within the French socialist movement in 1896. Though they were few, they were more than that.

For example, at the 1897 national *POF* congress, held in Paris, there were five women delegates, including Minck and Valette, plus a new face, Elisabeth Renaud, as well as two other women about whom nothing further is known. This was Renaud's début among the Guesdists, though her interest in them quickly flagged as she discovered what she considered to be their lack of interest in women's equality. (When, two years later, she helped to found the *Groupe féministe socialiste*, the subject of Charles Sowerwine's recent *Sisters or Citizens*, she led that group into the independent—Jaurèsist—wing of the movement, not into the *POF*.[83]) The resolution passed by that 1897 congress was sufficiently reactionary to warn off all but the most committed Guesdist women. It read, 'The aptitudes and the sexual burdens of woman and the superior interests of the species and of the society which she must safeguard, creates for her *vis-à-vis* the present conditions of production and of reproduction a situation distinct from that of man . . .' Therefore,

---

[82] Mary Foster, 'Women at the International Congress', in *Musée Social*, dossier 'Le Congrès international socialiste de Londres, juillet 1896', vols. i–ii, 'Articles divers parus dans la presse'.

[83] Renaud is, along with the *GFS*'s co-founder Louise Saumoneau, the focus of Charles Sowerwine's history of that movement at the turn of the century.

the Party puts on the agenda of the next congress, as well as in its written
or spoken propaganda, the question of knowing whether there is a reason
to elaborate a feminine programme, protecting the woman exploited as
waged worker and as woman dispossessed by her waged work of the fruit
of work, and forced to sell herself, her labour, and her sex, dispossessed
as mother of the product of her flesh if she is married, oppressed by all her
burdens of maternity outside marriage, doubly serving as producer and
reproducer.[84]

Well, that sort of convoluted wording surely threatened no one.
Not only did the resolution effectively table the issue until the
following year, but it suggested that the real issue was the
protection of mothers, babies, and working-class prostitutes.
Furthermore, it highlighted the new Guesdist approach to
women—by focusing not on their more threatening (and potentially
more equal) role within the waged labour force, but rather on their
traditional biological roles as mothers and objects of the lusts of
bourgeois men, who needed to be protected—by socialist men—
from the ravages of the present system. This approach could
hardly have offended any among the socialists' potential voters—
however much it offended against working women's own interests
or views of themselves.

Not surprisingly, what followed this resolution was not any
'written and spoken propaganda' but rather silence. Moreover, it
rang the death-knell on local socialist women's groups. Their last
gasp was heard at one Lille meeting toward the end of 1897 where
Citoyenne Reville told forty-nine men and sixteen women that
they must 'reanimate' what she called the 'fédération féminine
lilloise'. Henri Ghesquière seconded her appeal. But though
eleven women joined the *POF* at the end of the evening, nothing
further became of the moribund autonomous local women's
movement.[85]

Eighteen ninety-seven, then, saw the end of the only grass-roots
socialist women's organization in the Lille area in the early
decades of the Third Republic. Despite the high hopes and
militant rhetoric of the early years, it was a movement doomed to

---

[84] *15ᵉ Congrès national du Parti ouvrier, Paris, 10–13 juillet 1897, compte rendu*
(Lille, 1897).

[85] *ADN* M 154 73 'Police politique, propaganda socialiste, rapports, 1900'. The
local socialist press made no mention of this meeting, or of any other women's
group meetings that year. See *L'Égalité de Roubaix–Tourcoing* (1896).

end when the socialist political party ultimately began to cohere around a more properly Marxist analysis of society backed up by electoral politics, in which there was no room for the separate emancipation of non-voting women.

In dropping out of their groups in the period 1895–7, local women began to move away from the enthusiastically loyal position which had helped to put local socialists into municipal councils and into the *Chambre*. But their move out of Guesdist politics did not happen in isolation from their male comrades. Rather, local men also began to express their increasing disaffection from the Guesdist movement—a disaffection which shortly turned Guesde himself out of office, as we shall see in the next chapter.

6

WOMEN AND SOCIALISM, 1897–1914

i

THE disappearance of socialist women's groups from the workers' districts of Lille, Roubaix, and Tourcoing after 1897 reflected a broader decline in socialist fortunes among both male and female workers in the region. Five factors contributed to the Guesdists' problems. Firstly, the textile *patronat*, increasingly aware of the extent to which the *POF* could mobilize local workers, buried their differences in order to concentrate on electing non-socialist candidates to local and national office. Secondly, as the Guesdists continued tightening their hold on the local party's organizational structures and building more disciplined party cadres, the informally organized grass-roots activities of the movement—so long essential to socialist success at the ballot-box—declined. Furthermore, local leaders gradually purged dissenters from their ranks. The bloody public battles which accompanied this purging did little to endear the Guesdists to local working-class voters.

Thirdly, competition among the various socialist *tendances* at the national and international levels spilled over into local politics. Debates between national socialist leaders over Dreyfusism and Millerandism occasioned little unity among local leaders. In fact, the latter problem eventually split the once-solid Roubaix Guesdists in 1902. Henri Carrette, a supporter of ministerialism, was thrown out of the *mairie* and forced to form his own splinter socialist party under the auspices of the Guesdists' rival group, the independent socialists led by Jean Jaurès.

These political controversies were further exacerbated by a growing industrial depression. As unemployment increased and wages dropped for those still in work, the day-to-day struggle to survive drained many workers' energy for socialist politics. These harsh economic realities were further complicated by the increasingly strident local battle between the syndicalists organized in the metal-workers' union of Lille and the socialists in the national textile federation.

The conjuncture of these competing factors had immediate effects. Jules Guesde was the first victim, losing his *Chambre* seat to the textile magnate Eugène Motte in 1898 after a long and bitter campaign. Motte soon added insult to this injury by becoming Mayor of 'Red Roubaix' in 1903 following the party's split over ministerialism.[1] Only in 1912, after the unification of the socialist movement had healed the wounds of this divisive period, did local voters turn Motte out of Roubaix's *mairie*, electing instead the Guesdist Jean-Baptiste Lebas (who remained mayor until 1940).

Guesdist fortunes in Lille were only slightly less devastated. Gustave Delory lost the *mairie* in 1904, again following a series of local party squabbles. But he held on to the seat he won in the *Chambre* in 1902. Lille's voters also reacted quickly to the socialist unification, adding two more socialists to their parliamentary delegation in 1905—Jules Guesde and Henri Ghesquière.

In Tourcoing in these years the radical deputy and mayor Gustave Dron held on to the loyalty of most local voters. His efforts to duplicate many socialist reforms begun in the two neighbouring cities were successful in deterring most workers from shifting their allegiance to the Guesdist candidates. In fact, Dron was so successful that he held off the socialist tide until just before the German invasion of 1914. In that year, finally, Tourcoing's voters sent the Guesdist Albert Inghels to the *Chambre*. Even then, Dron remained mayor of the city until 1919.

For most of the years between 1896 and 1914, then, grass-roots loyalty to local Guesdist leaders declined sharply. Only after 1905 did the party begin to make up losses sustained during the troubled years around the turn of the century. And even in 1914 only Roubaix was solidly back in the socialist fold, with both the *mairie* and the parliamentary delegation in socialist hands. In Lille, the mayor was a conservative, though two of the three deputies were socialists.

These misfortunes at the formal political level, however, were countered to some extent by the continuing development and

[1] See André Morizet, 'Les Faits politiques. La scission de Roubaix', in *MS*, vol. i (Jan.–June 1902), pp. 394–5, as well as Robert Baker, 'A Regional study of working-class organisation in France: Socialism in the Nord 1870–1924' (Ph.D., Stanford University, 1967), pp. 106–42, and Robert Vandenbussche, 'Une Élection de combat dans le Nord: 27 avril et 11 mai 1902', *RdN* (Apr.–June 1974), pp. 131–40.

spread of a vital, informally based socialist popular culture. Though they did not always vote for socialist officials, most workers continued to participate actively in unofficial socialist manifestations, including mass parades, fêtes, amateur theatricals, musical evenings, and so on. Food co-operatives also continued to grow: if anything their benefits became even more immediately apparent in the bleak economic period after 1896. Thus, it was an ironic fact that, even as formal socialist politics grew increasingly separate from most workers' daily lives, socialist popular culture was everywhere the dominant mode of community expression in these years.

For women workers, their disappearance from the cadres and official groups of the *Parti ouvrier* was, to some extent, compensated for by their continuing role in local social and cultural life, in which they retained an essential place. Moreover, the loss of local women's groups from the formal political struggle of the region did not signal a loss of organized women from the national or international socialist scene. Quite the contrary in fact: the death of local women's groups was accompanied by the birth of France's first national socialist feminist group ('national' meaning, as usual, Paris-based), the *Groupe féministe socialiste* (*GFS*), whose history forms the core of Charles Sowerwine's recent work.[2]

In addition to the leaders of the new *GFS*, several new women militants appeared on the national scene, replacing those women whose deaths followed one after the other around the turn of the century. (Valette died in 1899, Minck in 1901, and Michel in 1905). Among these new faces were those of Elisabeth Renaud (whose flirtation with Guesdism was short-lived) and Louise Saumoneau, the two co-founders of the *GFS*, and Madeleine Pelletier, the only one who joined the Guesdist wing of the socialist movement.

The efforts of Renaud, Saumoneau, and others in the *GFS*, together with the more isolated work of Pelletier, kept the issue of

---

[2] Historians of working women's politics owe a great debt to Charles Sowerwine's work. It was he who first began the rediscovery of women socialists among the celebrated male denizens of the French left. Without his pioneering efforts and diligent, painstaking scholarship it is doubtful if such a book as this could ever have been written. See Sowerwine, *Sisters or Citizens? Women and Socialism in France Since 1876* (Cambridge, 1982).

women's place in the class struggle at the forefront of French socialist debates during the period preceding unification. At the same time, the problem of mobilizing women rose increasingly to the surface of Second International debates, as organized women's parties grew increasingly vocal in the socialist movements of Germany and Austria and, to a lesser extent, in the member parties of all European nations. These women's efforts culminated, in 1907, with the founding of the International Congress of Socialist Women (ICSW), which met concurrently with the International itself. This group succeeded in keeping women's demands—especially and increasingly for suffrage—prominent on socialist agendas throughout the pre-war period.

Of course, national and international activities had far less direct effect on local politics in the Nord than they did on socialist activities in Paris, especially as the local party no longer relied upon national women militants to spread the socialist message. None the less, the Nord department's position at the centre of Guesdist strength in these years meant that debates in the national and international parties both involved and influenced local party leaders. This fact in turn meant that many decisions taken at the international and national levels helped to shape the relations between regional parties and their constituents, including the women textile workers of the Lille *arrondissement*.

This chapter, then, necessarily has a wider focus than the previous one. Although the spotlight remains on women textile workers—both as subjects of their own politics and as objects of socialist attention—the stage is crowded with actors from outside the Lille, Roubaix, or Tourcoing areas.

ii

The first sign of decline in local political strength was measured by the fall in official party meeting attendance beginning in 1897. Where once popular local leaders had attracted thousands to meetings, now they began to draw crowds of only a few hundred. One of the best-attended meetings of that year, in fact, was one featuring the popular mayor, Gustave Delory. It attracted only 250 men and 100 women from the workers' districts of Lille.[3]

[3] *ADN* M 154 67 28, 'Parti ouvrier. Arrondissement de Lille'.

At the same time, however, informal socialist activities continued to lure sufficient crowds to arouse a growing concern among local authorities. And, ironically, given the disappearance of all local women's groups, most officials were particularly worried about women's participation in these socialist events. Throughout 1897, for example, police reports consistently noted an unusually large number of women present in socialist crowds of all types. One informer finally decided that women must have been 'enticed' thither by what he called 'frequent fêtes sponsored by the *mairie*'.[4]

On the whole, in fact, the local bourgeoisie was oblivious to the gradual withering of close relations between the *Parti ouvrier*'s cadres and local workers. Instead, many among the local professional classes, long on the opposite side of the political fence from the conservative, often monarchist textile mill owners, joined their efforts to a united move to destroy what they saw as the Guesdists' firm hold over the local electorate. As a result, the legislative campaign of 1898 saw a clearer class division than most earlier campaigns in Roubaix. Virtually all members of the bourgeoisie lined up on one side against the socialists.[5]

This new anti-Guesdist coalition deployed several weapons in the effort to elect Eugène Motte to the *Chambre*. Firstly, they tightened blacklisting in the mills of the city. This tactic was particularly effective in the face of widespread unemployment occasioned by the desperate crisis in the textile industry. Secondly, the *patronat* increased their pressure on workers to join prescribed *cercles* and to vote for their candidate. They held obligatory election meetings during the working day in the mills. They also organized spies within existing Catholic workers' *cercles* (then affiliated to the *patronat*'s new umbrella group, the *Union sociale et patriotique*, founded in 1893). Members of such groups collected electoral data for mill owners, including lists of voters and their polling places. On election day, owners organized groups of workers to go to the polls accompanied by a supervisor who tried to ensure a Motte vote. In the case of some workers whose politics

---

[4] Ibid., 68, 'Parti ouvrier à Lille, 1896–97 (et Roubaix et Tourcoing)'.

[5] Details of this election are found in IISH, 'Dossier Jules Guesde', and A. Compère-Morel, *Jules Guesde, le socialisme fait homme, 1845–1922* (Paris, 1937), pp. 427–8. See also Vandenbussche, 'Aspects de l'histoire politique du radicalisme dans le département du Nord (1870–1905)', *RdN* (Apr.–June 1965), pp. 223–68.

were suspect, they were prevented from leaving the factories to vote. One observer of the election, Guesde's friend Compère-Morel, further accused many mill owners of buying votes, and of re-registering loyal *Union* members in previously socialist voting districts in order to swing the vote against Guesde.

In addition to these practical measures, the *patronat* employed their own propaganda machine to spread an anti-socialist message throughout the workers' districts. In the long run, this propaganda had more serious consequences for socialist fortunes than did Guesde's defeat at the polls. It contained three key ideas which the socialists had difficulty countering. Firstly, Motte's supporters suggested that the socialists were anti-patriotic, a fact demonstrated by their membership in the Second International, as well as by their internationalist position. Secondly, the opposition argued that Guesde and his followers preached the end of the family. (Needless to say the *patronat* found plentiful ammunition in the curious ideas of Paul Lafargue, expressed in his Lille speech about women's sexual liberation.) Thirdly, the *patronat* tried to persuade the workers not to vote for Guesde on the grounds that he was not a proletarian, but instead a man who willingly accepted his parliamentary salary, which had amounted to 445,000 fr, between 1893 and 1898.

Although this last point, coming from multimillionaire textile magnates, doubtless aroused little more than scepticism among the working-class electorate, the former two points made an impact by raising doubts about socialist policies. In the case of the first accusation of internationalism, socialists could do nothing to counter the attack. They *were* committed to the international workers' struggle, a struggle which included German workers along with those of every other capitalist nation. The argument that the workers of Germany's industries were not the same as the hated leaders of the German state did not always weaken French workers' hatred. In French Flanders there were few happy memories of the German invasion of earlier years.

Guesdists did, however, attempt to counter accusations that they supported the end of the family, by arguing in favour of the traditional family. In the process, socialist speakers began increasingly to promise that socialism would return mothers and wives to their domestic duties, thus re-creating the working-class family's supposed pre-industrial idyll.

Although Guesdists were willing to compromise their earlier commitment to women's equality, they were not willing to compromise what they saw as the purity of their movement by forming any alliances with various local progressives.[6] Indeed, for most Guesdist leaders, the 1898 election provided an ideal opportunity to clarify once and for all the political identity of the *Parti ouvrier*, by insisting on the ideologial purity of the socialist platform. Moreover, eliminating moderate or dissenting opinion from party discourse tightened party discipline. Thus, even while these tactics virtually ensured defeat, they accomplished some of the party leaders' purposes.

But the cost of such tactics were heavy. Not only did Guesde cease to represent Roubaix workers in the *Chambre*, but his defeat demoralized many long-time Guesdists. Henri Ghesquière spoke for many among the most loyal party cadres when he lamented the widespread loss of enthusiasm for the *POF* which he discerned among local workers. Not only was this loss measured by Motte's victory, but it was also evident in the steep decline in party revenues.[7]

On the other hand, local socialists did not emerge from the 1898 elections entirely vanquished. Overall, election returns showed that the number of socialist voters had increased slightly, though changes in voting districts nullified the effects of this. More immediately, the *POF* gained eight new seats on the local *conseils des prud'hommes*, two in Tourcoing, and six in Lille.[8]

Ironically, given their increasing insistence that women's place was in the working-class home, Guesdist candidates stood for the *conseils* on a platform which included the proviso that women had the right to stand and to vote for these workers' councils. Gustave Delory articulated this position, telling one audience that working women 'are about half the personnel of the factories . . .'. 'Therefore', he added, 'women's presence on *conseils* will teach a lesson to mill owners, who presently regard women only as a source of pleasure or profit,' an attitude bolstered by the fact that 'women have no means of defending themselves because they have no rights'.[9]

[6] See Vandenbussche, 'Aspects', p. 247.

[7] *RS* (20–27 Apr. 1899).

[8] Ibid., (13–15 Sept. 1898).

[9] *ADN* M 154 70, 'Police politique. Roubaix, 8 juillet 1899'. See also 'Rapports, 1898–99'.

Thus, the socialist message for women workers in 1898 was contradictory. On the one hand, they heard that socialism was going to return them to their domestic *foyers*, where they could resume their traditional roles as wives and mothers. On the other, they heard strong support for their rights to participate in local workers' politics via the *conseils des prud'hommes*. The contradictory nature of these two positions characterized the relations between the party and working women throughout the period leading up to the unification of the Guesdists with other socialist parties.

iii

In the years immediately following the 1898 election, socialists grew increasingly distant from their constituents in the Lille area. This process reached a nadir in the black years of 1900 and 1901. So busy were Guesdist leaders arguing over national splits and issues that they failed to take any effective action to ameliorate the workers' desperate situation.[10] When the head of the Lille socialist textile union, Henri Lefebvre, wrote to Guesde about local workers' restiveness in the face of widespread misery in August 1900, he condemned what he saw as local socialist leaders' indifference to textile workers' plight. He told Guesde that masses of 8,000 unemployed textile workers thronged the streets of Roubaix every day. And, even though they gathered in the road outside the big socialist food co-operative, *La Paix*, they got no help from socialists inside. Lefebvre warned Guesde that such indifference and neglect of workers' needs would ultimately turn textile workers against the party—throwing them necessarily into the waiting arms of the 'anarchists' (of the *CGT*). He proposed that Guesde order the immediate distribution of food, as well as the creation of soup-kitchens, and so on.[11]

Unfortunately, and symptomatically, Lefebvre's warning went unheeded. When the mass march of the *Sans travail* was organized from Roubaix in October 1900, no *POF* leaders were involved.[12] Nor did the march to Paris elicit any party support. This

[10] Vandenbussche, 'Aspects', pp. 250–1.

[11] IISH, 'Dossier Jules Guesde, 313/8, Lefebvre to Guesde (Roubaix, 15 Aug. 1900).

[12] *AN* F⁷ 12501, 538–48. These reports show 10,000 unemployed workers marching from Roubaix alone.

remarkable gap between the workers themselves and the party which claimed to represent them underscored the extent to which the two sides had grown apart.

And although this 1900 breach affected relations between the party and workers of both sexes, it was widest between the party and its female constituency. Evidence of the fractured relations between *ouvrières* and the Guesdists was prevalent at the *POF*'s regional conference, held in Caudry in that year. Unlike all previous departmental party congresses, this one attracted no women delegates. As a result, every speaker addressed himself to 'citoyens'. Moreover, no discussion of women appeared among agenda items. In fact, only one woman was mentioned at all during the congress, and she was Paule Minck, listed among the party's 'occasional speakers' during the preceding year.[13]

The absence of women—either as delegates or as subjects for discussion—reflected the party's decision to expel any peripheral or divisive problems from party discourse. In Guesde's private notes concerning this Caudry congress, he noted the importance of this tactic which he thought would promote a more concentrated focus on the class struggle.[14]

However deleterious this policy on local rank and file enthusiasm for the *POF*, it did succeed in pushing the Guesdists to the forefront of the national struggle for dominance. As a result, Guesdists far outnumbered their socialist rivals at the Paris meeting of the Second International in September 1900, by 765 mandates compared with only 318 for all other socialists *tendances* combined.

Unfortunately, the absence of women from the regional Caudry meeting was mirrored in Paris. Guesdist ranks included not a single woman. All French women present at this meeting of the Second International belonged instead to one of the Guesdists' rival groups; most were among the independent socialists, led by Jean Jaurès.[15]

[13] *Congrès regional, Caudry, 5 août 1900, compte rendu* (Lille, 1900). Minck had come to Lille during the Flamidien case of 1899 which pitted Catholics against both socialists and anti-clericalists when a local priest was accused of murdering a schoolboy. Minck's speeches condemned the Church, particularly its manipulation of women.

[14] IISH, 'Dossier Jules Guesde', 313/25, 5 VIII 1900.

[15] *5ᵉ congrès socialiste international, Paris 23–27 septembre 1900, compte rendu analytique* (Paris, 1901).

Women's disappearance from Guesdist ranks by 1900 was accompanied by a sea-change in Jules Guesde's attitude toward working women's place in the socialist struggle. Nowhere was this change more obvious than in his pamphlet, *Problème et solution*, first published in 1895 but reprinted in 1900 and frequently thereafter until the war.[16] In this essay, Guesde argued Lafargue's line for the first time. He wrote that machines had not proved to be a liberating force, but had merely extended work from men to include women and children. Once machines had made women's and children's work possible, they had effectively 'emptied' the male workers' home 'of his wife and child', who became, instead the property of capitalists. Whereas before industrialization male wages had supported an entire family, now employers could buy the triple labour of 'man, woman, and child for the price of one male worker'.

This, then, comprised the problem—women and children no longer 'belonged' to male workers, but instead to male capitalists. And the solution? Socialism. Although none of the 'seven basic principles of socialism' which Guesde detailed in this brochure explicitly stated that women and children would be returned to the men after the socialist revolution, the implication of his essay was clear. Moreover, the pamphlet was openly addressed only to male workers. Women had vanished as historical subjects in Guesdist discourse.

Such attitudes, which Guesde shared with many other male socialist leaders, effectively hid working women from view. As blinkers, they were so effective that even the past was quickly lost. Women's mass participation in socialist efforts from 1880 to 1900 disappeared from the collective knowledge of socialist leaders.[17] Thus, when the socialist–feminist Mme Sorgue visited Lille in 1901, she was surprised to discover women present at the socialist meetings. A police spy reported that she told one audience that 'she was happy to see numerous women at this meeting—women who have come to acclaim the unity of revolutionary socialism'. She told the men present that the women 'want also to take their

---

[16] Brochure found in *AN* F[7] 12501, 'Actes socialistes dans les départements, Nord, 1900–1904'. See also *ADN* M 154 73, 'Police politique propagande socialiste. Rapports 1900' in which police spies increasingly lump women and children together in a single, secondary, category.

[17] Reports of various mass meetings found in *ADN* M 154 73.

place of combat in the social struggle between work and capital'. She revealed her complete ignorance of women's previous participation in local socialist activities by telling the crowd that women had long been 'agents of the clergy', 'controlled by the confessional'. Thus their presence as new recruits to the movement was especially important. Once in the socialist movement, Sorgue added, women could 'teach their sons not to become cannon fodder and their daughters not to become prostitutes'. Furthermore, they could 'engage their husbands to vote for the socialist platform'.[18]

Sorgue's failure to tell the working women in her audience what socialism might hold for them, or what direct activities they might undertake on their own behalf, mirrored male socialists' reluctance to include local working women in their discourse as anything more than marginal and secondary constituents. So invisible had women become to most party leaders' eyes, in fact, that the official party histories that began to appear among Nord socialists after 1901 included no mention of women at all, though they purported to include all socialist events in the years from 1879 to 1901![19]

This local policy of ignoring women's role in the collective socialist past was duplicated at the national level, among all of the movement's leaders, regardless of their party links.[20] Moreover, the leaders disdained organized women's participation in the present as well. For example, throughout the long, vexed process of unification, various leaders occasionally solicited the views of the *GFS* but then paid no attention to their response. This indifference meant that the *GFS*'s programme, designed to draw working women back into the socialist orbit, was ignored.

Basically, the *GFS* suggested that the socialists' increasing emphasis upon electoral politics necessarily excluded women. To counter this trend, they argued that socialist leaders should shift the emphasis back to the revolutionary message of socialism which

[18] *ADN* 154 76, 'Police politique' and *AN* F[7] 12522, 'Rapport Préfecture, Lille, 18 septembre 1901'.

[19] Fédération du Nord, *Congrès régional, Douai, 7 avril 1901, compte rendu* (Lille, 1901); *19me Congrès national du Parti ouvrier, Roubaix, 15–18 septembre 1901* (Paris, 1901).

[20] Milan Kundera in *The Book of Laughter and Forgetting*, trans. by Michael Heim (Harmondsworth, Middx, 1980), makes the point that oppressive relationships often operate by 'forgetting' the collective past of the oppressed.

they should spread among the workers of France. Secondly, they argued that the leadership was moving steadily away from democratic practices. To halt the development of dictatorial leaders, the party must begin consulting all federated socialist groups about every important decision. Thirdly, they demanded that the party adopt two strategies to mobilize women. All women, they argued, should be included in all party functions, whether they concerned voters or not. The *GFS* also thought that the newly unified socialist party should establish a separate 'tribune féminine', which would exist solely as a forum for working women's ideas.[21]

If the national party leadership had genuinely wished to attract more women into the movement in 1901, the *GFS*'s programme would have formed the core of a successful strategy. But they did not. As Charles Sowerwine has shown, male socialist leaders first marginalized the *GFS*, then excluded it altogether in 1905 by refusing to allow it to federate in the new *SFIO*.[22] (Youth groups, by contrast, were allowed to federate as autonomous groups within the new party.)

Thus, in the years preceding unification, the distance between national socialist leaders and a female constituency grew. In many ways, the process mirrored the division between local Guesdist leaders and their female (and male) constituents in the Lille area.[23] This latter gap became even more obvious when the third great general textile strike hit the Nord department in the autumn

---

[21] Letter from Louise Saumoneau to the *Comité general du Parti socialiste*, in *FS* (May 1901). See also Virinus, 'Le Droit des femmes', *FS* (July 1901).

[22] This is a necessarily abbreviated description of the process by which women's groups were excluded from the *SFIO*. Sowerwine describes the death blow in *Sisters*, pp. 97 ff. He also points out that autonomous youth groups were accepted into the new party structure.

[23] In Roubaix, debates over ministerialism provoked a split in the party. Henri Carrette was forced to resign as mayor in 1902. He then founded a local section of independent (Jaurèsist) socialists. Most local activists, however, did not go with Carrette but rather remained faithful Guesdists in what was in that year the *Parti socialiste de France*. In Lille the party was rocked by scandals. Henri Ghesquière's brother was arrested (and ultimately convicted) for fraudulent use of municipal funds. His arrest drew attention to nepotism among Guesdists. Six members of Ghesquière's family were employed by the *mairie*. Delory's brother-in-law Gustave Devernay, who was a municipal councillor, was similarly generous with political patronage. Six members of his family held city jobs. See *AN* F[7] 125010 247 '12 mars 1903'; *AN* F[7] 12501 212, 'août 1903', and 160, '14 décembre 1904'. See also Morizet, 'Les Faits politiques', pp. 394–5.

of 1903. It began entirely without foreknowledge on the part of the Guesdists—including even those who led the socialist textile union![24]

As a measurement of the abyss which existed between the socialist party leadership and the masses of textile workers throughout the Nord, this strike was telling indeed. At the very least, it revealed the complete failure of the Guesdists' long campaign against spontaneous, unplanned strikes. In the official Guesdist view such strikes uselessly drained energy and funds needed for the revolutionary class struggle. Indifferent to this often-repeated Guesdist policy, however, the workers took to the streets of Lille, Roubaix, and Tourcoing (as well as of most other major northern cities), catching the local Guesdist leaders completely off guard.

As we saw in chapter 4, the development of the strike witnessed no parallel development of the socialist participation in it. In fact, during the long months of the strike, socialist unions divided and regrouped almost continuously. By the time the 1904 parliamentary commission began its investigation of the strike, most of the socialist textile union movement of the area was highly fragmented, despite most unions' membership in the national textile federation. Union witnesses before the commission agreed on only one fact: that most textile workers in the area evinced no loyalty to any union or political party throughout the duration of the strike.

On the eve of unification, therefore, the Guesdist picture in Lille, Roubaix, and Tourcoing was not altogether an optimistic one. Virtually all of the grass-roots enthusiasm which had marked their organizing efforts in the earlier years had dissipated. Women, especially, stayed away from Guesdist politics in droves.

iv

Only after 1905 did the situation begin to change—slowly. The newly unified socialist party attracted many local people who had dropped out of the Guesdist party during the squabbles of the preceding years. Moreover, the new *SFIO* began to attract a steady number of new party members—even in Tourcoing, where

[24] IISH, 'Dossier Jules Guesde', 360/1. Guesde's notes say that the Lille area *PSdF* had no role in the strike.

party membership grew by a surprising 160 per cent in the years between 1906 and 1914.[25] Obviously, a unified party was far more attractive than one rent by internal dissension.

But, for local women, unification did not signal any change in party policy. Not only was the *SFIO* itself generally uninterested in organizing them,[26] but three further elements complicated the Guesdists' policy towards mobilizing working women in the years from 1905 to the war. These included (in decreasing order of importance) a bitter local struggle between the socialists and syndicalists (the former gathered into the textile federation, the latter prevailing among metal-workers), the activities of Paris-based socialist feminists (who lacked an organizational base because the *GFS* broke up after being rejected by the *SFIO*),[27] and, finally, the efforts of the women within the Second International, which culminated in the founding of the International Congress of Socialist Women (ICSW) in 1907 which met concurrently with the International itself until the war. This latter group was led by the organized women of the German social democratic party, who numbered 70,000 in 1903 (plus a further 225,000 women in the socialist-sponsored free trade union).[28]

The ground for syndicalist growth in the Lille area had been prepared by the Guesdists themselves—firstly, by their constant open bickering and, secondly, by the corrupt practices which came to light just before unification. In addition, their lack of participation in the general textile strike of 1903–4 did not

---

[25] *AN* F⁷ 13820, 'Textile, 1910–1914'.

[26] This is despite the increasingly vocal agitation of women in the Second International. See E. Dolléans, 'Féminisme et propriété', *MS*, vol. iii (Sept.–Dec. 1903).

[27] Described in Sowerwine, *Sisters*, p. 103.

[28] See Georges Weill, 'Le Mouvement féministe social en Allemagne', *FS* (May 1901); Weill, 'Les Partis socialistes en Allemagne. Les congrès des femmes socialistes et des socialistes allemands à Munich', *MS*, vol. ii (July–Dec. 1902), pp. 1892–1902. See also Karen Honeycutt, 'Clara Zetkin' (Ph.D., Columbia University, 1975); Annik Mahaim, *et al.*, *Femmes et mouvement ouvrier: Allemagne d'avant 1914, révolution russe, révolution espagnole* (Paris, 1979); Jean Quataert, *Reluctant Feminists in German Social Democracy 1885–1917* (Princeton, 1979); Jacqueline Strain, 'Feminism and political radicalism in the German Social Democratic movement, 1890–1914' (Ph.D., University of California, Berkeley, 1964); Werner Thönnessen, *The Emancipation of Women: the Rise and Decline of the Women's Movement in German Social Democracy, 1863–1933*, trans. Joris de Bres (London, 1973).

encourage textile workers to throw themselves into socialist union activities, which more and more seemed aimed at politics rather than at economic activities. When the socialist union leader, Victor Renard, led his organization out of the *CGT* at the Amiens congress of 1906 (ostensibly in opposition to that group's commitment to a general strike, which the socialists long opposed) the split between socialism and syndicalism became definitive.

From 1906 onwards, then, continual public quarrels between what the socialists called the 'anarchists' of the *CGT* and local socialist leaders lessened the possibility of a unified working-class movement in the Lille area. Socialists reacted defensively to the anarchist threat, trying to define every position in such a way as to distinguish it from that taken by rival syndicalist leaders. Ironically, in the one way in which they clearly differed from the syndicalists—their commitment to electoral politics—they were more likely to provoke hostility than support. Tired of the constant wrangles which had long been a feature of socialist meetings, local workers were unwilling to turn out for electoral meetings, despite their growing readiness to vote for socialist candidates.

Moreover, the *CGT* offered sound economic benefits which the socialists scorned in favour of the coming revolution. A strike, as most local workers knew, was a means of obtaining better condition or higher wages. An election, by contrast, did not necessarily gain anything immediately tangible. Moreover, those reforms which had helped socialists to win elections during the 1880s and nineties had long since been instituted—even in Tourcoing, where alert radicals, led by Gustave Dron, had skilfully co-opted socialist initiatives. Social welfare programmes in the post-unification period were more extensive than they were before 1892, and they extended to all the poor without regard to their moral qualities. Crèches had been built (though not nearly enough of them), cheap school dinners started, and programmes to distribute clothing and shoes to indigent children were under way. Both Lille and Roubaix, moreover, sponsored health camps at Dunkerque for local children found to have tuberculosis or other lung infections.

Because of the socialists' early success in accomplishing many of their promised reforms, many local workers neglected to give the party credit for them. Instead, the syndicalists' promises of higher wages and improved working conditions were more appealing to textile workers who had been suffering the effects of industrial crisis for so many years.

On the other hand, the war between the *CGT* and the *SFIO* did not attract most textile workers into one camp or the other. Instead, they straddled a position between the two groups—more often than not unifying not around syndicalist or socialist affiliations but rather around their common membership in the textile community. Collective self-interest, then, rather than union or socialist politics, increasingly characterized textile workers' behaviour after 1906. Even most public meetings imitated this unity, by including socialists, syndicalists, and unaffiliated workers.[29] One Roubaix meeting, held in 1907, was typical. At that event, a local textile worker told the audience that although 'all kinds of unions' existed in the Roubaix area, some 'reformist', some 'revolutionary', all of them shared a single purpose, 'to better the lot of all textile workers'. In his view, this goal took precedence over all other considerations.[30]

Meetings of this kind, which crossed the artificial, externally imposed categories of syndicalists and socialists, attracted considerably more local support than did official *SFIO* meetings. Even during *Broquelet* in May 1907, Delory found himself addressing a meeting of only 150 people gathered in Lille. With sorrow, he told his listeners that such low attendance was the 'natural result' of the dangerous division between syndicalists and socialists in the workers' *quartiers* of that city.[31]

In fact, the only socialist-sponsored meetings which attracted mass support in these years were those which promised an entertaining public fight between socialists and anarchists. Three thousand workers turned out in June 1907 to hear Guesde take on a crowd of local syndicalists. One shocked reporter noted with disgust that the eager crowd included 'plusieurs dames' who watched the 'rough-and-tumble fight' between rival groups with undisguised enthusiasm. That meeting, like most others like it, ended in a free-for-all.[32] Such scenes continued to enliven local politics throughout the post-unification years.

[29] Reports are found in *AN* F[7] 12495, 'Activité socialiste dans le département du Nord (1905–1914)'.

[30] Ibid., *pièce* 315.

[31] Ibid., *pièce* 295.

[32] Ibid., *pièce* 279.

Although many local workers relished these public battles between national party and union leaders they rarely took sides. Instead, they remained committed to the community solidarity so long characteristic of French Flanders. When the 1909 general strike broke out, it was typically without clear ties to either the socialists or the syndicalists. Instead, all local unions, red, yellow, and independent, joined together to support work stoppage. During that strike, moreover, whatever residual effects of wider political quarrels still lingered in the textile cities disappeared. Together the textile work-force concentrated all their energies on winning a uniform wage system similar to that won by Armentières workers in 1904. Though the strike failed—as it was certainly doomed to do, given the variety of products and processes in the textile mills of the area—it did demonstrate to many local leaders that workers were uninterested in factional wrangling. Instead, their loyalty to one another superseded any commitments to formal organizations.

Nevertheless, leaders of both the socialist party and the *CGT* continued their efforts to shift workers' loyalties into their respective movements after 1909. In the course of these efforts, women workers once again provoked the attentions of many male leaders who had for some time preferred to ignore their potential organized strength.

The *CGT*, for example, sent a fiery woman activist, Gabrielle Petit, on a speaking tour of the Lille area during the course of the 1909 strike.[33] Petit's appearances proved very popular with local workers, particularly *ouvrières*. In fact, her ability to attract considerable numbers of women to meetings surprised even *CGT* leaders who already knew of her successes elsewhere in France. One decided that 'women are attracted not by the name but rather by the sex of the speaker'. Moreover, he wrote, 'women together find it easier to formulate demands to help men in the struggle'.[34] This realization led the *CGT* to begin trying to identify and to train potential women militants among unionized women.

In addition to some *CGT* leaders' dawning recognition of women's potential, anarchists among them became increasingly fascinated by the success of women anarchists elsewhere in

---

[33] Petit's tour is reported in *AN* F^7 13820 'Textile—1910–1914'.

[34] Fernand Bellugue, 'Les Jeunes et les femmes', *VdP* (6–12 Apr. 1914).

Europe, particularly in England, where the calculated violence of the suffragettes was beginning to arouse mass press attention. News of the suffrage struggle quickly reached leaders of the organized French left. A series of admiring articles appeared in the national *CGT* press, applauding the suffragettes' militancy. Many writers concluded patriotically that French women might show themselves to be equally active in pursuit of syndicalist goals if only the movement learned how to mobilize them into the economic struggle.

In their ensuing efforts to bring more women into their movement, the syndicalists employed three tactics. Firstly, they depended upon women militants to spread their propaganda among France's *ouvrières*. Syndicalist women encouraged the formation of women's unions as well as of more informal women's groups, both of which were welcomed into the flexible structure of the *CGT*.

Secondly, a flood of syndicalist propaganda poured off the *CGT*'s presses after 1907, aimed at mobilizing women workers. Some of this propaganda was not without bias, of course. More than one reporter patronized women's militant activities, effectively marginalizing them from the mainstream of unionist efforts. In addition, articles favourable to women workers' strikes and demands usually provoked a backlash of letters and articles hostile to women's presence within the labour movement.[35] Nevertheless, the *CGT*'s new-found commitment to drawing women into the syndicalist fold did give many women a forum for their views. Moreover, news stories brought women's activities to national attention. Furthermore, *CGT* newspapers—including *La Voix du peuple* and *La Bataille syndicaliste*—increasingly pushed reforms of particular help to women workers. Among these were both crèches for infants and extended child care facilities for older

---

[35] This male hostility was not widespread in the textile industry. But it was present elsewhere. See Jeanne Bouvier, *Mes mémoires—ou cinquante-neuf années d'activité industrielle, sociale, et intellectuelle d'une ouvrière* (Vienne, 1936); Hélène Brion, *La Voie féministe* (Paris, 1978), as well as the arguments of historians including Marilyn Boxer, 'Foyer or Factory: working-class women in nineteenth century France', *Western Society for French History, 21–23 November 1974* (Austin, Texas, 1975), pp. 192–203. See also Madeleine Guilbert, *Les Femmes et l'organisation syndicale avant 1914* (Paris, 1966), and Marie-Hélène Zylberberg-Hocquard, *Femmes et féminisme dans le mouvement ouvrier français* (Paris, 1981), and *Féminisme et syndicalisme en France* (Paris, 1978).

children during school holidays. Interestingly, most such demands were voiced on behalf of 'fathers and mothers of families' rather than on behalf of women alone.[36]

Finally, the *CGT* continued to support a strong commitment to women's right to work—for equal pay—at all jobs. Even when the Couriau affair split the syndicalist movement into warring camps in 1913 (one side backing the Lyon printers' union in its decision to expel Louis Couriau for allowing his wife Emma Couriau to work as a printer, the others supporting her right to work at the job for which she was trained, as well as her right to belong to the union, regardless of her husband's affiliation), the *CGT* deliberately avoided taking up a position against women printers.[37]

Despite these efforts, however, the *CGT* had only minimal success in mobilizing most working women for their cause. On the eve of the First World War, many syndicalist leaders began to explore the reasons for their failure. One militant, Francis Million, argued that all efforts to organize working women into unions must take account of four factors, two negative and two positive.[38] The most important negative factor stemmed from the fact that terrible conditions in most French industries forced most women to concentrate all their energies on staying alive. So absorbing was this struggle for existence that few women found time or energy for other activities. Secondly, Million suggested, most women were victims of a lifetime of education aimed at inculcating 'womanly submission'. Thus they often found rebellion difficult. Women's automatic passivity had to be broken down before they could be organized effectively.

On the positive side, however, Million pointed to the millions of French women who *had* overcome their submissiveness and gone on strike against their conditions. In most women's strikes, he wrote (albeit in patronizing tones), women had proved themselves to be as 'tenacious and courageous' as men. Furthermore, as more

---

[36] See D. Seurin, 'Le Repos hebdomadaire', *VdP* (10 Aug. 1902); Conférence de citoyenne Sorgue sur les huit heures', *VdP* (29 July 1906); Octave Soyer, 'Garderies enfantines', *VdP* (11 Aug. 1912).

[37] Details of this affair are found in Holly Larsen, 'Emma Couriau' (unpublished honours paper, History department, University of California, Berkeley, spring 1979), and in Guilbert, *Les Femmes*.

[38] Francis Million, 'L'Éveil de la femme', *BS* (20 Sept. 1913). Million was a Lyon printer who campaigned against his union's decision to prevent Emma Couriau from taking a job in the industry.

and more women joined the waged work-force the potential membership of the *CGT* grew. Increasingly it was only what Million described as 'men's fantasies' which saw women 'au foyer'. In real life they were everywhere *but* inside the domestic world. Once men overcame their fantasies, then, they would be able to see 'real women in their real lives', and thus include them in their organizations.

Such attitudes and policies finally began to enjoy some success among *ouvrières* just before the war began. Just as the Guesdists' strong defence of women's rights in the 1880s had attracted women to socialist activities, so the *CGT*'s efforts finally began to draw more working women into their fold. Many of the militant socialist feminists in the Isère, for example, shifted their allegiance from the male-dominated socialist textile union, whose leader, Victor Renard, had long disdained them, to the *CGT*. One of the most articulate of the Isère's women leaders, a Vienne *institutrice*, spoke for most of the region's organized working women in an article published in *La Voix du peuple* in 1914.[39] Venise Pellat-Finet thanked the paper for being 'consistently open to women'. 'In the midst of the general indifference of political parties', she wrote, 'it seems to us particularly clear that it is the *CGT* which seeks a remedy for the dolorous situation of working women.' Her comments were echoed by a Vienne textile worker, Claudette Coste, who wrote to the paper to say that her co-workers shared Pellat-Finet's views. She added that she represented more than just textile workers, as she was also a member of Vienne's *conseil des prud'hommes et prud'femmes*.

The faith of these women was justified by the actions of the *CGT* at the confederation's 1914 congress. In an effort aimed at recruiting more of France's waged women (who were 53 per cent of all women in France), the *CGT* resolved an affirmative action programme which echoed the programme outlined by the socialist workers at Marseilles in 1879. The programme required every member union to choose women as leaders. Moreover, the unions were told to select women as delegates to every *CGT* meeting or congress.[40] Had the war not intervened, such progressive policies

---

[39] *VdP* (1–8 Feb. 1914). See also Marie Guillot, 'Au travail', *VdP* (27 Apr.–3 May 1914).
[40] Reported in 'L'Organisation de la femme', *VdP* (18–24 May 1914), and *VdP* (13–19 July 1914).

might well have begun to bear fruit in bringing more *ouvrières* into unions, just as similar Guesdist policies had attracted the women textile workers of French Flanders into the *Parti ouvrier* several decades before.

V

Of course this has been but the briefest overview of a vastly more complex story of relations between the *CGT* and France's *ouvrières* between 1906 and 1914.[41] Nevertheless, the *CGT*'s efforts provided a contrast to the indifference which characterized *SFIO* policy toward those same women through most of these years. In fact, only on the eve of the war, and because of a conjuncture of several further pressures in addition to the one provided by the *CGT*'s example, did the *SFIO* begin to change its attitudes—and even then, only to a limited extent.

Among the pressures on the newly unified *SFIO* was the continuing agitation of a few socialist feminists who remained active despite the débâcle of 1905–6. True, there were not many such women active in these years, but their influence on socialists was out of proportion to their numbers. This influence was nowhere more visible than in the strong reactions they provoked among organized men. Any reading of the socialist press in these years, for example—particularly the *SFIO*'s official paper, *L'Humanitè*—underscores the success of some women socialists in pricking the consciences of the party's leaders. Usually, these leaders reacted to women's public demands by arguing strongly against feminist activists who they said detracted from the more important class struggle. *L'Humanitè* and other socialist journals warned women repeatedly against forming any alliances with feminist groups or adopting feminist demands which, they said, were 'bourgeois'.

The *SFIO*'s policy of placing the class struggle before women's demands frequently aroused the wrath of those few articulate women leaders who remained within the socialist movement. These women reminded male leaders—especially the Guesdists among them—of the earlier socialist commitment to women's liberation. They recalled Guesdist promises to emancipate women

---

[41] See Guilbert, *Les Femmes*, and Zylberberg-Hocquard, *Féminisme*.

not only from capitalist oppression but also from the private oppression of the domestic *foyer*. Among the most articulate spokeswomen for these views was Madeleine Pelletier, who had joined the Guesdist wing of the *SFIO*.[42]

Pelletier, born of working-class parents in Paris in 1874, first attacked a bastion of French male chauvinism when she registered for medical training at the end of the nineteenth century. Once she had qualified as a doctor, she registered to sit exams to qualify as a psychiatrist. In 1906 she attained this goal and was duly certified to work in insane asylums—the first French woman to achieve this goal.

Educated, articulate, often outrageous (she followed the pattern set earlier by George Sand and Madame Adam and wore men's jackets and ties over long black skirts), Pelletier threw herself enthusiastically into the socialist struggle. She chose the Guesdists because of their progressive position on women's rights. Her loyalty to that group within the *SFIO* won her a position as a delegate from the Guesdist stronghold, the Nord federation. In 1906, she was one of five women included among that region's delegation at the *SFIO*'s Limoges congress.[43] And it was thanks to her efforts, as well as to those of many other women, that the issue of women's suffrage appeared on the Limoges agenda.

At Limoges, the debate on women's right to vote highlighted the wide divisions and conflicting ideas among delegates from all over France. Pelletier spoke for the Nord delegation, which continued to express (though less vociferously) its old commitment to women's equal rights. The content of Pelletier's speech, however, reflected her awareness that amidst even the most committed Guesdists were men with prejudices against women's equality. Much of her speech had a defensive tone. She began by stating that women neglected socialism because socialism neglected them. Why? Because women could not vote. Echoing Paule

---

[42] Details of Pelletier's life are found in Sowerwine, *Sisters*, pp. 110–11, James McMillan, *Housewife or Harlot. The Place of Women in French Society, 1870–1940* (Brighton, 1981), pp. 90–1, Marilyn Boxer, 'When Radical and Socialist Feminism were joined: the extraordinary failure of Madeleine Pelletier', in Jane Slaughter and Robert Kern, eds., *European Women on the Left* (Westport, Conn., 1981), pp. 19–50. Her own works are collected in *Madeleine Pelletier, l'éducation féministe des filles et autres textes*, ed. Claude Maignien (Paris, 1978).

[43] *3e Congrès national du Parti socialiste (SFIO), Limoges, 1–4 novembre 1906, compte rendu analytique* (Paris, 1906).

Minck's words of 2½ decades before, Pelletier added that assertions about women's intellectual inferiority were but 'tired old arguments'. (Paule Minck had called them 'ringing banalities'.) Such arguments, she insisted, were not grounded in fact, but instead rested on impressions created by women's servitude. More importantly, *men's* intellect had never been the criterion by which their collective fitness to vote had been measured.

Furthermore, she said, one often heard the 'laws of nature' invoked to explain women's disenfranchisement. But if there was no God, as socialists claimed, then what was this 'nature'? True, women possessed the ability to reproduce. But did this mean that 'nature' had decided that 'women should make the soup and clean the shoes? That women would have no horizon beyond the kitchen and bedroom?'

In Pelletier's view, those who objected to women's vote voiced their fear of the unknown. Moreover, those who argued that women's vote promised a 'reactionary peril' were wrong. Pelletier argued that it was nowhere true that 'all women fling themselves into churches'. 'If this were true', she noted, 'the churches would be too small to contain them.' The majority of women, she thought, were indifferent to religion.

Pelletier concluded by pointing out that a commitment to women's suffrage would give a practical voice to socialists' theoretical commitment to women's equality. Working women's actions, which had force but not political force, would then take on a new dimension.

Pelletier's words elicited several reactions. A speaker from the Vosges said that while Pelletier's opinions might hold true in Paris, they were not accurate descriptions of the situation in the provinces. Her assumption that most women were not religious, for example, did not hold true in his region, where the clerical question was 'more serious'. Because of this, he said, both he and the rest of his delegation would vote against women's suffrage.

Gustave Delory, speaking for the Lille Guesdists, countered the Vosges delegate's arguments. He reiterated what he said was the most important point in Pelletier's speech: to wit, that women must not be required to earn their right to vote, but rather must be granted it just as men had been. Furthermore, he added, the act of voting itself was an important form of political education to which women should have equal access.

A most surprising speech followed Delory's brief remarks. M. Boyer, a delegate from Brittany, spoke in favour of women's suffrage. He pointed out that Brittany 'as everyone knows', was a traditionally religious area. But in his region, he argued, a woman 'goes to mass because she knows nowhere else to go, and the Church welcomes her'. Thus, in those areas of France where tradition prohibited them from socializing in most public places, including café-bars, women found a venue for their sociability at the church.[44] These same women, Boyer thought, would not necessarily vote against the socialists merely because they attended church. In fact, he insisted that most women would vote for the socialists, particularly because of the party's campaign against alcoholism. Furthermore, mothers among the new voters would vote socialist in order 'to free their children'.

In the end, the resolution of this 1906 congress in favour of women's vote passed with only six dissenting votes (presumably all from the Vosges). Women militants' joy at this result was short-lived. By the close of the year, the *SFIO*'s total failure to implement this resolution showed Madeleine Pelletier that 'our party', as she called it in a distressed letter to Jules Guesde, paid only lip-service to women's rights. Because women could not vote, she told him, they were constantly shunted aside by male party leaders. She begged Guesde 'to bring your great influence to bear' upon this problem, and to 'make women's suffrage an issue in the *Chambre*'. That she was pessimistic about Guesde's willingness to do this was apparent in the compromise she offered him at the end of the letter. 'If not the national vote,' she wrote, 'then at least the municipal vote . . .'[45]

Unfortunately, Pelletier's pessimism was borne out by subsequent events. The years following the 1906 resolution saw no real gestures directed toward implementing women's suffrage. Moreover, the party directed no efforts toward gaining women's rights in any sphere. Relations between the party and women more

[44] Much of the historiography of women's sociability in Europe argues a similar case—that women went to church because they found there a place to meet that was not closed to them by custom. See Olwen Hufton, 'Women in the Counter-revolution' (paper given to the History Society of Trinity Hall, Cambridge, March 1980), and Temma Kaplan, 'Women in Spanish anarchism', in Renate Bridenthal and Claudia Koonz, eds., *Becoming Visible* (Boston, 1977), pp. 402–21.

[45] IISH, 'Dossier Jules Guesde', 386/3, Pelletier to Guesde (4 Oct. 1906).

recently recruited to the *SFIO* quickly became as strained as those between party leaders and older women militants, whose disillusion was ensured during the process of unification. Although many of the younger women continued their efforts to establish the priority of women's rights within the socialist movement, the *SFIO* continued to ignore their attempts. Neither official party policy nor unofficial party activities showed any lessening of the *SFIO*'s indifference.[46]

Relations between the male *SFIO* hierarchy and women militants reached a nadir in 1907. Although the national party congress agreed to yet another resolution favouring women's suffrage it rejected all efforts to attach a specific programme of action through which that goal might be attained.[47]

Not surprisingly, such hypocrisy ultimately drove many women out of the socialist movement altogether—mostly into the welcoming arms of the feminists. Others stayed within the movement, but began to respond to party leaders' negative attitudes by altering their own views in rather curious ways. As had happened in the 1890s, women's attempts to accommodate the views of hostile male leaders inevitably distorted their arguments.

Even the strong-minded Madeleine Pelletier fell victim to most male leaders' apparent indifference to women's suffrage. As a result, she produced a startling volte-face at the 1909 *SFIO* congress in Saint-Étienne. Again representing the Nord federation, Pelletier joined her voice to those arguing *against* women's suffrage. She told the congress that she now saw that women's vote was merely a reformist measure that could contribute little to the revolutionary class struggle. Instead of gaining the vote, she told her listeners, women should become subject to military conscription. Once all women were potential conscripts, they would quickly put an end to the practice by refusing to serve.[48] Not

---

[46] See, for example, Louise Chaboseau-Napias, 'Les Femmes et le socialisme', *H* (19 Feb. 1907).

[47] *4ᵉ Congrès national du Parti socialiste (SFIO), Nancy, 11–14 août 1907, compte rendu analytique* (Paris, 1907), and *5ᵉ Congrès national du Parti socialiste (SFIO), Toulouse, compte rendu sténographique* (Paris, 1908).

[48] *6ᵉ Congrès national du Parti socialiste (SFIO), St-Étienne, 11–14 avril 1909, compte rendu sténographique* (Paris, 1909). Pelletier's presumption that women were 'naturally' anti-war is shared by a number of recent feminist writers, many of them French. It is part of the convictions which underlie the women's anti-cruise missile campaign at Greenham Common, near Newbury, England.

surprisingly, this new idea met only bemusement, and quickly dropped from sight.

The following year, 1910, saw little change in the *SFIO*'s policies towards women. As was the case in 1907, the party took no notice of the meeting of the International Congress of Socialist Women which met concurrently with the International in Copenhagen in that year.[49] In fact, not until 1912 did the *SFIO* give any indication that they thought at all of increasing their efforts to organize working women. In that year, at long last, the *SFIO* began to issue occasional welcoming signals to potential women socialists, especially to those who had been active before 1906 in the moribund *Groupe féministe socialiste*.

The *SFIO*'s 1912 shift in policy was due in part to pressure from the *CGT*'s campaign to recruit more working women, as well as from women leaders like Madeleine Pelletier, and from women leaders of the Second International. In these years, the International increasingly debated women's rights issues, especially suffrage. The *SFIO*'s new interest in women was helped by the fact that many former leaders of the *GFS*, especially Elisabeth Renaud and Louise Saumoneau, had followed Pelletier's lead and had foresworn many of their more radical feminist demands in order to accommodate the more moderate position of the *SFIO*. As a result, these women regrouped in 1912 under a new organization, the *Groupe des femmes socialistes*. The name change was significant. It gave public recognition to their collective willingness to bury the feminist struggle within the class struggle—just as the *SFIO* had long wished them to do.[50]

By taking this position, however, the *GdFS* did win concessions previously denied the *GFS* by the socialist party leaders. Firstly, they convinced Jaurès to introduce a suffrage bill into the *Chambre*, which he did in December 1912.[51] His speech supporting the bill, however, was hardly encouraging to socialist feminists. He

---

[49] See *7ᵉ Congrès national de Parti socialiste (SFIO), Nîmes, 6–9 février 1910, compte rendu sténographique* (Paris, 1910) in which no mention is made of the coming ICSW meeting.

[50] Sowerwine details their re-emergence in *Sisters*.

[51] Jaurès's *Chambre* speech is reprinted in 'Le Droit politique des femmes', *H* (9 Dec, 1912). Further discussions are found in E. Peluso, 'Ce que pense Clara Zetkin du mouvement des femmes socialistes en France', *H* (12 Mar. 1913); A. Bracke, 'Le Suffrage des femmes', *H* (6 July 1913); A. Compère-Morel, 'Socialisme et féminisme', *H* (18 Feb. 1914).

argued that women had earned the right to vote by demonstrating their 'natural' pacifism, which might hold the key to preventing the war then looming on the European horizon.

Jaurès's position held two dangers for the politics of women's rights. Firstly, it was grounded in stereotypes of women's 'nature' which bolstered more reactionary politics in the *belle époque*. Except for some Guesdists, few male politicians of the period denied the notion that women belonged in a 'separate sphere'. Socialists among them merely added that women's separate sphere was 'equal' to men's, even if it was biologically determined whereas men's sphere was not. Secondly, Jaurès's speech implied that women should be granted this right because they had earned it. Unlike men, women must be granted only those 'rights' for which they showed themselves to be suited. In this case, their natural lack of aggression fitted them to vote in a dangerous period.

Nevertheless, so delighted were they by Jaurès's support for women's suffrage that the *GdFS* accepted his arguments without a murmur. This unquestioning stand won them a second important concession in January 1913. The *SFIO* decided to allow the group to join the party as a separately organized women's auxiliary. In order to ensure that this group would never supersede the party's control, however, the *SFIO* imposed a key condition on all prospective members. Only those women who already paid dues to the *SFIO* were allowed to join the *GdFS*. This policy not only guaranteed that only disciplined party members would participate in the women's group, but it also effectively prohibited the vast majority of France's *ouvrières* from joining. Even those few who could find enough money for *SFIO* dues could not find still more money for *GdFS* dues. Moreover, even if they could have afforded the extra dues, why would women choose to join an auxiliary group that had no programme of autonomous action or even any definite power to shape party decisions?

Still, for all its inherent weaknesses, this new *GdFS* did begin to work for a positive change in *SFIO* policies towards women. At the very least, the group provided a forum for the expression of women's problems within the larger socialist movement. Then too, the *GdFS* was nationally visible, not only to most party members but also to leaders of the rival *CGT*, which began to report their activities with great enthusiasm. Despite the fact that the *GdFS* was a potential rival to the *CGT*-sponsored women's group, the *comité d'action syndicaliste* (founded in 1907),[52] the *CGT*'s newspapers gave the group wide coverage. Syndicalists were particularly pleased when the *GdFS* provided aid and support for the striking women at the Lebaudy sugar-refineries in 1913. Both *CGT* national newspapers, moreover, supported the group's demands for the vote as well as for other legal rights.[53]

In addition to the increasingly intense efforts of the *GdFS*, Madeleine Pelletier and others who remained outside the group continued their individual efforts to push the *SFIO* into action to mobilize France's working women into the struggle for their rights. Finally, in 1914 their efforts bore fruit. In that year, the *SFIO* articulated a new theoretical position on the place of women within the revolutionary struggle. One version of the party's new position appeared in a pamphlet written by 'Suzon', with an introduction by Guesde's long-time friend, Compère-Morel.[54] Together, 'Suzon' and Compère-Morel stated the *SFIO*'s commitment to recruiting working women into the party. Furthermore, they insisted that there was no need for women to join the feminist struggle since the proletarian revolution would inevitably liberate them at the same time as it freed the working class from the exploitation of industrial capitalism. Moreover, the authors argued, women were no longer 'the slaves of men' as they had been in the nineteenth century when they were 'housewives and mothers before all else'. Instead, in the twentieth century they were primarily workers, who demanded their right to work in order to guarantee their independence and dignity. (This, of course, echoed the old Guesdist line of the 1870s and 1880s.) On the other hand, socialist feminists 'knew' that the proletarian revolution must always take precedence over the emancipation of women.

In other words, the *SFIO* was telling women that although they

---

[52] Led by Maximilienne Biais, this group was formed in 1907 to attract women into the *CGT*. See 'Mouvement social: Parti socialiste', *BS* (10 June 1913).

[53] Detailed descriptions of the Lebaudy strike are found in *BS* 'Une grève des femmes' (14 May 1913), and continuing through the month. Earlier protests against women's conditions at Lebaudy are found in *FS* (Aug. 1902). This journal also covered the later strike. See 10 July 1913.

[54] I could not discover the identity of 'Suzon', author of *Socialisme et féminisme* (Paris, 1914).

could demand their right to equality, they must not do so in any way that would dilute the more important class struggle. After all, there was no need to do so. 'Suzon' insisted that those who said that women must struggle for their own liberation on the grounds that men would not willingly liberate them were wrong. Proletarian men would, in fact, automatically liberate women after the revolution. But 'Suzon' did not stop there. Instead, this writer condemned all women who organized on their own behalf as 'Valkyries and viragos'. To this broad indictment, Compère-Morel added his voice. He wrote, 'the feminist movement is everywhere a bit repellent and provoking: here, tearful, sentimental, and inane outpourings; there, violent and grotesque demonstrations. But never, or nearly never, a serious or sane action, vigorous and efficacious, methodical and real.'[55]

Echoes of Victor Renard's comments about the 1911 women's food riots in the Nord! Only male leadership, Compère-Morel implied, could contain women's unbridled natures, which invariably exceeded propriety when they were left to their own inferior devices.

Instead of yielding to such temptations, 'Suzon' asserted, women should assume their 'privileged role', which made them 'capable of giving to man a glimpse of plenitude ennobled by love and good will'. To teach women to perform this special role, socialist militants should spread 'discreet but fecund' propaganda, in 'the workshop, the field, the factory, the school'. 'Suzon' concluded, 'thus we beat the call of feminine consciences without a break, calling for recruitment, as well as for socialist and syndicalist education.'

The implications of this pamphlet were extremely problematic for women socialists. Firstly, women were assured that they need have nothing to do with organized feminists, whose unruly behaviour repelled men. Instead, they must 'ennoble' male socialists who would then grant them liberation when it was time. Women socialists were even discouraged from acting as Valkyries— whose mythical mission, after all, was merely to conduct fallen male soldiers to Valhalla, not to fight in the front lines. Instead, women were told to hover genteelly in the background of the class struggle, 'glimpsed' but never heard, until the revolution trans-

[55] Compère-Morel, 'preface', ibid., p. 4.

formed these shadowy victims of oppression into grateful objects of male socialists' largesse.

The confusion of these arguments was not entirely gratuitous. Indeed, any theoretician seeking to discover arguments for women's liberation within Marxist discourse quickly encountered several spanners in the doctrinal work. Firstly, they confronted a problem in the most basic principle of workers' organization: as a revolutionary class, the proletariat must organize itself for its own liberation which it alone could bring about in the socialist revolution. By extension, then, oppressed women must organize themselves for *their* own liberation. But if they did so, they became feminists organized around the problems of gender, rather than socialists organized around the problems of class. Worse still, the feminist struggle obviously crossed class lines—bringing *bourgeoises* into the struggles of working-class women.[56]

As the *SFIO* saw it, the only solution to this problem was to insist that women's liberation was 'automatically', if unspecifically, linked to the emancipation of the proletariat. At the same time, the party allowed women to organize themselves, but only into a group whose goals were clearly tied to those of the larger socialist movement, and whose members were primarily loyal party members.

On the face of it, of course, there was no reason why the class struggle as such must necessarily include an organized women's movement. The link which most socialists made between the two had its basis in the history of the French left, but not in Marxist theory. On the other hand, socialists might have argued that proletarian women must enjoy those bourgeois rights denied them during the various revolutions of the late eighteenth and nineteenth centuries before they could ever join as equals in history's next stage—the socialist revolution. But if socialists had adopted this position, it would have meant a long struggle for women's equal rights at the expense of the organization of the proletariat. Furthermore, such a struggle would necessarily have doubled the size and potentially the strength of the bourgeoisie, by gaining bourgeois women their civil and political rights. Given this fact, it

[56] Bourgeois feminist activities are detailed in Patrick Bidelman, 'The Feminist movement in France: the formative years, 1858–1899' (Ph.D., Michigan, 1975), and Maïté Albistur and Daniel Armogathe, *Histoire du féminisme français*, vol. ii (Paris, 1977).

was never likely that socialists would undertake such a potentially self-defeating struggle.

Moreover, as Guesde had recognized in the 1870s, women's oppression went beyond their exclusion from the economic and political life of bourgeois society. Private families, including working-class families, were the site of a smaller but no less oppressive set of power relations, which underpinned the exploitation of women by male family members. These power relations, which were in no way linked solely to industrial capitalist production relations (the views of socialists like Lafargue to the contrary notwithstanding), did not lend themselves to a Marxist analysis. There was therefore no theoretical structure upon which socialists might base a programme of women's liberation from their domestic oppression. And, in the realm of practical politics, such a liberation was not necessarily a means for attracting proletarian voters to socialism. In fact, quite the opposite, as most socialist politicians recognized.

Given these various difficulties, it is not surprising that the *SFIO* failed entirely to design either a coherent plan of action aimed at ending women's social and political inequalities or a theoretical statement to legitimate such a programme. At the same time, of course, the *SFIO* needed women party members and supporters. Thus they compromised with a series of cursory gestures that satisfied neither male leaders hostile to women's inclusion in the party nor most socialist women.

At the upper levels of the party, then, relations between women and the party's male leaders remained difficult throughout the period following unification, despite a rather tentative reawakening of interest in 1912. But what of the situation at the local level? To what extent had national neglect affected socialist activities in the Lille area after 1905?

vi

In this same period, relations between the Guesdists of the Nord federation of the *SFIO* and local women textile workers were shaped by three factors. Firstly, after 1905, economic conditions in the mills of Lille, Roubaix, and Tourcoing slowly began to improve. Higher profits brought both more work and increased militancy among workers anxious to recoup the losses they had suffered during the black years around the turn of the century. The workers' growing restiveness in turn provoked a backlash from the employers. This took the form of increased vigilance in the mills— a vigilance complicated by the vastly increased size of most work-forces.

Not only did the *patronat* tighten discipline on the shop-floor, they also tried once again to speed up the work process—usually by doubling the number of machines tended by each worker. In this way, mill owners hoped to maintain their rising profits and to meet the growing international competition without investing profits in new machinery or improved factory conditions.

Taken together, these factors produced conditions in the mills that were, in many ways, even worse than those which had earlier darkened life in the textile mills of Lille, Roubaix, and Tourcoing. Though unemployment began to decrease after 1905, most worker's lives remained grim.

A third factor which helped to shape local politics in the post-unification period was a change in the social fabric of the three cities which occurred around the turn of the century. By 1905, especially in Tourcoing, much of what might be called the 'village character' of workers' *quartiers* had begun to vanish, a victim of the rapid growth of the three cities. Even Tourcoing had swollen irretrievably beyond its nucleus, with workers' suburbs and new factories growing in every direction from the ancient town centre. Moreover, in none of the three cities did workers regularly find work in mills near their *courées* and tenements. Instead, most travelled great distances to and from work. This, in turn, diluted some of the community-based solidarity which in the nineteenth century had developed among workers who both lived and worked together. The most direct consequence of this break in the web of social and work relations was that both politics and strikes began increasingly to transcend community limits and to merge into a more diffuse form.

On one level, as we have seen, workers confronted these changes with an increased class solidarity, which spread across city boundaries as well as across boundaries of union or party. The development of cheap and efficient public transport (encouraged by the socialist municipalities of Lille and Roubaix, as well as by the radical leaders of Tourcoing) aided this broadening of the workers' community base.

On another level, however, the growth of a much larger mass base posed a problem for socialists. A vast population of textile workers, no longer grounded in distinct *courée* or *quartier*-identified communities, proved less malleable than earlier, smaller groups of workers. Although socialists' organized efforts to capture voters in all three cities were ultimately successful, the outcome of various organizational or electoral activities was rarely as certain as it had once been. The potential capriciousness of potential voters discouraged many local Guesdist leaders from venturing into controversial issues. Needless to say, then, women's equal rights did not sit high on Guesdist agendas in these years.

Thus most local socialist politicians in the years after 1905 were rarely seen to pay much practical attention to organizing working women. Only when women showed their faces in mass events, including strikes, fêtes, and occasional mass meetings did the local socialist press remark their presence, although customarily as 'many women and children', rather than as *ouvrières*.

On the other hand, during elections socialists continued to solicit the help of local women, whose work in campaigns was always crucial to electoral success. In the 1907 election, the Guesdists courted local women's support by emphasizing the importance of the old *POF* demand that working women have the right to stand and vote for *conseils des prud'hommes et prud'femmes* (a right they won in that year). Election posters highlighted this demand. Most also demanded that these new *conseils* be granted the right to choose 'inspecteurs et inspectrices de travail', whose wages would be paid by the state.[57]

Such efforts encouraged many local women once again to play an active role within the party. Three women represented the Nord federation at the *SFIO*'s national congress at Toulouse in 1908.[58] Among them was Citoyenne Delory, who had been active earlier in the *Comité des femmes de Lille* in the 1890s. (Of the other two women delegates, however, nothing further is known.)

In general, the national *SFIO*'s campaign against bourgeois feminism found few echoes in the Nord federation. Only once, in fact, did local Guesdists evince any sign that they felt a threat from

---

[57] *ADN* M 154 88, 'Affiches 1907'.
[58] *5ᵉ Congrès national du Parti socialiste (SFIO), Toulouse, 15–18 octobre 1908, compte rendu sténographique* (Paris, 1908).

organized *bourgeoises*. In 1906 the local party called a meeting to protest against the newly founded *Office du travail féminin*. Headed by the most prominent of France's non-socialist feminists, Marguerite Durand, this new subministry was intended to support women workers, especially when they clashed with men in attempts to take jobs in various hitherto exclusively male occupations, such as printing. But this protest meeting attracted almost no attention from local workers. Even a sympathetic reporter counted only 170 men and 30 women participants.[59]

Other events and activities which stimulated great interest in Paris likewise fell flat in French Flanders. The exploits of the English suffragettes, for example, which intrigued many reporters in both the socialist and syndicalist national press, evoked no interest.[60] More surprisingly, perhaps, the creation of the *CGT*'s *comité d'action syndicaliste* in 1907 had no effect locally, although its organizers appeared in Lille in 1914.[61] The failure of this syndicalist attempt to gain working women's allegiance under-scored the loyalty most textile workers continued to feel for their unions, most of which were linked to the socialist movement. Moreover, these syndicalist *comités* were organized to function in *bourses du travail*, which remained small and ineffectual in the textile cities in the *belle époque*.

Looking at the years immediately following unification, then, it is clear that, in the eyes of local socialist leaders, working women formed a peripheral if necessary group within the area's socialist party. As a result, women as a group with problems distinct from those of male workers virtually disappeared from view, although they continued to join most mass-based socialist activities in these years.

Only in 1913 did local socialist women's groups once more emerge on the local scene. The stimulus came from the newly reformed *Groupe des femmes socialistes* in Paris. These socialist

[59] *ADN* M 154 88, 'Affaire Durand'.

[60] The exploits of the suffragettes were reported in 'Les Suffragettes à *L'Humanité*', *H* (18 June 1907); Jean Longuet, 'Féminisme et socialisme—Un entretien avec une "suffragette" ', *H* (19 June 1907).

[61] This *comité* was founded to organize working women, especially those in the domestic out-putting system who were isolated from most propaganda. See Maximilienne Biais, 'Communications – Comité d'action féministe syndicaliste', *VdP* (18 July–4 Aug. 1907). See also G. Dumoulin, 'Ligue féminine d'action syndicale', *VdP* (11–17 May 1914).

women sent an appeal to women in the Lille area. 'All over France', they declared, 'local women are following the German model and forming women's groups.' (This was, of course, a significant change. Excluded by law from membership in political parties, women within the German social democratic movement had always organized as an auxiliary within the party. Moreover, they had never claimed a feminist identity for themselves. The leaders of the new French *Groupe des femmes socialistes*, on the other hand, included both Elisabeth Renaud and Louise Saumoneau, both of whom had once led the more militant and autonomous *Groupe féministe socialiste* which had been prevented from joining the *SFIO* in 1906.)

An organizational meeting for the new *GdFS* was subsequently held in Lille in April 1913, on a Sunday afternoon.[62] Those who attended that meeting founded a local group, which they called the *Groupe des femmes socialistes propagandistes de Lille*. Their leader—unlike many of the women leaders of the 1890s women's groups—did not come from among local textile workers. Instead Marguerite Dupuis was the lifelong companion of a local Guesdist writer, Charles Verecque. Like him, Dupuis had originally come to the area from Abbeville at the end of the nineteenth century. In 1913 Dupuis was apparently not employed. Verecque was the editor of the local socialist newspaper, *Le Travailleur*.[63]

What was important about the choice of Marguerite Dupuis as leader of the local *GdFS* was the fact that she represented an important change in the nature of local Guesdist leadership. Both she and Verecque were not only outsiders but were also not industrial workers. Thus the intimacy with which the earlier Guesdist leaders of both sexes worked among their comrades in the textile workers' *quartiers* of the area was absent in this later period. For the local textile *ouvrières*, this change was particularly problematic. Given the distinctive nature of women's day-to-day problems, they were less likely to feel at ease with a leader who lived in a world very different from theirs than they were with a woman who lived among them.

The sparse information about this new Lille area group suggests

[62] *FS* (15 Apr. 1913).

[63] Dupuis, also known as Dupuis-Verecque, was among the first members of the *Parti ouvrier*. She was a delegate at the Lille *PSdF* congress in Lille in 1904, and at the *SFIO* congresses of 1910 and 1911.

that its leaders enjoyed very little success among local women textile workers in 1913 and 1914. Indeed, as one might expect, the activities pursued by this group had only peripheral relevance to the daily lives of women workers. The Lille group's primary commitment was to pacifism. Their propaganda, moreover, followed Jaurès's traditionalist line, arguing that women were 'naturally' against war because they were 'givers of life'. It is not known how the group planned to implement their pacifism, since they did not demand the vote, or any other extension of women's rights. In fact, the only practical campaign they sponsored was on behalf of the widow and daughter of the local poet Eugène Pottier (author of the lyrics to the Internationale), who were left without resources upon his death.[64]

Although the very fragmentary evidence cannot be adduced to support any broad generalizations about the character of the Lille group, it does suggest that these women in no way challenged the national *SFIO*'s policy of relegating to socialist women only those activities assigned them by tradition. In no way did the new *Groupe des femmes socialistes* (locally or nationally) signal the emergence of a militant women's movement organized to demand an equal role within the socialist struggle.[65]

On the other hand, socialist reactions to the new women's group in the Lille area were rather different from those of the Jaurèsists of the national party. In fact, the founding of the Lille *GdFS* stimulated the Nord federation to launch a broad campaign to recruit more women into its party sections. This effort, begun in 1913, provoked a revival of the old Guesdist strategies to attract *ouvrières* into the movement. Led by Delory in Lille, party leaders proposed to take three positive steps aimed at giving local working women a larger say in the party. Firstly, the federation dictated that all party sections identify every local woman who was potentially a socialist militant. Once she was identified, the party undertook to train her in organizing techniques—just as they already trained potential male militants. Once trained, these women together would be sent throughout the industrial cities of the Nord to recruit working women into the party.

[64] *FS* (20 July 1913).

[65] In October 1913 the *SFIO*'s new attitude toward women was highlighted by the *Humanité* column aimed at them. Called 'En Famille', the column offered household and child care hints.

Secondly, the Nord federation required that all unions affiliated to the *Parti socialiste* (including of course, the national textile federation) ensure that all working women—unionized or not— were inscribed on *prud'hommal* lists so that they could exercise their recently won right to vote for the *conseils des prud'hommes et prud'femmes*. Furthermore, the federation ordered every socialist union or party section to put forward at least one woman candidate in every *prud'hommal* list.[66]

Even more important than such positive policies, the local Guesdists were among the first organized French socialists to address a problem which they had neglected during the earlier years of organizing in the 1880s and 1890s. This was the problem posed by non-waged women of the local working class. For the first time, Guesdist leaders began to address their propaganda to housewives. Moreover, unlike national socialist leaders, these local politicians did not categorize housewives as passive victims. (Jean Jaurès, by contrast, described them as 'women of sorrow and stupor'.[67]) In fact, quite the contrary. No doubt mindful of women's behaviour in the 1911 food riots, Lille area leaders assumed housewives' militancy. Moreover, they declared their support for women's continuing efforts to control food prices. Furthermore, they specifically invited all non-waged women to join socialist food co-operatives which, they argued would provide the logical venue for such organized price-control campaigns.

Local socialist propaganda, then, drew all women of the working class together in its efforts to recruit women into the party. 'Politics', one local leader told a crowd of *ouvrières* and housewives, 'are not only for men, but are also your business. Are you not interested in protective labour legislation? In a living wage? In help during childbirth? Old age . . . Join the party that defends your interests, the *Parti socialiste*.'[68]

On the eve of the Great War, then, *ouvrières* once more began to play a clear role in local socialist activities. But in this reawakening most of the earlier impetus had been lost. No longer did women form their own groups, impelled by the Guesdists' revolutionary visions of liberation from the mill and from domestic

---

[66] Marcel Deschamps, 'Le Congrès des socialistes du Nord', *H* (1 Oct. 1913).

[67] See Jaurès, 'Les Femmes et la guerre', *H* (1 Dec. 1912).

[68] 'La Fédération du Nord lance un appel aux femmes', *H* (24 Nov. 1913).

slavery. Rather, the energy came from Paris and from above. Male leaders of what had become a highly centralized, controlled socialist party stamped their approval on womens' auxiliaries. Gone were 'Women's Revenge', 'Women's Emancipation', and 'Women's Rights'. In their place was one carefully delimited section of the *Groupe des femmes socialistes*, whose leaders had achieved a place in the *SFIO* only at the cost of their feminism.

It would, of course, be intriguing to know the precise extent to which local women responded to these initiatives of the *GdFS*. Were many local women attracted by the socialists' new efforts to recruit them into the party and into the ancillary women's groups? Did some textile *ouvrières* manage to find the extra centimes each month to join such groups?

Unfortunately, the answers to these questions lie buried. As Charles Sowerwine and others have remarked, membership figures of the *SFIO* in 1914 vary considerably, and are rarely broken down by sex. Moreover, no membership figures exist for the *GdFS*. And in the Nord department many local records were lost in two successive German occupations—in both world wars. Although one can only estimate numbers of women members, therefore, most historians would agree that no estimate supports an optimistic view of women's response to the *SFIO*'s 1913 initiatives. Sowerwine, for example, has estimated that the total number of women members in the *SFIO* in the period from 1905 to 1914 totalled only between 2 and 3 per cent of the national membership. Although there was an increase in party membership in 1914—from 72,765 members in January to 90,725 in July—there is nothing to suggest that women comprised any substantial proportion of this growth. In fact, Sowerwine has concluded that the female membership of the *SFIO* throughout 1914, in all of France, never totalled more than 2000 women.[69]

Of course, as we have seen, official membership figures in no way reflected the extent to which local women in the Lille area participated in the broader socialist movement. And in these informal, often unorganized mass activities women consistently played a vital and visible role after 1880. Moreover, despite their growing neglect by party leaders after 1896, few months passed

[69] Sowerwine, *Sisters*, Appendix Z: 'French socialist women in figures', pp. 198–201.

when women did not militate on their own behalf—in strikes, in parades, in demonstrations, food riots, and so on. Furthermore, as we have seen, most election campaigns at the local level depended heavily upon women's participation. In fact, only between 1898 and unification, the period when many socialists went down to defeat in local elections, were women absent from election reports. At the moment when Guesdists once again began to win elections, local working women once more appeared on the scene—both as direct beneficiaries of many socialist election promises, and as important activists in the election campaigns.

Of course, at no time did official membership figures in the Lille area's socialist parties reflect the extent of male socialists' sympathies either. Men voted socialist in far greater numbers than they joined the party. Then, too, those who did join the party often represented an entire family of socialists. Usually, these members were men. Not only did custom dictate this choice, but also men's right to vote as well as their higher pay ensured its practice throughout the *belle époque*.

On the other hand, it would be wrong to suggest that working men and women played identical, or even separate-but-equal roles within the political life of the three textile cities in our period. Not only were women underrepresented among party members, but they were rarely found among party militants and never among party leaders. Thus, however militant and loyal women showed themselves to be, particularly in the late 1880s and early 1890s, male socialists never offered them any genuine share in party leadership. Even the most active women remained on the margins of formal party activities. And the more formal these party pursuits became after the mid-nineties, the fewer women were visible in the middle or bottom ranks of the party.

Finally, women's different life experiences limited the scope of their political participation in these years. Not only were they the poorest among the textile workers, but they were also the most severely disciplined. Guarded carefully in the mills, they were also watched in their private lives in the *courées* and slums where they laboured to maintain family and community life. Unacceptable behaviour in the mills could cost them their jobs. 'Immoral' behaviour in the other often closed the charitable purse upon which so many women textile workers depended for survival.

Moreover, on the simplest day-to-day level, women's lives left them with less time and considerably less energy for political battles. Constant child-bearing, plus a double daily work-load, ensured that most textile workers enjoyed only precarious health. Further, the illiteracy of most textile *ouvrières*—caused, in part, by their domestic burdens during childhood—limited the extent to which they could join in political study groups. What political ideas they did have, they obtained from oral propaganda, which fortunately was prevalent in French Flanders in our period. But, even during political meetings and discussion, women's attentions were restricted by the 'mobs of kids' (in the words of one textile *ouvrière*) who accompanied women everywhere. Preoccupied with keeping children quiet and amused, most women could only rarely give full attention to socialist speakers. Worse, few mothers could participate in the important discussions which followed such speeches. It is likely that only their own women's group meetings gave them an opportunity to learn how to talk about and to understand the complicated new ideas of proletarian revolution which spread throughout Lille, Roubaix, and Tourcoing in the *belle époque*. Once those groups disppeared, women workers lost a venue where they could learn more sophisticated modes of political participation and expression. It is not surprising, then, that they remained committed to mass protest rather than to more formally organized kinds of political behaviour.

Of course, many of these various elements which constrained working women's lives changed over time, as we have seen. In the earliest years of the 1880s, communities remained small and closely knit. Moreover, women, like other family members, were more likely to find jobs in mills within walking distance of their homes. Thus, friends and families worked in close proximity and could socialize during work breaks as well as during trips to and from the mills. Although women's working days were longer in the years before factory legislation, they enjoyed more of the informal support which neighbours could provide. Moreover, shorter travelling time allowed more leeway in women's choice of activities outside work.

Over the years, however, many of the old neighbourhoods grew beyond their familiar identity. Vast immigration changed many workers' *quartiers* and crowded them beyond all recognition. Furthermore, vast new workers' districts sprawled on the fringes of all three cities—many laid out in a grid pattern unfamiliar in

French Flanders. This geographic sprawl meant that an increasingly well-organized socialist party was needed to knit together the politics of workers who lived and worked in increasingly scattered areas. But the organization of such a party necessarily destroyed much of the intimacy between local socialist leaders and the people of the *courées* and tenements. Moreover, because none of the new party's leadership was female, the distance between the socialist party cadres and women workers grew even greater than that between men and their leaders.

Women's work experiences also changed over the thirty-four years before the war. Mills grew larger. Conditions in the mills worsened and wages dropped. Once it became clear to most local workers that the depression that struck the industry in 1880 was going to last, a deep fear of unemployment—or even of short time—set in. Even the upswing in the textile industry which began in 1910 did little to alter workers' insecurity.

As the lowest-paid workers, women felt even less secure about their ability to support themselves—and often their children. Moreover, once protective labour legislation began to dictate shorter hours for women and children, many women lost their jobs to men whom employers could exploit with virtual impunity. Thus, in our period, the number of women textile workers actually dropped relative to the number of men workers. Women's unemployment was exacerbated in the Lille region by the general unavailability of alternative women's work.

Together, these factors help to explain what many outsiders perceived as women textile workers' general passivity in the face of their conditions. One *Parisienne* who visited the Lille mills in 1914 wrote, 'they laughed when they saw me. It was the laughter of castaways, who know themselves irremediably lost, they and their nests of urchins. It was the laughter of slaves, who believe that all is finished, and who no longer hold even the feeblest hope. Their laughter sickened me . . . "go away", it said, "we know we are lost".'[70]

And, of course, this view was similar to that held by many *SFIO* leaders in the final years before the war. But, given the long history of local women's militancy—culminating in the massive food riots only a few years before—why did so many observers fail

---

[70] Capy, 'Industrie textile—Quelques réflexions', *BS* (20 Apr. 1914).

to see women's militant potential? There are several likely explanations for such misperceptions. To most outsiders, the Flemish workers' *quartiers* were closed. Although warm and welcoming to inhabitants, most *courées* and *estaminets* discouraged strangers' visits. Then, too, women workers, watched and spied upon throughout their lives, were doubly suspicious of prying eyes. It was not worth their jobs to suggest to outsiders that they were planning collective resistance amongst themselves. Thus they naturally met visitors with closed lips or laughter.

But what of socialist leaders? Why were they met with a similar suspicion and mistrust? The answer lies in the fact that, after the 1905 unification, the local Guesdists lost control of the socialist movement. Thus, many faces among socialist agitators and organizers in the Nord were new ones. Moreover, many of them did not come from among the textile workers' community—and that fact alone rendered them suspect. In addition, most male socialists treated the women textile workers as though they were primarily concerned with domesticity—their husbands, their children—rather than with their jobs. This stereotypical and reactionary view of women was bolstered by women's dis-appearance from party histories. Because *ouvrières* fell victim to male socialists' collective amnesia, women's earlier activities on behalf of liberation struggles vanished from sight. However much they may have 'chattered for socialism and for women's liberation', after the turn of the century, few party leaders were listening. As a result, virtually no one took seriously any suggestion that working women might be mobilized at the centre of *SFIO* politics.

Finally, socialists began to offer working women a very different message after the turn of the nineteenth century—a message which they rejected just as the party, in its turn, increasingly rejected them. This message, supported by male party leaders' actions, told women that their place was in the working man's home, where they could fulfil their 'natural duties' to him and to *his* children. Few working women found this message attractive. Thus they ceased working toward full membership of the party and directed their energies elsewhere in the mass protests of their class.

It is conceivable, of course, that the new Lille section of the *GdFS* might eventually have altered the poor relationship between *ouvrières* and the *SFIO*, had it had a chance to do so. Unfortunately, however, the outcome of this second wave of party organization among working women can never be known. Once German armies invaded Lille in the autumn of 1914, all party organizational efforts ceased. Instead, local socialists used party cadres and resources to try to alleviate the worst effects of the German army's occupation. These included efforts to try and halt the mass deportation of local women (of all classes), who were used as agricultural labourers elsewhere in occupation zones. They were more effective, however, in their attempts to distribute food through the network of socialist food co-operatives and via traditional workers' soup-kitchens. Politics as such, needless to say, remained underground for the duration.[71]

---

[71] An evocative portrayal of life during the German occupation is found in Maxence van der Meersch, *Invasion '14* (Paris, 1935).

CONCLUSION

AT no time during the first three decades of socialist organizing in the textile cities of French Flanders did the movement's leaders develop either a coherent theory or a consistent practice to ensure working women's equal place in the wider class struggle. Nevertheless, there was one period in the years between 1880 and 1897 when the Guesdists nearly managed to establish a place for working women in the socialist cause. In these early years, flexible organizational forms, backed by the party's forceful commitment to women's right to participate equally in every sphere of French life, gave the *Parti ouvrier* an effective political practice for attracting female adherents.

Indubitably the most important factor in the movement's recruitment of women in these years was Jules Guesde's personal determination to bring working women into the centre of socialist politics. For potential women recruits the crucial element in Guesde's message was his insistence that women's genuine emancipation depended upon their achieving economic independence from men. The *POF*'s demand that women be paid a living wage naturally aroused *ouvrières*' enthusiasm. Moreover, the *POF* was the first workers' organization to couple this goal with women's personal liberation from their 'double toil'.[1]

In the Lille area, working women responded with alacrity to the party's promise to ameliorate their situation. With the Guesdists' support, women organized their own study groups and joined their united efforts to the socialists' work in the workers' communities of Lille, Roubaix, and Tourcoing. Their collective enthusiasm lasted for nearly a decade.

Given the extent of the Guesdists' initial success in mobilizing local working women, their subsequent failure is perplexing. How

---

[1] The concept of women's 'double proletarianization', so often articulated by Guesdist leaders in these years, derived from Flora Tristan, although it has more often been attributed to Marx and Engels. See Dominique Desanti's 'L'Utopie saisie par les féminisites ou les Utopiennes: Suzanne, Pauline, Jeanne, Flora et les autres', in Gisèle Halimi, ed., *Fini le féminisme?* (Paris, 1984), pp. 46–58.

was it possible for party leaders to lose women's support so quickly? In the case of the Lille region, three broad elements combined to stifle most organizational work among women workers.

The most immediately apparent problem arose from Jules Guesde's decision to reorganize the *POF*. Out of a loose and open federation of all sorts of socialist groups—including women's groups along with study groups, Free Thinkers, youth groups, and so on—Guesde created a more formally structured, centrally controlled political party. The primary goal of this party was winning elections.

The effects of his policy, instituted in 1889, were not instantly devastating to local women's groups. Indeed, for several years after they increased their membership. But eventually, like all those socialist groups which could not readily be turned into party sections, the women's groups began to disappear into the category reserved for various 'cultural' groups, peripheral to the party's central political concerns. However important such groups remained in the larger socialist world of French Flanders, they were necessarily marginal to the primary work of the party, which increasingly involved developing effective election strategies. Because women could not vote, and because their equal rights posed a potentially controversial issue in some constituencies, their groups gradually moved away from the focus of local socialists' attentions.

This process of reorganizing the *POF* dealt a second blow to local women's hopes of finding an equal role within the party. The new *Parti ouvrier*, led by a disciplined and loyal hierarchy of militants, excluded local women from its cadres. However vociferous the Guesdists' continuing promises to end women's oppression, they failed to propose specific remedies for women's subordination within the party itself. Indeed, the one woman Guesde finally chose to sit on the administrative council of the *POF* took no position which might have revealed the leadership's hypocrisy on this issue. In fact, Aline Valette's 'feminism' was distinctly reactionary and appealed to the more misogynist among Guesdist supporters. At the same time, neither her presence on the *POF* council nor her opinions did anything to halt the growing disaffection from the party felt by previously committed local working women.

The explanation for women's gradual exclusion from the socialist movement does not, however, lie entirely in the realm of practical politics. From the outset, working women presented a group of complex problems to party tacticians as well as to socialist ideologues. Perhaps the most significant of the dilemmas was one that combined a practical problem with a theoretical contradiction. This was women's obvious preference for sex-segregated groups. Women's groups, as such, implied a primary commitment to the emancipation of women—which necessarily relegated the class struggle to a secondary place. Moreover, within these groups, women were free to address what they saw as women's special needs within the proletarian community—needs which frequently threatened to shake the status quo within the working-class family. When they did this, they began to undermine the Guesdists' appeal for the party's male constituents who, after all, benefitted from traditional domestic arrangements which depended upon women's passive acceptance of virtually all domestic work.

In Roubaix and Lille, local Guesdist leaders attempted to forestall the growth of such revolutionary women's demands by channelling women's activities into traditional directions. Thus, they encouraged women's participation in the campaign for free school lunches. Moreover, they supported women's demands for various services that did not threaten male domination, including demands for free maternity care or more crèches. But whenever women veered onto more potentially dangerous territory they met with indifference. Thus, for example, when the Rémy women strikers asked the party to help them win their strike, the Guesdists shunted them off into the safer 'women's campaign' for children's school meals.

Underlying most local male leaders' reaction to women's groups were several concerns which remained unvoiced throughout the *belle époque*. For one thing, few male leaders were not shaken by women's autonomous activities within groups which they clearly preferred to mixed-sex groups led by men. Male reactions to militant behaviour ranged from patronizing approval of a women's protest to overt hostility. Victor Renard's response to the 1911 food riots included both kinds of reaction. On the one hand he approved women's efforts in unctuous tones. On the other, however, he expressed the widely held view that groups of women without 'rational' male leadership could only produce erratic, unproductive, and uncontrolled behaviour. Like many officials of the Third Republic, as well as Compère-Morel and 'Suzon', Renard revealed a deep-seated fear of women's collective resistance. In mass demonstrations, passive housewives were transformed by the male imagination into 'viragos' who threatened the male order.

Of course, the Guesdists had another means of preventing the development of potentially threatening women's groups while at the same time recruiting women into the socialist movement. They were free to include women in mixed-sex groups. In the Lille area these included both textile unions and socialist party sections. But within such groups the effects of women's lifelong oppression could never be overcome. Hélène Brion has described these effects: 'The hell of the *foyer*, as it is presently constituted, weighs on women throughout their lives and prevents every manifestation of independent thought or action.'[2]

Added to such lifelong habits of subordination to male family members, women had primary responsibility for children. This posed practical difficulties during mixed-sex meetings, when most women were preoccupied with keeping children quiet, whilst the men got on with the serious business of politics.

Of course, the structures of such groups need not have mirrored sexual relations in the wider society. Leaders who were sincerely committed to ending women's inequality had options. They could have identified and trained women militants and leaders. They might have offered key women party or union jobs which would have freed them from mill work and from the fear of blacklisting which limited their political activities. They might even have established travel funds for women needing to attend distant meetings, or provided child care so that such women could be away from home for the time required. But they did none of these things.

Early on, then, socialist theory and socialist practice proved to be entirely inadequate to the task of liberating women either from their exploitation in the factories or from their oppression within the working-class communities. Not surprisingly, these various inadequacies rose to the surface at the same time as working

---

[2] Hélène Brion, *Hélène Brion: la voie féministe*, ed. Huguette Bouchardeau (Paris, 1978), p. 59.

women's groups were becoming active within the movement at the local level. And, as women were increasingly distanced from the centralized party power structure, they began to drop out of the organized movement altogether.

Between 1897 and 1912 a curtain fell over the problems of organizing working women into the socialist movement in French Flanders. Only in the latter year did several factors provoke a reawakening of party leaders' interest in their female constituents. But this time, instead of building on earlier successes or correcting earlier mistakes, most leaders chose to relegate to socialist women only those spheres of influence assigned them by tradition. Thus, socialist attempts to organize women between 1912 and 1914 were grounded in stereotypical assumptions about women's natural proclivities. These included a bent for domestic self-sacrifice as well as a preference for pacifism.

Although this second-phase vision of women's roles was undoubtedly popular among many segments of the socialist movement of the time, it did nothing to recruit great numbers of working women into the party. Moreover, it could not ever produce a progressive or revolutionary politics of women's liberation as it depended totally on the most reactionary interpretation of women's own history.

At no time, therefore, did the organized Marxist wing of the French left ever go beyond the early efforts to organize women's groups at the local level. Perhaps it was too much to expect of working men whose acquaintance with both the theories and the practices of class liberation was still very slight. Indeed, it is to the early Guesdists' credit that they at least paid lip-service to women's emancipation in an industrial capitalist society. That they failed to develop a politics grounded in theory that was adequate to this broad and difficult project was not surprising. (Indeed, even present-day feminists have yet to articulate a coherent, analytically viable theory of women's liberation which could underpin what are increasingly sophisticated and efficacious organizational strategies.) Moreover, no nascent political party, hoping to come to power in the *belle époque*, could afford to alienate the voting half of their constituency by forcing men to reshape their private behaviour. And even had they determined to accomplish this end it was not clear what means they had at their disposal.

In addition, most socialist leaders genuinely expected that the socialist revolution was imminent around the turn of the century. For them, the key problem was to organize the proletariat quickly and effectively so that the revolution would not fail. Peripheral issues, including the knotty problem of emancipating women, took a second place to this essential socialist project.

Unfortunately, however, the revolution did not come. Thus the *Parti ouvrier*'s (and later the *SFIO*'s) failure to confront the problems inherent in their promises to women sowed seeds which subsequent socialist parties have reaped ever since. The most obvious residue of this earlier failure is the constant tension between women's divided loyalties: to their sex on the one hand, to their class on the other.[3] Choosing feminism then, as now, meant rejecting socialism, since women's oppression does not fit into class divisions, but rather affects women of all classes (though never equally and never in identical ways). Choosing socialism means working within a male-dominated party which may or may not be convinced by women's united efforts to share power equally with women. Moreover, because Marxist theory, to which the organized French left looks for legitimacy, does not include an analysis of women's personal oppression, neither socialist women nor sympathetic socialist men can bolster their efforts with the necessary 'scientific' arguments. Instead, women's liberation remains on the purely ethical plane.

Nevertheless, many thousands of contemporary French women remain convinced that they must work within the socialist movement. And for these women, as well as for some men socialists, the experiences of Lille area textile *ouvrières* hold important lessons. At the most minimal level, the day-to-day political practice of socialist parties must exclude what would today be described as 'phallocentrism'. Moreover, every practical means of ensuring women's equal participation—from providing child care during meetings to establishing affirmative action quotas—must be used. Finally, women—who remain the only group still not entirely equal before French law or in the provisions

---

[3] Hélène Brion described the socialist message as working women heard it during the First World War: 'Le socialisme suffit à tout! Le vrai féminisme, c'est d'être socialiste! Vous n'avez pas besoin d'être féministe, il doit vous suffire d'être socialistes, pleinement, intégralement . . . toute la question sociale est là!', in ibid., p. 51.

of French education—must at last be drawn completely into the bourgeois democratic society. And this must be accomplished before—not after—the revolutionary 'rupture'. As François Mitterrand promised recently:

Il reste maintenant à faire passer les droits dans les faits. On ne peut en deux ans changer un mode d'habitudes et de pratiques. Mais aucun retard ne droit être toléré. L'action entreprise pour plus de justice et plus d'égalité sera poursuivie.[4]

ii

It remains to consider two further elements. Firstly, how far does this history of relations between a local party organization (though one based in a national party) and women textile workers offer generalizations which might apply to the larger picture in France around the turn of the nineteenth century? Secondly, what does the story add to our knowledge of the circumstances and behaviour of working women in France, or indeed in Europe, in this period?

In the first case, it seems clear that the special nature of the textile industry in the Lille area created conditions which were unusual in French industry. For one thing, the mixed nature of the work-force as well as the integration of most jobs in the mills meant that the development of political consciousness was to some degree common to all workers. In addition, the fact that the Lille area was early on a centre of Guesdist organization meant that the particularly progressive stand of the *Parti ouvrier* on women's rights was heard in the earliest days of socialist organizing. Moreover, the Guesdist method of assimilating Flemish popular culture to socialist ends necessarily drew all members of the working-class community into contact with socialism at least at some points in their lives. The continuing existence of a vital socialist subculture in the Lille area meant that, even after women were left behind by official party policy after 1897, they often remained active in the less formally defined movement. In fact, by the turn of the century, most textile workers of both sexes were 'informal' socialists even if they never paid dues to the party or to a socialist union.

[4] Message adressé par M François Mitterrand, Président de la République Française, au Colloque International organisé par le mouvement "Choisir" (UNESCO, 15 Oct. 1983).

It seems clear, then, that both ethnicity and the peculiarities of textile production in the cities of French Flanders helped shape the Guesdists' relations with local working women. Perhaps the most significant of the two factors was the form of production, which mingled men and women together from early in their childhoods. However much wages and shop-floor conditions differentiated women workers from their men co-workers, their work experience remained, on the whole, a shared one. This, in turn, meant that socialist voters in this region did not find women's participation in politics either shocking or repellent.

But linking a progressive political practice *vis-à-vis ouvrières* to a certain form of mixed-sex production relations raises certain other intriguing possibilities. Were such politics characteristic of other areas where industries employed men and women together in relatively equal numbers?

It was certainly the case that regions such as the Rhône department had long been strongholds of organized women's political activities. The Lyon silk *ovalistes*, for example, were the first women's group to join the First International, in 1869.[5] In our period, the Lyon textile unions included active and militant women among the leadership. Moreover, in our period, Lyon textile workers of both sexes were predominantly Guesdists, just as they were in the Nord. Throughout the *belle époque*, the activities of the Lyon textile leaders (particularly in support of women's textile unions of the neighbouring department of the Isère) suggests that they were, if anything, even more committed to bringing women into equal participation in political activities.

But the situation in various areas where women worked in sex-*segregated* industrial production raises even more interesting possibilities. In the silk mills of the Isère, the Gard, and the Ain, as well as in the tobacco-producing regions of France, militant women organized unions and agitated on behalf of their equal economic (and, in many cases, political) rights. In silk-working areas, in fact, the socialist union's rejection of women's equal participation in the federation sent groups of organized women workers straight into the more welcoming arms of the syndicalist movement, especially after 1907. (This option was unavailable to

---

[5] Their history is detailed in Claire Auzias and Annik Houel, *La Grève des ovalistes, Lyon, juin–juillet 1869* (Paris, 1982).

textile *ouvrières* in Lille, Roubaix, and Tourcoing, where the entire union movement was in the hands of Guesdist anti-syndicalists.)

Given these women's militancy in the *belle époque*, it may well be that the socialists' greatest missed opportunity lay in these areas. Especially in the Isère, a long-standing close alliance between the organized *institutrices* and the women's silk-workers' union meant that most silk-workers were literate and informed— an ideal potential constituency for a Guesdist party wishing to mobilize women for their own liberation as well as for the class struggle.

On the other hand, there was a third potential constituency for socialists, among the non-waged women—the housewives of proletarian France. In mining areas, for example, where married women were less likely to work for wages, the *SFIO*'s post-1911 paeans of praise for working-class housewives may well have attracted substantial support. Moreover, some peasant women may have been attracted to the later socialists' more traditional view of their roles as *ménagères*. Unfortunately, no recent historian has undertaken to investigate these questions, and they remain open to every speculation.

iii

In the broader history of working women in the *belle époque*, this study prompts several thoughts. Firstly, explanatory links between women's primarily domestic roles and their putative lack of political interest fall away in the face of evidence from the Nord department. Most women saw their relation to production and reproduction in a more complex way than much recent historiography has suggested. Furthermore, they acted on their self-image within the public arena—on behalf of interests arising from both their roles. Moreover, they were in no way the passive hand-maidens of their male relatives, meekly led into the politics chosen by their fathers and husbands. In fact, quite the contrary. When male socialist leaders began to patronize and marginalize their organized efforts, women collectively rejected them.

Furthermore, the women textile workers of the Lille area were not oblivious to feminists or to feminism. Both women militants and many male leaders spread the call for women's equal rights throughout the workers' *quartiers* of the three cities. Although much recent historiography assigns French Flanders feminists only a marginal place, on the fringes of Parisian society, this study supports Charles Sowerwine's contention that the feminist message spread rapidly from Paris into the provinces during the *belle époque*, where it helped shape the collective behaviour of working women, even after the socialist movement had lost interest in them.

Finally, and most importantly, the behaviour of all the textile workers of these three cities demonstrates a minimal division by gender within the larger textile workers' community, despite women's enslavement to domestic work. Women socialized in the same places frequented by men, and spent their leisure hours with them as well as with their children. They worked together, marched together, went to meetings together, and created a vital cultural life together. To a far greater extent than many historians have suggested, working women—at least in the Lille *arrondissement*—lived within their communities rather than within a separate 'women's world'.

Of course, this is not to minimize women's experience of a gender-based identity. They did create their own socialist women's groups. They frequently struck together rather than together with men. Moreover, they held women-only strike meetings, and excluded men from their food riots. Furthermore, they shared the events of women's lives, including pregnancy and birth, as well as the various duties assigned them by tradition, including the care of the dead. But they managed to balance their various roles far more easily than many historians have assumed. Women textile workers expressed this balance when they sent a message to women in a nearby mining community: '*Ouvrières* like us,' they wrote, 'like us wives and mothers of workers . . .'[6] It was not working-class women who made clear distinctions but rather only male leaders.

Thus, when clear-cut gender distinctions began to colour socialist politics after unification, they remained to a large extent distinctions imposed from above, where both prejudice and the exigencies of electoral politics encouraged the socialists' neglect of the potential female constituency among the industrial proletariat.

It would appear, then, that this study bears out two contentions:

---

[6] Lille women's call to mining women is reported in *VdP* (14–21 Sept. 1913).

firstly, that the political history of working women can be written via a close and sometimes tedious day-to-day study of their lives and behaviour, despite the great difficulties imposed by a dearth of many of the records upon which similar political histories of male workers have rested; and, secondly, that it is not sufficient to adduce women's low membership figures in socialist parties or unions as conclusive evidence for the argument that working women were apolitical. Instead, this study underscores the importance of looking beyond voting returns or party membership lists—at what Eric Foner has described as 'the ways in which power in civil society is ordered and exercised', as well as at the ways in which that same power is wielded within the cultural and social relations of worker's private lives.[7]

[7] Eric Foner, *Politics and Ideology in the Age of the Civil War* (New York, 1980), p. 9.

APPENDIX

MARRIAGE AND WAGED WORK,
THE DEBATE

THIS vexed question of whether or not most married working-class women worked for wages stems from the fact that most British women of that class ceased waged work upon marriage in the last years of the nineteenth century. Because Britain is usually taken as the model for those changes wrought by industrialization, many historians have assumed that French women followed a similar trajectory. But in fact there is no evidence for such a generalized pattern. Virtually all non-quantifiable evidence for the end of the nineteenth century suggests that waged women continued in work throughout their lives. But it is important to ascertain whether or not quantifiable data (suspect as they are in this period) support this contention that most working-class women continued to work after marriage.

To that end, I have examined both data available for the Nord department as a whole and similar data for the Seine-Inférieure, a department with some rather similar occupational structures to those of the Nord. Data for the Nord are taken from France, *Recensement général de la population 1901* (Paris, 1902). Data for the Seine-Inférieure are taken from France, *Annuaire statistique 1905* (Paris, 1906).

In the Nord in 1901, 36.8 per cent of the total female population (aged 1 to 100) either was or had been married. What is remarkable is that the comparable percentage of married women among industrial *ouvrières* was only slightly less (33.6 per cent). If marriage were taken to presume the likely departure from the work-force, it should follow that single *ouvrières*, upon marrying, left the factories in droves. The predominant age of marriage for French women as a whole in 1901 was between 20 and 24. Of all married French women, 62.48 per cent had married by the age of 25. Assuming that the industrial *ouvrières* married at about the same age as women in general, we should see a sharp drop in their numbers after the age of 25. In fact, however, the sharpest drop comes by or before the age of 20 (43.2 per cent of all industrial *ouvrières* in the Nord were 19 or younger). Clearly, one could hypothesize that these women married very young indeed, but in that case we have to face the converse problem: that 57 per cent of all *ouvrières* in the Nord were over 20, and, by extension, for the most part married.

Thus, either local working women married young and dropped out of waged work in droves—in which case we would need to assume that a very large number never married (and there is no evidence to support this)—or, assuming that most *ouvrières*, like other French women, married in their early to mid-twenties and had stayed on in the factory until then, they appear in large part to have remained at work thereafter.

The rate of fall-out from the ages of 20 to 65 is remarkably steady, except for a sharp fall in the numbers of women at work in their forties relative to those working in their thirties. This fact confirms the low life expectancy posited in the text. Women who survived into their forties (married or otherwise) appear to have worked steadily until they died. The smallest decline in *ouvrières* is registered between the cohorts 40–49 and 50–59.

It should be stressed again that these figures are indicative, not conclusive; we shall in fact never know exactly how many married *ouvrières* there were in each age category, and must therefore make assumptions regarding such figures with caution.

On the other hand, one check can be made by looking at another area of France. An analysis of the 1905 data concerning the Seine-Inférieure revealed the following: There were 274,000 women between the ages of 25 and 64, of whom 168,000 were 'active' in all fields. Since only 92,000 women were single in 1905, we are forced to conclude that, even in the absurdly unlikely event that every unmarried woman was at work, 42 per cent of married women must have been employed as well. Even if we count all widows and divorcees as single women, and further assume that all of them worked full time, 29.2 per cent of the married women would still have had to be at work in order to make up the active female population.

An even more speculative analysis is possible if one assumes that 59 per cent of the female population of the Seine-Inférieure was 'ouvrière', as was the case in the Lille *arrondissement* in this period. Given that assumption, plus the assumption that *ouvrières* married in the same percentage as women in the department as a whole, one can estimate that there were some 60,000 married, divorced, and widowed women at work in service and industrial occupations. From this it can further be assumed that 58 per cent of all *ouvrières* who married remained at work.

The evidence from the Seine-Inférieure, then, far from suggesting that the Nord's figures were anomalous, indicates that if anything my estimates for the Nord erred on the side of caution. Evidence from other departments, of course, might suggest otherwise. It does, however, seem clearly the case that there is little statistical support in France for the a priori assumption that marriage involved withdrawal from the labour force for most working women. In view of the abundance of qualitative evidence to the contrary, the onus would seem to be on proponents of such a thesis to provide more evidence in support of it than they have hitherto done.

BIBLIOGRAPHY

1: ARCHIVAL SOURCES

Archives nationales

C 3019	'Enquête sur la situation des classes ouvrières, 1872–75'.
C 4039–40	'Élections générales 1881 par canton, département du Nord'.
C 5306 a.76	'Élections législatives 1885'.
C 5322 a.92	'Élections législatives 1889, Marne-Nord'.
C 5358 a.128	'Élections législatives 1898, Nord'.
C 6399	'Élections législatives 1906, Nord (Lille)'.
F^7 12488	'Congrès ouvriers 1876–1879'.
12489	'Congrès socialistes 1880–1882'.
12490	'Congrès guesdistes 1884, 1890–1899'.
12494	'Congrès divers'.
12495	'Activité socialiste dans le département du Nord, 1905–1914'.
12501	'Activité socialiste dans les départements, 1900–1915: Nord, 1900–1904'.
12522	'Congrès divers, 1876–1902'.
12528–30	'Premier mai (1898–1905)'.
12538	'Le Mouvement syndicaliste (par département) 1905–1912'.
12723	'Agitation révolutionnaire par département, 1893–1914'.
12767	'Industries textiles: renseignements généraux, questions ouvrières 1900–1910'.
12793	'Syndicats jaunes'.
12886	'Parti ouvrier français 1896–1899'.
12887	'Socialisme 1900–1901'.
12889	'Socialisme 1901–1902'.
12890	'Socialisme 1902'.
13072	'SFIO: congrès 1905–1920'.
13819	'Travailleurs du textile, activité des syndicats et congrès, 1905–1908'.
13820	'Textile 1910–1914'.
F^{12} 4660	'Grèves et coalitions 1880–1881'.

	4664	'Grèves 1880–1889'.
	4667–89	'Grèves 1890–1899'.
	4938	'Établissements insalubres et dangereux'.
F²²	150	'Syndicats ouvriers'.
	167	'Grèves 1905–1906'.
	169	'Grèves 1907'.

Archives de la préfecture de police

Ba	37	'Congrès de Marseille 1879'.
	201	'Socialisme 1885–1892'.
	182/202	'Grèves des ouvriers et ouvrières en laines et cotons, 1883–1898'.
	1178	'Le socialisme: (i) 1880–1895. (ii) 1896–1901'.
	1290	'Dossier Aline Valette'.
	1351–1446	'Grèves et Syndicats'.
	1476	'Le Socialisme en province'.

Archives départementales du Nord

M	37	'Professions de foi des candidats, Élections législatives 1889–1914'.
	89	'Élections Municipales'.
	154	'Partis politiques. Socialistes et mouvement syndical, Agitation ouvrière, 1901–1906'.
	157	'Partis politiques. Dossiers individuels'.
	159	'Partis politiques. Manifestations 1889–1908'.
	160	'Fête du 14 juillet, 1880–1904'.
	161	'Fêtes diverses 1871–1910'.
	201	'Police administrative. Prostitution et police de mœurs, 1818–1908'.
	203	'Police administrative. Recherche dans l'intérêt des familles'.
	222	'Sociétés particulières'.
	225	'Sociétés de secours mutuels'.
	226	'Sociétés de secours mutuels en Lille'.
	253	'Santé, 1878–1907'.
	264	'Santé, 1884'.
	310	'Santé. Fièvre puepérale 1899'.
M	417	'Santé. Textiles'.
	547, 22–24	'L'Industrie textile'.
	572	'Industries. Situation: Enquêtes et rapports'.
	581	'Industrie textile. Ouvriers tisseurs, 1878. Usines: Renseignements statistiques 1891'.
	591	'L'Industrie textile. Inspection 1891'.

	594	'Travail dans l'Industrie. Inspection'.
	595	'Syndicats: Généralités et correspondance'.
	596	'États des syndicats'.
	597	'Travail dans l'industrie'.
	599	'Unions de syndicats ouvriers—notices, dossiers par localité (Roubaix–Tourcoing)'.
	600	'Syndicats mixtes—notices, dossiers par localité (Lille, Tourcoing)'.
	601	'Bourses du travail, 1905, Lille'.
	602	'Bureaux de placement, 1854–1904'.
	603	'Rapports entre patrons et ouvriers, 1848–1893'.
	604	'Livrets d'ouvriers, 1826–1886'.
	605	'Condition des ouvriers, 1848–1892'.
	606	'Salaires. 1831–1890'.
	610	'Ouvriers—Apprentis, ouvriers, étrangers, 1818–1906'.
	611	'Travail des femmes adultes dans les manufactures—Enquêtes, rapports 1882–1883, 1892'.
	614	'Accidents, 1845–1908'.
	615	'Protection du travail, 1862–1909'.
	616	'Chômage, 1831–1900'.
	617	'Grèves'.
	619	'Grèves. Questionnaires et rapports de police, 1867–1908'.
	625	'Grèves. Textiles, 1900–1909, 1862–1910'.
	646	'Statistique générale de la France 1884–1903'.
1	U 78	'Conseils des prud'hommes, Roubaix'.
1	U 79	'Conseils des prud'hommes, Tourcoing'.
2	U 155	'Dossiers criminels'.
		'Plan no. 470 (Lille-Roubaix-Tourcoing)'.

International Institute of Social History, Amsterdam
'Dossiers Jules Guesde, 1880–1914'.

Bibliothèque Marguerite Durand
'Dossier Madame Sorgue'.

Musée Social

Collection 6808. 'Articles divers parus dans la Presse française sur les congrès nationaux du *POF*, 1896, 1898, 1899, 1900, 1902'.

Le Congrès international socialiste de Londres, juillet 1896, vols. i–iv: 'Articles divers parus dans la presse', 'Publications faites à l'occasion du Congrès', 'Rapport des commissions diverses'.

2: PRINTED SOURCES

Congresses

(a) International socialist congresses

Congrès international ouvrier socialiste, Paris 1889, compte rendu (n.p., n.d.).

5ᵉ Congrès socialiste international, Paris 23–27 septembre 1900, compte rendu analytique (Paris, 1901).

Congrès socialiste international, Amsterdam 14–20 août 1904.

Rapports et projets de résolution sur les questions de l'Ordre du jour. Supplément (Bruxelles, 1904).

7ᵉ Congrès socialiste international, Stuttgart, 16–24 août 1907, compte rendu analytique (Bruxelles, 1908).

Parti socialiste SFIO, Fédération de la Seine. Documents concernant le Congrès national de Nancy et le Congrès international de Stuttgart, 1907 (Paris, 1907).

8ᵉ Congrès socialiste international, Copenhague, 28 août–3 septembre 1910, compte rendu analytique (Gand, 1911).

Conférence internationale des femmes socialistes, Copenhague 25–26 août 1910 (Gand, 1911).

(b) National congresses of Parti ouvrier français

Congrès ouvrier socialiste de France, 3ᵉ session, Marseille, 20–31 octobre 1879 (Marseille, 1880).

5ᵉ Congrès national, Reims, 30 octobre–6 novembre 1881, compte rendu (Paris, 1882).

6ᵉ Congrès national, St-Étienne, 25–30 septembre 1882, compte rendu (Paris, 1883).

7ᵉ Congrès national du Parti ouvrier, Roubaix, 29 mars–7 avril 1884 (Paris, 1884).

8ᵉ Congrès national du Parti ouvrier, Lille, 11–12 octobre 1890 (Lille, 1890).

9ᵉ Congrès national du Parti ouvrier, Lyon, 26–28 novembre 1891 (Lille, 1891).

10ᵉ Congrès national du Parti ouvrier, Marseille, 24–28 septembre 1892 (Lille, 1892).

11ᵉ Congrès national du Parti ouvrier, Paris, 7–9 octobre 1893 (Lille, 1893).

12ᵉ Congrès national du Parti ouvrier, Nantes, 14–16 septembre 1894 (Lille, 1894).

13ᵉ Congrès national du Parti ouvrier, Romilly, 8–11 septembre 1895 (Lille, 1895).

14ᵉ Congrès national du Parti ouvrier, Lille, 21–25 juillet 1896 (Lille, 1896).

284 *Bibliography*

15ᵉ Congrès national du Parti ouvrier, Paris, 10–13 juillet 1897 (Lille, 1897).

16ᵉ Congrès national du Parti ouvrier, Montluçon, 17–20 septembre 1898 (Paris, 1898).

17ᵉ Congrès national du Parti ouvrier, Épernay, 20–27 août 1899 (n.p., n.d.).

18ᵉ Congrès national du Parti ouvrier, Ivry-sur-Seine, octobre 1900 (Paris, 1900).

19ᵉ Congrès national du Parti ouvrier, Roubaix, 15–18 septembre 1901 (Paris, 1901).

20ᵉ Congrès national du Parti ouvrier, Issoudun, 28 septembre–4 octobre 1902 (n.p., n.d.).

(c) National congresses of the SFIO

1ᵉʳ Congrès national du Parti socialiste (SFIO), Paris, 23–25 avril 1905, compte rendu analytique (Paris, 1906).

2ᵉ Congrès national du Parti socialiste (SFIO), Chalon-sur-Saône, 29 octobre–1 novembre 1905, compte rendu analytique (Paris, 1906).

3ᵉ Congrès national du Parti socialiste (SFIO), Limoges, 1–4 novembre 1906, compte rendu analytique (Paris, 1906).

4ᵉ Congrès national du Parti socialiste (SFIO), Nancy, 11–14 août 1907, compte rendu analytique (Paris, 1907).

5ᵉ Congrès national du Parti socialiste (SFIO), Toulouse, 15–18 octobre 1908, compte rendu sténographique (Paris, 1908).

6ᵉ Congrès national du Parti socialiste (SFIO), St-Étienne, 11–14 avril 1909, compte rendu sténographique (Paris, 1909).

7ᵉ Congrès national du Parti socialiste (SFIO), Nîmes, 6–9 février 1910, compte rendu sténographique (Paris, 1910).

8ᵉ Congrès national du Parti socialiste (SFIO), St-Quentin, 16–19 avril 1911, compte rendu sténographique (Paris, n.d.).

9ᵉ Congrès national du Parti socialiste (SFIO), Lyon, 18–21 février 1912, compte rendu sténographique (Paris, n.d.).

10ᵉ Congrès national du Parti socialiste (SFIO), Brest, 23–25 mars 1914, compte rendu sténographique (Paris, n.d.).

(d) Regional congresses of Parti ouvrier (Nord federation)

Congrès régional, Denain, 28 août 1898, compte rendu (n.p., n.d.).

Congrès régional, Lens, 16 avril 1899, compte rendu (n.p., n.d.).

Congrès régional, Roubaix, 18 févier 1900, compte rendu (n.p., n.d.).

Congrès régional, Caudry, 5 août 1900, compte rendu (Lille, 1900).

Congrès régional, Douai, 7 avril 1901, compte rendu (Lille, 1901).

Congrès régional (Parti socialiste de France), Valenciennes, 31 mai 1903, compte rendu (Lille, 1903).

Congrès régional (Parti socialiste de France), Lille, 3 juillet 1904, compte rendu (Lille, 1904).

(e) Other Socialist congresses

1er Congrès départemental, Parti socialiste (SFIO) Fédération du Nord, Denain, 22 octobre 1905, compte rendu officiel (Lille, 1905).

2e Congrès général des organisations socialistes françaises, Paris 28–30 septembre 1900, compte rendu sténographique (Paris, 1901).

(f) Congresses of textile syndicats

Conférence du Syndicat ouvrier des peigneurs de lin, cotonniers, tissérands et filtiers, Roubaix, 15 mai 1882, compte rendu (n.p., n.d.).

2e Congrès national de l'industrie textile, Roubaix, 20–24 novembre 1893, compte rendu officiel (Lille, 1894).

5e Congrès national de l'industrie textile, St-Étienne, 15–17 août 1903, compte rendu (St-Étienne, 1903).

6e Congrès national ouvrier de l'industrie textile, Reims, 14–16 août 1904, compte rendu (Lille, 1904).

8e Congrès national ouvrier de l'industrie textile, Tourcoing, 12–15 août, 1906, compte rendu (Lille, 1906).

10e Congrès national ouvrier de l'industrie textile, Troyes, 15–17 août 1907, compte rendu (Lille, 1908).

11e Congrès national ouvrier de l'industrie textile, Lyon, 15–18 août 1909, compte rendu (Lille, 1909).

12e Congrès national ouvrier de l'industrie textile, Roubaix, 13–16 août 1911, compte rendu (Lille, 1911).

13e Congrès national ouvrier de l'industrie textile, Fourmies, 15–17 août 1912, compte rendu (Lille, 1912).

14e Congrès national ouvrier de l'industrie textile, Limoges, 15–16 août 1913, compte rendu (Lille, 1913).

(g) Other congresses

2e Congrès international des œuvres et institutions féminines, Paris, Palais des congrès de l'Exposition universelle de 1900, compte rendu des bureaux, vols. i–iv (Paris, 1902).

Congrès international de la condition et des droits des femmes, Paris, 5–8 septembre 1900 (Paris, 1901).

Actes du Congrès international des œuvres et institutions féminines, Paris, Exposition universelle, 1889 (Paris, 1890).

Congrès de l'Association internationale pour la protection légale des travailleurs, section française (Paris, n.d.).

Official Documents and Publications

France

Assemblée nationale, Chambre des députés, session de 1904: *Procès-verbaux de la commission chargée de procéder à une enquête sur l'état de l'industrie textile et la condition des ouvriers tisseurs*, vol. 11 (Paris, 1906).

Assemblée Nationale, Sénat, session de 1896: *Proposition de loi, adoptée par la Chambre des députés (ayant pour objet: 1er d'assurer à la femme mariée la libre disposition des fruits de son travail; 2e de la protéger contre certains abus de la puissance maritale)*, no. 47 (2 Mar. 1896).

Ministère de l'armement et des fabrications de guerre, Protection et utilisation de la main d'œuvre féminine dans les usines de guerre (Paris, 1917).

Ministère du commerce, *Annuaire statistique 1886* (Paris, 1886).

Ministère du commerce, *Les Associations professionnelles ouvrières*, vol. ii (Paris, 1901).

Ministère du commerce, Office du travail, *Poisons industriels* (Paris, 1901).

Ministère du commerce, *Rapports sur l'application pendant l'année 1895 des lois réglementant le travail* (Paris, n.d.).

Ministère du commerce, *Recensement des industries et professions 1896* (Paris, n.d.).

Ministère du commerce, *Résultats statistique du recensement des industries et professions, 29 mars 1896* (Paris, 1897).

Ministère du commerce, Statistique générale de la France, *Annuaire statistique 1901* (Paris, 1901).

Ministère du commerce, *Statistique des grèves 1896* (Paris, 1897).

Ministère du commerce, *Bulletin de l'Office du travail*, Jan. 1894–Dec. 1894, vols. i–xii (Paris, n.d.).

Ministère du commerce, *Bulletin de l'Office du travail*, vol. iii, 1896 (Paris, 1897).

Ministère du travail, *Bulletin de l'inspection du travail, 1902–1906* (annual) (Paris, 1902–1906).

Ministère du travail, *Bulletin de l'Office du travail*, May 1907 (Paris, 1907).

Ministère du travail, *Bulletin de l'inspection du travail, 1908* (Paris, 1908).

Ministère du travail, *Bulletin de l'office du travail, 1909–1911* (annual) (Paris, 1909–1911).

Ministère du travail, *Bulletin de l'inspection du travail et de l'hygiène industrielle, 1912* (Paris, n.d.).

Ministère du travail, *Bulletin de l'inspection du travail, 1913–1914* (annual) (Paris, 1914).

Ministère du travail, *Bulletin*, 20th year, vol. xii, Dec. 1913 (Paris, 1913).

Ministère du travail, *Enquête sur la reduction de la durée du travail le samedi* (Semaine anglaise) (Paris, 1913).

Ministère du travail, *Salaires et coût de l'existence à diverses époques jusqu'en 1910* (Paris, 1911).

Ministère du travail, *Statistique générale de la France, Résultats statistiques du recensement général de la population, 1911* (Paris, 1912).

Ministère du travail, *Statistique générale de la France, Statistique des familles et des habitations en 1911* (Paris, 1912).

Ministère du travail, *Statistique des grèves 1902* (Paris, 1903).

Ministère du travail, *Statistique des grèves 1904* (Paris, 1905).

Ministère du travail, *Statistique des grèves 1906* (Paris, 1907).

Ministère du travail, *Statistique des grèves 1911* (Paris, 1912).

Ministère du travail, *Statistique générale de la France, Résultats statistiques du recensement général de la population, 4 mars 1906*, vol. 1 (Paris, 1907).

3: NEWSPAPERS AND JOURNALS

L'Action syndicale (1904–1910).

L'Avenir social (1896–1905).

L'Avenir du travailleur (13 Feb.–17 July 1887).

La Bataille syndicaliste (June 1911–Apr. 1914).

Le Cri du forçat (6 Apr.–3 Aug. 1884).

Le Cri de l'ouvrier (30 Nov. 1884–5 Apr. 1885).

Le Cri du travailleur (24 July 1887–6 Sept. 1892).

L'Égalité (18 Nov. 1877–1 Nov. 1882).

L'Égalité de Roubaix-Tourcoing (1896–1914).

L'Exploité (10 Aug.–23 Nov. 1884).

La Femme socialiste (May 1901–Sept. 1902, Mar. 1912–Dec. 1914).

Le Forçat (July 1882–July 1883).

La Guerre sociale (1906–1913, sporadic).

L'Humanité (1904–1914).

Le Monde ouvrier (Jan.–June 1899).

Le Mouvement socialiste (1899–1913).

L'Ouvrier des deux mondes (Feb 1897–July 1898, Jan.–July 1899).

L'Ouvrier textile (1903–1914).

Le Petit Jaune (1901–1911).

Le Prolétaire (Nov. 1878–Dec. 1884).

La Revanche du forçat (15 July–9 Sept. 1883).

Le Réveil du forçat (30 Aug. 1885–20 June 1886).

Le Réveil du Nord (1889–1914).

La Révolte (1890, sporadic).

La Revue socialiste (1885–1914).

Le Travailleur (i) (26 June–26 Dec. 1886).

Le Travailleur (ii) (23 Aug. 1891–27 Apr. 1895).
Le Travailleur (iii) (14 July 1900–1914).
La Voix du peuple (1900–1914).

4: CONTEMPORARY BOOKS AND PAMPHLETS

Addams, Jane, 'The Modern City and the Municipal Franchise for Women' (Baltimore, 1906), in Mari Jo and Paul Buhle, eds., *The Concise History of Woman Suffrage* (Urbana, Ill., 1978).

Albistur, Maïté and Daniel Armogathe, eds., *Nelly Roussel, l'éternelle sacrifiée* (Paris, 1979).

—— *Suzanne Voilquin. Mémoires d'une saint-simonienne en Russie* (Paris, 1977).

Ardouin-Dumazet, *Voyage en France, région du Nord* (Paris, 1903).

Audiganne, Armand, *Les Populations ouvrières et les industries de la France dans le mouvement social du dix-neuvième siécle* (Paris, 1854).

Baggio, C., *Petit catéchisme socialiste ou la conquête des femmes au socialisme* (Paris, 1888).

Bebel, August, *La Femme dans le passé, le présent et l'avenir*, trans. H. Ravé (Paris, 1891).

Berthod, S.H., *Légendes et traditions surnaturelles des Flandres* (Paris, 1862).

Blanqui, Adolphe, *Des classes ouvrières en France pendant l'année 1848* (Paris, 1849).

Blum, Léon, *Les Congrès ouvriers et socialistes français, 1876–1900*, 2 vols. (Paris, 1901).

Bocquet, Léon, *Villes meurtries de France. Villes du Nord: Lille, Douai, Cambrai, Valenciennes, Bergues, Dunkerque* (Brussels and Paris, 1918).

Bolligelli, Émile, ed., *Correspondence, Friedrich Engels, Paul et Laura Lafargue*, vol. iii, *1891–95* (Paris, 1959).

Bonneff, Léon and Maurice, *La Vie tragique des travailleurs* (Paris, 1914).

Bourdon, Mathilde, *Marthe Blondel, ou l'ouvrière de fabrique* (Paris, 1862).

Bouvier, Jeanne, *Mes mémoires, ou cinquante-neuf années d'activité industrielle, sociale et intellectuelle d'une ouvrière* (Vienne, 1936).

Brion, Hélène, *La Voie féministe*, ed. Huguette Bouchardeau (Paris, 1978).

Brisson, P., *Histoire du travail et des travailleurs* (Paris, 1906).

Compain, Louise-Marie, *La Femme dans les organisations ouvrières* (Paris, 1910).

Compère-Morel, Adéodat, *Jules Guesde, le socialisme fait homme, 1845–1922* (Paris, 1937).

—— *et al., Encyclopédie socialiste, syndicale et coopérative de l'Internationale ouvrière*, vol. ii (Paris, 1913).

Constant, Louis, ed., *Mémoires de femmes, mémoire du peuple* (Paris, 1979).

Crawford, Virginia, 'Feminism in France' in *Fortnightly Review*, lxi (Jan.–July 1897), pp. 524–34.

Dalôtel, Alain, ed., *Paule Minck, communarde et féministe, 1839–1901* (Paris, 1981).

Descamps, Désiré, *Les Crimes de la misère* (Lille, 1892).

Desrousseaux, Alexandre, *Mœurs populaires de la Flandre française*, 2 vols. (Lille, 1889).

Destrée, Jules, *Le Socialisme et les femmes* (Brussels, 1897).

Diard, Ennemonde, 'La Main-d'œuvre féminine' in *L'Œuvre Économique*, vol. xxxviii (10–25 July 1918).

Dictionnaire biographique illustré (2nd edition, Paris, n.d.).

Drioux, M., *Le Mouvement féministe et le socialisme* (Orleans, 1896).

Duhet, Paule-Marie, *Cahiers de doléances des femmes en 1789 et autres textes* (Paris, 1981).

Engels, Friedrich, *The Condition of the Working Class in England* (Moscow, 1973).

—— *The Origins of the Family, Private Property and the State* (New York, 1972).

Gérard, Claire, *Syndicalisme féminin et bourses du travail* (Paris, 1912).

Ghesquière, Henri, *La Femme et le socialisme* (Lille, 1893).

—— *La Mine et les mineurs* (Lille, n.d.).

—— and A. Compère-Morel, *L'Action syndicale* (Lille, 1911).

Gide, Charles, *Les Institutions de progrès social* (Paris, 1912).

Guesde, Jules, *La Femme et la société bourgeoise*, ed. Marcel Cachin (Paris, 1923).

—— *Quatre ans de lutte de classe à la Chambre, 1893–1898* (Paris, 1901).

—— and Paul Lafargue, *Le Programme du Parti ouvrier. Ses considérants et ses articles* (Lille, 1902).

Kauffman, Caroline and Paule Minck, *Importance de l'éducation physique scientifique combinée avec l'éducation intellectuelle morale. Idées générales sur les travaux du congrès international féminin de Londres* (Rapport au conseil municipal par les déléguées du Groupe de la Solidarité des femmes, Paris, 1899).

Klein, Viola, *The Feminine Character: History of an Ideology* (New York, 1946).

Lafargue, Paul, *La Question de la femme* (Paris, 1904).

—— 'Socialism in France from 1876–1896' in *Fortnightly Review*, lxii (July–Dec. 1897), pp. 445–58.

—— *Textes choisis*, ed. Jacques Girault (Paris, 1970).

Le Garrec, Evelyn, ed., *Séverine. Choix de papiers* (Paris, 1982).

Leroy-Beaulieu, Paul, *Le Travail des femmes au XIXe siècle* (Paris, 1873).

Leundan, l'abbé, *Histoire de l'institution Notre Dame des Victoires de Roubaix* (Roubaix, 1891).

MacDonald, J. Ramsay, ed., *Women in the Printing Trades: A Sociological Study* (London, 1904).

Maday, Dr André de, *Le Droit des femmes au travail: Étude sociologique* (Paris, n.d.).

Marcus, Jane, ed., *The Young Rebecca: The Writings of Rebecca West 1911–1917* (London, 1982).

Meersch, Maxence van der, *Bodies and Souls*, trans. E. Wilkins (New York, 1948).

—— *Invasion '14* (Paris, 1935).

—— *Maria, fille de Flandre* (Paris, 1937).

—— *Quand les sirènes se taisent* (Paris, 1933).

Michel, Louise, *Mémoires* (Paris, 1977).

Michelet, Jules, *La Femme* (Paris, n.d.).

Milhaud, Caroline, *L'Ouvrière en France* (Paris, 1907).

Minck, Paule, *Le Travail des femmes (discours prononcé par Mme Paul [sic] Minck à la réunion publique du Vauxhall, 13 juillet 1869)* (n.p., n.d.).

Motte, Fernand, *Souvenirs personnels d'un demi-siècle de vie et de pensée, 1886–1942* (n.p., n.d.).

Motte, Gaston, *Roubaix à travers les âges* (Roubaix, 1946).

Pawlowski, Auguste, *Les Syndicats féminins et les syndicats mixtes en France* (Paris, 1912).

Pelletier, Madeleine, *Madeleine Pelletier, l'éducation féministe des filles et autre textes*, ed. Claude Maignien (Paris, 1978).

Pelloutier, Maurice, *La Vie ouvrière en France* (Paris, 1900).

Petit, Gabrielle, *Les Conseils d'une mère: pour nos fils et pour nos filles* (Paris, n.d.).

Petitcollot, Maurice, *Les Syndicats ouvriers de l'industrie textile dans l'arrondissement de Lille* (Paris, 1907).

Poisson, Charles, *La Salaire des femmes* (Paris, 1906).

Popp, Adelheid, *La Jeunesse d'une ouvrière*, trans. Mina Valette (Paris, 1979).

Pottier, Eugène, *Œuvres complètes*, ed. Pierre Brochon (Paris, 1966).

Roubaix socialiste, ou quatre ans de gestion municipale ouvrière (Lille, n.d.).

Roussel, Nelly, *Quelques discours* (Paris, n.d.).

Rouzade, Léonie, *Petit catéchisme de morale laïque et socialiste* (Meudon, 1895).

Schirmacher, Kaethe, *Le Travail des femmes en France* (Extrait. Bibli. Marguerite Durand, Dossier Schirmacher).

Siegfried, André, *Tableau politique de la France de l'Ouest sous la Troisième République* (Paris, 1913).

Seilhac, Léon de, *La Grève du tissage de Lille* (Paris, 1910).
—— *Les Congrès ouvriers en France, 1876–97* (Paris, 1899).
Simon, Gustave and Jules, *La Femme du vingtième siècle* (Paris, 1982).
Stanton, Theodore, *The Woman Question in Europe* (New York, 1884).
'Suzon', *Socialisme et féminisme* (Paris, 1914).
Theremin, le citoyen, *De la condition des femmes dans les républiques* (Paris, Year VII).
'Le Travail féminin en concurrence avec le travail masculin', 3ᵉ entretien, *Libres Entretiens* (10 Jan. 1909), pp. 132–74.
Tristan, Flora, *The Workers' Union*, trans. Beverly Livingston (Urbana, Ill., 1983).
Uhry, Jules, *Les Grèves en France et leur solution* (Paris, 1903).
Valette, Aline, *Cahier des doléances féminines 1ᵉʳ mai 1893* (Fédération française des sociétés féministes, Paris, 1893).
—— *Socialisme et sexualisme* (Paris, 1895).
Vallin, A., *Le Femme salariée et la maternité* (Paris, 1911).
Vandervelde, Émile, *Souvenirs d'un militant socialiste: 1ᵉ partie, mes débuts dans la vie socialiste, 1881–1914* (Paris, 1939).
Varenne, L., *Pour l'ouvrière: éducation sociale de la femme* (Paris, 1903).
Verhaeghe, Dr D., *Le Secrétariat ouvrier d'hygiène de la bourse du travail de Lille* (Lille, 1908).
Villermé, Dr Louis-René, *État physique et moral des ouvriers des manufactures de coton, laine . . .* vol. i (Paris, 1840).
Vincent, Mme, *Électorat et éligibilité des femmes aux conseils des prud'hommes* (Paris, 1897).
Watteeuw, Jules, *Tourcoing au XIXᵉ siècle* (Tourcoing, 1904).

5: SELECTED SECONDARY SOURCES

(a) Books

Actes du Colloque international d'histoire religieuse, Grenoble 30 septembre–3 octobre 1971 (Grenoble, 1974).
Albistur, Maïté and Daniel Armogathe, *Histoire du féminisme français* (Paris, 1971).
Auzias, Claire and Annik Houel, *La Grève des ovalistes, Lyon, juin–juillet 1896* (Paris, 1982).
Banks, J. A., *Prosperity and Parenthood. A Study of Family Planning Among the Victorian Middle Classes* (London, 1954).
Basch, Françoise, *Relative Creatures* (New York, 1974).
Beauvoir, Simone de, *The Second Sex*, trans. H. M. Parshley (London, 1953).
Bédarida, François and Jean Maîtron, eds., *Christianisme et monde ouvrier* (Paris, 1971).

Blanquart, Louisette, *Chiffres et commentaires sur la 'Presse féminine'* (Paris, 1978).

Borgé, Jacques and Nicolas Viasnoff, eds., *Archives du Nord* (Paris, 1979).

Bouchardeau, Huguette, *Pas d'histoire, les femmes . . .; 50 ans d'histoire des femmes, 1918–1968* (Paris, 1977).

Boxer, Marilyn and Jean Quataert, eds., *Socialist Women: European Socialist Feminism in the Nineteenth and Twentieth Centuries* (New York, 1978).

Branca, Patricia, *Women in Europe Since 1750* (London, 1978).

Bridenthal, Renate and Claudia Koonz, eds., *Becoming Visible: Women in European History* (Boston, 1977).

Carter, Edward, *et al.*, *Enterprise and Entrepreneurs in 19th- and 20th-Century France* (Baltimore, 1976).

Catrice, Paul, *Roubaix au delà des mers* (Roubaix, 1969).

Chabert, Alexandre, *Les Salaires dans l'industrie française (les textiles)* (Paris, 1960).

Codaccioni, Félix-Paul, *De l'inégalité sociale dans une grande ville industrielle: le drame de Lille de 1850 à 1914* (Lille, 1976).

—— *et al.*, *Histoire d'une métropole: Lille, Roubaix, Tourcoing* (Toulouse, 1977).

Colin, Madeleine, *Ce n'est pas d'aujourd'hui* (Paris, 1975).

La Condition féminine (Paris, Centre d'études et de recherches marxistes, 1978).

Corbin, Alain, *Les Filles de noce: misère sexuelle et prostitution (19ᵉ siècle)* (Paris, 1982).

Davis, Alan, *American Heroine* (New York, 1973).

Diagoras, Léon, *La Genèse d'une métropole* (Roubaix, 1969).

Droz, Jacques, *Le Socialisme démocratique* (Paris, 1966).

Dublin, Thomas, *Women at Work* (New York, 1979).

Dubois, Ellen, *Feminism and Suffrage* (Ithaca, NY, 1978).

Dumont, Yvonne, ed., *Les Communistes et la condition de la femme* (Paris, 1970).

Dumortier, Jacques, *Le Syndicat patronal textile de Roubaix-Tourcoing de 1942 à 1972* (Lille, 1975).

Evans, Richard, *The Feminist Movement in Germany* (London, 1976).

'Femmes, capitalisme, mouvement ouvrier' in *Critique communiste,* numéro spécial (1987).

Figes, Eva, *Patriarchal Attitudes* (Greenwich, Conn., 1970).

Fini le féminisme? Compte rendu intégral du colloque international 'Féminismes et socialismes' organisé par le mouvement Choisir les 13–15 october 1983 (Paris, 1984).

Flexner, Eleanor, *A Century of Struggle* (New York, 1968).

Fohlen, Claude, *L'Industrie textile au temps du Second Empire* (Paris, 1956).

Gadille, Jacques, *La Pensée et l'action politiques des évêques français au début de la Troisième République, 1870–1933*, 2 vols. (Paris, 1967).

—— *Guide des archives diocésaines françaises* (Lyon, 1971).

Gildea, Robert, *Education in Provincial France, 1800–1914: a Study of Three Departments* (Oxford, 1983).

Gillet, Marcel, ed., *L'Homme, la vie et la mort dans le Nord au 19ᵉ siècle* (Lille, 1972).

Gordon, Linda, *Woman's Body, Woman's Right* (Harmondsworth, Middx., 1977).

Gornick, Vivian and Barbara Moran, eds., *Women in Sexist Society* (New York, 1971).

Guilbert, Madeleine, *Les Femmes et l'organisation syndicale avant 1914* (Paris, 1966).

—— *Les Fonctions des femmes dans l'industrie* (Paris, 1966).

Gurr, Ted, *Why Men Rebel* (Princeton, 1970).

Halimi, Gisèle, *Choisir: la cause des femmes, le programme commun des femmes* (Paris, 1978).

Harrison, Brian, *Separate Spheres* (London, 1978).

Hilaire, Yves-Marie, *Une Chrétienté au XIXᵉ siècle? La vie religieuse des populations du diocèse d'Arras, 1840–1914*, 2 vols. (Lille, 1977).

Hunt, Eddie, *British Labour History, 1815–1914* (London, 1981).

Hufton, Olwen, *The Poor of Eighteenth-Century France, 1750–1789* (Oxford, 1974).

Jenness, Linda, ed., *Feminism and Socialism* (New York, 1972).

Joll, James, *The Second International, 1889–1914* (London, 1968).

Judt, Tony, *Marxism and the French Left* (Oxford, 1986).

—— *Socialism in Provence, 1871–1914* (Cambridge, 1979).

Kaplan, Temma, *Anarchists of Andalusia* (Princeton, 1977).

Kemp, Tom, *Economic Forces in French History* (London, 1971).

Knibiehler, Yvonne and Cathérine Fouquet, *Histoire des mères du Moyen Âge à nos jours* (Paris, 1977).

Kolakowski, Leszek, *Main Currents of Marxism*, 3 vols. (Oxford, 1978).

Kraditor, Aileen, *Ideas of the Woman Suffrage Movement* (New York, 1965).

Kriegel, Annie, *Aux origines du communisme français*, 2 vols. (Paris, 1964).

—— *Le Pain et les Roses* (Paris, 1968).

Kundera, Milan, *The Book of Laughter and Forgetting*, trans. Michael Heim (Harmondsworth, Middx., 1980).

Laserre, André, *La Situation des ouvriers de l'industrie textile dans la région lilloise sous la monarchie de juillet* (Lausanne, 1952).

Laslett, Peter, *The World We Have Lost* (New York, 1965).

Le Bras, Gabriel, *Études de sociologie religieuse* (Paris, 1955).

Lederer, William, *The Fear of Women* (New York, 1968).

Lefranc, Georges, *Le Mouvement socialiste sous la Troisième République*, vol. i, *1875–1920* (Paris, 1971).

—— *Le Mouvement syndical sous la Troisième République* (Paris, 1967).

Lequin, Yves, *Les Ouvriers de la région Lyonnaise, 1848–1914*, 2 vols. (Lyon, 1977).

Lewenhak, Sheila, *Women and Work* (Glasgow, 1980).

Lichtheim, George, *From Marx to Hegel* (New York, 1974).

—— *Marxism: An Historical and Critical Study* (New York, 1969).

—— *Marxism in Modern France* (New York, 1966).

—— *The Origins of Socialism* (London, 1968).

Liddington, Jill and Jill Norris, *One Hand Tied Behind Us* (London, 1978).

McMillan, James, *Housewife or Harlot. The Place of Women in French Society, 1870–1940* (Brighton, 1981).

Macciocchi, Maria, *Letters to Louis Althusser* (London, 1969).

Mahaim, Annik, *et al.*, *Femmes et mouvement ouvrier: Allemagne d'avant 1914, révolution russe, révolution espagnole* (Paris, 1979).

Maitron, Jean, ed., *Dictionnaire biographique du mouvement ouvrier français* (Paris, 1964–).

Mayeur, Françoise, *L'Enseignement secondaire des jeunes filles sous la Troisième République* (Paris, 1977).

Mayeur, Jean-Marie, *Les Débuts de la Troisième République* (Paris, 1973).

Milward, Alan and S. B. Saul, *The Economic Development of Continental Europe* (Totowa, NJ, 1973).

Mitchell, B. R., *European Historical Statistics, 1750–1970* (New York, 1978).

Nettl, J. P. *Rosa Luxemburg*, 2 vols. (London, 1966).

Okin, Susan, *Women in Western Political Thought* (Princeton, 1979).

Perrot, Michelle, *Enquêtes sur la condition ouvrière en France au dix-neuvième siècle* (Paris, n.d.).

—— *Les Ouvriers en grève*, 2 vols. (Paris, 1974).

—— and Annie Kriegel, *Le Socialisme français et le pouvoir* (Paris, 1966).

Pierrard, Pierre, *La Vie ouvrière à Lille sous le Second Empire* (Paris, 1965).

—— *La Vie quotidienne dans le Nord au XIXe siècle* (Paris, 1976).

—— *Les Chansons en patois de Lille sous le Second Empire* (Arras,)1966).

—— *Lille et les Lillois* (Paris, 1967).

Quataert, Jean, *Reluctant Feminists in German Social Democracy 1885–1917* (Princeton, 1979).

Rabaut, Jean, *Histoire des féminismes français* (Paris, 1978).

Rebérioux, Madeleine, *La République radicale?* (Paris, 1975).

Rice, Margery S., *Working Class Women* (London, 1939).

Rowbotham, Sheila, *Women, Resistance and Revolution* (New York, 1972).

Schorske, Carl, *German Social Democracy, 1905–1917* (Cambridge, Mass., 1955).

Segalen, Martine, *Love and Power in the Peasant Family: Rural France in the Nineteenth Century*, trans. Sarah Matthews (Oxford, 1983).

Shorter, Edward and Charles Tilly, *Strikes in France, 1830–1968* (Cambridge, 1974).

Sklar, Katherine, *Catherine Beecher: A Study in American Domesticity* (New Haven, Conn., 1973).

Slaughter, Jane and Robert Kern, eds., *European Women on the Left* (Westport, Conn., 1981).

Smith, Bonnie, *Ladies of the Leisure Class: The Bourgeoises of Northern France in the Nineteenth Century* (Princeton, 1981).

Soldon, Norbert, *Women in British Trade Unions, 1874–1976* (Dublin, 1978).

Sorlin, Pierre, *La Société française, 1840–1914*, vol. i (Paris, 1969).

Sowerwine, Charles, *Les Femmes et le socialisme* (Paris, 1978).

—— *Sisters or Citizens? Women and Socialism in France Since 1876* (Cambridge, 1982).

Stearns, Peter, *Revolutionary Syndicalism and French Labor: A Cause Without Rebels* (New Brunswick, NJ, 1971).

Strumingher, Laura, *Women and the Making of the Working Class: Lyon, 1830–1870* (Montreal, 1979).

Sueur, Georges, *Lille, Roubaix, Tourcoing: Métropole en miettes* (Paris, 1971).

Sussman, George, *Selling Mothers' Milk* (Champaign, Ill., 1982).

Taïëb, Edith, *Hubertine Auclert. La Citoyenne, 1848–1914* (Paris, 1982).

Talmy, l'abbé R., *L'Association catholique des patrons du Nord, 1884–1895: une forme hybride du catholicisme social en France* (Lille, 1962).

Taylor, Barbara, *Eve and the New Jerusalem. Socialism and Feminism in the Nineteenth Century* (London, 1983).

Tentler, Leslie W., *Wage-earning Women* (Oxford, 1979).

Thomas, Edith, *Louise Michel*, trans. Penelope Williams (Montreal, 1980).

—— *Les Pétroleuses* (Paris, 1963).

Thönnessen, Werner, *The Emancipation of Women: the Rise and Decline of the Women's Movement in German Social Democracy, 1863–1933*, trans. Joris de Bres (London, 1973).

Tilly, Louise and Joan Scott, *Women, Work and Family* (New York, 1978).

Toulemonde, Jacques, *Naissance d'une métropole: Roubaix and Tourcoing au XIXe siècle* (Tourcoing, n.d.).

Van den Driessche, J.-E., *Histoire de Tourcoing* (Tourcoing, 1928).

Weber, Eugen, *Peasants into Frenchmen, the Modernisation of Rural France, 1870–1914* (London, 1977).

Willard, Claude, *Les Guesdistes: le mouvement socialiste en France (1893–1905)* (Paris, 1965).

—— *Socialisme et communisme français* (Paris, 1969).

Wohl, Robert, *French Communism in the Making, 1914–1924* (Stanford, 1966).

Woodcock, George, *Pierre-Joseph Proudhon* (London, 1956).

Woolf, Virginia, *A Room of One's Own* (New York, 1945).

Zeldin, Theodore, *The Oxford History of Modern France*, vol. 1, *Ambition, Love and Politics* (Oxford, 1978).

Zévaès, A., *Histoire du socialisme et du communisme en France, 1871–1947* (Paris, 1947).

Zylberberg-Hocquard, Marie-Hélène, *Féminisme et syndicalisme en France* (Paris, 1978).

—— *Femmes et féminisme dans le mouvement ouvrier français* (Paris, 1981).

(b) Articles

Abray, Jane, 'Feminism in the French Revolution', *American Historical Review*, lxxx (1975), pp. 43–62.

Ademar, Hélène, 'La Liberté sur les barricades de Delacroix', *Gazette des beaux-arts*, xliii (Feb. 1954), pp. 83–92.

Applewhite, Harriet and Darlene Levy, 'Women of the Popular Classes in Revolutionary Paris, 1789–1795', in Carol Berken and Clara Lovett, eds., *Women, War and Revolution* (New York, 1980).

Boxer, Marilyn, 'Foyer or Factory: working-class women in nineteenth century France', *Proceedings of the Second Meeting of the Western Society for French History, 21–23 November, 1974* (Austin, Texas, 1975), pp. 192–203.

Brenne, Jules, 'Les Candidatures ouvrières dans le Nord', in *Revue du Nord*, ccxxi (Apr.–June 1974), pp. 185–93.

Buriez-Duez, Marie-Pascale, 'Le Mouvement de la population dans le département du Nord au XIXe siècle' in Marcel Gillet, ed., *L'Homme, la vie et la mort dans le Nord au 19e siècle* (Paris, 1979), pp. 17–33.

Cayrol, R. and Y. Tavernier, 'Sociologie des adhérents du Parti Socialiste Unifié', in *Revue française de science politique*, 19, iii (June 1969), pp. 699–707.

Codaccioni, Félix-Paul, 'L'Élection de Paul Lafargue en 1891', in *Revue du Nord*, ccxx (Jan.–Mar. 1974), pp. 43–7.

Colpin, Françoise, 'Les Femmes d'Albi', in *L'Humanité dimanche*, no. cxlvi (15–21 Nov. 1978), pp. 14–25.

Cross, Miriam, 'Testament of Shirley Williams', in *The Observer* (22 Mar. 1981), p. 15.

Derfler, Leslie, 'Reformism and Jules Guesde 1891–1904' in *International Review of Social History*, xii (1967), pp. 66–80.

Enthoven, Jean-Paul, 'Tu ne feras point périr ton fruit: un entretien avec Jean-Louis Flandrin', in *Le Nouvel Observateur* (22–28 Oct. 1979).

Franca, Pieroni Bortolotti, 'Feminismo e socialismo dal 1900 al primo dopo guerra', in *Critica Storica*, 1 (31 Jan. 1969), pp. 29–41.

Franchomme, Georges, 'L'Évolution démographique et économique de Roubaix dans le dernier tiers du XIXe siècle', in *Revue du Nord* (Apr.–June 1969).

Furet, François and Jacques Ozouf, 'Literacy and industrialisation: the case of the Département du Nord in France', in *Journal of European Economic History*, v (Spring 1976), pp. 5–44.

Gales, Kathleen and P. H. Marks, 'Twentieth-century trends in the work of women in England and Wales', in *Journal of the Royal Statistical Society*, series A, vol. cxxxvii, part 1 (1974), pp. 60–70.

Guilbert, Madeleine, 'Les Femmes actives en France, bilan 1978', in *La Condition féminine* (Paris, 1978).

Hamilton, George H., 'The Iconographical orgins of Delacroix's "Liberty leading the people"', in Dorothy Miner, ed., *Studies in Art and Literature* (Princeton, 1954).

Hilaire, Y.-M., 'Les Missions intérieures face à la déchristianisation pendant la deuxième moitié du XIXe siècle dans la région Nord', in *Revue du Nord*, xlvi (1964).

—— 'Les Ouvriers de la région du Nord devant l'église catholique—XIXe et XXe siècles', in François Bédarida and Jean Maîtron, eds., *Christianisme et monde ouvrier* (Paris, 1971), pp. 223–38.

Hilden, Patricia, 'Women in Europe: a Review', in *Social History*, vol. 4, iii (Oct. 1979), pp. 526–7.

—— 'Women's History or the History of the Family?' in *International Labor and Working-Class History* (Nov. 1979), pp. 1–11.

Hobsbawm, Eric, 'Man and Woman in socialist iconography', in *History Workshop Journal*, vi (autumn 1978), pp. 131–40.

—— 'Sexe, symboles, vêtements et socialisme', in *Actes de la recherche en sciences sociales*, xxiii (Sept. 1978), pp. 209–218.

Honeycutt, Karen, 'Clara Zetkin: A socialist approach to the problem of women's oppression', in *Feminist Studies*, 3, iii–iv (spring/summer 1976), pp. 131–44.

Hufton, Olwen, 'Women in Revolution, 1789–1796', in *Past and Present*, liii (1971), pp. 90–108.

Judt, Tony, 'A Clown in Regal Purple: social history and the historians', in *History Workshop Journal*, vii (spring 1979), pp. 66–94.

Kaplan, Temma, 'Women and Spanish anarchism', in Bridenthal and

Koonz, eds., *Becoming Visible*, pp. 402–21.

Knibiehler, Yvonne, 'Les Médecins et la "nature féminine" au temps du Code Civil', in *Annales ESC*, iv (July–Aug. 1976), pp. 824–45.

Lentacker, F., 'La Main d'œuvre belge à Roubaix', in *Revue du Nord* (Apr. 1950), pp. 130–44.

Lesaege-Dugied, Aline, 'La Mortalité infantile dans le département du Nord de 1815 à 1914', in Gillet, ed., *L'Homme, la vie et la mort dans le Nord au 19ᵉ siècle*, pp. 81–93.

McLaren, Angus, 'Doctor in the House: medicine and private morality in France, 1800–1850', in *Feminist Studies*, ii (autumn 1975), pp. 39–54.

—— 'Some secular attitudes towards sexual behaviour in France, 1760–1860', in *French Historical Studies*, viii (autumn 1974), pp. 604–25.

Meyer, Alfred, 'Marxism and the women's movement', in Dorothy Atkinson, *et al.*, *Women in Russia* (Brighton, 1978), pp. 85–114.

Moodie, Thomas, 'The Reorientation of French socialism, 1888–90' in *International Review of Social History*, xx (1975), pp. 347–69.

Perrot, Michelle, 'Les Ménagères et la classe ouvrière', in *Les Femmes et la classe ouvrière* (Colloque de Vincennes, 16 Dec. 1978).

Phayer, J. Michael, 'Lower class morality: the case of Bavaria', in *Journal of Social History* (autumn 1974), pp. 79–95.

Pierrard, Pierre, 'L'Enseignement primaire à Lille sous la monarchie de juillet', in *Revue du Nord*, ccxx (Jan.–Mar. 1974), pp. 1–11.

Pierreuse, Robert, 'La Situation économique et sociale à Roubaix et Tourcoing à la Belle Époque', in *Revue du Nord*, ccxix (Oct.–Dec. 1973), pp. 423–4.

Reddy, William, 'Family and Factory: French linen weavers in the Belle Époque', in *Journal of Social History* (autumn 1974), pp. 102–12.

Richards, Eric, 'Women in the British economy since about 1700: an interpretation', in *History*, lix (Oct. 1974), pp. 337–57.

Rouche, Michel, 'La Recherche historique sur la femme, l'amour et le mariage', in *Revue du Nord*, liii (Apr.–June 1971), pp. 313–17.

Scott, Joan and Louise Tilly, 'Women's work and the Family in nineteenth-century Europe', in *Comparative Studies in Society and History*, 17, i (1973), pp. 36–64.

Shorter, Edward, 'Illegitimacy, sexual revolution and social change in modern Europe', in *Journal of Interdisciplinary History*, ii (1971), pp. 237–75.

Sontag, Susan, 'The Third World of Women', in *Partisan Review* (1974), pp. 473–7.

Sowerwine, Charles, 'The Organisation of French socialist women 1880–1914: a European perspective for Women's movements', in *Réflexions Historiques*, iii (summer 1976), pp. 3–24.

Tilly, Louise, 'The Food Riot as a form of political conflict in France', in *Journal of Interdisciplinary History*, ii (1971), pp. 23–58.

—— 'Structure de l'emploi, travail des femmes et changement démographique dans deux villes industrielles: Anzin et Roubaix, 1872–1906', in *Mouvement social* (Dec. 1978), pp. 33–58.

Vandenbussche, Robert, 'Aspects de l'histoire politique du radicalisme dans le département du Nord (1870–1905)', in *Revue du Nord* (Apr.–June 1965), pp. 223–68.

Willard, Claude, 'Les Attaques contre Notre Dame de l'Usine', in Bédarida and Maîtron, eds., *Christianisme et monde ouvrier*, pp. 244–50.

Zylberberg-Hocquard, Marie-Hélène, 'L'Ouvrière dans les romans populaires du dix-neuvième siècle', in *Revue du Nord*, numéro spécial, 'Histoire des femmes du Nord' (July-Sept. 1981), pp. 603–36.

(c) Unpublished dissertations

Baker, Robert, '*A Regional study of working-class organisation in France: Socialism in the Nord, 1870–1924*' (Ph.D., Stanford, 1967).

Bidelman, Patrick, '*The Feminist movement in France: the formative years, 1858–1899*' (Ph.D., Michigan State, 1975).

Boxer, Marilyn, '*Socialism faces Feminism in France, 1879–1913*' (Ph.D., University of California, Riverside, 1975).

Dehove, Gérard, '*Le Contrôle ouvrier en France: l'élaboration de sa notion*' (Thèse, Univ. de Lille, June 1937).

Honeycutt, Karen, '*Clara Zetkin*' (Ph.D., Columbia, 1975).

Jonas, Raymond, '*From Radical Republic to the Social Republic: the example of the Isère*' (Ph.D., University of California, Berkeley, 1984).

Lambert, Jean, '*Quelques familles du patronat textile de Lille-Armentières, 1789–1914*' (Thèse doctorat, Univ. de Lille, 1954).

Larsen, Holly, '*Emma Couriau*' (Honours thesis, Dept. of History, UC Berkeley, spring 1979).

Lewenhak, Sheila, '*Trade-union membership among women and girls in the UK, 1920–1965*' (Ph.D., London, 1971).

Melucci, Alberto, '*Idéologies et pratiques patronales pendant l'industrialisation capitaliste: le cas de France*' (Thèse 3e cycle, École Pratique des Hautes Études, Paris, 1974).

Quataert, Jean, '*The German socialist women's movement, 1890–1918: issues, internal conflicts*' (Ph.D., UC Berkeley, 1974).

Romero-Maura, J., '*Urban working-class politics in Catalonia, 1899–1909*' (D.Phil., Oxford, 1970).

Siemiatycki, Myer, '*Guesdism and anti-collectivism in Roubaix-Wattrelos*' (MA thesis, Sussex, n.d.).

Sullivan Smith, Bonnie, *'The Women of the Lille bourgeoisie, 1850–1914'* (Ph.D., Rochester, 1975).

Sohn, Anne-Marie, *'Féminisme et syndicalisme'* (Thèse, 3ᵉ cycle, Paris X, 1973).

Strain, Jacqueline, *'Feminism and political radicalism in the German social democratic movement, 1890–1914* (Ph.D., UC Berkeley, 1964).

INDEX

abortion, 41–2
agriculture, 93–4
Agulhon, Edith, 134 n
Ain (department), 274
alcoholism, 47, 104, 247
Amiens, 127, 212; congress of, 238
anarchists, 173; and Louise Michel, 182, 231, 238; and women, 240–1
Ardouin-Dumazet, 28, 54, 57, 85, 87–8
Armentières, 38, 139, 157, 161, 162–3, 190, 240
Assemblée générale des syndicats des femmes, 128–9
Association des patrons chrétiens, 85
Auclert, Hubertine, 3, 184, 196
Audiganne, Armand, 48, 51

Ballon (Belguim), 141
Barrois frères mill, 104
Barrois-Lepers mill, 113
La Bataille syndicaliste (newspaper), 241
Baud, Lucie, 134 n
Bayart-Parent mill, 113
Bebel, August, 198
Belgian workers, 10, 11, 18–20, 65, 88, 131
Belgium, 6, 16, 56, 141, 146; immigration from, 9, 18–19, 65
Biais, Maximilienne, 251 n
Binet wool mill, 157
birth-control, *see* contraception
birth-rate, 18, 20–1, 37–8
blacklisting, 102, 109, 121, 173, 187, 208, 228
Blanqui, Adolphe, 18
Bocquet, Léon, 55, 89
Bonduel, Citoyenne, 205
Bonnafoux, Marie, 134 n
Bonneff, Léon and Maurice, 33, 45, 120
bourses du travail, 109, 257
Boyer, M., 247
Brion, Hélène, 270, 272 n
Brisson, Paul, 99
Brittany, 247
Brontë, Charlotte, 78

Broquelet, 7, 54–6, 239; socialist assimilation of, 172, 186
bureau de bienfaisance, 41, 59, 82–3, 97, 210

cabarets, see *estaminets*
café-bars, see *estaminets*
Cahiers des doléances féminines, 197–8, 210
Calais, 190, 211, 217
Cambrai: diocese of, 122; illegitimacy rate, 41
Capart, Victor, 156–7, 171, 175
Capy, Marcelle, 27, 47, 49, 53–4, 111, 121
Carrette, Henri, 87, 125, 151, 171, 175, 202, 211, 215, 224, 235 n
Carrette, Mme Henri, 4, 186, 202–3, 206
Catholic Church, 173; charities, 59–60; clergy, 61–2, 78, 83, 109, 112, 114, 118–20, 234, 246; education and, 50, 75; illegitimacy and, 41; marriage and, 40; mill-owners and, 8, 69, 74–5, 77, 81, 112; mill-owners' wives and daughters and, 79;
Rerum Novarum, 76, 84, 85 n, 114, 129; struggle with socialists, 187; textile workers and, 113–15, 147–8, 163; Tourcoing, 87–8, 113; and women, 8, 81, 181, 234, 246; youth groups in, 146
Catholic workers' movement, 212
Chaboseau-Napias, Louise, 134 n
Chabrouilland, Félix, 50 n
charities, 40–1, 98–9; hospices, 83; maternity aid, 84–5; night refuges, 83; patronal charities, 76, 85; as political weapon, 187;
see also *bureau de bienfaisance*
children, 39, 45–6; charities for, 40; education, 49–50; *fêtes*, 54–6; socialism and, 183, 238; textile workers, 22–3, 102, 106, 109
Clermont-Ferrand, 180
Codaccioni, Félix-Paul, 21